Indicators of Justice

Indicators of Justice

Measuring the Performance
of Prosecution, Defense,
and Court Agencies Involved
in Felony Proceedings

Sorrel Wildhorn
Marvin Lavin
Anthony Pascal

Lexington Books
D.C. Heath and Company
Lexington, Massachusetts
Toronto

Library of Congress Cataloging in Publication Data

Wildhorn, Sorrel.
 Indicators of justice.

 Includes index.
 1. Criminal justice, Administration of—United States. 2. Criminal statistics—United States. I. Lavin, Marvin, joint author. II. Pascal, Anthony H.,
joint author. III. Title.
KF9223.W53   1977   345'.73'05   76-57898
ISBN 0-669-01363-3

Published simultaneously in Canada.

Printed in the United States of America.

Paperbound International Standard Book Number: 0-669-01361-7

Clothbound International Standard Book Number: 0-669-01363-3

Library of Congress Catalog Card Number: 76-57898

Contents

v

84379

List of Figures

List of Tables

Preface

This book presents some of the results of a research study on the measurement of performance of prosecution, defense, and court agencies involved in felony proceedings. The research study was funded by a grant from the National Institute of Law Enforcement and Criminal Justice, the research arm of the Law Enforcement Assistance Administration of the United States Department of Justice. The study is part of Rand's continuing research program in criminal justice.

The broad objectives of this book are: (1) to identify and evaluate sets of statistical performance measures (to be estimated from case file data and other agency records) as indices of progress in several important issue areas; and (2) to demonstrate their applicability in two county jurisdictions. The jurisdictions in which performance measures were applied were Multnomah County (City of Portland), Oregon and Dade County (City of Miami), Florida. Each major agency—the Circuit Court, the prosecutor's office, and the public defender's office—in both jurisdictions cooperated fully in the research study.

The book may be viewed from several perspectives. First and foremost it is intended as a guide to practicing professionals and policymakers in court, prosecution, and defense agencies throughout the United States who are interested in measuring their agency's performance. Second, it should be of interest to criminal justice researchers, since we illustrate how analytical techniques may be usefully applied to reveal and explain performance in two jurisdictions. Third, it should be of interest to police administrators too, since the work of the police impinges heavily on all the agencies, particularly the prosecutor's performance in screening and charging and in plea bargaining. Finally, it should be of general interest to informed lay persons who would like to understand more clearly how these agencies are performing.

Points of view or opinions stated in this book are those of the authors and do not necessarily represent the official position or policy of the United States Department of Justice; of the Circuit Court, State Attorney's Office, or Public Defender's Office of Dade County; or of the Circuit Court, District Attorney's Office, or the Metropolitan Public Defender's Office of Multnomah County.

Summary

Focus and Purposes

The primary focus of this book is on the selection, estimation, and analysis of performance measures as statistical devices that aid in the interpretation of data drawn from court system operations[1] (i.e., from case files and other records in court, prosecution, and public defender agencies). Performance measures may be viewed either as quantitative descriptors of what is being done in felony proceedings or as progress indices of how well these functions are being performed. (For example, the number and proportion of all felony filings that are disposed of by dismissal, plea of guilty, conviction at trial, and trial acquittal or dismissal are examples of the former, whereas the proportion of felony trials exceeding the speedy trial standard is an example of the latter.)

This book emphasizes the latter role of performance measures. Its emphasis is to be contrasted with, for example, the application of standards and goals as articulated in the series of volumes issued since 1968 by the ABA on standards for criminal justice[2] or those which resulted in 1973 from the work of the National Advisory Commission on Criminal Justice Standards and Goals. Few of these hundreds of individual goals and standards relating to the criminal proceeding are couched in quantitative terms or lend themselves to quantitative interpretation—the primary exception being those concerning the "speediness" of the proceeding.

The objectives of this book are:

1. To identify, screen, and evaluate sets of performance measures (to be estimated from case files and other agency records) as indices of progress.
2. To demonstrate the applicability of these indices in two jurisdictions, selected to be Multnomah County, Oregon and Dade County, Florida.

---

[1] The study on which this book is based focused secondarily on performance measures of the court system as viewed through the eyes of lay participants in the felony proceeding—victims, other lay witnesses, jurors, and defendants. That is, their attitudes toward the court system are performance measures of interest, which can be elicited through survey techniques. And, with proper statistical analysis, their attitudes can be related to their individual experiences with, and treatment by, the system. Preliminary work was completed on devising and applying personal interview questionnaires to defendants and mail survey questionnaires to the other three classes of lay participants. Preliminary statistical analysis of responses was also completed. However, because of the preliminary nature of the work, we have omitted it from this book. Readers interested in this survey research should consult the study's two final reports. See Sorrel Wildhorn et al., *Indicators of Justice: Measuring the Performance of Prosecution, Defense and Court Agencies Involved in Felony Proceedings (A Guide to Practitioners)*, R-1917-DOJ, The Rand Corporation, June 1976; and Sorrel Wildhorn et al., *Indicators of Justice: Measuring the Performance of Prosecution, Defense and Court Agencies Involved in Felony Proceedings (Analysis and Demonstration)*, R-1918-DOJ, The Rand Corporation, June 1976.

[2] See footnote 1, Chapter 1, for a listing of these volumes.

Scope

The scope of this study was confined to adult felony proceedings; thus we considered neither misdemeanor nor civil proceedings. We addressed only the primary activities of the court system, thus excluding supporting activities and functions performed by court clerks, court reporters, bailiffs, or paralegals in the prosecutor's office or the public defender's office. Of the several potential roles and uses of statistical performance measures, two broad types of applications were made: *retrospective* comparisons of the full court system and of its component agencies (rather than of individual practitioners) *within* the jurisdiction at different times;[3] and *retrospective interjurisdictional* comparisons of court systems and component agencies at the same time.

The study focused on a limited set of persistently important issue areas (described below) and sought to select and apply sets of performance measures that would illuminate them.

The Issue Areas and the Policy Interests of Practitioners and Agencies

We selected important issue areas that involve significant aspects of the performance of the court system. For some—delay, efficiency, evenhandedness, charging accuracy—practitioners and observers would all agree on the direction of improvement to be sought, even though they might not agree on a structure of goals (and their relative importance) for the felony proceeding. For others— the charging threshold, the impact of plea bargaining, sentence variation—they could agree only that further illumination is desirable. Also, certain agencies and types of practitioners would find particular issues to be of greater interest than others, either because of relevance to their own performance or because of concerns about current policy.

Charging Standards

Prosecutors' offices in most jurisdictions need objective evidence of the standards being implemented to discern, for example, whether they conform to policy and what the impacts on the system are if policy changes. For example, if the charging threshold is lowered, how is court workload, delay, and plea bargaining affected? Measures of the operation of the charging threshold over time also can reveal trends in police performance as a by-product.

[3] In two contexts: when no major change (i.e., routine monitoring) is introduced; and when a major policy change or innovation (procedural, legislative, administrative) is to be evaluated.

Charging Accuracy

Is the nature of the disposition of cases being unduly affected by the accuracy with which charges are filed against defendants? Is the court workload being magnified by the consequences of inaccurate charging? Such questions concern not only prosecutors, but also judges, defense counsel, and court administrators in assessing charging policy and practices in their jurisdiction.

Plea Bargaining

What is the nature and frequency of the practice in the jurisdiction? Quantitative evidence available to practitioners is often scant on this question. And the public rarely has seen even the rudiments of an objective picture. What is the court system gaining or losing from plea negotiation? How are delay and efficiency of resource use being affected? Is punishment significantly lighter than in the absence of such negotiation? All practitioners, and the public as well, have a vital stake in these questions, even though plea bargaining policy is primarily a prosecutorial responsibility.

Sentence Variation

Judges and other practitioners want to know the degree of consistency in sentencing in their court system as compared to others, how sentencing practices change over time, and how they vary among judges within a court system. If, in addition, quantitative evidence were available to explain how much of the observed variation was accounted for by various legitimate and illegitimate factors, such illumination could help to reduce disparities or enhance the effectiveness of specific devices (e.g., sentencing panels, appellate review of sentences) aimed at reducing sentence disparity.

Evenhandedness

All practitioners and lay participants in the system, as well as the general public, are concerned that the courts be evenhanded in the delivery of justice, although the bench would have the primary responsibility in ensuring that it occurs. If "illegitimate" factors (e.g., the defendant's ethnicity, pretrial custody status, type of defense counsel) that should not significantly affect how cases are disposed or sentences imposed have done so, then steps can be taken to guard against such occurrences in the future.

Delay

Justice should be speedy, but few jurisdictions have comprehensive objective evidence on the duration of their cases. Even less can they isolate the effects of the separate factors (e.g., nature of offense, type of disposition, type of defense counsel, or backlog problems) that may tend to delay individual cases. Although some factors that might cause delay are not readily controllable (e.g., court caseload), others are (e.g., continuance policy). Better measurement of delay and its determinants can help the court administration, for example, improve the allocation of resources.

Efficiency

Court system managers—the presiding judge, court administrator, district attorney, and chief of the public defender office—have responsibility for efficiency of operations. They must seek to make resources, including manpower, appropriate to the workload, given some standard for individual productivity.

Thus, each set of performance measures we discuss in this report has an "audience" among practitioners (and often in the general public too). Access to various sets of statistical indicators can assist in the assessment of performance, and in the design and evaluation of new policies and innovations in the myriad aspects of criminal prosecution, defense, adjudication, and sentencing.

Study Methods and Sources of Information

The information used in this book was obtained from literature relevant to performance measurement, interviews with practitioners, and case files and other records in various agencies.

Practitioner Interviews

Structured interviews with 33 seasoned criminal justice practitioners in 13 jurisdictions were conducted to elicit their views toward the value of performance measures, the selection of issue areas and relevant performance measures, and the choice of the two demonstration jurisdictions.

Data Collected from Agency Records and Case Files

Rand data collection teams obtained data manually on roughly 2000 cases from various records made available by cooperating officials in the two demonstration jurisdictions and at the state level. In addition, a pilot case auditing activity was conducted in which a team of outside practitioner/consultants examined 20 burglary-type cases disposed of by plea of guilty in each jurisdiction for the purpose of making judgments about the appropriateness of decisions that were made by participants at various stages in the felony proceeding. The case audit activity also included extensive interviews with practitioners in both jurisdictions.

Once performance measures were calculated from the raw data elements, standard and specially developed software packages (i.e., computer programs) were used to cross-tabulate the performance measures and to analyze (i.e., explain) their variation across cases.[4]

The Performance Measures

Because of space limitations in this summary, we will not list the many performance measures selected to illuminate each of the issue areas. The reader is referred to Chapter 4 of this book for a discussion of the selection criteria used to screen candidate sets of measures; of the selected sets of performance measures and the data elements necessary for computing their value; and of the rationale of what they can reveal, as well as conceal, about performance in each issue area.

General Findings and Implications

On the Feasibility of Applying Performance Measures

Our study has shown that it is feasible to apply performance measures to data already available in court agencies' files, even though incomplete, and to draw inferences about whether and how performance in specified issue areas changed in a jurisdiction. To a lesser extent too, we have shown that it is feasible (within carefully specified limits) to make interjurisdictional comparisons of performance using the measures specified in this study. The careful collection of specified data elements, the computation, grouping, and cross-tabulation of performance measures, and the analysis (using multivariate statistical techniques) of what factors account for the variation in key performance measures can provide greatly strengthened informational bases for officials in court, prosecution, and public defender agencies to improve criminal proceedings.

We were more successful in applying performance measures to certain policy

---

[4]For example, multivariate regression analysis was employed to isolate the independent effect of selected factors that were hypothesized to affect three key performance measures of outcomes in the felony proceeding: probability of conviction, sentence severity (given conviction), and delay (i.e., elapsed time between arrangement and final disposition).

issues than to others because of inherent differences in the precision or ambiguity of the performance measures (e.g., in those which measure changes in delay compared with those which measure changes in the charging threshold) or because of differences in the availability of data (e.g., the availability of data on sentence agreements in Multnomah compared with its unavailability in Dade for measuring plea bargaining impacts).

The actions to be taken jointly by the court, prosecution, and public defender agencies in a jurisdiction to strengthen the informational and analytical base for measuring their performance may be visualized as an *integrated performance measurement program* (IPMP). A fairly comprehensive IPMP would consist of:

1. An enumeration of required data elements (or categories) and performance measures.
2. Standardized data collection and output forms for each policy issue area of interest (the ones we considered and/or others of interest to particular jurisdictions).
3. Flexible, modular software packages (i.e., computer programs) for computing, displaying, and analyzing performance measures within each issue area—e.g., for performing cross tabulations and for applying multivariate regression models that help to explain conviction probability, delay, and sentence severity imposed.
4. Guidelines for conducting case audits at each major decision point (screening, guilty plea, trial, sentencing) in the proceeding—using either outside practitioner/consultants or inhouse supervisory personnel.

If data collection procedures and software packages were flexible and modular in design, the scale and scope of an IPMP could be tailored to individual jurisdictions. For example, the three agencies in a using jurisdiction could decide whether to embrace all elements (e.g., to include case auditing) and whether to measure performance in all the listed issue areas (e.g., to include the measurement of case processing efficiency in the prosecutor's and public defender's office, as well as in the court). What would be vital to proper tailoring is a clear enunciation by agency officials of the management and policy issues upon which performance measurement should focus.

This study is a first step toward the design of an IPMP. We have enumerated required data elements and performance measures and, with varying degrees of success, have devised and applied statistical models to explain key performance measures. More work needs to be done, however, and its nature is discussed below.

On Methodology and Data Availability

Case Audits. Our pilot case auditing exercises (of cases in which there was a plea of guilty) in the demonstration jurisdictions strongly suggest that it provides complementary information about qualitative factors that aid in the interpretations of the statistical performance measures. (By their very nature, case audits are much more expensive per case included than the data collection required to develop statistical performance measures. Thus, with limited resources, audit samples are inevitably too small to stand alone as a substitute for statistical performance measures.)

One benefit results because the average practitioner probably regards case auditing to be a natural and nontechnical way of revealing performance. His confidence in the correctness of what is shown by statistical performance measures is undoubtedly increased when the results of (even quite limited) case auditing corroborate the statistical story. Another possible benefit of case auditing is that it may help reveal the explanations for the "behavior" of statistical indices. And, finally, it may considerably strengthen the credibility of interjurisdictional comparisons made by means of statistical measures. (Our suggestions for broadening case auditing to test its value more fully are discussed below.)

Data Availability. A salient lesson in our attempt to demonstrate the application of performance measures in two selected jurisdictions was that many necessary or desirable data elements normally recorded in various files were missing from the customary records and some were simply not recorded at all. And this is likely to be the situation in other jurisdictions as well.

Among the data elements that had been (at best) incompletely recorded and preserved were: defendant-related characteristics, such as ethnicity, prior criminal record, occupation and employment, family status, income, and transiency; the number of appearances per victim or other witness in the course of a proceeding; data describing how judges apportion their time among judicial tasks; and attribution of continuances to the responsible movant(s). However, even with incomplete recording of these data, we were able to adequately apply performance measures to issue areas requiring these data (with the exception of judicial weighted caseload).

Among the data elements that were not recorded at all were: the apportionment of time among the principal activities of prosecutors, public defenders, and jurors; background characteristics of suspects whose cases were screened out prior to arraignment on felony charges; full information on the outcome of plea bargaining, including the nature of any sentence agreement reached; judicial statements of the rationale for sentences in individual cases; detailed reasons for case dismissals in lower court; and duration of appearances of victims and other witnesses. The unavailability of these data made it impossible to analyze issue areas such as the use of time by prosecutors and public defenders and evenhandedness in screening and permitted only partial analysis of the plea bargaining balance and charging accuracy in one jurisdiction. With special data collection through surveys of lay participants it was possible to assess such issue areas as the use of their time and their attitudes toward the court system and its practitioners.[5]

---

[5] See Rand reports R-1917-DOJ and R-1918-DOJ.

Desirable Extensions

We feel that a fuller foundation for the design of an operational IPMP would be provided by the following extensions in scope and refinement in methodology to our demonstration work:

1. Classes of data that were not recorded or were incompletely recorded in Multnomah and Dade Counties should be collected and analyzed elsewhere. Evenhandedness in screening should be analyzed with a proper body of data containing appropriate defendant-related characteristics. The allocation of prosecutors' and public defenders' time to their various activities is another performance area warranting examination and would need a proper body of data.

2. The assessment of case auditing should be broadened in the screening area (to include rejected cases) and also extended to the trial area, so that our inferences as to the value of case auditing as a complement to statistical performance measurement can be tested more fully.

3. Improved statistical models should be constructed to help explain performance outcomes in criminal proceedings. Those we developed for explaining sentence outcomes and delay in proceedings worked fairly well but need further refinement. Because we were unsuccessful in explaining the determinants of conviction probability, we believe much more theoretical and empirical work is necessary. We speculate that data on the seriousness of the crime incident, on mitigating and exacerbating circumstances of the defendant and the crime incident, and on factors describing the strength of the case at the time of screening are relevant for constructing better conviction probability models.

On How Potential Capabilities of Planned Information Systems Compare with an IPMP

One major consideration for local agencies that may be interested in moving toward an IPMP is that considerable resources already have been or will be devoted to existing or planned information systems, such as CCH/OBTS, SJIS, and PROMIS.[6] It is clearly important to know how their potential performance measurement capabilities (which issue areas can be analyzed in what depth?) compare with an IPMP under two conditions: (1) the basic systems with only those data elements already collected, assuming simple software packages (with a cross-tabulation capability) are available; (2) modest, inexpensive upgrading of the basic systems (by adding a few new data elements to be collected,[7] plus a more sophisticated software package, e.g., statistical models and standard multivariate statistical analysis routines for estimating the independent effect of important factors on delay and sentence severity imposed).

[6] See Chapter 8 for definitions and descriptions of these information systems.

[7] See footnotes to tables and Chapter 8 for the few additional data elements that can be collected inexpensively.

Capabilities of the Basic Systems Planned.[8] Given the data elements collected by these information systems and the availability of (at best) simple software packages, all the systems have a valuable capability for measuring performance in the delay estimation and charging accuracy issue areas and a partial capability in the areas of plea bargaining, sentence variation, evenhandedness, and the determinants of delay. In addition, SJIS is capable of very gross estimates of the use of judicial time; and PROMIS has a good capability in the charging threshold area and a partial capability in addressing evenhandedness in screening (whereas CCH/OBTS and SJIS have no capabilities in the screening area).

Capabilities if Planned Systems are Upgraded. Upgrading any of the basic systems (as noted above) would enable better analysis of the plea bargaining balance, the independent effects of important factors on delay, and the independent effects of legitimate and illegitimate factors on sentence severity imposed for all the systems. In addition, upgrading of PROMIS would improve the capability to analyze evenhandedness in screening.

Capabilities of an Improved IPMP. If an IPMP were improved and extended in the ways noted above, its performance measurement capabilities would have greater breadth because many data elements specified for it are not collected by the basic (or upgraded) existing or planned systems. Although each system could function as a partial IPMP, none of the systems are designed to measure (as would an IPMP) performance in the following areas: the effect of legitimate factors on conviction probability; continuances (except for PROMIS); the use of lay participant (victim, witness, juror) time; and the use of practitioner (judge, prosecutor, public defender) time.[9]

On the Costs and Utility of Various Information Systems

Careful estimates of the range of incremental costs for implementing and operating a partial or full (improved) IPMP or of upgrading existing or planned systems (as noted above) were beyond the scope of this study. However, based on actual resources used in various activities of this study and on rough guesses of costs of activities not covered in this study, we can bound the range of likely costs within, say, a factor of two.

For a jurisdiction with one of the existing or planned information systems, incremental (i.e., over and above the costs of the basic system) annual costs on the order of $10,000 might be incurred for upgrading the system and assessing performance annually. This assumes that appropriate software packages are made available without cost and that any practitioner time devoted to additional

---

[8] We assess system capabilities in terms of the issue areas addressed in this study; capabilities of these systems to address other issue areas are not assessed.

[9] And the attitudes (and their determinants) of lay participants, too.

raw data generation is "free." Given the relatively low marginal costs associated with upgrading an existing or planned system and the major benefits outlined above, it is probably cost-effective for a jurisdiction to pursue this alternative.

For a jurisdiction without an existing information system (but with access to a computer) that desires to implement and operate a full improved IPMP, operating costs on the order of $50,000 per year are implied, once it is set up.[10] (First-year costs should be considerably higher because of nonrecurring set-up costs.) This rough estimate assumes (as with the previous case) that software and practitioner time are free and that the number and size of case file and survey response samples to be collected and analyzed are similar to that collected and analyzed in this study. Of course, additional samples or larger samples would increase costs, and exclusion of certain issue areas from an IPMP would reduce costs.

Whether implementing a full IPMP has adequate utility—i.e., whether incremental benefits sufficiently outweigh incremental costs—is a judgment that can be made by an implementing jurisdiction only after such an approach is installed and operated over several years. At that point the costs will be much less uncertain and its benefits can be assessed by the policymakers involved.

Specific Findings from the Application of Performance Measures in Two Jurisdictions

In the interests of brevity, we do not summarize the findings obtained from the applications of performance measures in the two demonstration jurisdictions, but refer to the reader to Chapters 5 and 6 of this book.

[10] This includes the administration and analysis of mail surveys of 150 to 200 samples each of victims, witnesses, and jurors and 45 defendant interviews. Excluding these items would reduce the annual operating costs to about $40,000.

Acknowledgments

We are especially indebted to members of our distinguished Study Advisory Group, who helped substantially in giving direction to our study efforts and in commenting on earlier drafts of the study reports. In addition, they suggested many of the experienced criminal justice practitioners we interviewed during the study. The Advisory Group members were: District Attorney Louis Bergna (Santa Clara County, California); Professor Alfred Blumstein (Carnegie-Mellon University); The Honorable Winslow Christian (Justice, California Court of Appeals); District Attorney Harry Connick (New Orleans, Louisiana); John Flynn (Attorney, Phoenix, Arizona); Edward McConnell (Director, National Center for State Courts); Public Defender Sheldon Portman (Santa Clara County, California); Harvey Solomon (Executive Director, Institute for Court Management); Professor Harry Subin (New York University Law School, formerly Office of U.S. Attorney); District Attorney Preston Trimble (Cleveland County, Oklahoma); The Honorable Ernst Watts (Dean, National Center for State Judiciary); and Jerry Wilson (Chief, Metropolitan Police Department, retired, Washington, D.C.).

The names of the many individuals who often granted us considerable time in which to interview them about their experience and views as criminal justice practitioners as these related to our study are listed in Appendix D. We are deeply appreciative for their cooperation.

Our gratitude extends to the many officials of the court systems and other agencies in Multnomah County, Oregon, and Dade County, Florida, who made possible our demonstration work in these jurisdictions, aided in collecting and interpreting data from their files, and commented on earlier drafts of our reports. In Multnomah County, they included: Harl Haas, District Attorney; J.G. McClain, Chief Deputy, Senior Deputies M.D. Shrunk, K.C. Frankel, and J.E. Grayson, and Deputy J.C. Ray and Kelly Bacon, all of the District Attorney's Office; The Honorable C.B. Olsen, Presiding Judge; Judges John Beatty and John Jones of the Circuit Court; Michael Hall, Court Administrator, and James Murchison, Assistant Court Administrator, both of the Circuit Court; Charles Barnard, Chief Criminal Clerk, and Gwen Biehre of the Office of the Chief Criminal Court; James Hennings, Metropolitan Public Defender, Robert Lockwood, Assistant Public Defender, and Samuel Imperati, Executive Officer; O.R. Chambers, Executive Assistant, and Louis Lewandowski, Manager, ADP Services of the Oregon Division of Corrections; Commander Kerner, Rocky Butte Jail, Multnomah County; and Sheriff Lee Brown, Multnomah County.

In Dade County they included: Richard Gerstein, State Attorney, Janet Reno, First Assistant State Attorney, and James Regan, Administrative Manager, State Attorney's Office; The Honorable Grady Crawford, Chief Judge, The Honorable Gene Williams, Administrative Judge of the Criminal Division, and

The Honorable Edward Coward, Judge of the Criminal Division, and The Honorable Seymour Gelber, Judge of the Juvenile Division, Circuit Court, Eleventh Judicial Circuit of Florida; Wilber McDuff, Court Executive Officer, Richard Brinker, Clerk of the Circuit and County Courts, James Sykes, Operations Officer of the Magistrate's Division, Montague Eadie (formerly Operations Officer of the Criminal Division), Circuit Court, and Cheryl Johnson of the Pretrial Release Program; Phillip Hubbart, Public Defender, Richard Gillen, Business Manager, and David Weed, Office of the Public Defender; Captain Gallagher, Director, Dade County Jail; and G.R. Worley, Administrator, Research and Statistics Section, Florida Department of Offender Rehabilitation.

Invaluable efforts were contributed by the members of our data collection teams. In Multnomah they were either students from the Northwest School of Law (Lewis and Clark College) or students in Administration of Justice at Portland State University. The team included: M. Craven, C. Francis III, C. Henry, M. Ketelle, J. Sokol, and K. St. Amant. In Dade they were students from Miami University Law School (or, in one instance, a graduate who was already a member of the Florida Bar). The team included: A. Cohen, J. Kaiser, K. Rizzo, J. Sloto, D. Weinberger, and J. Wulchak.

We are obligated to William Hutchins, California Bureau of Criminal Statistics, for materials that are a foundation for the sentence severity indices devised in our study.

We acknowledge the significant participation of Professor Gerald F. Uelmen, Loyola University Law School, and Raymond Sinetar, Office of the District Attorney, Los Angeles County, who were consultants to this study and especially contributed to the planning and implementation of the practitioner interviews and the case auditing activities in the demonstration jurisdictions.

Especially deserving of mention for their contributions are Professor Harry Subin, New York University Law School, who reviewed earlier drafts of the study reports; Rand Consultant, Professor Peter Haynes, Criminal Justice Department, Arizona State University, who assisted during the formulation of the research tasks; and Cheryl Martorana of LEAA's National Institute of Law Enforcement and Criminal Justice, who reviewed earlier drafts of the study reports and suggested several improvements.

Many of our Rand colleagues aided us in varied and important ways. B. Mori and E. Woo excellently performed the vital computer programming for the analysis of the case file data collected in the demonstration jurisdictions. Stephen B. Klein and Sandra H. Berry planned, administered, and analyzed the surveys of lay participants that are reported in the Rand reports cited above. Stephen J. Carroll, Charles E. Phelps, Daniel Relles, and John E. Ware provided professional guidance in resolving statistical problems that arose in the course of our work. Gene H. Fisher, Peter W. Greenwood, and D. Mike Landi served as technical reviewers of drafts of the study report. William Ahern and Robert J. Gladstone assisted during the formulation of the research tasks.

Indicators of Justice

1   Introduction

A Guide to this Book

This book presents some of the results of a broad study of performance measurement of criminal justice agencies involved in the felony proceeding—postarrest through disposition (and sentencing if it occurs). The primary focus of the book is on the selection, estimation, and analysis of performance measures as statistical devices that aid in the interpretation of data drawn from court system operations (i.e., from case files and other records in court, prosecution, and public defender agencies). Performance measures may be viewed either as quantitative descriptors of what is being done in felony proceedings or as progress indices of how well these functions are being performed. For example, the number and proportion of all felony filings that are disposed of by dismissal, plea of guilty, conviction at trial, and trial acquittal or dismissal are examples of the former, whereas the proportion of felony trials exceeding the speedy trial standard is an example of the latter.

This study emphasizes the latter role of performance measures. Its emphasis is to be contrasted with, for example, the application of standards and goals as articulated in the series of volumes issued since 1968 by the ABA on Standards for Criminal Justice[1] or those which resulted in 1973 from the work of the

The study on which this book is based focused secondarily on performance measures of the court system as viewed through the eyes of lay participants in the felony proceeding—victims, other lay witnesses, jurors and defendants. That is, their attitudes toward the court system are performance measures of interest, which can be elicited through survey techniques. And, with proper statistical analysis, their attitudes can be related to their individual experiences with, and treatment by, the system. Preliminary work was completed on devising and applying personal interview questionnaires to defendants and mail survey questionnaires to the other three classes of lay participants. Preliminary statistical analysis of responses was also completed. However, because of the preliminary nature of the work, we have omitted it from this book. Readers interested in this survey research should consult the study's two final reports. See Sorrel Wildhorn, et al., *Indicators of Justice: Measuring the Performance of Prosecution, Defense and Court Agencies Involved in Felony Proceedings (A Guide to Practitioners)*, R-1917-DOJ, The Rand Corporation, June 1976 and Sorrel Wildhorn, et al., *Indicators of Justice Measuring the Performance of Prosecution, Defense and Court Agencies Involved in Felony Proceedings (Analysis and Demonstration)*, R-1918-DOJ, The Rand Corporation, June 1976.

[1] The individual volumes (and their dates of approval) include *ABA Standards Relating to Pretrial Release* (1968), *Providing Defense Services* (1968), *Fair Trial and Free Press; Pleas of Guilty* (1968); *Speedy Trial* (1968); *Joinder and Severence* (1968); *Trial by Jury* (1968); *Sentencing Alternatives and Procedure* (1968); *Appellate Review of Sentences* (1968); *Post-Conviction Remedies* (1968); *Discovery and Procedure Before Trial* (1970); *Probation* (1970); *Criminal Appeals* (1970); *Electronic Surveillance* (1971); *The Prosecution Function and the Defense Function* (1971); *The Function of the Trial Judge* (1972); *The Urban Police Function* (1973); *Court Organization* (1974); *Trial Courts* (Tentative Draft, 1975).

1

National Advisory Commission on Criminal Justice Standards and Goals.[2] Few of these hundreds of individual goals and standards relating to the criminal proceeding are couched in quantitative terms or lend themselves to quantitative interpretation—the primary exception being those concerning the "speediness" of the proceeding.

In this chapter we describe briefly the roles or uses of performance measures, the broad purposes, scope, and methods of the study, and the relationships between the issue areas considered in this book and the interests of agencies and practitioners responsible for making policy. In Chapter 2 we provide a general background discussion and a limited literature review to show how our work relates to prior efforts. Chapter 3 provides a discussion of the practitioner interviews and their results. From the practitioner's viewpoint Chapter 4 is the heart of the book. In it we discuss the links between the selected issue areas and various goals of the criminal justice system and of the felony proceedings; the general criteria used for screening performance measures; we list the sets of performance measures selected for each issue together with the data elements needed to compute their values; we briefly discuss the techniques used to estimate, display, and explain changes in the performance measures; and we provide a brief rationale on what the measures may reveal, as well as conceal, about performance.

Chapter 5 illustrates one of the major roles of performance measures—an application in one jurisdiction (Multnomah County) to illuminate and explain how performance changes from year to year. Here we discuss the inferences (as well as the qualifications or ambiguities inherent in these inferences) that can be drawn from this illustrative application. In Chapter 6 we illustrate yet another role of performance measures—an application comparing performance in the two jurisdictions in one year. The discussion focuses on why performance comparisons between these specific jurisdictions can be made for some issue areas and not for others and why caution must be used in interpreting observed differences in performance.

In Chapter 7 we discuss the role of criminal case auditing in performance measurement and illustrate its application in one of the jurisdictions. Finally, Chapter 8 presents some of the general findings and implications that emerged from the study. It includes a discussion of lessons learned and the need for certain extensions to the work completed, and most importantly, it illustrates for jurisdictions that may be interested in applying our performance measurement approach: (1) which issue areas can be analyzed using information systems currently installed or planned in some jurisdictions; (2) to what extent modest and inexpensive extensions in data elements collected by these systems could improve the scope and depth of performance measurement capabilities; and

[2] The six individual reports of the National Advisory Commission are entitled: *A National Strategy to Reduce Crime; Criminal Justice System; Courts; Police; Corrections; Community Crime Prevention* (1973).

(3) those performance measurement applications to issue areas that would require new (and more costly) data collection and analysis efforts, because current or planned information systems do not suffice for such applications. It must be emphasized that certain software packages (such as those applied in this study) would be required for analyzing performance, whichever of the three alternatives is pursued.

Roles and Uses of Performance Measures

The potential roles and uses of statistical performance measures in the felony proceeding can be categorized as follows.

Within a Jurisdiction

1. Routine tracking or administrative monitoring of pending cases in the prosecution, defense, and court agencies.
2. Retrospectively comparing the performance of the full court system, its component agencies, and its individual practitioners at different times, e.g., when no major policy change or innovation is introduced; or when a major policy change or innovation (procedural, legislative, administrative) is to be evaluated.
3. Prospectively estimating the performance impacts of a major policy change or innovation.

Among Jurisdictions

1. Retrospectively comparing the full court systems and component agencies in different jurisdictions, e.g., comparing different jurisdictions within a state (say, of interest to a state-level Judicial Council or Supreme Court); or evaluating whether a particular policy or innovation in one jurisdiction has similar effects in another.
3. Helping to show the condition of the criminal justice process at the state and national levels.

Other

1. Prompting and guiding research on ways to enhance the administration of justice in felony proceedings.

Even though the collection and use of statistical data describing the operations of court, prosecution, and defense agencies has increased over the last decade, the major use of these data has been to provide (often rudimentary) assessments of how speedily and efficiently a jurisdiction disposes of its pending caseload. There has been less inclination to employ statistical indicators to measure other aspects of felony proceedings relating to the quality of justice, notwithstanding the upsurge in production of (largely qualitative) standards and goals bearing on these proceedings, as mentioned above. Basically, statistical descriptors have been widely used to depict what is going on in felony proceedings. Thus there is a marked gap between the articulation of (largely qualitative) goals and standards, on the one hand, and the measurement of progress toward goals, on the other. Given this observation, the broad purpose of our study was to reduce that gap.

Purposes and Scope of the Study

The specific purposes of the study were:

1. To identify, screen, and evaluate sets of performance measures as indices of progress.
2. And then to demonstrate their applicability in two selected (county) jurisdictions.

As "outside" analysts, we could, at best, aim to demonstrate the feasibility of applying performance measures. Whether this application is "practical" and whether the benefits of applying performance measures would outweigh the incremental costs can thereafter be assessed by having officials in one or more jurisdictions adopt the approach, use it over some period of time, and then make the necessary cost/benefit judgments. Incremental costs of applying the full range of performance measures would vary from jurisdiction to jurisdiction, depending on the type of information system that was planned or already installed and the extent to which the jurisdiction would desire to measure performance in issue areas outside the capabilities of existing information systems. Careful estimates of the range of such incremental costs were beyond the scope of this study. However, we provide (in Chapter 8) very rough incremental cost estimates for two bounding cases: a gross estimate of costs for implementing a relatively comprehensive performance measurement system from "scratch," assuming that a jurisdiction has access to a computer but has not installed (or does not plan to install) an information system; and a gross estimate of the incremental cost associated with "upgrading" (i.e., adding a few data elements that can be collected inexpensively and special software packages) existing or planned information systems, such as CCH/OBTS, SJIS, or PROMIS.[3]

---

[3] See Chapter 8 for definitions and description of these systems.

Resource limitations necessarily limited the scope of this study. Attention was confined to adult felony proceedings; thus we did not consider misdemeanor proceedings nor civil proceedings. We addressed only the primary activities of the court system, thus excluding supporting activities and functions performed by court clerks, court reporters, bailiffs, or paralegals in the prosecutor's office or the public defender's office. Two broad types of performance applications were made: retrospective comparisons of the full court system and of its component agencies (rather than of individual practitioners) within the jurisdiction at different times; and retrospective interjurisdictional comparisons of court systems and component agencies at the same time. To the extent that our statistical modeling was successful in predicting and explaining certain performance measures of outcomes, we developed a very limited capability to do prospective performance analysis.

The study focused on a set of persistently important issue areas. Our view of their importance was confirmed by the results of personal interviews with some 33 practitioners (judges, prosecutors, defense counsel, court administrators, and legal scholars) in 13 large urban court systems throughout the United States and by the views of an advisory panel of distinguished practitioners. These issue areas were:

Prosecutorial (or other) case screening: limited to the subissues of adherence to charging standards and charging accuracy.

Plea bargaining: viewed as a balance between gains to, and other "operational impacts" (some possibly harmful) on, the court system, on the one hand, and system "concessions" to defendants, on the other.

Sentencing variation: how much variation; to what extent "legitimate" as opposed to "illegitimate" factors explain the variation.[4]

Evenhandedness or consistency of disposition and sentencing: to what extent such outcomes are affected by illegitimate factors.

Delay (or measures of elapsed time) between major events in the felony proceeding.

Case processing efficiency (as reflected in the use of judicial, prosecutorial, and defense counsel time) and the use of lay participant (jurors, victims, other witnesses) time.

---

[4] There is considerable controversy over whether certain factors are legitimate or illegitimate in sentencing decisions; for others there is general agreement. For purposes of this study, we have assumed that defendant's age, prior criminal record, community ties, and the nature of the original and convicted charges, and counts are legitimate factors and that ethnicity, pretrial custody status, type of defense attorney, type of disposition (trial or guilty plea), and correctional facilities crowding are illegitimate factors. See the discussion in Chapters 4 and 5.

Relationships between Issue Areas and the Policy
Interests of Practitioners and Agencies

These issue areas are important in the administration of criminal justice because
they involve significant aspects of the performance of the court system. For
some issue areas—delay, efficiency, evenhandedness, and charging accuracy—
practitioners and observers would all agree on the direction of improvement to
be sought. For others—the charging threshold, the impact of plea bargaining, and
sentencing variation—they could agree only that further illumination is desirable.
Also, certain agencies and types of practitioners would find particular issues to
be of greater interest than others, either because of relevance to their own
performance or because of concerns about current policy and how current
policy impacts compare with impacts of past policy.

Charging Standards

Prosecutors' offices in most jurisdictions need objective evidence of the standards being implemented to discern whether they conform to policy and what the
impacts on the system are if policy changes. For example, if the charging
threshold is lowered, how are court workload, delay, and plea bargaining
affected? Measures of the operation of the charging threshold over time also can
reveal trends in police performance.

Charging Accuracy

Is the nature of the disposition of cases being unduly affected by the accuracy
with which charges are filed against defendants? Is the court workload being
magnified by the consequences of inaccurate charging? Is inaccuracy in the
charging process abusing defendants' rights? Such questions concern not only
prosecutors but also judges, defense counsel, court administrators, et al. in
addressing charging policy and practices in their jurisdiction.

Plea Bargaining

What is the nature and frequency of the practice in the jurisdiction? Quantitative
evidence available to practitioners is often scant on this question. And the public
rarely has seen even the rudiments of an objective picture. What is the court
system gaining from plea negotiation? How are delay and efficiency of resource
use being affected? Is punishment significantly lighter than in the absence of
such negotiation? All practitioners, and the public as well, have a vital stake in

these questions, even though plea bargaining policy is primarily a prosecutorial responsibility.

Sentence Variation

Judges and other practitioners want to know the degree of consistency in sentencing in one court as compared to others, how sentencing practices change over time, and how they vary among judges within a court system. If, in addition, quantitative evidence were available to explain how much of the observed variation was accounted for by various legitimate and illegitimate factors, such illumination may enhance the effectiveness of various devices (e.g., sentencing panels and appellate review of sentences) aimed at reducing sentence disparity.

Evenhandedness

All practitioners and lay participants in the system, as well as the general public, are concerned that the courts be evenhanded in the delivery of justice, although the bench might have the primary responsibility in ensuring that it occurs. If illegitimate factors (e.g., the defendant's ethnicity, pretrial custody status, or type of defense counsel) have significantly affected how cases were disposed or the sentences imposed, steps can be taken to guard against such occurrences in the future.

Delay

Justice should be speedy, but few jurisdictions have comprehensive objective evidence on the duration of their cases. Even less can they isolate the effects of the separate factors (e.g., nature of offense, type of disposition, type of defense counsel, or backlog problems) that tend to delay individual cases. Although some factors that might cause delay are not readily controllable (e.g., court caseload), others are (e.g., continuance policy). Better measurement of delay and its determinants can help the court administration, for example, improve the allocation of resources.

Efficiency

Court system managers—the presiding judge, court administrator, district attorney, and chief of the public defender office—have responsibility for efficiency of operations. They must seek to make resources, including manpower, appropriate to the workload, given some standard for individual productivity.

Thus, each set of performance measures we discuss in this book has an "audience" among practitioners and often in the general public. Access to various sets of statistical indicators can assist in the assessment of performance, the design of new policies, and the evaluation of innovations in the myriad aspects of criminal prosecution, defense, adjudication, and sentencing.

Study Methods and Sources of Information

In the initial conceptualizing period of the study we undertook the construction of a hierarchy of recognized goals of the criminal justice system as a whole, and of felony proceedings as a whole. This goal structure was intended to be the framework to which would be related individual performance measures, then to be assembled into sets that would assess how closely the proceedings in a jurisdiction approached the goals.[5] In an early review by our Advisory Group (made up of distinguished jurists, prosecutors, defense attorneys, law professors, analysts, and experts in court administration), it was clear that no general consensus among practitioners on any specific goal structure was forthcoming.[6] Thus a "fail-safe" quality was lacking: if no specific goal structure was accepted, the credibility of the study would suffer. In response, we reshaped the study's scope by focusing on several persistently important areas (noted above) to which we could apply performance measures to assess at least desired direction of movement.

A series of interviews with seasoned criminal justice practitioners and the analysis of their responses comprised the second phase of this study. There were six interviews with judges, seven with court administrators, five with defense counsel, six with prosecutors, and two with academicians—the interviews being distributed in 13 jurisdictions across the country.[7] The interviews, which ranged from several hours to a full day in duration, informed us about the views of experienced practitioners toward the use and value of performance measures, the selection of issue areas, and the relevant performance measures and focused our consideration on the choice of the two demonstration jurisdictions.

In the demonstration phase we collected operational data from case files and other records in the prosecution, public defender, and court agencies made available by cooperating officials in the two jurisdictions.[8] These included 1,200 cases filed in felony court (samples of 100 each of burglary or breaking and

[5] For a brief discussion of goals and their links to the issue areas, see Chapter 4.

[6] See Appendix D for a roster of the Advisory Group members.

[7] See Appendix D for identification of the interviewees.

[8] For a complete description of the methods and sources used to collect these data, see Appendix B.

entering, robbery, and all felonies in each jurisdiction in each of two years) containing data on the nature and number of original and convicted charges, plea bargaining information, dates of major events in the case, disposition, sentence, and a variety of defendant-related characteristics. In addition, separate samples were collected for continuances and victim/other witness appearances, where necessary, as were samples for screening actions (100 each of police-booked burglary and robbery cases in two years in both jurisdictions) and for rejection reasons (samples or census of burglary and robbery "rejections" or "no informations" in two years in both jurisdiction). In addition, a pilot case audit activity was conducted as noted above, and it included extensive interviews with practitioners in both jurisdictions.

Once performance measures were calculated from the raw data elements, standard and specially developed software packages (i.e., computer programs) were used to cross-tabulate the performance measures, to estimate whether observed changes were statistically significant, and to analyze or explain the performance measure variation across cases. For example, multivariate regression analysis was employed to uncover the independent effect of selected factors that were hypothesized to affect performance measures of outcomes in the felony proceeding. These outcome measures included probability of conviction, sentence severity (given conviction), and delay (i.e., time elapsed between arraignment and final disposition).

2

Background and Literature Review

Contexts for the Use of Criminal Justice Data

Our central concern is with statistical indicators that measure the performance of the primary criminal court agencies, namely, the court itself, the office of the prosecutor, and the office of the public defender, as well as court-appointed and privately-retained defense counsel. For the moment, we characterize *performance measures* simply as statistical devices that help in the interpretation of quantitative information about systems operations. Later, we shall expand and deepen this characterization.

Collecting and processing criminal justice data is a burgeoning activity. Why? A leading writer in the field answers the question in this way:

Despite the uncertainty of objectives, the inherent difficulty of the crime problem itself, and limited resources to cope with it, there are more pressures on criminal justice agencies to measure and evaluate their own activities than on almost any other public system in our society. . . . corrections and other criminal justice agencies have strong mandates not only to report their activities but to assess their effectiveness, and thus to justify in measureable form their very existence. Normally it is not sufficient for the police to report how many crimes they investigated; they must also indicate how many they solved. Prosecutors often feel obligated to give a win-loss report in order to be reelected; judges face the responsibility of appellate reversal of their actions if they are deemed improper by a higher court; and prisons must make effectiveness claims of both security and rehabilitation. The time spent by criminal justice agencies counting and evaluating their activities probably exceeds that of any other public system, yet, as pointed out earlier, the amount and reliability of criminal justice reporting is less than adequate. One consequence of this pressure to report is that illusory improvements or failures can be shown simply by changing methods of record keeping, making rates appear to increase or diminish. . . . In any event, by selective statistics or by other means, there is great pressure within and between criminal justice agencies toward self-maintenance, toward winning a larger share of available tax-based resources. . . . There are other minor intra-agency objectives that may become important in understanding or evaluating a criminal justice agency or its processes. Because they are public agencies, all criminal justice offices and bureaucracies have public relations needs. Agency image is important not only for receiving budget support, but also for maintaining respect of the public at large, particularly if their cooperation is sought in helping to achieve crime control goals. Image making is not directed outside exclusively, but is equally important for those who work in the agencies, to maintain the morale and *esprit de corps* necessary to attain even limited success in achieving objectives. . . .[1]

To reiterate, the primary thrust of this book is to the question of how criminal justice data, and more particularly how statistical performance measures, may be used to analyze the operations in the criminal proceeding. As an aid to placing this research in a larger context, we summarize in Table 2-1 a comprehensive discussion of alternative approaches to analyzing the criminal justice process given by D.J. Newman.[2] Each identified approach differs in the degree to which it relies on the use of operational data and in the nature of the data used. We note that our study approach most closely relates to the Agency Practices Approach and the Recurrent Themes Approach as characterized by Newman.

Historical Perspective on Judicial Statistics

The efforts, historically, to collect court data reflect a snail's pace growth of the recognition that this type of criminal statistics has rewarding uses. In his recapitulation of these efforts, J.A. McCafferty describes the primitive beginnings at the federal level in the 19th century, involving mostly a handcounting of cases docketed and disposed of by the separate courts.[3] Apparently, no significant advance in collecting and processing federal court data occurred until the 1930s, when punched-card methods were introduced. A few state jurisdictions began collecting court statistics in the 1920s, followed by a landmark Ohio study that purported to show the feasibility of a permanent state reporting program.[4] The Bureau of Census, pursuant to a 1931 act of Congress, initiated the collection and compilation of statistical information on state court operations, with the participation of about 30 states (at one time or another). This program was abandoned in 1946, both because of poor cooperation by state courts and the limited availability of resource support.[5]

Advances in the collection and use of judicial statistics during the 1930s and 1940s were meager despite the farsighted recommendations of the National Commission on Law Observance and Enforcement (the Wickersham Commission), given in its Report on Criminal Statistics. But in the 1950s and 1960s, as the business of the criminal courts grew increasingly heavy and as substantive and procedural law reforms were made and felt, there developed an impetus to

[1] From Donald J. Newman, *Introduction to Criminal Justice*, pp. 47-48; reprinted by permission of the publisher, J.B. Lippincott Company, Philadelphia, 1975.

[2] Newman, *Introduction to Criminal Justice*, pp. 115-130.

[3] J.A. McCafferty, "The Need for Criminal Court Statistics," *Judicature*, Vol. 55, No. 4, November 1971.

[4] *Ohio Criminal Statistics, 1931*, Johns Hopkins Press, Baltimore, 1932.

[5] H. Alpert, "National Series of State Judicial Criminal Statistics Discontinued," *Journal of Criminal Law and Criminology*, Vol. XXXIX, No. 2, 1968.

Table 2-1
Approaches to Criminal Justice Analysis[a]

I. *Criminal Procedure* (Statutes and Case Law) Approach

Studying procedural law that relates to each decision point from the police investigation of crimes to parole and discharge from sentence; highlighting issues that are current and controversial.

II. *Agency Practices* Approach

Studying the day-to-day practices of police, prosecutors, judges, correctional personnel, defense counsel, and other participants in the criminal justice process; seeking to ascertain the criteria applied by these practitioners in performing their functions and to explain deviations from normal practices.

Three methods of analyzing agency practices:

1. Statistical—tabulate how frequently each discretionary alternative occurs at major decision stages of the criminal justice process.
2. Descriptive—describe the qualitative range of discretionary alternatives at each major decision stage and identify reasons for variations.
3. Evaluative—assess the effectiveness of decisions made at the major stage.

III. *Models* Approach

Constructing simplified, aggregative representations of the criminal justice process that purport to show how it operates according to a dominant proposition or analogy.

Examples: H.L. Packer's *Crime Control* and *Due Process* Models; J. Griffiths' *Family* Model.

IV. *Managerial Styles* Approach

Isolating and contrasting the styles of managerial behavior within criminal justice agencies.

Examples: (J.Q. Wilson) police enforcement styles—watchman, legalistic, and service; (L. Ohlin et al.) probation and parole officers—punitive, protective, and welfare; (V. O'Leary and D. Duffee) correctional organizations—reform, rehabilitative, restraint, and reintegration.

V. *Recurrent Themes* Approach

Identifying issues that are pervasive across the criminal justice process.

Example: Approach of F.J. Remington et al., using five themes:

1. Evidence sufficiency
2. Consent
3. Fairness and propriety of procedures
4. Effectiveness and efficiency of procedures
5. Discretion

VI. *Analysis of Dominant Functions* Approach

Perceiving each decision point in the criminal justice process as it relates to the different purposes assigned to crime control efforts, which purposes become functional imperatives in the daily operation of the system.

Example:

1. Punitive function
2. Deterrent function
3. Community protection function
4. Corrective function
5. Due process function.

[a]Derived from the discussion in Newman, *Introduction to Criminal Justice*, pp. 115-130.

obtain informational bases by which to improve the administration of the courts. Yet, even as late as the mid-1960s, the availability of judicial statistics, especially on a national scale, was limited.[6] But in the past decade, forces for change—including those exerted by the President's Commission and by the National Advisory Commission—have constructively reshaped the situation. One effect has been the implementation of research and development programs such as Project SEARCH.,[7] which has shown the technological feasibility of computerized information systems that can meet the needs of the criminal justice system and its component agencies. But even if there remain no serious technological impediments to the collection and processing of criminal justice data, economic and bureaucratic obstructions persist to the present time and limit the availability of court data in particular. Of course, such limitations differ widely in the various jurisdictions.

That it is now a propitious time to expand the uses of criminal justice data has been widely expounded. The following extract from the *Report on the Criminal Justice System*, National Advisory Commission on Criminal Justice Standards and Goals, January 1973, speaks to this point:

All criminal justice agencies, those with operational responsibilities and those with planning or policy responsibilities require substantial data to function properly as part of the overall criminal justice system. In general, criminal justice agencies require information on the events that initiate and terminate criminal justice processes; on people (suspects, victims, offenders, etc.) who are relevant to the operation of the criminal justice system; . . . and on *the operation of the agencies themselves* [emphasis added]. p. 37.

And to conclude this brief historical review, we draw from a modern text, Dean D. Nelson's *Cases and Materials on Judicial Administration and the Administration of Justice*, a quotation at p. 863 to show how judicial statistics ought now be viewed:

. . . The compiling and publishing of intelligently gathered and adequately organized judicial statistics is an important item in a program of improving our administration of justice. But at the outset one must enter a *caveat* that we must not expect too much from such statistics. . . . We cannot use even the best and most scientifically compiled statistics to solve the fundamental problems of jurisprudence. They cannot give us a measure of values of competing claims, or a

[6] See the discussion in P. Lejins, *National Crime Data Reporting System: Proposal for a Model*, Appendix C; *Crime and Its Impact—An Assessment*, Report of the Task Force on Assessment, The President's Commission on Law Enforcement and Administration of Justice, 1967.

[7] Project SEARCH (System for Electronic Analysis and Retrieval of Criminal Histories) was launched in 1969 by LEAA funding. It has sought to integrate the criminal statistics reporting systems of a number of states by means of an on-line information system for the exchange of offender files.

criterion of justice, or a theory of what we are seeking to bring about by means of law. But it does not follow that we have no use for statistics. . . . We must learn how to use statistics to control the quality of the output of the operations by which the legal order is maintained and carried on. . . . A workable system of intelligent gathering, compiling, and reporting statistics is one of the first steps toward making justice effective for its purpose [Pound, *Judicial Councils and Judicial Statistics*, 28A.B.A.J.98, at 102-104].

The foregoing discussion has been concerned with the role and uses of statistical information in the criminal justice context generally and in the criminal court system particularly. Henceforth our attention will focus on the statistical device of performance measures.

Performance measures may be regarded as having dual aspects. On the one hand, they are convenient and concise quantitative descriptors of the outputs from various stages of a criminal proceeding and of supporting activities. On the other hand, they are indices of how well the criminal justice process is working, that is, of progress toward goals. But their utility in the latter role is limited unless they are buttressed by the application of revealing statistical tools, such as regression analysis, factor analysis, cross-tabulation, etc. Such further analyses should generally help to explain what underlying factors are responsible for observed changes in the magnitudes of the performance factors. Later in this book (see Chapters 4, 5, and 6) we shall show how the application of statistical estimation techniques to performance data enables one to better understand the significance of variations in performance measure magnitudes.

The Present Study in the Perspective of Prior Efforts:
A Limited Literature Survey

We are not going to present a comprehensive compilation and critique of the existing criminal justice studies and writings that bear upon statistical performance measures for criminal proceedings. Rather, by means of a limited literature review, we will provide a perspective on the work that has preceded our study and thereby effect an understanding of where our efforts fit.

As noted above, statistical performance measures in the field of criminal justice (and criminal proceedings particularly) may be regarded as *quantitative descriptors* or as *indices of progress*. In plain terms, quantitative descriptors help to answer the question What are we doing?; progress indices, the question How well are we doing?—all in the context here of criminal proceedings. It will be helpful to retain this broad dichotomy for the purposes of our review.

Performance Measures as Quantitative Descriptors:
What Are We Doing?

Descriptors Unrelated to Quantitative Models. Quantitative descriptors of criminal court operations may be viewed as falling generally into two classes (with some important middle-ground exceptions). First, there are measures that describe the activities of a criminal court system as it actually is organized and operates without attempting to depict it in terms of a quantitative model. These measures may present either intermediate or final outputs of the proceedings— for example, the number of defendants charged, the number of case dispositions, the number of jury trials, the number of defendants incarcerated, etc., all in a specified period. Or they may describe resource inputs to the process—for example, overall expenditures, payroll expenditures, employment levels, use of physical facilities such as courtrooms, numbers of practitioners of various types (judges, prosecutors, public defenders, etc.) engaged in the proceedings, etc. Input descriptors are not of themselves "performance" measures, but they do enable output data (which are performance measures) to be further refined into measures of productivity and efficiency. This first class of quantitative descriptors is found with varying degrees of completeness in national-level publications,[8] not only applying to the federal courts, but also individually and aggregatively to the states and lower jurisdictions; state-level reports;[9] and local-level publications emanating from the county (or its governmental equivalent), the municipality, the individual court system, and even an agency within a court system.[10] While these statistical descriptors provide a "snapshot" of court system operations at one point or period in time, it is customary to present them in company with the corresponding snapshots of preceding periods and thereby

[8] An important example would be *Sourcebook of Criminal Justice Statistics, 1974*, National Criminal Justice Information and Statistics Service, LEAA, U.S. Department of Justice (prepared by M. Hindelang et al., Criminal Justice Research Center, Albany, N.Y.). To illustrate, one would find a tabulation therein of criminal cases filed in U.S. District Courts by offense and by fiscal year, and a tabulation of the disposition of persons formally charged by the police (in 2832 cities) by offense. An example of a resource-input report that could aid the preparation of performance measures is *Expenditure and Employment Data for the Criminal Justice System*, U.S. Law Enforcement Assistance Administration and U.S. Bureau of the Census. To illustrate, this report contains a tabulation of the judicial expenditures of 312 large county governments, by character and object, for fiscal year 1972-1973.

[9] See, for example, *Crime and Delinquency in California*, Bureau of Criminal Statistics, Division of Law Enforcement, Department of Justice, State of California (issued annually), which contains statistical information about crimes, arrests, court dispositions, jail populations, and personnel engaged in law enforcement activities; or see *Judicial Statistics, Fiscal Year 1973-1974*, Office of Court Administrator, Supreme Court of Michigan, which contains a tabulation of the average elapsed time in months from date of filing to date of trial for criminal jury and nonjury cases in the 46 circuit (county) court systems in that state.

[10] An example would be the *Annual Report, The Recorder's Court of the City of Detroit, Michigan*, which includes tabulations such as total felony dispositions for a calendar year by type of disposition and by individual judge and felony arraignments for a calendar year by offense and by month. Examples of reports at the court agency level that present statistical descriptors of performance are two from Multnomah County, Oregon, viz., *The Public Defender, A Program Analysis*, Office of Planning, Evaluation, and Program Development, Board of County Commissioners (1974); and *Your District Attorney's Office*, Harl Haas, District Attorney (1974). These both contain workload measures for the staff attorneys.

to suggest trends in activities—the descriptors thus may serve as "indicators." Many types of users (government executives, legislators, court administrators, the media, the public, etc.) employ this first class of statistical descriptors for a variety of purposes (policymaking, management, administrative, public relations, political, etc.).

Descriptors Related to Quantitative Models. By contrast, a second class of statistical descriptors are those that derive from, or are associated with, the quantitative modeling or simulation of a court system. The presence of this analytical formulation or representation of the court system distinguishes the second class from the first. Jennings has briefly surveyed quantitative models of criminal courts and has identified three types, namely, those that address case flow, case scheduling, or courtroom activities, respectively.[11] Case-flow models, which have been especially applied to the problem of allocating court resources, range in complexity and depth from descriptive types that clarify the inter-relationships within a court system (and thereby help to identify bottlenecks) to types that relate the flow of cases to the specific use of resources in the system (and thereby help to explore the effects of alternative uses of resources).[12] Jennings also reviews the use of models that simulate court operations for the purpose of improving case scheduling or calendering.[13] And, finally, he touches upon the applications of simulation to other aspects of court activities, e.g., the efficient use of jurors.[14]

For our purposes, we note that the application of quantitative models to a specific court system requires actual operating data to be collected from the system and incorporated into the model. The significance to us of the

[11] J.B. Jennings, *Quantitative Models of Criminal Courts*, P-4641, The New York City-Rand Institute, May 1971.

[12] Instances of (case-flow) simulation models of court operations, primarily applied to resource allocation problems, can be found in the following publications, included among those surveyed by Jennings: J. Navarro and J. Taylor, "Data Analyses and Simulation of the Court System in the District of Columbia for the Processing of Felony Defendants," *Task Force Report: Science and Technology*, President's Commission on Law Enforcement and the Administration of Justice, Washington, D.C., 1967; J. Jennings, *The Flow of Arrested Adult Defendants through the Manhattan Criminal Court in 1968 and 1969*, the New York City-Rand Institute, R-638-NYC, January 1971; and J. Jennings, *The Flow of Defendants through the New York City Criminal Court in 1967*, The New York City-Rand Institute, RM-6364-NYC, September 1970.

[13] *Final Report on the Development of a Criminal Court Calendar Scheduling Technique and Court-Day Simulation.*, Programming Methods, Inc., New York, N.Y., March 1971 is cited as containing a detailed simulation model of the operations of a portion of the New York City Criminal Court, which was developed primarily to test the effects of alternative methods of scheduling cases.

[14] A court is modeled in terms of the number of courtrooms in which jury trials are held each day, the times required for *voir dire*, the probability of accepting a prospective juror, and the lengths of trials in the article by F. Merrill and L. Schrage, "Efficient Use of Jurors: A Field Study and Simulation Model of a Court System," *Washington University Law Quarterly*, Vol. 1969, No. 2, cited by Jennings.

availability of analytical models of specific or generalized criminal court systems is that statistical descriptors are generally an explicit part of their analytical structure or are readily implied by it. Depending on the type of model, these may be measures of the relative flow of cases in various branches of the model, time consumed between events in the proceeding, workloads, backlogs, relative frequencies of various outputs, etc.

In this vein, the work of Blumstein and his associates in constructing flow models of the criminal justice system should be cited.[15] Numerous court system descriptors stem from their analytical representations, including workload measures for case processing (e.g., prosecutor-hours per guilty plea, judge-days per trial) and cost measures (e.g., cost to the court for processing a defendant by type of offense charged). Such models generally entail the determination of branching ratios within the system (e.g., the likelihood that a defendant at point A in the criminal proceeding will move to point B); these ratios in effect characterize the relative flows of cases and serve as quantitative descriptors of the court system simulated.

A narrower example is that of a simulation model addressing the vital issue of court delay.[16] While this model suggests informative measures of delay, it is not a source for measures of other aspects of court performance.

A final example is a statistical model of judicial productivity and elapsed time to disposition in the U.S. District Courts, in which the author devises several statistical descriptors of productivity and delay and attempts to explain the independent effects of important variables in these descriptions.[17] This model, like the preceding one, is not a source for measures of other aspects of court performance.

Quantitative Descriptors from a Middle Ground. The two classes of descriptors—related and unrelated to quantitative models—are not exhaustive. One may find in the literature significant studies in which quantitative descriptors were identified or devised not strictly on the basis of analytical models but nevertheless with a clear recognition of court processes and agencies as a "system." This recognition underscores the need for a full and balanced statistical picture of criminal proceedings, which in turn suggests an array of

[15] Alfred Blumstein and Richard Larson, "Models of a Total Criminal Justice System," *Operations Research*, Vol. 17, No. 2, 1969; J. Belkin and A. Blumstein, "Methodology for the Analysis of Total Criminal Justice Systems," Urban Systems Institute, Carnegie-Mellon University, 1970; J. Belkin, A. Blumstein, and W. Glass, "JUSSIM, An Interactive Computer Program for Analysis of Criminal Justice Systems," Urban Systems Institute, 1971.

[16] *System Study in Court Delay—LEADICS (Law Engineering Analysis of Delay in Court Systems*, Notre Dame University Law and Engineering Schools (in four volumes), prepared for LEAA, January 1972.

[17] R.W. Gillespie, *Judicial Productivity and Court Delay: A Statistical Analysis of the Federal District Courts*, Final Report: Grant Number 74-NI-0025, National Institute of Law Enforcement and Criminal Justice, LEAA, U.S. Department of Justice, March 5, 1975.

measures that reveal what the system is doing. A classic study of this type was conducted by Subin, who sought to show how a judicial process (felony and serious misdemeanor proceedings in the District of Columbia Court of General Sessions) might be described quantitatively.[18] Two similar instances (again reflecting the efforts of Subin and others) are presented in an appendix to the President's Commission Task Force Report on the Courts.[19] These studies produced descriptions of municipal criminal court systems mainly by means of a statistical framework.

An important example of the middle-ground approach is that of Greenwood, Wildhorn, et al., who viewed the prosecutor's office in a systems context;[20] they described in statistical terms how the felony prosecutorial process functioned in Los Angeles County and attempted to demonstrate the value of analysis in informing policymakers how the policies of the prosecutor's office were working. A variety of statistical descriptors was employed in analyzing the prosecutor's screening decision; the lower court's decision to hold the defendant to answer on felony charges, treat him as a misdemeanant, or dismiss the case and discharge him; the plea bargaining process; the trial outcome; the court's sentencing decision; the effect of factors such as the defendant's prior record, race, type of defense counsel, and pretrial custody status on type of disposition and outcome; and the consistency or evenhandedness with which defendants were treated in various branches of the District Attorney's Office and the Superior Court within the county. (The study also hypothesized two polar descriptive models of prosecutorial management and philosophy and attempted to explain differences in felony dispositions and outcomes across branch offices in terms of these polar models.)

A contrasting, middle-ground approach is that of DonVito, who views urban criminal courts in a system context (but without a quantitative model).[21] DonVito begins by advancing a set of seven measures and then attempts to

---

[18] H. Subin, *Criminal Justice in a Metropolitan Court—The Processing of Serious Criminal Cases in the District of Columbia Court of General Sessions*, Office of Criminal Justice, U.S. Department of Justice, Washington, D.C., October 1966.

[19] "Administration of Justice in the Municipal Court of Baltimore" and "Administration of Justice in the Recorder's Court of Detroit," Appendix B, *Task Force Report: The Courts*, The President's Commission on Law Enforcement and Administration of Justice, Washington, D.C. 1967.

[20] P.W. Greenwood, S. Wildhorn, et al., *Prosecution of Adult Felony Defendants in Los Angeles County: A Policy Perspective*, Lexington Books, D.C. Heath and Company, 1976.

[21] P. DonVito, "An Experiment in the Use of Court Statistics," *Judicature*, Vol. 56, No. 2, August-September 1972. The selected measures are: the amount of time taken to dispose of criminal cases; the extent to which those convicted had entered pleas of guilty; the percentage of jail prisoners awaiting trial; the the backlog of criminal cases relative to the court's caseload; the average number of cases disposed of per judge; and the extent to which probation is used as an alternative to imprisonment. The number of cities from which data were available varied from 3 to 28, depending upon the descriptor.

ascertain how well these measures, as a set, describe the performance of the courts in a number of urban areas from which he draws data.

Another distinctive example in the middle-ground genre is provided by the Report of the State's Attorney's Office of Baltimore City, which portrays that office as an element of a larger system and explains how specified statistical descriptors serve to indicate its performance as an agency of the court system.[22]

Performance Measures as Indices of Progress toward
Goals: How Well Are We Doing?

Assessing progress toward goals and standards is the second function that we have attributed to statistical performance measures (as a basis for classifying relevant literatures).[23] Again we perceive a dichotomy that facilitates the discussion, namely: goals that are associated with a (primarily qualitative) model; and goals that are set forth without specific reference to a model or conceptual representation. This review will touch upon selected references that articulate various criminal justice goals toward which the system should progress. And the review will lead us to conclude that there is an important gap in the literature, namely, on how performance measures may be selected or devised to assess progress toward criminal justice goals.

Goals and Standards Not Associated with Models. The leading sources of standards and goals not associated with a specific model of the criminal justice system or its components are the ABA Standards for Criminal Justice, which appeared in a series of volumes since 1968,[24] the *Standards and Goals of the National Advisory Commission on Criminal Justice Standards and Goals*,[25] which resulted from the work of a commission appointed in 1970 by the administrator of LEAA, and the ABA Standards of Judicial Administration, being drawn up by an ABA commission.[26] Reference to statements of goals and

---

[22] *Report of State's Attorney's Office of Baltimore City*, Under the Administration of Milton B. Allen, January 1971 to July 1974. The Office appears to rely on measures such as disposition rate, conviction rate, jury trial rate, and plea rate, with appropriate break-outs of some gross measures.

[23] Our purposes here do not require that we make a distinction between goals and standards. We may regard a *standard* as being one type of goal that has been established by authority or that has been set forth officially (in some sense), for example, by constitution, legislation, court decision, court rule, governmental commission, professional committee, etc.

[24] See footnote 1, Chapter 1.

[25] See footnote 1, Chapter 1.

[26] The first completed volume is *Standards Relating to Court Organization* (Approved 1974); a second volume, *Standards Relating to Trial Courts* is in tentative draft form; the third and final volume, *Standards Relating to the Administration of Appellate Courts* is in rough draft.

standards has been facilitated by the preparation of a comparative analysis standard-by-standard of the first two works.[27] For our purposes, we note that a substantial proportion of these hundreds of individual goals and standards relate to the criminal proceeding, but few are couched in quantitative terms or lend themselves to a quantitative interpretation—the primary exception being those concerning the "speed" of the proceeding. For example, an ABA standard relating to pleas of guilty sets forth, as to the relationship between defense counsel and client, that: "Defense counsel should conclude a plea agreement only with the consent of the defendant, and should ensure that the decision whether to enter a plea of guilty, or *nolo contendere* is ultimately made by the defendant."[28] By contrast, an NAC standard relating to the time frame for prompt processing of criminal cases states that: "The period from arrest to the beginning of trial of a felony prosecution generally should not be longer than 60 days."[29] Having raised the question of how performance measures might assess progress toward such goals as these, we postpone comment to a later point in this chapter.

An excellent example of an expression of goals (and subgoals) for a court system that is not associated with a qualitative model is to be found in an internal memorandum of the Institute of Judicial Administration, Inc.[30] In this instance, the selection and application of performance measures have been facilitated by rephrasing the general goals as more specific issue statements.[31]

[27] *Comparative Analysis of Standards and Goals of the National Advisory Commission on Criminal Justice Standards and Goals with Standards for Criminal Justice of the American Bar Association*, American Bar Association, Section of Criminal Justice, Washington, D.C., 1973.

[28] Ibid., 240.

[29] Ibid., p. 249.

[30] Internal Memorandum, D. Weinstein to Requirements Analysis Subcommittee, April 24, 1974, The Institute of Judicial Administration, Inc., New York, N.Y.

[31] The goals, subgoals, and corresponding issue statements are as follows:

Goal: Efficient use of resources.
  Subgoal: Court unification and reorganization.
  Issue: Is the caseload reasonably well allocated among judicial districts and personnel? Are there districts too large or too small to operate efficiently?
  Subgoal: Reduction of unnecessary idleness of resources.
  Issue: Are judicial and other resources standing idle because of insufficient resources or poor management?

Goal: Accurate and conscientious decisionmaking.
  Subgoal: Adequate time and resources devoted to individual cases.
  Issue: Are individual cases receiving adequate time and attention?
  Subgoal: Equal protection of the laws.
  Issue: Are judges or other decisionmakers letting personal bias unduly influence decisionmaking?
  Subgoal: Due process of law.

(continued on page 22)

Goals and Standards Associated with Qualitative Models. An articulation or at least an implication of goals is usually entailed in the qualitative or descriptive models approach to the characterization and analysis of criminal justice. We shall rely on a recent article by J. Senna to provide a concise classification of qualitative models of criminal justice.[32] Senna identifies three broad classes of these models, namely: *systems* models, which typically characterize a criminal justice system as an interrelationship of police, court, and corrections agencies; *process* models, which perceive a series of decisionmaking points and emphasize the various sequential stages through which an offender passes in the attempt to achieve some expressed goals; and *organization* models, which embody applications of organization and management. The systems model approach has generally been frustrated, Senna feels, by the fact that criminal justice is implemented by a loose federation of agencies with some mutual concerns, but which tend to operate more or less independently with a multiplicity of sometimes conflicting objectives.

By contrast, process models have been more fruitfully pursued. H. Packer has developed two widely discussed models termed *crime control* and *due process.*[33] The crime control model is founded on the belief that repression of criminal conduct is the most important function of criminal justice; the due process model is based on the concept of the primacy of the individual along with limited official power. The first emphasizes the need to maintain a high rate of apprehension and conviction of offenders, with a premium on the speed and finality of the criminal proceeding; the second underscores the protections for the accused at every stage of the criminal proceeding.

Another author, J. Griffiths, has devised a *family* model in opposition to both of Packer's models.[34] In Griffith's model, the interests of society and the offender need not be incompatible, and the state should seek to act in the best interests of the offender, as a juvenile court attempts to do. By contrast, Griffith

---

Goal: Neutrality in decisionmaking.
  Subgoal: Elimination of unnecessary delay.
  Issue: Is there unnecessary delay in the processing of cases which is favoring particular classes of litigants?

Goal: Minimize social and economic costs to outside participants in the judicial process.
  Issue: Are the demands of the judicial system on witnesses, jurors, and litigants too great in terms of time, money, and dislocation?

Goal: Maintenance and growth of judicial system.
  Issue: Is the judicial system receiving enough financial and other support to continue to serve the public effectively and efficiently?

[32] J. Senna, "Models in Criminal Justice: Building Blocks for Change," *Judicature*, Vol. 59, No. 1, June-July, 1975.

[33] H. Packer, *The Limits of the Criminal Sanction*, Stanford University Press, Stanford, 1968.

[34] J. Griffiths, "Ideology in Criminal Procedure or a Third Model of the Criminal Process," *Yale Law Journal*, Vol. 79, January 1970.

suggests Packer's models are two versions of a "battle" model that depicts a conflict of interests.

Other process modeling has been contributed by W. Miller[35] (who distinguishes a "left" ideological pattern from a "right" ideological pattern in implementing the criminal justice process), by F. Remington et al.,[36] (who identifies five basic analytic themes for viewing the criminal justice process—see Section V of Table 2-1), and by A. Goldstein[37] (who contrasts "inquisitorial" models with "accusatorial/adversarial" models).

Senna's survey identifies several leading examples of the organizational model approach. One such development was given by the Organization for Social and Technical Innovation.[38] Another is a management model of criminal justice proposed by McCaffey, wherein the emphasis is primarily on the roles, functions, skills, programming, budget control, and other management considerations.[39]

Given this spectrum of descriptive models, what do they express in the nature of goals as the directions for criminal justice efforts, which goals in turn generate requirements for progress measurement? Senna finds in his survey that systems models seek to accomplish a wide span of criminal justice objectives including crime prevention, deterrence, rehabilitation, reintegration, and punishment. But the core of the difficulty in developing systems models is that these goals tend to be conflicting, and different agencies within a criminal justice system pursue them with different emphases.

On the other hand, process models are found generally to underscore both deterrence and restraint of offenders while emphasizing also fairness and strict procedural safeguards. And Senna observes that organizational models, by focusing on goals of efficiency and effectiveness, seek to avoid moral dilemmas posed by the imposition of criminal sanctions.

Measuring Progress toward Goals and Standards. The main thrust of our limited review of the literature serving as a source of goals and standards for criminal justice (and for criminal proceedings in particular) is that one generally obtains gross and qualitative expressions or inferences of goals from these references,

[35]W. Miller, "Ideology and Criminal Justice Policy: Some Current Issues," *Journal of Criminal Law and Criminology*, Vol. 64, June 1973.

[36]F. Remington, D. Newman, et al., *Criminal Justice Administration*, Bobbs-Merrill, Indianapolis, 1969.

[37]A. Goldstein, "Reflections on Two Models: Inquisitorial Themes in American Criminal Procedure," *Stanford Law Review*, Vol. 26, May 1974.

[38]*Implementation Report Submitted to the President's Commission on Law Enforcement and the Administration of Justice*, The Organization for Social and Technical Innovation, 1967.

[39]A. McCaffey, *Administration of Criminal Justice—A Management Systems Approach*, Prentice-Hall Publishing Co., 1974.

which do not of themselves suggest how progress might be measured by performance data. At a minimum, the analyst finds it necessary to seek or devise a structure of more specific and measurable subgoals and then perhaps to translate these subgoals into concrete issue statements that clarify what operational data are relevant.[40] And then there remains the problem of selecting specific performance measures or sets of measures that reveal the appropriate informational content of these data (which will be considered in Chapter 4).

To our knowledge, the literature is largely lacking in studies that address the problems of translating general statements of objectives into specific measures of progress. One important purpose of our study is to help close the gap. In particular, we set forth in Chapter 4 a set of criteria for selecting preferred performance measures from among the wide choices that may be available to assess performance relative to a goals issue. And our study as a whole illustrates the process of arriving at and applying sets of performance measures that illuminate several important issue areas that are widely acknowledged to be closely linked to criminal proceeding goals.

Summary

Therefore, the present study may be viewed in the perspective of the literature review as follows. Our focus has not been on the use of performance measures simply as quantitative descriptors of criminal proceedings, that is, as aids to answering the question What are we doing? Rather, our study's thrust has been toward the role of performance measures as progress indices—toward their contribution in answering the question How well are we doing? Our study does not advance a fresh set of goals and standards (except to the limited degree given in Chapter 4, a product of the first exploratory stage of our work); neither does it propound another model, either quantitative or descriptive, of the court system. Most significantly, what the present study sets out to do is to close some of the research gap between articulating goals and standards, on the one hand, and selecting and applying progress indices, on the other.

As to its links with previous work, our study may be viewed as a natural outgrowth, both in scope and depth, of a previous Rand study (described above) of adult felony proceedings in Los Angeles County.[41] The present study is broader in scope in that certain issues (such as delay) are considered here, whereas the earlier study simply did not address them at all. It provides more depth in several ways: by advancing more of a conceptual basis for selecting performance measures and for drawing inferences about performance; by analyzing some specific issue areas (such as plea bargaining) in greater detail; and by applying multivariate statistical estimation techniques and thereby attempting to explain the independent effects of important variables on some of the major performance measures.

---

[40] See, for example, footnote 31.

[41] P. Greenwood, S. Wildhorn, et al., *Prosecution of Adult Felony Defendants.*

3

Professional Views on Performance Measures: Interviews with Practitioners

The Purpose of the Interviews

A series of interviews with experienced criminal justice practitioners (including academicians in the field) was conducted early in the study after our research efforts had been reshaped on the basis of the counsel given by the Advisory Group organized for the study.[1] The purposes of the interviews were set out to be the following:

1. To learn at first-hand the views and attitudes of a variety of judges, court administrators, defense counsel, prosecutors, and academicians toward the use and value of statistical performance measures in criminal court systems.
2. To elicit reactions from these experienced professionals about our (reoriented) study program, including their views on:
    a. Our tentative selection of significant issue areas in which to demonstrate applications of performance measures.
    b. Our preliminary choices of specific performance measures purporting to illuminate these issue areas.
    c. Our insights concerning the validity of interjurisdictional comparisons by means of performance measures.[2]
3. Finally, to appraise possible choices of two jurisdictions in which the study team would seek to demonstrate the application of performance measures.

Primarily, these practitioner interviews were regarded not as a source from which we would derive final study output but rather as a foundation for decisions and choices in the subsequent phases of our work. The interviews, in fact, provided the first empirical data of the study.

Implementation of the Interviews

In preparation for the practitioner interviews, a set of brief discussion papers was written, to be sent beforehand to the interviewees so that they might be

---

[1] Appendix D contains the roster of our Advisory Group and a listing of the practitioner interviewees.

[2] See Chapter 4 for an outline of key factors in making interjurisdictional comparisons of performance measures.

prompted to collect their thoughts on the issue areas that we planned to address.[3] In addition, an interview instrument of nearly 100 questions (keyed to a set of exhibits) was constructed. It was intended that these questions would be flexibly administered by an interviewer as seemed appropriate, given the available interview time, the interests of the practitioner, and the practitioner's role in the system. Our next step was to "pretest" these materials with a sample of practitioners in the Los Angeles area—a trial court judge, a senior prosecutor, a federal public defender, two court administrators, and an academician with both prosecution and defense experience. The interview materials and the technique of applying them were both refined as an outcome of these pretest interviews.

Next came a series of countrywide inquiries to a list of well-known practitioners, whose names had been suggested mostly by the Advisory Group and by study consultants. Their replies were almost invariably affirmative when asked: "Would you be willing to submit to an interview of several hours or more for the described purposes of Rand's study?" Five study team members then conducted interviews over a period of roughly two weeks in the jurisdictions listed in Table 3-1. By design, the interviewing was almost entirely concentrated in major metropolitan areas. Most quarters of the country were represented.

Including the pretest interviewees, a total of 33 professionals were queried in the course of 26 interviews, which ranged from an hour and a half to an entire

Table 3-1
Jurisdictions in Which Practitioner Interviews Were Conducted

Maricopa County (Phoenix), Arizona
Los Angeles County (City of Los Angeles), California
District of Columbia
Dade County (Miami), Florida
Fulton County (Atlanta), Georgia
Cook County (Chicago), Illinois
Wayne County (Detroit), Michigan
New York County (City of New York), New York
Clackamas County (Oregon City), Oregon
Multnomah County (Portland), Oregon
Philadelphia County (City of Philadelphia), Pennsylvania
Harris County (Houston), Texas
Milwaukee County (City of Milwaukee), Wisconsin

[3]These background papers presented definitions and ideas in the areas of prosecutorial screening, plea bargaining, sentencing variation, evenhandedness, case processing efficiency, delay, and interjurisdictional comparisons, respectively. Their content is reflected in Chapter 4 of this book.

day in duration.[4] We invited the respondents to choose the issue areas they preferred to discuss (among those we proposed) in addition to replying to our other areas of inquiry. The distribution of their choices, which is of itself instructive, is given in Table 3-2.

Table 3-2 reveals that the judges we interviewed preferred to express their views most frequently in the subject areas of sentencing and of case processing efficiency and delay; court administrators tended to parallel judges in their emphases but with greater concentration on efficiency and delay (which could be expected); defense counsel showed less propensity to concentrate than the other practitioners in our sample; and prosecutors gravitated toward two areas of special concern to them, namely, screening and plea bargaining.

The practitioners comprising our interview sample spanned the primary professional roles within criminal proceedings; furthermore, they were geographically diverse. But they do not purport to be a representative cross section of the national population of criminal justice practitioners. By contrast with the nominal practitioner, those that we selected were more experienced and had evinced greater interest in the problems of analyzing criminal justice operations. Such a sample bias was consistent with the purposes of the interviews, which were directed toward obtaining professional guidance and not to produce an accurate nationwide picture of practitioners' attitudes. Therefore, we must emphasize that, *because of the small size of the interview sample and its special qualities, one should not regard the views expressed to us (summarized below) as*

Table 3-2
Number of Interviews in which a Given Issue Area Was Elected

Practitioner	Efficiency and Delay	Evenhand-edness	Screening	Plea Bargaining	Sentencing
Judges (6 interviews)	5	3	0	1	6
Court administrators (7 interviews)	7	3	0	2	3
Defense counsel (5 interviews)	2	3	1	3	1
Prosecutors (6 interviews)	1	0	4	5	1
Academicians (2 interviews)	0	0	1	2	1
Total	15	9	6	13	12

[4]With the exception of the pretest sessions, which were conducted jointly by all interviewers, each session was conducted by a single interviewer who manually recorded notes as the dialogue proceeded, usually in the office or chambers of the interviewee during the business day.

being attributable to practitioners in general. Nevertheless, when the interviewees were nearly unanimous in their responses to a query, we are inclined to give that position special weight and regard it as likely to be representative.

Below, without seeking to be exhaustive, we shall give some general findings from the interviews and indicate how they influenced our subsequent undertakings.

General Observations, Findings, and Impacts

Our interviews were marked by a wide diversity of views on most substantive issues that were raised, differences being expressed not only among types of practitioners but also within each type. We anticipated this variety of response and were, in fact, reassured by its presence.

We were particularly struck by the division of views and the strength of feeling about the role of case auditing relative to the role of statistical performance measures as informational devices in criminal proceedings. (See Chapter 7 for a characterization and application of case auditing.) Some interviewees asserted that case auditing was indispensible, even when other informational tools, such as statistical performance measures, were used. Others were less extreme but felt that case auditing was the most reliable technique for revealing how a court system had been performing. Still others placed a higher value on performance measures but thought that their main utility was for internal management control. And finally, some were performance-measure enthusiasts who perceived important benefits not only in their application to internal control but also in measuring progress toward external goals and in facilitating interjurisdictional comparisons of criminal justice performance.

The more experience that an interviewed practitioner had had with the operational use of performance data and statistical performance measures, the less pervasive appeared to be his distrust and the more specific and realistic his reservations about such use.

Nearly all interviewees professed an appreciation of our need to limit the scope and aspirations of this performance measures study and concurred, at least by default, in its design. Perhaps the deepest misgivings were expressed about the omission of misdemeanor proceedings and of support staff operations, both of which were felt by some interviewees to be inseparable from the elements included in the study.

There was a weak consensus that, among the five issue areas that we identified, the least promising for our research purposes would be evenhandedness or possibly case processing efficiency and delay. This relative disaffection with evenhandedness seemed to stem from three bases: (1) even where the problem was recognized, there tended to be little policy leverage on it; and (2) in most jurisdictions the problem was regarded as not being significant; and

(3) some practitioners felt that a practical definition of the problem was difficult to frame and have accepted. It was less apparent why case processing efficiency and delay was given a lower rank by some interviewees; evidently they felt that this topic was already the subject of enough work that our contribution would be marginal. But, observing the absence of a clear consensus and the lack of suggestions as to alternative issue areas,[5] we interpret the interviewing results as not, of themselves, calling for the elimination of any of our five issue areas from further attention.

As a whole, the interviewed practitioners seemed to oppose complexity in the measures that purported to capture plea bargaining performance and the accuracy of screening.

If a formal management information system (which included the production and distribution of statistical performance information) were to be implemented in a jurisdiction that lacked one, the interviewees tended to believe it should be operated on a routine periodic basis under centralized control, but not necessarily with centralized data collection. Nearly all doubted the availability of additional funding in their own jurisdiction for such purposes; some surmised that a reallocation of current resources might be feasible, if such an information system clearly promised an overall reduction in court system costs.

In general, the practitioners anticipated that having demonstrations in (two) selected jurisdictions, as we contemplated doing, would be useful, but there was no consensus that these demonstrations would be instrumental in persuading other jurisdictions to adopt a more extensive program of collecting and applying performance data. Rather, the feeling was that local budgetary factors would be almost completely determinative in any decision to undertake such activities.

The foregoing general findings led us to conclude that:

1. We would add a case auditing effort of modest dimensions to the demonstration phase of the project, primarily to show the complementarity of the two approaches. But this would not reflect a diminution of our belief (shared by many interviewees) that statistical performance measures, objectively employed, have a rich and insufficiently tapped potential for policymakers, managers, practitioners, and the public.

2. While we concurred that a picture of the performance of felony proceedings would not be as complete and accurate as might be desired if measures of support staff operations and of misdemeanant and juvenile processing were omitted, our resource limitations continued to preclude the expansion of the study scope to include the latter areas. We would, however, accept the lessened applicability of the study in some situations.

---

[5] The only alternative issue area to which a shared view of importance seemed to attach was the court itself, viz., judicial background, judicial appointment method, judicial competence, judicial temperament, etc., and the relations among these factors. But this issue area is not particularly amenable to quantitative analysis.

3. As mentioned earlier, an absence of a persuasive consensus about eliminating any of the proposed five issue areas and a lack of suggestions for alternative or additional areas amenable to statistical analysis were observed in the interview responses. Therefore, we would continue consideration of all five through at least the demonstration phase. Difficulties in collecting relevant data or a paucity of useful results might impel later abandonment of an issue area.

4. Despite an abundance of technical difficulties in measuring plea bargaining performance and screening accuracy, as underscored by the interviewees, we would continue to seek measures that were more informative than the gross ones now employed, while sacrificing simplicity only when we could not avoid doing so.

5. We would not count on our work in the two demonstration jurisdictions as being of such scope and detail that it could prove compellingly the advantage of having an information system embodying statistical performance measures, at various alternative levels of implementation cost. The size of our data bases in the demonstration systems would have to be governed to an important degree by constraints on our study resources. We might fortuitously uncover instances of gross inefficiency, the elimination of which could help underwrite a better information system in the demonstration jurisdiction. But even this result could not be expected to persuade other jurisdictions to act.

4

The Performance Measures: Selection, Rationale, Limitations and Data Elements Required

Our exposition of performance measures in this chapter is not intended to be a complete handbook that presents a full spectrum of available performance measures for criminal proceedings and methods for devising additional ones. Indeed, depending upon the data base that is constructed, there would be a virtually unlimited number of statistical descriptors of that data; and many, if not all, of those descriptors would be interpreted as performance indicators for some purposes. The scope and objectives of this book lead us to focus our treatment of statistical performance measures more narrowly, that is, on exemplary sets of measures (whose data elements are collected from case files and other agency records) that we find to be useful in illuminating the specific issue areas with which this book is concerned—case processing efficiency and delay, prosecutorial case screening, plea bargaining, evenhandedness, and sentence variation. The discussion here is, almost in its entirety, from the intrajurisdictional point of view. However, at the end of this chapter we describe briefly some interjurisdictional considerations.

First, we set forth societal goals of the criminal justice system (which tend to conflict when they are pursued jointly). Next, for each of the system goals, we formulate one or more supportive goals of the criminal proceeding and indicate how they are linked to the issue areas we considered. Then, we present a set of criteria to guide the selection of performance measures in general and which shaped our choices in particular. Next we discuss in detail some illustrative complexities that are involved in devising a set of performance measures for an issue area—in this instance, prosecutorial screening. This discussion is intended to be suggestive of problems in the other issue areas as well, which we do not consider in the same depth. Finally, the main content of the chapter is the presentation and explanation of sets of performance measures for each issue considered within the specified areas, including a specification of the data elements contained in these measures. The explanations will touch upon how changes in the values of the given measures communicate information about the related issue.[1] And we shall note where difficulties were encountered in collecting the required data elements in the demonstration jurisdictions.[2]

---

[1] Chapters 5 and 6 contain a fuller discussion of using performance measures to draw inferences about performance issues (in the context of the demonstration jurisdictions).

[2] See also Appendix B.

Societal Goals for the Criminal Justice System

Formulating and classifying the societal goals for the criminal justice system may be done in various ways depending on one's purpose. Our purpose is to create a framework within which criminal justice issues can be readily understood and assessed. The utility of performance measures to be devised will be judged ultimately in terms of the issues themselves rather than by reference to the contextual framework. Thus, the design we choose for the latter need not be regarded as crucial.

We perceive five broad societal goals, complementing and conflicting in varying degrees:

1. Control crime.
2. Exact retribution from criminals.
3. Accord fairness to defendants, victims, and the public.
4. Conserve resources, both external and internal to the criminal justice system.
5. Promote public trust and confidence in the system.

Further, as shown in Figure 4-1, we distinguish subgoals or different ways of furthering the broad goals.[3]

At least four ways of *controlling* crime are identified in the various theories of punishment:

1. Control criminals (by using incarceration, pretrial diversion, probation supervision, parole supervision, etc.).
2. Achieve general deterrence (by punishing criminal conduct and thereby deterring society from such conduct).
3. Achieve specific deterrence (by convicting and punishing specific individuals and thereby deterring them from further criminal acts).
4. Rehabilitate criminals.

These means of controlling crime are not mutually exclusive; for example, probation supervision is a device that may help to control an offender, to rehabilitate him, and to deter further criminal conduct.

Exacting retribution needs little elaboration. Its roots run deeply into history, but there is a tendency to disavow this goal. Nonetheless, some practitioners and much of the public still strongly embrace this aim for criminal justice.

According fairness is a fundamental principle of American jurisprudence, civil and criminal. Here the phrase subsumes the accuracy of criminal proceedings, procedural due process, the evenhandedness of outcomes, and redress of

[3] Just as balances must be struck among the broad goals when they conflict, so too must balance be struck among subgoals in the attainment of a general goal.

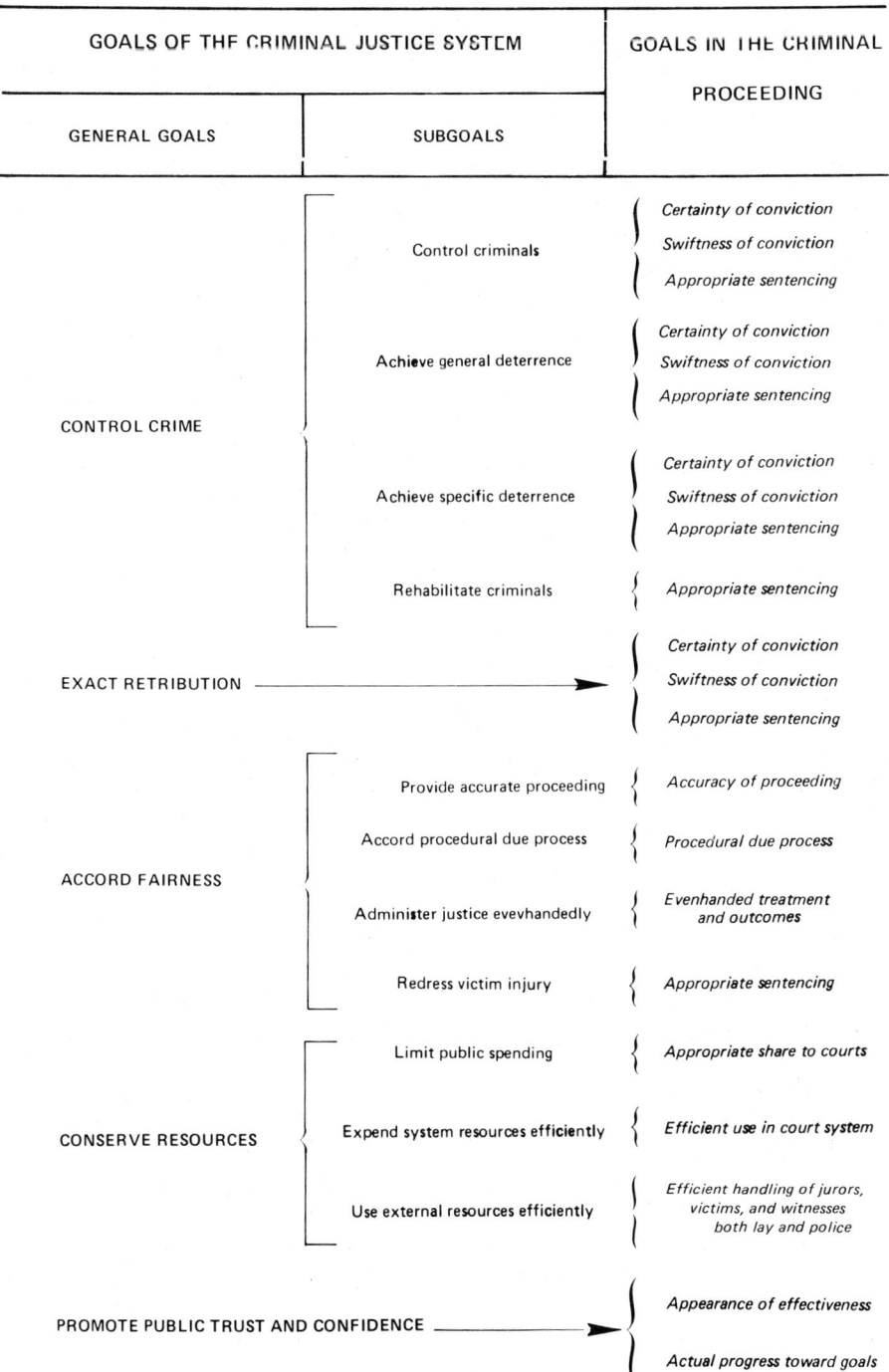

GOALS OF THE CRIMINAL JUSTICE SYSTEM | GOALS IN THE CRIMINAL PROCEEDING

GENERAL GOALS | SUBGOALS

CONTROL CRIME

Control criminals
- Certainty of conviction
- Swiftness of conviction
- Appropriate sentencing

Achieve general deterrence
- Certainty of conviction
- Swiftness of conviction
- Appropriate sentencing

Achieve specific deterrence
- Certainty of conviction
- Swiftness of conviction
- Appropriate sentencing

Rehabilitate criminals
- Appropriate sentencing

EXACT RETRIBUTION
- Certainty of conviction
- Swiftness of conviction
- Appropriate sentencing

ACCORD FAIRNESS

Provide accurate proceeding
- Accuracy of proceeding

Accord procedural due process
- Procedural due process

Administer justice evenhandedly
- Evenhanded treatment and outcomes

Redress victim injury
- Appropriate sentencing

CONSERVE RESOURCES

Limit public spending
- Appropriate share to courts

Expend system resources efficiently
- Efficient use in court system

Use external resources efficiently
- Efficient handling of jurors, victims, and witnesses both lay and police

PROMOTE PUBLIC TRUST AND CONFIDENCE
- Appearance of effectiveness
- Actual progress toward goals

Figure 4-1. A Hierarchy of Goals.

victim injury. Thus, it relates to the defendant (and his counsel), to the public (and its legal representative, the prosecutor), and to the victim.[4]

Conserving resources is at least three-faceted. One subgoal is to limit overall public expenditures on criminal justice to a reasonable and appropriate level.[5] Then, at this level of support, the criminal justice system should operate efficiently. Among other things, this subgoal of internal efficiency implies that cost and inconvenience should be balanced among all elements of the system, i.e., one agency should not optimize its operations at the expense of the others. Finally, the system should also operate as to use external resources efficiently, thereby minimizing its impact on those who are not part of the system but who must participate in the proceedings.

Promoting public trust and confidence, perhaps the most intangible of the five broad goals, is distinguished by its dependence on the achievement of the other four. Jurisdictions in which the principal practitioners are elected to office would tend to weight this goal heavily.

Goals of the Criminal Proceeding

Goals of the criminal proceeding are identified in Figure 4-1 and also linked to criminal justice system goals and subgoals. But we cannot demonstrate the degree to which the system goals and subgoals are affected by degrees of achievement of the criminal proceeding goals, either absolutely or compared with the achievement of the companion goals of police and corrections agencies. Some linkages shown in Figure 4-1 are simply a matter of definition; others are founded on reasonable belief, e.g., that swiftness of conviction furthers specific deterrence. Also, in some instances the higher and lower goals are the same.

The criminal proceeding goals shown in Figure 4-1 are generally self-explanatory, but several deserve comment. *Accuracy* can be viewed as having two aspects: acquitting the legally innocent, and convicting the legally guilty. In practice, these two aspects are not independent, for the higher the assurance demanded in convicting the legally guilty, the more likely it is that a legally innocent individual will be erroneously convicted; and conversely, the higher the assurance demanded in acquitting the legally innocent, the more likely it is that a legally guilty individual will escape conviction. Clearly, there must be a balancing of the two demands, but as criminal proceedings attain greater accuracy, the balancing becomes less consequential.

We intend that the subgoal use nonsystem resources efficiently not be interpreted as a mandate to independently optimize the handling of lay persons who participate in the criminal proceeding. This goal, more correctly interpreted, involves a balancing of cost and inconvenience between the resources

---

[4] Fairness to a victim implies restitution or compensation for the injury to his person or property. Restitution by the defendant may be part of the punishment imposed upon him; compensation may be drawn from public funds by legislative mandate. The first source of relief is within the scope of the court system; the second goes beyond.

[5] Issues of allocating public resources among the criminal justice system and other governmental agencies are beyond the scope of this book.

external and internal to the system. For example, the operative principle in judicial administration is often found to be that a judge's time is the dominant factor, and therefore criminal proceedings should be scheduled to optimize the judge's use of time. The result may be inefficient handling of lay participants. Another example is that continuances freely granted for the convenience of the prosecutor or defense counsel may create unreasonable inconvenience to lay participants. Few would dispute that a broader balancing is desirable; the issue is whether more complex scheduling considerations can be implemented.

The criminal proceeding goals purporting to advance the system goal of promoting public trust and confidence are to present an appearance of effectiveness and to progress toward system goals. In other words, the criminal proceeding is not likely to be held in public esteem if it doesn't "look good," as well as produce constructive results. We believe that the impressions formed by lay participants and the public are colored as much by the appearance of operations as by the outcomes. A judge who is technically competent and fair may nevertheless appear otherwise to the unenlightened layman; the role of defense counsel tends to be misunderstood by the public; prosecutorial functions are sometimes distorted in media reporting, and so on. And it is a matter of wide experience that ill-conceived or misreported public statements by prominent practitioners, perhaps in the heat of political campaigns, do significantly affect public trust and confidence in the criminal justice system.

The Links between Goals and the Issue Areas Considered

Having indicated the links between systemwide goals and goals of the criminal proceedings, we turn next to the links between the issue areas considered in this book and these goals. Some issue areas may be linked to several goals; others may be linked to only one.

The screening threshold issue relates closely to the criminal proceeding goals of certainty and swiftness of conviction, accuracy of proceeding and efficiency, and through them to the systemwide goals of crime control, exacting retribution, according fairness, and resource conservation. For example, if the threshold for rejection is set high, conviction may be more certain, conviction may be swifter (because more cases are rejected, leaving fewer in the system), and resources conserved or public spending limited (because fewer cases enter the courts). With the exception of swiftness of conviction, the issue of screening accuracy relates to the same goals too. More accurate charging increases certainty of conviction, accuracy of conviction, and efficiency (the latter because less time of the court system is wasted on nonconvictions).

The issue of plea bargaining relates to virtually all the criminal proceeding goals, including certainty and swiftness of conviction, appropriate sentencing, accuracy, and efficiency. Plea agreements produce convictions that are at least certain, swift, and efficient. However, it is not immediately clear whether sentencing will be more or less appropriate and whether proceedings will be more or less accurate. The issue of evenhandedness is primarily linked to the general goal of according fairness. The issue of sentence variation relates to the goals of appropriate sentencing and evenhandedness in sentencing, and through them to the systemwide goals of crime control, exacting retribution, and according fairness.

The twin issues of case processing efficiency and delay clearly relate to the swiftness of conviction and efficiency of the court system. There may be less direct linkages, too. Greater efficiency and less delay, for example, may also impinge on certainty of conviction, accuracy of proceeding, and the according of procedural due process, although it is arguable whether the effect is favorable or unfavorable.

Finally, since all the issues relate to actual progress toward goals and to the appearance of effectiveness, they also impinge on the systemwide goal of promoting public trust and confidence.

Selection Criteria for Performance Measures to be Applied to Criminal Proceedings

A performance measure should be relevant and the more proximate, directly linked, and applicable the measure is, the better it is. The meaning of these terms as we use them is as follows.

A *relevant* performance measure is one with significant probative value concerning a matter that is in issue or that requires illumination. For example, the average elapsed time from arraignment to disposition is a measure relevant to issues of court resource use. The proportion of cases dismissed prior to trial is a measure that has little relevance to issues of sentence variation.

A performance measure may be more or less *proximate*, depending on how close the events it captures are to the matter of interest. For example, the proportion of complaints rejected by the prosecutor for reasons of insufficient evidence is an immediate output of screening and is therefore proximate to the matter of screening performance. By contrast, the rate at which trial dismissals occur is a measure of events more remote from the screening process and is therefore less proximate to the prosecutor's screening performance.

A performance measure is more *directly linked* to an aspect of the criminal proceeding if its magnitude is more strongly correlated with that aspect. For example, the guilty plea rate would be more directly linked with judicial case processing efficiency than would be (say) a measure of sentencing severity.

The *applicability* of a performance measure refers to its usefulness in the analytical task undertaken. For example, if one's purpose is to make interjurisdictional comparisons of judicial productivity, then the number of weighted cases processed per available judge-year may be a more useful measure for this purpose than simply the unweighted average number of dispositions per judge year would be.

Two further criteria are the specificity and clarity of a performance measure. We intend that these terms be given the following interpretation.

The fewer the aspects of the proceeding on which the informational content of a performance measure is focused, the more *specific* it is. For example, case rejection rate is a measure more specific to the screening process, on which it is singularly focused, than is a measure such as the proportion of cases in which the defendant pleads to charges different from the ones originally filed, which reflects both the charging and plea bargaining aspects.

Clarity connotes that the construction and usage of a performance measure is readily understood by the average practitioner. For example, median number of days between arrest and final disposition of all felony cases is a clear measure of delay. On the other hand, a sentence severity "score" is a less clear performance measure of sentence severity than the elements that comprise it (e.g., two years of prison followed by five years on probation).

It is appropriate in the use of sets of performance measures to apply the criteria of consistency and complementarity.

Performance measures are *consistent* if they can properly be used to measure the same element of performance. For example, the average severity of sentencing broken out by defendant's race for convicted charge A might not be consistent, for the purpose of revealing a lack of evenhandedness, with the same measure for convicted charge B if there were a statutory minimum sentence for one charge and not for the other. On the other hand, the complete set of screening outputs produced by a prosecutor's office during a specific period would be a consistent set of measures of screening performance.

Performance measures are *complementary* when they mutually contribute to the analysis of an issue. For example, the proportion of jury trials among all trials and the average number of continuances in a proceeding are two measures that are complementary for purposes of analyzing the duration of criminal proceedings.

Finally and importantly, there is the criterion of implementability, which brings into consideration the cost and availability of data embodied in a performance measure.

When a jurisdiction can, with reasonable cost and effort, collect and process the data necessary to employ a specified performance measure, then we say that this measure is *implementable*. For example, the median time elapsed between arraignment and final disposition is a measure that is readily implementable in most jurisdictions, since the dates of major case events are nearly always recorded in standard case files. By contrast, there may be formidable difficulties in obtaining reliable data on the economic status of defendants in some jurisdictions; measures (say, of evenhandedness) that require such information might not be implementable in these circumstances.

For brevity, we shall not discuss the specific application of these selection criteria each time that we introduce sets of performance measures in the discussion. Instead, they will be examined in selected instances.

Performance Measures for Selected Issue Areas

Prosecutorial Case Screening

As mentioned in the opening of this chapter, we shall discuss the application of performance measures to the prosecutorial case screening function in some depth, with attention to two salient aspects of this screening, namely, the charging threshold and the accuracy of charging. These matters are important in their own right, but they also are richly revealing about limitations in the application of statistical performance measures more generally. As a foundation, we shall first briefly review the nature of the screening function.

The Nature of the Screening Function. The responsibility to initiate formal criminal proceedings adheres to the prosecutor in most jurisdictions for most types of offenses.[6] Traditionally the screening function involves broad prosecutorial discretion (with which the courts have been highly reluctant to interfere). "The primary responsibility of a prosecutor in charging is to determine whether or not there is sufficient evidence to convict the accused of the particular crime in question and to authorize the filing of appropriate charges."[7] A decision to charge is said to require that four criteria be met: the evidence satisfies the prosecutor that the accused is guilty of the crime to be charged; there is legally sufficient, admissible evidence of a *corpus delecti*; there is legally sufficient, admissible evidence of the accused's identity as the perpetrator; and the nature of the admissible evidence makes the probability of conviction by a reasonable and objective fact finder sufficiently high notwithstanding foreseeable plausible defenses.[8] But there are other important dimensions to the charging decision. Most fundamentally, the prosecutor will consider whether charging a suspect in a specific case would serve one or more goals of the system. In his consideration, the prosecutor may weigh many factors that are largely external to the merits of the evidence, such as:[9]

1. Attitude of the victim.
2. Cost to the criminal justice system (including possible loss of public support and respect) for initiating prosecution.

---

[6] That this should be a prosecutorial responsibility is recommended in the *Standards Relating to the Prosecution Function*, approved draft, ABA Project on Standards for Criminal Justice, Institute of Judicial Administration, 1971, p. 32.

[7] *Uniform Crime Charging Standards*, prepared and published by the California District Attorneys' Association, December 1974, p. 13.

[8] Ibid., p. 13.

[9] F.W. Miller, *Prosecution—The Decision to Charge a Suspect with a Crime*, The Report of the American Bar Foundation's Survey of Criminal Justice in the United States, Little, Brown and Company, Boston, 1969. Listed items are derived from chapter and section headings.

3. Undue harm to the suspect.
4. Adequacy of the incarceration potential in alternative nonprosecutorial procedures (e.g., insanity commitment).
5. Effectiveness of criminal sanctions (relative to available noncriminal sanctions).
6. Willingness of suspect to cooperate in achieving other enforcement goals.

The prosecutor's charging decision sometimes will be complicated by the fact that, at the time the decision must be made, the criteria for charging (summarized above) cannot be fully applied because of uncertainties unresolvable at that time.[10] To arrive at a decision, the prosecutor may then rely on local prosecutorial policy, e.g., he may at all times follow a policy of filing the most serious charge that the available evidence would support were the uncertainties to be resolved in favor of the prosecution, or he may apply a policy of not charging if a clear violation of constitutional rights has occurred in making the arrest, etc. Also, when the charging decision is complicated by uncertainties in the case, the prosecutor may be particularly influenced by the current work load in his office and the court, for his decision directly affects the future load.

Given this brief review of the nature of the prosecutorial screening, we next address the application of statistical performance measures to the two selected aspects, the charging threshold and the accuracy of charging.[11]

The Charging Threshold. One pervasive concern with the prosecutorial screening function is the translation of charging policies and standards into actual practice. Since it is highly discretionary, the decision to charge or not to charge a felony suspect reflects many policy elements, even though the latter may not be explicitly and fully articulated in some jurisdictions.[12] For illustrative purposes, we shall regard policies or standards that govern the charging threshold as being in the nature of goals or objectives. We may then ask how well these goals are being realized; that is, Is the charging threshold that is applied the one that is intended? One approach to illuminating this question could be purely procedural; for example, all charging decisions by screening deputies in cases that

---

[10] For example, uncertainty in making the charging decision may be present because a legal issue requires a later court ruling to resolve, or because the availability of affirmative defenses is unknown, or because the admissibility of decisive evidence cannot be ascertained short of a judicial determination, or because the reliability of prosecution testimony is problematical without follow-up police investigation, etc.

[11] See N. Abrams, "Prosecutorial Charge Decision Systems," *UCLA Law Review*, Vol. 23, No. 1, October 1975, for an indepth discussion of a third aspect, viz., the timing of the charge decision.

[12] The California District Attorneys' Association, *Uniform Crime Charging Standards*, is a leading example of charging standards developed for statewide use. Another example of articulated prosecutorial standards, including charging policies, is *The Prosecutor's Discretion—A Statement of Policy of the Office of District Attorney of Harris County*, by Carol S. Vance, District Attorney, Harris County, Texas, April 1974.

meet specified criteria are immediately reviewed at the supervisory level and possibly modified. Another approach might rely on case auditing, that is, on the indepth after-the-fact review of the charging decision in appropriate samples of the case flow.[13] And a third approach could be the statistical monitoring of the entire case output (or a sample thereof) of the screening operation, using performance measures with a level of detail that would depend on the specificity of the charging policies being monitored. Whatever the approach, maintaining a gross statistical picture of the case output from screening serves the purpose of alerting officials to changes in the nature of this output over time, and thereby to possibly unintended movement of the charging threshold.

This gross statistical picture is most simply depicted in terms of a classification of the case output from screening. The corresponding performance measures may be taken to be the size of each class, expressed as a proportion of the number of suspects screened. The set of classes might be as follows:

1. Suspects unconditionally rejected for felony prosecution because of evidence deficiencies.
2. Suspects unconditionally rejected for felony prosecution for reasons other than evidence deficiencies (further classified by major reason).
3. Suspects rejected for felony prosecution in favor of misdemeanor prosecution.
4. Suspects for whom prosecution is deferred in favor of diversionary (rehabilitative) programs.
5. Suspects charged with at least one felony count.[14]

These are such natural measures for the purpose of monitoring the impact of charging threshold policies that we need not discuss the application of the suggested selection criteria (namely, relevance, proximity, direct linkage, applicability, specificity, clarity, consistency, complementarity, and implementability), except to note that implementation may entail a more complete and precise recording of screening data than had previously been the practice. The desired information is, however, readily available to the screening deputy.

Proceeding from the gross statistical monitoring of the screening function in order to show adherence to charging standards, we next address a more specific and subtle charging issue, namely, abuse of discretion to reject prosecution of felony suspects. The decision to reject may, for simplicity, be viewed as having one of three bases:

[13] Chapter 7 discusses a demonstration of case auditing conducted within our study.

[14] This class would ordinarily be broken out in greater detail to reflect the seriousness of the charges as defined in the jurisdiction (e.g., capital; 1st, 2d, 3d degree; class A, B, or C; etc.), as well as their number.

1. The case has significant (and incurable) evidentiary defects.[15]
2. The case conforms to a recognized specific reason for rejection other than insufficiency of evidence.
3. The case, whether or not it might culminate in a conviction, evokes a judgment call from the prosecutor that to initiate prosecution would not be in "the interests of justice."

Applying such a classification to help reveal abuse of charging discretion requires that in each instance of rejection there be recorded the (accurate) reason for its occurrence. Most prosecutor's offices already use a more or less standardized list of evidence flaws in articulating the reasons for rejection, for example:[16]

1. No *corpus delicti*
     No specific intent (if this is an element of the offense)
     No criminal act
2. No connecting evidence
     Statement deficiency
     Witness deficiency
     Physical evidence deficiency
3. Insufficient evidence[17]
     Facts weak
     Evidence not available
     Incomplete investigation
     Witness not available
     Evidence inadmissible

Similarly, in connection with the second basis for rejection, a set of specific nonevidentiary reasons is widely recognized, for example:[18]

---

[15] Or the case may have curable evidentiary defects and is tentatively rejected and sent back to the police for further investigation.

[16] Extracted from "Prosecutorial Discretion in the Initiation of Criminal Complaints," unsigned comment, *So. Calif. Law Review*, Vol. 42, 1969.

[17] The meaning of *insufficient* does of course vary among prosecutors' offices. The legal burden of proof on the prosecution at the charging stage is *probable cause* to believe that the suspect committed the alleged crime. Some prosecutors look ahead to the probability of being able to present proof of guilt beyond a reasonable doubt; and look also to the expected reaction of the trier of fact to the defendant and to the evidence presented. These prosecutors are thereby applying a charging standard of whether or not a jury (or judge) would convict this suspect of this crime.

[18] The California District Attorneys' Association, *Uniform Crime Charging Standards*, pp. 42-46.

1. Contrary to legislative intent
2. Antiquated statute
3. Victim requests no prosecution
4. Need for granting immunity to suspect (to support other prosecutions)
5. *De minimus* violation
6. Present confinement on other charges
7. Pending conviction on other charges
8. Highly disproportionate cost of prosecution.

But for the third rejection basis, one cannot expect to find objective, standardized reasons, since the rejection results from a judgmental balancing of factors in an exercise of true prosecutorial discretion. The result is typically characterized only as a rejection in the "interests of justice."

Here, then, is a potential impediment to the use of statistical performance measures for revealing abuse of discretion in rejecting felony suspects. If the broad, undifferentiated "interests of justice" reason were frequently employed by the prosecutor, it might effectively conceal the presence of abuse. Another impediment would be, of course, the inaccurate recording of the true reasons for rejection.

The charging standards issue upon which our study primarily focused in its demonstration phase was whether and how the charging threshold might be changing over time within a jurisdiction. To this end, we adapted the foregoing theoretical discussion as follows.

We viewed the gross output of case screening (whether done by the prosecutor's office or the court) as falling into one of three classes: cases filed on the most serious charge(s) booked by the police, cases filed on a lesser degree or charges (broken out by level of seriousness), and cases rejected unconditionally. These outputs were taken to be the appropriate performance measures. This scheme is shown in Table 4-1, along with the data elements implied by these measures.

How do inferences about a shift in charging threshold over time follow from the use of these measures? For example, if police arrest policies and booking standards remained unchanged, one would expect to see a rise in the rejection rate and the filing rate at lesser levels and a decline in the filing rate at the booked-charge level when the charging threshold for a specified offense catetory was elevated from one period to another. But if police arrest practices changed too and, say, responded to the change in the charging threshold by less frequent presentation of weaker cases, then changes in the gross measures of case screening shown in Table 4-1 would be more ambiguous and difficult to interpret. Knowledge of changes in police arrest practices would be required to remove their effect on the inference about a charging threshold shift. A fuller discussion of the interpretation of these charging threshold performance measures is given in Chapter 5 and 6, where their application to the demonstration jurisdictions is presented.

Table 4-1
Performance Measures in Case Screening: Charging Standards or Threshold

Performance Measures	Required Data Elements
By category of highest offense at police booking as a percentage of cases screened over a specific time period:	Number of cases screened
Filing rate on most serious booked-charge level	Number of cases filed at most serious booked charge
Filing rate on less than most serious booked-charge level[a]	Number of cases filed at less than most serious booked-charge level
Gross rejection rate	
	Number of cases rejected
Reasons for rejection (in percentage of cases rejected):[b]	Number of cases rejected
Evidence deficiency (illustrative subcategories: no *corpus delicti*, no connecting evidence, insufficient evidence, inadmissible evidence, returned to police for need of more investigation)	Number of cases rejected for evidence deficiency
Nonevidence deficiency: specific reasons (illustrative subcategories: victim requests no prosecution, need to grant immunity, suspect currently confined or pending conviction on other charges, contrary to legislative intent)	Number of cases rejected for specific nonevidence deficiency reasons
Nonevidence deficiency: general reasons (illustrative category: interests of justice)	Number of cases rejected for general or interests of justice reasons
Case audit results	Judgment about the charging standards used, given the observed screening decision

[a]May be broken down in greater detail to reflect the seriousness of the charge. For example, if there are three felony levels of seriousness (A, B, and C) and if the most serious charge level is, say, felony A, this measure may be broken down into three categories: felony B, felony C, and misdemeanor.

[b]Depending on whether the screening agency (prosecution, lower court) has a pretrial diversion program, which agency makes the diversion decision, and at what point in the felony proceeding diversion may occur, an additional category of "rejection" reasons may be added.

Table 4-1 also shows a breakdown of the rejection rate by reasons for rejection, which we sought in order to obtain insights about the possible abuse of discretion in rejecting cases and the quality of cases submitted by the police. To illustrate the interpretation of this more detailed performance measure, we observe (as noted earlier) that a dramatic rise in the frequency of rejections "in the interests of justice" might signal an abuse of discretion. Or if the proportion of rejections for inadequate evidence lessened and the proportion of rejections for other specific reasons increased, while the "interests of justice" rejections remained constant, this might be a signal that the quality of cases submitted by the police had improved. And if the overall rejection rate rises at the same time, an elevation in charging threshold might also be indicated thereby.

The required data elements for the performance measures shown in Table 4-1 would generally lead to a straightforward collection approach. In some jurisdictions, to judge from our experience in the demonstration phase,[19] reasons for rejection previously may not have been recorded in sufficiently clear, complete, and accurate form, so attention to this collection problem would be required. However, it is clearly possible to record these reasons completely and accurately, as evidenced in those jurisdictions that have implemented the PROMIS system.

The Accuracy of Charging. We have selected charging accuracy as a second issue area to illustrate the use and limitations of statistical performance measures applied to prosecutorial screening. The question to be considered is How accurate are the charges as originally filed, given the decision to initiate a (felony) prosecution? First, what is *accurate* charging? For the purposes of the discussion here, we adopt a simplified definition as follows: A prosecutor has charged a defendant *accurately* if there is sufficient evidence to convict him of the most serious charges filed.[20] Second, given this definition, we may ask: What data are relevant to the measurement of charging accuracy? Is the collection of these data feasible? The key to answering these questions seems to be the following proposition: Errors in filing charges affect later stages of a criminal proceeding and must be inferred from events subsequent to the charging. But this proposition involves an intrinsic difficulty; namely, the outcomes of subsequent events in criminal proceedings are governed by a variety of factors, only one of which would be the accuracy of the charges originally filed. For example, an acquittal may occur not only because of an inaccurate charging decision but also because of prosecutorial shortcomings in preparing the case, arguing motions, or conducting the case at trial. Or, superior defense counsel performance may be the explanation. The occurrence of an acquittal by itself thus lacks specificity as a charging accuracy datum. But we also observe that this ambiguity could be largely eliminated by accurately recording the true reason for the acquittal.

Trial outcomes, however, are but one class of the many events that may be affected by the accuracy of original charging—others being the outcomes of the preliminary hearing, pretrial hearings on motions of various types, plea negotiations, etc. And each of these events is also affected by processing factors other

---

[19] See Appendix B.

[20] We have already noted while briefly reviewing the nature of the screening function that there may exist at the time of the charging decision various uncertainties concerning the law involved in the case or concerning the availability and admissibility of evidence. These uncertainties may prevent the prosecutor from making a reliable determination of the most accurate charges to file. Also, note that our definition requires that a prosecutor, in seeking to charge accurately, go beyond his minimal legal duty of charging when there is "probable cause." (By contrast with our definition, Abrams, "Prosecutorial Charge Decision Systems," pp. 49-55, views the accuracy of the charge decision as being the correctness with which the future "disposition" of the defendant is predicted.)

than charging accuracy, often to a greater degree than by the latter. In consequence, we are led to the use of a set of performance measures that collectively capture the effects of inaccurate charging, as well as information extraneous to this issue.

Table 4-2 presents this set of performance measures, together with the required data elements. Basically, these measures reflect four types of dispositions subsequent to charging: nonconvictions (includes pretrial dismissals; *nolle prosequi* cases, if applicable; pretrial diversions or interventions, if applicable; and trial acquittals, dismissals, and mistrials); convictions on all charges as filed (both by guilty plea and trial); conviction at the most serious filed charge level, but with some charge or count reductions; and conviction at lesser charge levels than as initially filed.[21]

The measures given in Table 4-2 are relevant to the issue of charging inaccuracy in the sense mentioned earlier, i.e., they capture information on how

Table 4-2
Performance Measures in Case Screening: Charging Accuracy

Performance Measures	*Required Data Elements*
By category of highest offense of charging as a percentage of cases charged or disposed over a specified time period:	Number of cases charged or number of dispositions
Overall nonconviction rate	Number of nonconvictions
Pretrial dismissal rate	Number of pretrial dismissals
Nolle prosequi rate (if applicable)	Number of *nolle prosequi*
Pretrial diversion or intervention rate (if applicable)	Number of pretrial diversions
Trial acquittal, dismissal, and mistrial rate	Number of trial acquittals, dismissals, mistrials
Conviction rate on all charges as filed	Number of convictions on all charges as filed
By plea of guilty	As above, by plea
By trial	As above, by trial
Conviction rate on at least one of the most serious charges, but with charge or count reductions	Number of convictions on at least one of the most serious charges, but with charge or count reductions
By plea of guilty	As above, by plea
By trial	As above, by trial
Conviction rate on lesser charges than the most serious filed	Number of convictions on lesser charges
By plea of guilty	As above, by plea
By trial	As above, by trial
Case audit results	Strength and appropriateness of filed charges in average case

[21] These measures may be broken out in greater detail to reflect the seriousness of the convicted charge. See first footnote to Table 4-1.

this inaccuracy affects subsequent defendant-related events. They are more or less proximate, depending upon when these events occur in the chain of consequences of the charging decision. Their directness of linkage would depend upon the relative importance of factors other than charging accuracy in the occurrence of the events. Since these measures are constructed from mutually exclusive and exhaustive counts of defendant dispositions, they satisfy the criteria of consistency and complementarity. Their meaning seems clear, but (as discussed above) shortcomings in specificity are present. For example, the final measure could be dominated by the plea bargaining process, which might be motivated by reasons other than the redress of charging inaccuracy. Finally, since these measures involve only counts of defendant dispositions, they should be readily implementable.

Given the ambiguity of these measures, as noted above, one would have to observe large changes in their magnitudes over time to conclude that charging accuracy has changed; or if it is known from other sources that other factors affecting the measures have remained essentially constant, smaller changes in the measures over time would suffice to indicate a movement in charging accuracy. On the other hand, should one of the "extraneous" factors change substantially, for example, as did the plea bargaining policy in one of our demonstration jurisdictions between the periods studied, then this change could nullify the applicability of one or more of these measures to charging accuracy performance (see Chapter 5 for further discussion).

Dispositional data that comprise the required data elements shown in Table 4-2 for the charging accuracy measures tend to be among the most available, accurate, and complete items of information in the criminal proceeding. Our experience in the demonstration jurisdictions was that the individual case folders generally sufficed as sources of such dispositional data (see Appendix B).

Finally, we sought to deepen understanding about the performance measures proposed in Table 4-2 by postulating theoretical (statistical) equations that related these conviction and nonconviction probabilities (or rates) as dependent variables to a broad set of possible determinants. The latter independent variables reflected the characteristics of the defendant, his pretrial status and type of counsel, the original charges filed against him, whether he was tried, the influence of case backlog, etc. We then tested these models (by means of regression analysis), using the data obtained from case samples drawn from the two demonstration jurisdictions. We found that our postulated equations did not provide an adequate explanation of the determinants of conviction probability. (By contrast, similar statistical models worked rather well in explaining the determinants of sentence outcomes and delay in proceedings.) It is likely that our failure to include (because of lack of data) such possible determinants as the seriousness of the crime incident, the mitigating or exacerbating aspects of the crime incident and the defendant, and case-strength factors at time of charging was responsible for the disappointing outcome. It is clear that more theoretical and empirical work must be done if a useful statistical model of conviction probabilities is to be constructed.

Case Processing Efficiency and Delay

Within the issue area termed *case processing efficiency and delay*, our study and particularly its demonstration phase have focused on a limited set of topics, primarily: judicial efficiency in criminal proceedings;[22] and delay in proceedings and the use of lay participant (jurors, victims, and other witnesses) time. For these topics, we next set out the performance measures selected for the conduct of this study, together with the data elements they imply and explanatory comments.

Judicial Efficiency. One way of assessing judicial efficiency in criminal proceedings could be simply to divide the total number of dispositions in a period (say, a year) by the number of judge-years devoted to the criminal caseload. But this measure is very gross and unrevealing—when its magnitude changes, one does not know whether this was caused by a change in the relative frequencies of different types of cases processed (for example, the mix of crime types) or by changes in policies or procedures affecting the frequency with which various judicial activities occur in a specified case type or the time consumed in a specified type of judicial activity.

A more reliable measure of judicial efficiency is available and is already being employed in some jurisdictions (including California, where the Judicial Council employs it to help establish the required number of judicial positions in local jurisdictions). This measure has the virtue of compelling the collection of those data and the performance of those calculations that generally reveal what is responsible for changes in judicial efficiency. Specifically, the measure is the number of weighted cases processed (counted either by filings or dispositions) per available judge-year.

To explain the nature of this performance measure, we first describe what is meant by *weighted-caseload processing time*. For each activity (or step) in a criminal proceeding, one may associate both an average duration of that activity and the relative frequency with which it occurs per disposition. (Table 4-3 shows illustratively the classifications of judicial activities for this purpose, which have been used in three weighted-caseload studies). The weighted processing time for

---

[22] Although we discuss only judicial efficiency here, similar approaches are available for measuring prosecutorial and public defender case processing efficiency. For example, Peat, Marwick, Mitchell & Co. has used a statistically based approach to ascertain prosecutorial and public defender staffing requirements in several California counties. (See their report, *Staffing Requirements Projection Approach for Professional Prosecution and Defense Services*, September 1974, a study done for the County of Santa Clara, California, under LEAA funding.) Unquestionably, case processing efficiency is a product of the efficiency with which *all* court agencies perform, rather than the bench alone.

Table 4-3
Classifications of Judicial Activities in Criminal Proceedings

California Judicial Council Study[a]	Florida Weighted Caseload Statewide Study	Multnomah County (Oregon) Circuit Court[b]
Short matters (plead not guilty, continuance, calendar call, sentencing and probation hearing, diversion hearing, other pretrial motions, trial confirmation conference)	Case-related, with party and counsel present:	Arraignment
Plead guilty	First appearance hearing	Motion hearing
Dismissal transfer	Preliminary hearing	Plea hearing
§ 995 PC (penal code) motion	Arraignment	Other hearings
§ 1538.5 PC motion	Motion hearings	Court trial
Court trial (regular, transcript, transcript and testimony)	Plea hearings	Jury trial
Select jury and jury trial	All other hearings	Sentencing hearing
Habeas corpus hearing	Pretrial conference	
	Detention hearing	
	Adjudicatory hearing	
	Disposition hearing	
	Nonjury trial	
	Jury selection	
	Jury trial	
	Sentencing/presentence investigation	
	Postdisposition/trial hearing, motions	
	Other case-related	
	Case-related, office work:	
	Predisposition (legal research, drafting, etc.)	
	Postdisposition (legal research, drafting, etc.)	
	Conferences	
	Jury related:	
	Grand jury	
	Mass jury selection	
	Statewide grand jury	
	Coroner's jury	
	Non-case-related:	
	Correspondence	
	Travel	
	General research and study	
	Conferences	
	Court administration	
	Ex officio	

[a]*Judicial Weighted Caseload System Project*, Final Report Prepared for the Judicial Council of California, Arthur Young & Company, Sacramento, May 1974. This list of activities pertains to criminal (felony) proceedings in superior court. The cited report gives similar lists for other types of proceedings in superior court as well as the various proceedings in municipal courts.

[b]See Chapter 5.

a judicial activity is the product of its average duration and its relative frequency of occurrence per disposition. For example, taking a guilty plea might on the average consume 20 minutes of the court's time and occur six times per ten dispositions. If so, the weighted processing time per disposition would be 12 minutes for a guilty plea. By summing the weighted processing times for the various activity types, we obtain the weighted caseload processing time per disposition (for all types of dispositions). Then, to estimate the weighted caseload processing time per filing, we multiply the preceding result by the ratio of dispositions to filings.[23]

The second ingredient of the judicial efficiency measure for criminal proceedings is the *available judge-year time.* This is the total time per year per judge less the time consumed by civil matters, vacations, sick leave, official traveling, professional meetings, etc.

The judicial efficiency measure is then calculated simply by dividing the available judge-year time by the weighted caseload processing time per filing. This measure generally satisfied the selection criteria that we gave earlier, although implementation may present difficulties.

In jurisdictions where the nature of the case mix by offense tends to vary significantly over time or locality, it would be desirable to maintain·the judicial efficiency measure separately for different classes of offenses[24] and possibly for different geographic divisions of the court system. By so doing, one makes the measure more sensitive to changes in efficiency.

For the purposes of this study, we felt that the next important step forward in the use of judicial performance measures would be the wider application of the measure the number of weighted cases processed per available judge-year. This would enable court systems to better determine the impact of policies that alter the relative mix of activities within the proceeding (e.g., the impact of a change in plea bargaining policies and a consequent change in the frequency of related activities); to better translate projections of future case loads into requirements for practitioners and other court personnel; and to better estimate the impact of procedural changes (e.g., the adoption of omnibus hearings) that would alter the time consumed in affected court activities.

---

[23] This simple procedure rests on the assumption that nondisposed cases resemble disposed cases in the consumption of judicial time.

[24] Currently, jurisdictions that collect the necessary data and calculate weighted criminal caseload for judges do so only for criminal cases as a whole and not by offense type or class. On the other hand, different types of proceedings are already being handled separately, as in the Superior Courts of California for criminal, juvenile delinquency, probate, personal injury-death-property damage, eminent domain, civil complaints, civil petitions, and appeal proceedings and in the Municipal Courts for felony preliminary-felony reduction, traffic, intoxication, other misdemeanor, civil, small claim, juvenile traffic, and illegal parking proceedings. (See *Judicial Weighted Caseload System Project*, Final Report Prepared for the Judicial Council of California, Arthur Young & Company, Sacramento, May 1974.)

We attempted to apply the weighted caseload approach in one of the two demonstration jurisdictions but rejected the results because of deficiencies in the available raw data. The key difficulty was the unwillingness of the judges of this court to have the use of their time directly monitored. Indirect sources of data (e.g., logs of the clerk's activities while court was in session) and inferences about the allocation of off-bench time devoted to various matters turned out to be too inaccurate (see Appendix B and Chapter 5 for a discussion of the data collection and analysis, respectively). The lesson appears to be that the cooperation of the bench is essential, and this cooperation probably hinges on persuading the judges beforehand of the value of weighted caseload information and the preservation of their anonymity in the data recording process.

Delay and Use of Lay Participant Time. The speediness of felony proceedings is a highly visible attribute by which criminal justice is necessarily judged, and it is a matter of urgent concern to officials and the public. In many jurisdictions, delay has increased because resources allocated to court system agencies have not kept pace with rising caseloads or because practitioner time is not used efficiently. We adopted three basic gross measures of delay or elapsed time between specified events: median number of days,[25] minimum time for the lengthiest 10 percent of cases (i.e., the shortest of the longest 10 percent of cases), and the percentage of cases exceeding some standard (set by court rule or statute). The specified intervals we selected were: from arrest and from arraignment to dismissal, to plea of guilty, to trial, to sentencing, and to final disposition (the sum of cases dismissed, acquitted, and sentenced). In addition, the time between conviction (by any means) and sentencing is of salient interest. Speedy trial standards usually refer to the arrest-to-trial period, but it is revealing also to estimate the percentage of cases exceeding the standard that are disposed of otherwise. These performance measures should be calculated for all felonies and for each major offense category as defined at the point of charging to determine which offense categories account for more or less delay.

In addition, it is useful to apply multivariate statistical techniques to determine the independent effects of certain factors on delay. We have hypothesized that four factors may influence delay: pretrial custody status (because defendants out on bail or on their own recognizance may have incentives to delay proceedings); type of defense attorney (because court calendar conflicts or incentives stemming from attorney compensation arrangements may lead to more delay by private attorneys or because one category of attorney might know the system better than another); type of disposition (cases tried may take longer than guilty plea cases); and heavier or lighter caseloads or more or less court backlog as measured directly or as reflected in a time trend (proxy) variable.

---

[25] Instead of mean or average number, because the mean is too sensitive to the presence of a few cases of very long duration.

Continuance measures, which are indirect measures (and causes) of delay, provide additional insights into performance. They should be estimated separately for contested and uncontested cases (because of large differences between the two types of cases). Where possible, the "movant" or "requestor" should be identified (e.g., prosecution, defense, court, or joint) to reveal which agencies are most responsible for continuance-induced delays.[26] The continuance measures we adopted were: the percent of cases continued; the number of continuances per case; and the average number of days continued per case.

Measures of the use of victims' and other witnesses' time that we adopted were: the number of appearances per case disposition, the time consumed per appearance, and the number of total appearance hours consumed per disposition (the product of the previous two measures)—each measure calculated separately for victims and other witnesses. At best, court records may contain information on the number of victim/witness appearances per disposition. Data on time per appearance is generally not recorded, at least in the two jurisdictions we examined. It can be measured directly (the preferred approach) by filling out time sheets for each appearance, or it can be estimated from the response of victims and witnesses to mail surveys (as we did). However, the latter approach is flawed because it relies on the memories of respondents. These performance measures should be calculated for the entire (or a sample thereof) felony caseload to obtain a general picture, but it may also be estimated for particular offense types that are thought to consume much victim or witness time.

Conventional measures of juror usage essentially measure the over-supply of jurors in an indirect fashion. For example, the *juror usage index* (JUI) used in federal courts is defined as the available number of jurors per day (summed over a month) divided by the number of juries in trial per day (summed over a month). A more informative and direct set of measures we adopted is simply the average fraction of time a juror spends in idleness (although in the courthouse), in jury selection, and in trial. The latter two measures should be calculated separately for civil and criminal matters in jurisdictions that use the same juries for both types of cases. Data on the use of juror time is normally not recorded, at least in the two jurisdictions we examined. Again, it can be measured directly (the preferred approach) or it can be estimated from juror responses to mail questionnaires (as we did).

---

[26] This complete classification of continuances in terms of the responsible party would be advantageous for many purposes. At the same time we must recognize the complex nature of continuance reasons. For example, in being "responsible" for a continuance, a defense attorney may have legitimate reasons (e.g., to prepare and file a motion) or illegitimate reasons (e.g., to collect a fee) or reasons that cut both ways, e.g., "judge shopping" to avoid unduly harsh judges. The usual prosecutor's reason is the unavailability of witnesses, which might mean that they cannot be found despite the prosecutor's efforts or that he has not tried sufficiently to find them. If the complete attribution of continuances is impractical, then the identification at least of defense-moved continuances would be the next best level of detail. In our application of continuance measures in one jurisdiction, the data were adequate to attribute responsibility; in the other, the data were incomplete (see Chapters 5 and 6).

Table 4-4 presents the performance measures that this study used for the above-discussed topics in the issue area of delay, continuances, and the use of lay participant time, as well as the data elements that are required to apply the measures. In both jurisdictions we worked in, data from case files and agency records were adequate to estimate measures of delay and continuances (but not attribution in one jurisdiction). No data were available in agency records to estimate the use of juror time or the time consumed per appearance of victims and other witnesses; these data were collected in surveys of these lay participants. Data from agency records on number of witness or victim appearances per disposition were fragmentary; in one jurisdiction the data were available only for trials, whereas in the other the data were available for both contested and uncontested cases but only in a small fraction of the cases sampled. Thus we also collected frequency of appearance data using the victim and witness mail surveys.

Plea Bargaining

Plea bargaining (the terms *plea negotiation* and *case settlement* will be used here synonymously) is currently an issue area attracting much professional and lay attention and engendering wide public debate. Numerous jurisdictions have conducted or are conducting experiments to ascertain the effects of curtailing or eliminating some or all forms of plea bargaining.[27]

For simplicity and to serve the purposes of this study, we shall define a *plea bargain* to be an agreement between the defendant, on the one side, and the court system, on the other, that elicits a plea of guilty from the defendant.[28] The result of this agreement is generally (though not necessarily) a less severe punishment than that which might otherwise have been imposed on the defendant. A plea agreement may entail a dismissal of some of the original charges (or counts), possibly producing a reduction in the gravity of the most serious charge. It may provide for the dismissal of other pending cases against this defendant or a commitment by the prosecutor not to file other cases. Or it may entail a sentence commitment by the court or a limitation on the prosecutor in recommending or opposing sentences. Some plea bargaining issues are not quantitative in nature and cannot be illuminated by performance measures. But some aspects of plea bargaining are quantifiable. We shall discuss an analytical framework in which to view the quantitative side of the plea bargaining process.

What the defendant has gained from a plea agreement (even if only the

[27]The Office of the U.S. Attorney in San Diego, California, the District Attorney's Office in Fresno County, California, the District Attorney's Office in Los Angeles County, California, and the District Attorney's Office in Multnomah County, Oregon are instances.

[28]This definition excludes straight pleas of guilty to the specified charges for which no consideration is offered to the defendant.

Table 4-4
Performance Measures of Delay and the Use of Lay Participant Time

Performance Measures	Required Data Elements
Elapsed Time between Events:	
For all felonies and specific offense categories over a specified time period:	
1. Median number of days	
2. Minimum number of days for longest 10 percent of cases	
3. Percent of cases exceeding standard[a]	
These measures to be calculated between the following events:	*For each case in each sample, applicable dates of arrest, arraignment, dismissal, guilty plea, trial (commencement and end dates), sentencing*
Arrest and arraignment } and { Dismissal / Guilty plea / Trial / Final disposition	
Conviction and sentencing (Meas. 1 only)	
Continuances:	
Separately for all, contested and uncontested, cases in a random sample of all felonies over a specified time period:	
4. Percent of cases continued	Number of cases continued ÷ number of cases
5. Continuances per case	Number of continuances ÷ number of cases
6. Number of days continued per case	Number of continued days (= number of continuances × number of days per continuance) ÷ number of cases
7. Percent of continuances attributed to defense, prosecution, court, joint	Identity of "movant" or "requestor"
Use of Lay Participant Time	
Victims and Other Witnesses	
For all felonies over a specified time period:	
8. Number of appearances per disposition	Separately for victims and other witnesses
9. Time consumed per appearance	Separately for victims and other witnesses
10. Total number of appearance-hours per disposition	(Measure 8) × (Measure 9)
Jurors	
For all trials over a specified time:	
11. Percent of time idle	
12. Percent of time in jury selection	Separately for civil and criminal trials
13. Percent of time in trial	Separately for civil and criminal trials

[a]The speedy trial standard (defined by court rule or statute) usually applies only to the arrest-to-trial period, but it is of interest to compute this measure as if the same standard applied as well to the period between arrest and dismissal, arrest and guilty plea, and arrest and final disposition.

removal of uncertainty about his sentence) we say is a *concession* by the criminal justice system. At the same time, the system tends also to gain from the agreement by conserving its resources and possibly in other ways. This is not to say that plea agreements are necessarily prompted by the system's desire to conserve resources, for there are many other reasons within the accepted administration of criminal justice that account for plea agreements.[29] Nonetheless, whatever may be the motivation of the prosecutor for entering into a plea agreement, increasing the proportion of cases that are settled by plea negotiation has the effect of creating operational advantages for the system, for example:

1. The average time to reach final disposition would tend to shorten.
2. The rate of trials and the trial backlog would tend to lessen.
3. The use of witnesses and jurors would be reduced, etc.

For analytical purposes, we can thus regard a plea agreement as an exchange or balance (though not necessarily a conscious one) of concessions to the defendant and operational advantages and/or disadvantages to the system resulting from a certain conviction by a plea of guilty rather than a less certain conviction by trial. This exchange or balance is the quantitative framework for plea bargaining that our study has adopted.

But how might concessions to the defendant be measured? The outcome of plea bargaining to the defendant might be characterized, for example, as a changed description of his alleged criminal conduct; or a change in the number and legal nature of the charges against him, possibly reflecting other pending or potential cases; or a change in the punishment that he might otherwise incur. We have concluded that, among these and other possibilities for measuring concessions, the preferred approach to assessing the "amount" of concession to the defendant is to use the resulting change in imposed punishment (i.e., the sentence change) attributed to the plea agreement. One compelling reason for this choice is that a direct sentence commitment is frequently used as a the form of the concession in many jurisdictions (and seems to be the leading objective of the typical defendant).

For analytical purposes, we define the *concession* to the defendant to be the punishment foregone by him, i.e., the concession is the difference between the following two levels of punishment severity:

---

[29] See D.J. Newman, *Conviction—The Determination of Guilt or Innocence Without Trial*, Little, Brown and Company, Boston, 1966, for a comprehensive treatment of this subject. Examples of reasons (other than conserving resources) for granting concessions to the defendant, as discussed by Newman, are: avoidance of his acquiring a repugnant social label (e.g., sex deviant) as a result of conviction on the original charge; avoidance of a felony record; avoidance of a mandatory sentence; his youth and inexperience; his "respectability"; his low mentality; the disrepute of the victim, complainant, or witnesses; his prior illegal relationship with the victim; or the view that his conduct is regarded as normal within his subculture.

1. The sentence imposed on the defendant as a result of his guilty plea in return for the prosecutor's reducing the gravity of the charges; or lessening the number of counts; or arranging or consenting to a sentence commitment; or agreeing to drop or not to file other cases; or providing some combination of these considerations.
2. The sentence that would have been imposed in the absence of the plea agreement, i.e., had the defendant gone to trial (or, alternatively, had he made a straight plea to the original charges).[30]

To apply this definition we are compelled to simplify the multidimensionality of sentences and to devise a means of estimating the sentence that would have been imposed on the defendant in the absence of the plea agreement.

First, consider the problem of sentence complexity. Sentence elements include prison time, jail time, supervised or unsupervised probation, registration, fines, restitution, community services, and rehabilitative programs with conditions on the defendant (e.g., entering a drug therapy program); furthermore, any given sentence may contain several of these elements. Given the complex forms that sentences take in practice, it is difficult to perform arithmetical operations on them or even to compare them in severity. The analysis of sentences for many purposes is greatly facilitated by the use of a sentence severity index, that is, a one-dimensional numerical scale onto which the various elements of a sentence can be projected and combined. But this process of integrating different kinds of punishment into a single measure requires that they be given weights relative to one another. For example, what should be the relative severity of one year of prison incarceration compared with a $10,000 fine? Any single set of these weights is controversial, for if it is appropriate to one class of defendants in one community, it is inevitably inappropriate to another class in that community or the same class in another community. This difficulty is significant, but we feel it can be overcome by the use of several alternative sets of weights that span reasonable differences in belief about how onerous one type of punishment is relative to another. We next describe the four alternative sets used in this study (their application is illustrated in Chapters 5 and 6).

The first of our four weighting schemes (Index A) approximates one developed by the California Bureau of Criminal Statistics (BCS) but never applied in their publicly available summaries of sentencing. Our *Sentence*

---

[30] In his review of an earlier draft of the study report on which this book is based, Professor H. Subin pointed out that the concession to the defendant would be better measured by taking the reference level of punishment to be that which the judge and/or prosecutor *threatened* to have imposed. Granting this, it seems clear that the collection of data on "threatened" punishment presents formidable difficulties. See, in this connection, M. Finkelstein, "A Statistical Analysis of Guilty Plea Practices in Federal Courts," *Harvard Law Review*, Vol. 89, No. 2, December 1975, wherein the argument is developed that prosecutors may be using threats of lengthy sentences to obtain convictions in cases in which the government's evidence is quite insubstantial.

Severity Index A was defined to be the sum of the following component scores:[31]

Jail incarceration score:	1 per month of jail time imposed.
Custody time (credit) score:	−1 per month of custody prior to disposition.
Probation time score:	0.167 per month of probation imposed (i.e., 2 per year).
Fines score:	1 per $1000 in fines (with maximum score of 5).
Prison incarceration score:	18 plus 1 per year of prison time imposed.

Sentence Severity Index B differs from Index A in that both the probation and fines scores have only half the magnitude of those of Index A, but the increase in prison incarceration score per year imposed is three times as large. *Index C* differs from Index A in that both the probation and fines scores are taken to be zero, while the increase in the prison score per year imposed is five times as large as for Index A. Finally, *Index D* differs from Index A in that again the probation and fines scores are taken to be zero, while the prison incarceration score is the same as the jail incarceration score per month of incarceration imposed (i.e., the incarceration score is 12 per year imposed whether jail or prison). Indices C and D embody the view that fines and probation times are not punishment (even though they may involve "costs" to the defendant, perhaps in the sense that bail bond fees and legal fees are costs but technically not punishment).

Table 4-5 summarizes the weighting formulas by which the four severity indices are calculated. By way of illustration, for a sentence of 6 months in jail plus 5 years probation, the magnitude of A would be 16; B would be 11; and both C and D wwuld be 6. For a sentence of 10 years in prison, A would be 28; B would be 48; C, 68; and D, 120.

Next, consider the problem of estimating the sentence that would have been imposed on the defendant in the absence of the case settlement—the second difficult aspect of applying our definition of concession to the defendant. Conceptually, given reliable historical data concerning trial outcomes for defendants who are similar (in traits and charges) to this defendant, one could accurately estimate the hypothetical outcome had the latter gone to trial. In

---

[31] Translated into words, this formula reflects the value judgment that a one month incarceration in jail is as harsh as 6 months probation time or a $1000 fine; or that one year of prison time (score = 19) is 58 percent harsher than one year of jail time (score = 12), while two years of prison time (score = 18 + 2 = 20) is 67 percent more onerous than one year in jail. We have followed the BCS approach in defining the components of the Index to be additive.

57

Table 4-5
Four Alternative Sentence Severity Indices[a]

Components	Description of Indices			
	A	B	C	D
	Modified BCS	Probation and Fines Half of A; Prison Rate 3 Times A	Probation and Fines Zero; Prison Rate 5 Times A	Probation and Fines Zero; Prison and Jail Equal and Heavy
Jail time score (per month imposed	1	1	1	1
Custody time score (credit per month of custody before disposition)	−1	−1	−1	−1
Probation time score (per month imposed)	.167	.083	0	0
Fines score (per $1000 in fines; maximum score = 5)	1	.5	0	0
Prison time score	18 plus 1 per year	18 plus 3 per year	18 plus 5 per year	12 per year
Illustrative sentences: 6 months jail + 5 years probation	16	11	6	6
10 years prison	28	48	68	120

[a]The Sentence Severity Index is the sum of the five component scores.

practice, however, the appropriate data are sparse in most court systems, one reason being that relatively few criminal cases culminate in trials and, of these, relatively few involve defendants similar to this one. This paucity of data is exacerbated because plea bargaining tends to be inherently selective, i.e., some defendants who go to trial do so because their traits and criminal conduct have precluded their obtaining a concession in return for a plea. Thus trial outcomes are appropriate for deriving the desired estimates only to the extent that trial defendants resemble defendants obtaining concessions.

One way of circumventing this data base problem is to adopt the view that defendants enter the plea bargaining process with the option of making a straight plea to the original charges and with the expectation that punishment resulting from a straight plea, if made, would be less severe than that imposed after conviction at trial.[32] Thus, at least from the defendant's viewpoint, the

---

[32] E.J. Younger, Attorney General of California, speaks to this point by citing the responses of federal judges to a *Yale Law Journal* questionnaire that indicated that 66 percent thought the fact that the defendant had pled rather than been tried was a relevant factor in an accepted practice to give lighter sentences to those pleading guilty. E.J. Younger, "Change Plea Bargaining Law," *Los Angeles Times*, Part X, "Opinion," December 14, 1975.

concession to him could be properly measured by reference to his straight-plea option. From the prosecutor's viewpoint in his prosecutorial role, it might be argued that the concession should be measured by allowing for the likelihood that the defendant might be acquitted or be convicted of lesser charges as the result of trial. It can be further moderated by the prosecutor's responsibility to be also a "minister of justice," which may encourage him to feel that the most severe punishment obtainable is not necessarily the most desirable. The upshot of using the straight-plea punishment as a reference level for calculating the amount of concession is, of course, that this enables the analyst to apply a larger data base than when using the trial-conviction alternative.

In the demonstration phase of our study we viewed performance measures of plea bargaining from the two perspectives: those which indicate what happens over time and those which indicate how the systemwide exchange or balance of gains or other (possibly harmful) operational impacts on the one hand and concessions to defendants on the other hand has changed over time. Table 4-6

Table 4-6
Performance Measures in Plea Bargaining: The Frequency of Plea Bargaining

Performance Measures	*Required Data Elements*
By category of highest offense charged as a percentage of dispositions over a specified time period:	Number of dispositions
1. Straight plea rate (to all charges and counts) with no other bargain	Number of guilty plea dispositions in each designated category
2. Straight plea rate	

With sentence agreement
   With agreement to drop other cases
   With combination of the above	

3. Plea rate to at least one count of most serious charge with other charges and/or counts reduced	

With no other bargain
   With sentence agreement
   With agreement to drop other cases
   With combined sentence/drop other cases agreements	

4. Original charge plea rate (Sum of items 1, 2, 3)	
5. Plea rate to lesser charges (charge bargaining rate)	

With no other bargains
   With sentence agreement
   With agreement to drop other cases
   With combined sentence/drop other cases agreements	

6. Gross plea rate (Sum of items 4 and 5)	Total number of guilty pleas

displays performance measures relating to what happens over time to the gross plea rate and the frequency of different types of plea bargains—i.e., the straight-plea (to all charges and counts) rate (with no other bargain); the straight-plea rate with other bargains (such as a sentence agreement or an agreement by the prosecutor not to oppose a defense-recommended sentence, or an agreement to drop other pending cases); the plea rate to at least one count of the most serious charge, with other charges and/or counts reduced (with and without other bargains); and the plea rate to lesser charges (with and without other bargains).

Table 4-7 displays measures of the systemwide impacts of plea bargaining. On the one hand are measures of operational impacts, some of which may be viewed as "gains" and some as "losses" depending on the direction of the changes in the performance measures and one's philosophical view. A change in plea bargaining policy (and the resulting change in plea bargaining rates) could affect pretrial dismissal rate (and diversion or *nolle prosequi* rate, where applicable); trial rate; trial conviction rate; overall conviction rate; measures of sentence severity imposed (e.g., percent of guilty pleaders incarcerated, the average sentence severity score imposed); delay in proceedings (e.g., measures such as the period from arrest to final disposition or arraignment to final disposition); and the use of witnesses and jurors time (e.g., measures such as the number of victim/witness hours consumed per disposition and the fraction of time jurors spend in jury selection and trial). Most observers would agree that if delay were reduced by a change in plea bargaining policy, this would constitute a gain to the system, as long as the quality of justice was not adversely affected. However, if a change in plea bargaining policy led to a decrease in average sentence severity imposed, there is considerable controversy as to whether this constitutes a system gain or loss. On the other hand are the concessions granted to defendants. In the demonstration phase of the study we used the straight-plea sentence as our reference level of punishment in the application of the performance measures shown in Table 4-7.[33] Nevertheless, even when this reference level is used, we believe it is still important for a jurisdiction to determine whether and to what extent imposed sentences differ for like cases that go to trial if it is to fully appreciate plea bargaining impacts, particularly since the conventional wisdom holds that the system exacts a penalty in punishment imposed on those who exercise their rights to a trial.

Tables 4-6 and 4-7 also display the data elements implied by our choice of measures. A serious limitation on our plea bargaining performance analysis in one demonstration jurisdiction turned out to be the failure of the system to record the occurrence and nature of the principal type of plea bargain in that system, i.e., sentence agreements. Without this data element, only a fragmentary picture of plea bargaining performance could be drawn, as is discussed in

---

[33] The alternative approaches mentioned in the definition of concession given earlier proved to be infeasible because of data availability problems.

Table 4-7

Performance Measures in Plea Bargaining: Balance of Systemwide Effects and Systemwide Concessions to Defendants

Performance Measures	*Required Data Elements*
Systemwide Operational Effects:	
By category of highest offense charged over specified period of time:	
Pretrial dismissal, diversion, *nolle prosequi* rates	Number of cases in each category/number of dispositions
Trial rate (total, bench, jury)	Number of trials (total, bench, jury)/number of dispositions in each category
Trial conviction rate (total, bench, jury)	Number of trial convictions (total, bench, jury)/ number of trials in each category
Overall conviction rate	Number of convictions/number of dispositions
Sentence severity imposed:	
Percent of guilty pleaders incarcerated	Number of guilty pleaders incarcerated/number of guilty pleaders
Average sentence severity score imposed	Sentence elements by type and amount imposed on guilty pleaders
Delay or elapsed time measures:	
Median arrest to final disposition period Median arraignment to final disposition period	Median elapsed time (days) between these events
Number of victim-hours per disposition	(Number of victim appearances/disposition) X (time per appearance)
Number of other witness-hours per disposition	(Number of witness appearances/disposition) X (time per appearance)
Percentage of juror time in jury selection and trial	Juror time in jury selection and trial ÷ total time (including idleness)
Systemwide Concessions to Defendants:	
Sentence concession per guilty pleader	Difference between average sentence severity score of all straight pleaders and of all guilty pleaders
Sentence concession:	Difference between average sentence severity score of all straight pleaders and
Per charge bargainer	Average severity score of all charge bargainers
Per count bargainer	Average severity score of all count bargainers
Per sentence bargainer	Average severity score of all sentence bargainers
Per combination of above	Average severity score of all combinations

Chapter 6. In the other jurisdiction the analysis was much more successful because the occurrence of sentence agreements was recorded (as well as other types of plea bargains), although the nature was not.

Evenhandedness

Evenhandedness is a quality of court operations that is characterized by the following question: Do defendants in *similar* circumstances fare comparably in criminal proceedings?[34] In devising a statistical approach to this issue area we sought to classify defendants so that within each class they would be sufficiently similar that the intermediate and final outcomes within a class ought not be significantly different. It would then be appropriate, given outcome data in a specific jurisdiction, to examine the differences within a class for significant indications of unevenhandedness.

Taking this approach, we first identified various outcomes within a criminal proceedings that might manifest unevenhandedness. Specifically, these were as follows:

1. The proportion of suspects rejected
2. The proportion of suspects charged with at least one felony count
3. The proportion of defendants dismissed (including *nolle pros.*)
   a. Prior to arraignment
   b. Following arraignment
4. The proportion of defendants making a straight plea
5. The proportion of defendants entering a plea agreement
6. The proportion of defendants tried
7. The proportion of defendants acquitted
8. The proportion of defendants convicted in trial of charges less serious than the original charges—by type of trial
9. The magnitude of the Sentence Severity Index
   a. For conviction by plea (also separately for straight pleas and plea agreements)
   b. For conviction by trial

Next we addressed the problem of identifying those defendant qualities that appear to justify differences in the outcomes reflected by the above list, e.g., rejected or not, charged or not, dismissed or not, etc. These qualities (which we term *legitimate*) would thus serve to classify defendants so that within each class the defendants are sufficiently similar that the above outcome measures ought not differ significantly (among groups of defendants within a class). On the basis of Rand's earlier work[35] and the views of practitioners interviewed in the course of this study, we designated the following factors to be *legitimate factors*, or the defendant qualities for which differences in outcomes were justified:

1. Nature of the criminal conduct
   a. Most serious charges (i.e., those for which the most severe punishment could be imposed)
   b. Strength of the evidence[36]

---

[34] Note that lack of evenhandedness in police practices is beyond the scope of this study. For example, police rejection of cases may reflect uneven treatment of suspects prior to the involvement of the court system.

[35] Reported in P. Greenwood, S. Wildhorn, et al., *Prosecution of Adult Felony Defendants.*

[36] We treat this factor only in the case-auditing substudy of the demonstration phase of this study (see Chapter 7). It would affect disposition but not (in theory at least) sentencing.

2. Prior record[37]

    a. None

    b. Minor

    c. Major

    d. Prison

3. Age

    a. Youth

    b. Adult

    c. Senior

4. Sex[38]

5. Defendant's community ties, as reflected by an index that includes income, education, transiency, employment status, marital status, and number of dependents[39]

---

[37]Our definitions, which are simplifications of the classification scheme developed by the California Bureau of Criminal Statistics, are here as follows:

No prior record: fewer than three prior arrests and no convictions.

Minor prior record: three or more arrests or some convictions but none imposing more than 90 days of jail time.

Major prior record: any convictions with more than 90 days jail time or more than two years probation but no prison time.

Prison record: any prior prison incarceration.

More elaborate categories were used in P. Greenwood, S. Wildhorn, et al., *Prosecution of Adult Felony Defendants*, again based on the BCS scheme (see Table 21, p. 40, of that reference). Prior record could be expressed in terms of specific types of offenses or (as we have done) nonspecifically. For some purposes, for example, analyzing sentence variation, specific-offense prior records would be desirable but would engender greater complexity both in data collection and analysis. In our demonstration work we used the nonspecific-offense prior record categories. The fact that a defendant has a prior criminal record may have an impact in various ways at a number of points in a felony proceeding. The police may be prompted to make a more thorough investigation of the offense; the charging may be performed with greater care; the defendant may be more likely to remain in jail during the proceeding because of ineligibility for OR release or inability to meet a higher bail requirement; the defendant may elect not to testify because of his vulnerability to impeachment by evidence of his prior record; or the sentencing judge may be strongly influenced by the defendant's history of criminal conduct. All these and other effects could lead to an outcome significantly different from that for a defendant with no prior record.

[38]There is a marked division of view on whether or not sex is a justifiable ground for distinction. This dispute is inconsequential for our purposes, since female defendants are relatively infrequent.

[39]Some practitioners would regard community ties as being a legitimate basis for differences in sentences (e.g., probation versus incarceration) but not necessarily for other aspects of the proceeding. For a discussion of the community ties index, refer to Appendix C, which contains our analysis of data from the demonstration jurisdictions for the purpose of estimating the relative weights of the above-listed independent variables in their relationship to the community-ties dependent variable.

For example, one class of defendants defined by this list of factors would be composed of male youths who were charged with armed robbery, had no prior record, and had weak community ties. We would expect such similar defendants to fare comparably in their criminal proceedings, as indicated by the performance measures listed above, if the court system is operating evenhandedly.

Finally, what are the appropriate factors within a class of similar defendants that should be examined to show lack of evenhandedness in outcomes? In other words, what defendant-related and other factors are illegitimate, or suspect, bases for differences in the outcome of criminal proceedings for similar defendants? We identified the following such *illegitimate factors:*[40]

1. Defendant's ethnicity (in affecting disposition and sentencing)
2. Defendant's pretrial custody status (in affecting disposition and sentencing)
3. Type of defense counsel (in affecting disposition and sentencing)
4. Type of conviction (by trial or straight plea of guilty—in affecting sentencing only)
5. Crowding of correctional facilities (in affecting sentencing only)

Most observers would agree that ethnicity alone should not affect dispositional or sentence outcomes under our system of justice. They would also concur that pretrial custody status per se should not affect whether an arrestee is charged or rejected; dismissed, convicted, or acquitted; or (if convicted) given a more or less severe sentence. In practice, pretrial custody status may relate to disposition and sentence. One argument holds that compared with defendants in custody those who are released are better able to strengthen their defense by locating witnesses. Another contends that defendants held in jail (particularly for offenses in which the probability of receiving a nonincarceration sentence is high) have more incentive to plead guilty, since this cuts short the total (pretrial and postconviction) incarceration period. In addition, the failure to obtain pretrial release may be a proxy for the viciousness of the offense or the evilness of the defendant (in ways not fully reflected by the actual original charges, the convicted charges, and the defendant's prior record).

Most observers would also agree that whether a defendant has the services of a public defender, a privately-retained counsel, or a court-appointed attorney should not influence disposition or sentence. But in reality, disposition or sentence may relate to the type of defense counsel. One argument is that a wealthier defendant who retains private counsel can provide more resources in

---

[40] Another factor, geographical evenhandedness, was investigated in an earlier Rand study (P. Greenwood, S. Wildhorn, et al., *Prosecution of Adult Felony Defendants*) of the performance of the Office of the District Attorney, Los Angeles County, which has numerous branch offices distributed over that county. This factor is not included in the present study since the criminal proceedings in the two demonstration jurisdictions are centralized.

building a defense. Another view is that public defenders (compared with the usually less specialized court-appointed or privately-retained counsel) may achieve better results for defendants because they know the court system and its principals better. For example, the public defender may be more skilled at "judge shopping" to avoid the more severe sentencers.

Most observers would also agree that, all other things equal, the type of conviction, whether by trial or straight plea of guilty, ought not affect sentence severity. The conventional wisdom, however, is that conviction by trial leads to more severe sentences, i.e., the system penalizes defendants who exercise their right to a trial. (However, in our application of measures of evenhandedness in the two demonstration jurisdictions, the analysis of a small sample of trial convictions revealed no penalty in sentence severity for these defendants compared with others who pleaded guilty to the original charges against them.)

Finally, the degree of crowding in correctional facilities ought not to affect sentences, but in reality, it undoubtedly does. In some jurisdictions where correctional facilities are extremely crowded, judges may feel compelled to impose probation or other nonincarceration sentences on the least dangerous defendants who would have otherwise been incarcerated.

The approach taken by this study in its demonstration phase was, in short, to take as indicators of a lack of evenhandedness the direction and magnitude of effects of each illegitimate factor on a set of performance measures of dispositional and sentence outcomes.[41] The effects of these illegitimate factors may be estimated by cross tabulations or by multivariate statistical techniques. The former can indicate only the presence of gross effects. For example, if the straight-plea rate of black burglary defendants is 70 percent and that of white burglary defendants is 50 percent, one cannot be sure that all the difference is due to ethnicity, because some of the difference may be due to other factors. Continuing with this example, if a much larger proportion of the black burglary defendants remain in jail and have public defender representation, the effects of these factors may confound the ethnicity effect. Multivariate statistical techniques, however, permit the identification of the unique or independent effect of each of these factors.

For dispositional evenhandedness we used the illegitimate factors ethnicity, pretrial custody status, and type of defense counsel. For sentencing evenhandedness we added type of disposition (straight plea, trial) to this list of three factors, believing that jurisdictions might wish to test the proposition that exercising the right to trial involves a penalty in punishment compared to a straight pleader. We also added degree of crowding in correctional facilities as an illegitimate sentencing evenhandedness factor, even though in practice, crowding may lead to lighter sentences.

---

[41] We believe that an examination of the evenhandedness of charging would also have been desirable. Unfortunately, data on defendant characteristics was too sparsely recorded at the screening stage in both demonstration jurisdictions.

Table 4-8 gives the performance measures together with the comparisons that need to be made to assess the effects of the illegitimate variables (required data elements are not repeated here since they were indicated in previous tables).

In the demonstration jurisdictions we found the principal data element problem in this issue area to be the incompleteness of case files and other data sources in recording defendant ethnicity (and other biographical information).

Sentencing Variation

That sentencing vitally affects the achievement of criminal justice system goals is universally recognized. Notwithstanding this recognition, there seems to be scant understanding and agreement about relationships between the type and severity of punishment imposed and how progress toward system goals is made. To say that no generally accepted theories or models exist and that judges tend to accord little weight to accumulated experience in sentencing is not an unfair assessment. This situation obviously reduces the opportunities for useful application of performance measures in the general area of sentencing.

Table 4-8
Measuring Evenhandedness in Dispositional and Sentence Outcomes

Performance Measures	*Magnitude and Direction of the Illegitimate Factor Effects*
By category of highest offense as booked by police and charged by prosecutor over a specified time period:	*(Each of the illegitimate factors must be identified for each case in the sample)*
Dispositional Outcomes:	
Rejection rate (based on number screened)	
Nonconviction rate (based on number of dispositions)	Black, Spanish, other, minority vs. majority
Pretrial dismissal rate	Held in jail vs. released on bail vs. released on
Pretrial diversion rate	OR
Nolle prosequi rate	
Conviction rate (based on number of dispositions)	Public defender vs. retained counsel vs. court-appointed counsel
By straight plea	
By any plea bargain (gross plea rate)	
By trial (and trial conviction rate)	
Overall	
Sentence Outcomes	
Sentence severity score	*As above but add:*
	Trial conviction (all, bench, jury) vs. straight plea
	Crowding in correctional facilities

One quality of sentencing activity is, however, relatively visible and readily lends to measurement. This is *sentencing variation*, i.e., the sentencing disparities that occur within statutory punishment limits. What is the significance of this variation? Generally, judges have some breadth of discretion in imposing sentence in individual cases. In exercising this discretion, judges concern themselves with appropriateness of punishment, which requires that they balance the gravity of the criminal conduct, the characteristics of the convicted defendant, the goals of criminal justice (both locally and nationally), and the expectations of the victim and the public, among other factors. At the same time, our system of justice includes an evenhandedness standard for sentencing, which requires that judges sentence not only rationally but also consistently.

Sentencing disparities are, on their face, ambiguous. They might reflect an intended and justified adaptation of a flexible punishment structure to individual cases. Or they might signify the presence of sentencing flaws, for example, the presence of unjustifiable inconsistencies among sentences or unreasonable interpretations of the appropriateness of punishment.

Our study undertook the limited task of identifying measures that could reveal sentencing variation in informative ways. Despite the complexity of issues in this area, we believe that sentencing performance measures are useful if they simply reveal in gross terms what the prevailing sentencing practices are in a specific jurisdiction. They then serve to "tip off" the appearance of abrupt sentencing aberrations or of major changes occurring more gradually over time.[42]

Our task in the issue area of sentencing variation has two aspects: identifying criteria that measure how much sentence variation for a specified conficted charge actually exists and explaining how much of the total observed variation is accounted for by various factors that should (i.e., legitimately) or should not (i.e., illegitimately) cause the variation. An appropriate approach begins by measuring the proportion of defendants receiving sentences in each of the following categories:[43]

[42] What a jurisdiction should do to remedy undue sentence variation, given statistical evidence of its presence, is far from a settled matter. See, for example, C.A. Korbakes, "Criminal Sentencing: Should the 'Judges' Sound Discretion' Be Explained?" *Judicature*, Vol. 59, No. 4, November 1975, wherein the author discusses the results of a survey of the chief judges of the 50 states by the American Judicature Society. The survey addresses several measures (e.g., stating reasons for sentences in writing, using sentencing panels, providing for appellate review of sentences) aimed at "better" sentencing. Opinions given by these judges were widely and sharply divided concerning these measures.

[43] In the earlier Rand study of adult felony defendants in Los Angeles County (P. Greenwood, S. Wildhorn, et al., *Prosecution of Adult Felony Defendants*), we also used a measure that is appropriate to a jurisdiction that gives the court the discretion to treat specified offense types as alternative misdemeanor/felony offenses; namely, the proportion of defendants receiving sentences at each of the following levels of conviction/sentence for a specified most serious charge:

Convicted of felony as charged, received felony sentence.

(continued on page 67)

1. Probation only
2. Rehabilitative program (possibly as a probation condition)
3. Community service (possibly as a probation condition)
4. Fine only
5. Probation and fine
6. Jail only
7. Jail and fine
8. Jail and probation
9. Jail, fine, and probation
10. Prison

In this approach, these sentence categories are broken out by the magnitude classes of their elements. This should be done for each major category of convicted offense, if one believes that the convicted charge most accurately reflects the criminal conduct of defendants. Or it should be done for each major category of highest charged offense, given a belief that the latter most accurately reflects the criminal conduct. This provides a gross statistical picture of the distribution of sentences, i.e., sentence variation. But to facilitate further analysis, each of the sentences can be assigned a corresponding sentence severity score (or a set of such scores for alternative sentence severity indices, as discussed earlier within the issue area of plea bargaining). The result would then be a sentence distribution in the form of the proportion of defendants receiving sentences that correspond to each specified interval of scores of a stated Sentence Severity Index. A useful statistical measure of how much variation is reflected by this distribution of sentences (for a category of convicted offense or else of highest charged offense) is the so-called coefficient of variation, namely, the ratio of the standard deviation of the sentence severity scores divided by the average sentence severity score.

Sentences vary for many reasons.[44] As we noted above in the discussion of

Convicted of lesser felony, received felony sentence.

Convicted of felony as charged, received misdemeanor sentence.

Convicted of lesser felony, received misdemeanor sentence.

Convicted of misdemeanor (though charged with felony).

[44] One important study on unevenhandedness was submitted by NILECJ in June 1972 to the U.S. Senate Subcommittee on Criminal Law and Procedure (McClellan subcommittee). The Institute, reporting on sentencing variations in the federal courts during the four-year period 1967-1970, concluded that, among other findings, there was a significant lack of evenhandedness in sentence length according to the race of the defendant. Another such study was the "1972 Sentencing Study, Southern District of New York," unpublished report, compiled May-October 1972 by the Office of the U.S. Attorney, SDNY (published in part in the *American Criminal Law Review*, Vol. 11, No. 4, Summer, 1973, pp. 826-834). The latter study found that during the six-month period covered, there was a significant disparity in sentences (both as to rate and to length of incarceration) among classes of offenses, with "white-collar crime" being treated much more leniently than other types of theft, not only in the Southern District of New York but in all federal courts.

evenhandedness, some are acceptable (i.e., legitimate); they may include the defendant's age, prior record, an index of community ties (including employment, education, family status, transiency), the nature and number of charges against the defendant, and the judges' sentencing philosophies. Some are not so acceptable (i.e., illegitimate); most observers would agree that certain factors should not affect sentencing. They may include defendant race or ethnicity, pretrial custody status, type of defense counsel, method of conviction (guilty plea, trial), and changes over time in the crowding of correctional facilities. By applying standard multivariate statistical techniques it is possible to determine how much of the explained variation is accounted for by each of these factors (with the exception of judicial philosophy). (Data on all but the latter factor is normally recorded or could be easily recorded in agency files. Data on the judge's sentencing philosophy would be very difficult to quantify.) The remaining unexplained variation is then attributable to factors that could not be identified or measured, or to random effects. Chapters 5 and 6 illustrate, for the demonstration jurisdictions, how this approach is applied to measure the amount of sentence variation present and how much of this variation can be accounted for by various factors (see Tables 5-19 and 6-13).

Gauging Overall Performance

We have, as declared at the opening of this chapter, restricted our treatment to the selection, rationale, and limitations of statistical performance measures in illuminating several salient issue areas within criminal proceedings. Our intent was not to consider performance measures as routine informational devices in support of day-to-day management and control of court systems. Nevertheless, much of what has been presented in this section could be recast in the context of day-to-day management and control, *mutatis mutandis.*

Also, we have not undertaken to gauge the overall performance of a court system. The scope of this study was not overall in breadth. In some jurisdictions, the selected issue areas might encompass most operational problems being encountered; in others, the coverage could be significantly incomplete. In some jurisdictions, performance in these issue areas might be highly interrelated; in others, markedly independent.

Nevertheless, for completeness, we should touch upon the question of objective approaches to the aggregate interpretation of an entire battery of performance measures (and sets of performance measures) used in a jurisdiction to illuminate various aspects of criminal justice operations. We shall confine our comments to two possible approaches, neither of which appears to be a satisfying solution to this oft-felt need to characterize, in some overall sense, the criminal justice posture of a specific jurisdiction at some given point in time.

One approach might be the construction of an aggregate performance measure constructed out of separate indices of performance in selected areas of criminal justice activity. Of course, this approach immediately thrusts upon us a multitude of "apples and oranges" issues, the resolution of which tends to be strongly subjective. What activities within the process should be selected for inclusion in the aggregate measure? How may they be made commensurable? And, most difficult of all, how much importance should be attributed to one activity relative to another—for example, what weight should case processing efficiency be given relative to charging accuracy in the construction of an aggregate performance measure? Such dilemmas might be resolved by statements of position by responsible policymakers. Or they might be circumvented by the use of a small set of alternatives, spanning reasonable differences of opinion. But, in practice, a single composite measure of performance for a complex process serving a multitude of (sometimes conflicting) objectives would not gain acceptance. The criminal justice community shows a clear preference for retaining the separate identities of different functions and agencies and for integrating their performance (if any integration is attempted) subjectively according to the evaluator's view of their relative contributions.

In the rare case where clear changes are observed over time in performance measures (for say, the better) in all or virtually all the issue areas of interest, it is then possible to draw a qualitative inference that overall performance changed for the better. Our application of performance measures in one of the two jurisdictions uncovered such a case (see Chapter 5).

Another approach to obtaining a collective interpretation of a battery of performance measures might be to compare their magnitudes with "standards" that are implied by various descriptive models of the criminal justice process, for example, Packer's due process and crime control models, Goldstein's inquisitorial and accusatorial/adversarial models, Davis's administrative model, etc. Conceptually, one could observe changes in magnitude occurring over time in a battery of performance measures in a jurisdiction and then infer, if possible, the presence of trends toward one or another of the descriptive models. But there are serious difficulties, both conceptual and practical, in implementing this approach, as we learned in unsuccessfully attempting to apply it in the present study.

Interjurisdictional Comparisons by Means of Statistical Performance Measures

The inclination to compare the performance of criminal court systems among different jurisdictions is often strongly and widely felt. Statistical performance measures might be used for this purpose, but questions of validity arise in such use. Mechanical comparisons may always be made, but whether or not it is meaningful to compare the magnitude of a performance measure in one jurisdiction with its magnitude in another is an issue to be seriously considered.

Among the 50-plus major jurisdictions in this country, codes of criminal law differ widely. Criminal procedure· and court rules are similarly disparate. Interfaces between the police and the courts and between the courts and the correctional system vary from one locality to another. Law enforcement policies are necessarily adapted to local conditions, and these adaptations are not consistent over wide areas.

Some degree of uniformity certainly exists, and the trend is toward its increase. This movement reflects such developments as the Supreme Court's enunciation and clarification of constitutional rights, the growing adoptions of model codes and uniform laws, the pervasive influence of federal rules and practices, the publication of ABA standards and similar efforts, the educational and training programs conducted by professional societies and institutes, etc. Nevertheless, criminal justice systems can be strikingly different, particularly if they do not operate in the same state.

When are interjurisdictional comparisons of criminal court systems meaningful? We do not undertake to answer this question broadly, but instead offer two instances where these comparisons by means of statistical performance measures can be meaningful.

In the first instance, one may be addressing certain outputs of the court system that are significant in a societal sense independently of the institutional machinery that produced them. For example, the size of prison populations is societally significant in itself, independent of the details of the judicial process that sent people there. It may therefore be argued that a related measure, such as the rate at which prison sentences are imposed (and not suspended), leads to a meaningful comparison among different court systems, even though the latter differ in important respects.

In the second instance, one may be able to identify the "comparability" features that are significant to performance of a court system in a specified province of operations or, to use the term employed by this study, a specified issue area. Presumably, a comparison of these features or factors between two jurisdictions would provide the necessary appreciation of how meaningful would be a comparison of statistical performance measures that illuminate this province of operations. And it would provide the qualifications that should be articulated in presenting inferences from the comparison of measures. A provisional list of comparability features, keyed to the issue areas of this study, is given in Table 4-9 (see Table 6-6, for an application of this list to the comparison of Multnomah and Dade Counties).

Table 4-9
Comparability Features for the Issue Areas[a]

I. *Case Processing Efficiency and Delay*
  A. Practitioner productivity
    1. Differences in procedural steps or disposition points
    2. Pretrial motion practices (e.g., delaying such motions until trial)
    3. Conduct of jury *voir dire*
    4. Use of commissioners for judicial functions
    5. Method of assigning prosecutors and public defenders to cases
    6. Court calendaring system
    7. Caseload mix (by offense category)
    8. Backlog of pending cases
  + 9. Use of court coordinators

  B. Witness use
    1. Court calendaring system
    2. Continuance policy and procedure
    3. Availability rules (e.g., "on call" system)

  C. Juror use
    1. Conduct of jury *voir dire*
    2. Policy on jury pool size

  D. Delay
    1. Court calendaring system
    2. Continuance policy and procedure
    3. Differences in procedural steps or disposition points
    4. Availability of interlocutory appeals
    5. Liberality of pretrial discovery
    6. Existence and nature of time-limit standards; power to refile
    7. Caseload mix (by offense category)
    8. Scale of court system and backlog of pending cases

II. *Evenhandedness*
    1. Police arrest and screening policies
    2. Bail and OR policies
    3. Jury selection and composition
    4. Judicial selection and composition
    5. Payment or fee compensation system for defense counsel

III. *Prosecutorial Screening*
    1. Charging or filing standards
    2. Police arrest and screening policies
    3. Procedure for *nolle prosequi* (on motion or by court)
    4. Existence and nature of time-limit standards; power to refile

Table 4-9 (cont.)

III. *Prosecutorial Screening (continued)*

    5. Availability and nature of pretrial diversion programs

    6. Availability of precharging conference

    7. Organization of prosecutor's office

IV. *Plea bargaining*

    1-7. As above in III.

    8. Statutory sentencing structure

    9. Liberality of pretrial discovery

    10. Availability and nature of preliminary hearing

    11. Probation policy

    12. Judicial involvement in plea bargaining

  +13. Jail conditions

  +14. Caseload and backlog

  +15. Jury or judge sentencing

  +16. Method of providing defense counsel

V. *Sentencing Variation*

    1. Statutory sentencing structure

    2. Probation policy

    3. Plea bargaining practices

    4. Charging or filing standards

    5. Parole eligibility and practice

    6. Public attitudes toward gravity of various offenses and appropriate sentences for them

    7. Availability of sentence review

    8. Overcrowding of correctional facilities

  + 9. Method of filling judgeships

  +10. Postsentencing powers of trial judge

  +11. Availability of presentence reports

  +12. Judge or jury sentencing

  +13. Availability of alternatives to sentencing

---

aThose items to which the symbol + is prefixed were added at the suggestion of practitioners whom we interviewed.

5

Application of Performance Measures in Multnomah County

In Appendix A, we describe in largely qualitative terms the organization, operation, and policies of the court, prosecution, and public defender agencies in Multnomah County. In this chapter, using data collected from the agencies' records and from mail surveys of victims, witnesses, and jurors, we apply the statistical performance measures in this jurisdiction. For illustrative purposes, our analysis is largely built around a preliminary evaluation of the systemwide effects of a "no-plea-negotiation experiment" introduced by the District Attorney's office in late 1973. First, we describe briefly the objectives and nature of the experiment. Next, we provide the reader with a statistical overview of system resources, defendant-related characteristics, and the outputs of felony proceedings before and during the experiment. Then, taking each of the major issue areas discussed in the previous chapters, we attempt to show how performance has changed between these two time periods and to what extent performance changes are associated with the experiment or to other identifiable factors. Finally, we summarize these findings and comment on the extent to which we find it possible to characterize changes in overall performance.

The District Attorney's "No-Plea-Negotiation Experiment"

Toward the end of calendar year 1973 a special trial unit, known as the Impact Unit, was formed in the District Attorney's Office and became fully operational by January 1974. It was funded partially through the LEAA as part of Portland's (Oregon) High Impact Anti-Crime program. There were three broad operating goals: to improve the quality of cases coming to trial by providing legal advice and casework assistance to police investigators; to provide swift and appropriate prosecution of target crimes; and to reduce the frequency of negotiated pleas. The target (or Impact) crimes were dwelling burglaries, serious robberies, and "fencing."

Six additional deputy prosecutors and five support people were funded under the grant and assigned to the Impact Unit. In a departure from the usual procedure employed with cases other than target crimes, in which a case moves among DA units, an attorney in the Impact Unit retains a case from filing to final disposition. Also, deputies work with detectives on a day-to-day basis, assisting with case preparation whenever requested. We observed two other departures from the usual procedures in Impact cases: case folders are in a distinctive bright orange (clearly conveying to the judge and defense attorney that this is an Impact case); and more extensive presentence investigation reports are prepared more frequently in Impact cases than in other cases.

The program's goal of reducing negotiated pleas deserves some elaboration. In this aspect of the experiment the District Attorney's objective was to reduce only plea agreements involving charge reduction. The program goals were silent on other forms of plea agreements, such as to reduce the number of counts (but not the charge level), to recommend or not to oppose specific sentences, to not file or not prosecute other cases pending against the defendant, or combinations of the foregoing, in return for guilty pleas.

More specific objectives within the goals were also delineated. These included maintaining a high "original-charge" conviction rate of 85 percent, maintaining a rate of negotiated pleas (i.e., charge-reduction plea bargains) of less than 5 percent, reduction of the dismissal rate for insufficient evidence, and maintaining an arrest-to-trial period for Impact offenses equal to that for a comparison group of offenses. Since the nature of any plea bargain is recorded in a special form filed with the court and since we captured this information in our data collection effort, it was possible (as is discussed below) to determine how plea bargaining changed during the experiment and to trace its consequences on other outcomes.

A Statistical Overview

In Tables 5-1 through 5-6 we provide a statistical overview of caseloads and dispositions in the Circuit Court, inmate population of the Oregon felony correctional institutions, and a variety of defendant-related and other characteristics. The information was collected from two sources: from statistics provided by various criminal justice agencies in Multnomah County and the State of Oregon and from data samples collected by research team members from agency records. The collection procedures for the latter are described in Appendix B, together with descriptions of the samples themselves.

General characteristics of the court, prosecution, and public defender agencies are summarized in Table 5-1. Most of the information summarized is taken from the descriptions provided in Appendix A. Criminal case filings and backlog (i.e., pending or open cases) in the Circuit Court are shown in Table 5-2, and felony inmates confined in Oregon correctional institutions are shown in Table 5-3.

Notice that case filings have steadily increased between 1971 and 1975 and that backlog doubled between end-1973 and end-1975. The number of felony inmates in Oregon's correctional institutions (excluding those on work release) declined somewhat between 1972 and 1974 but increased steadily thereafter. By June 30, 1975 the number of inmates (2,054) exceeded the single cell capacity

Table 5-1

Characteristics of Criminal Justice Agencies in Multnomah County

Criminal Justice Agency	Characteristics
Circuit court	
Number of courts	1 chief criminal court (no trials except on stipulated facts)
	10 civil/criminal trial courts
Number of felony cases filed per year	2,500 (approx.)
Number of felony trials per year	300 (approx.)
Method of electing judges	Nonpartisan; 6-year term
Juries	
Term of duty	4-5 weeks
Pool of venirepersons	200
Jury size	12
Sentencing	
Statutory maxima by felony level	Life: life, no minimum
	A: 20 years
	B: 10 years
	C: 5 years
Court discretion	May impose maximum lower than statutory maximum; concurrent or consecutive sentences
Typical percentage of imposed sentence served (all felonies)	33
District attorney's office	
Number of prosecutors	
Total (felonies and misdemeanors)	50
Felonies only	27
Number of felony cases filed per year ÷ number of felony-assigned deputies	100 (approx.)
Public defender's office	
Number of felony cases adjudications	1,400
Number of attorneys	
Total	12
Felonies only	8
Number of felony cases adjudicated per year ÷ number of felony-assigned defenders	175 (approx.)

of 1,918 beds (including work release inmates) in the entire system, and by December 1975 inmates exceeded capacity by almost 300. During the past few years there has been no increase in state correctional facilities for felony inmates. Multnomah County facilities (Rocky Butte Jail) were nearly full, too. Until mid-1973 the average daily count ran somewhat over 400 inmates. After a remodeling in mid-1973, which reduced capacity to 340, in 1974 the average daily count rose to near capacity (288 in August and 335 in December).

Table 5-2
Criminal Cases[a] Filed and Pending in Multnomah County Circuit Court, 1971-1975

Fiscal Year	Number of Filings	Date	Cases Pending (backlog)
1971-72	2,466	Dec. 1972	597
1972-73	2,928	Dec. 1973	533
1973-74	3,250	Dec. 1974	774
1974-75	3,657	Nov. 1975	1,008

Source: Multnomah County Circuit Court records.
[a]Includes criminal appeals from lower court.

 Table 5-4 displays the mix of felony cases, by offense type, closed in 1973 and 1974. Offenses against persons in other than robbery declined from 16 percent in 1973 to 9 percent in 1974. Offenses against property also declined during that period—45 to 37 percent—mainly due to a decrease in burglary and theft offenses. The relative proportion of drug offenses, however, increased sharply from 26 to 38 percent during that period.
 In Table 5-5 we display trends in the characteristics of felony defendants processed in Circuit Court. Compared with 1973, burglary and robbery defendants in 1974 tended to be somewhat younger and less educated and had resided longer in Multnomah County, although these differences were not substantial. In 1974 fewer burglary and robbery defendants were black. Prior records of these defendants changed only slightly over the two years; about half had no prior record, and 15 to 17 percent had prior prison records. In 1973 about half of all

Table 5-3
Inmates[a] Confined in Felony Correctional Institutions in the State of Oregon, 1972-1975 Selected Dates

Date	Number of Inmates
Jan. 1, 1972	1,899
Jan. 1, 1973	1,595
Jan. 1, 1974	1,659
Jan. 1, 1975	1,886
June 30, 1975	2,054
Dec. 1, 1975	2,205

Source: Oregon Department of Corrections.
[a]Excludes inmates on work release.

Table 5-4
Distribution of Felony Cases by Type of Offense in Multnomah County, 1973-1974
(Percent of All Cases)

Type of Offense	1973	1974
Offenses against persons	25	20
Robbery	9	11
Other	16	9
Offenses against property	45	37
Burglary	21	16
Theft	16	13
Other	8	8
Drug offenses	26	38
All other offenses	4	5
Total	100	100

Source: Based on a random sample of 100 felony cases in each year (the "general" samples—see App. D).

felony defendants had public defenders, whereas in 1974 only a third did. In 1973 over 80 percent of all felony defendants made bail or were released on their own recognizance (OR), whereas in 1974 this was the case with only 70 percent.

In Table 5-6 we present an overview of felony case dispositions, sentences, and delay based on an examination of a random sample of almost 100 Circuit Court case folders in each of the two years. Pretrial dismissal rates remained almost constant over the two years at 35 to 38 percent, although the proportions dismissed for other reasons and for insufficient evidence changed somewhat in 1974 compared with 1973. The trial rate also declined from 13 percent in 1973 to 7 percent in 1974; this decline was fairly evenly split between jury and court trials. Trial conviction rates, however, remained fairly constant.

For all felonies, the overall rates of pretrial guilty pleas showed little change over the two years (52 to 53 percent), and the proportion pleading guilty to original charges as opposed to lesser charges also showed little change over this time period. (However, as we shall demonstrate below, the picture for the specific Impact offenses of dwelling burglary I and robbery I was very different.) With pretrial dismissal, guilty plea, and trial conviction rates fairly constant over the two years, overall conviction rates also showed little change—remaining at roughly 60 percent of all felony dispositions.

Somewhat over 60 percent of all felony defendant sentences were nonincarcerations—i.e., probation, fines, restitutions, etc., or combinations of these elements—and little change in these rates occurred over these two years. Of the

Table 5-5

Selected Characteristics of Felony Defendants in Multnomah County, 1973-1974

(Percent of All Defendants)

Characteristics of Defendants	1973	1974
Age[a]		
Under 21	40	46
21-29	47	39
30 and over	13	15
Ethnic group[a]		
Black	45	30
Spanish surname	4	0
Other minority	8	13
Nonminority	43	57
Transient[a] (i.e., less than 2 years in county)	15	11
Less than high school education[a]	57	50
Prior record[a]		
None	47	52
Minor	20	12
Major	18	19
Prison	15	17
Type of defense attorney[b]		
Public defender	50	33
Private (court-appointed or defendant-retained)	50	67
Pretrial custody status[b]		
In jail (or combination of jail and bail or OR[c])	17	30
Released on bail or OR	83	70

[a]Based on 100-case random samples for each exemplary offense in each period, and weighted by their relative frequency of occurrence as shown in Table 5-4.
[b]Based on a 100-case random sample of all felony defendants in each period.
[c]The defendant is in jail part of the time and free part of the time.

32 to 39 percent incarcerated, the relative proportion receiving jail sentences (rather than prison sentences) declined markedly in 1974 compared with 1973. Although we cannot demonstrate it conclusively, this phenomenon may be related to the fact that the total number of confinements in state felony correctional institutions was rising rapidly (see Table 5-3) during this period and

Table 5-6

Dispositions, Sentences, and Delays in Felony Proceedings in Multnomah Circuit Court[a]

(Disposition and Sentence Entries in Percent)

Type of Disposition, Sentence, and Delay	1973		1974	
Dispositions				
Pretrial dismissal rate	35		38	
For insufficient evidence		16		8
For other reasons		19		30
Trial rate	13		7	
Jury		5		2
Court		8		5
Trial conviction rate[b]	75		72	
Trial acquittal rate[b]	25		14	
Trial dismissal, mistrial rate[b]	0		14	
Pretrial plea of guilty rate	52		53	
To original charges		22		19
To lesser charges		30		34
Overall conviction rate	62		58	
N (dispositions)	(94)		(95)	
Sentences				
Suspended	2		0	
Nonincarceration (probation, fine, restitution, etc.)	66		61	
Incarcerated	32		39	
Jail (and any lesser punishment)		11		28
Prison (and any lesser punishment)		21		11
N (convictions or sentencings)	(57)		(53)	
Median elapsed time (days)				
From arrest to trial	56		84	
From arrest to final disposition	62		77	
From arraignment to final disposition	34		63	

[a]Based on random sample of 100 felony cases from each period.
[b]Based on number of trials.

approaching the single cell capacity of the entire system. (Again, as we shall demonstrate below, the sentencing picture for felony defendants charged with Impact offenses was very different.)

Median elapsed time from arrest to trial and from arrest to final disposition increased by 50 and 25 percent respectively between 1973 and 1974. In 1973 the median arrest-to-trial period was barely within the statutory standard of 60 days for individual cases, but in 1974 it rose to 84 days. (However, of even more significance for the operation of the Circuit Court itself, the median time from arraignment to final disposition almost doubled between 1973 and 1974. As we shall indicate below in a more detailed discussion of the delay issue, part of the rise in elapsed time seems to be related to the steady rise in the number of case filings and amount of backlog. For example, between the end of 1973 and the end of 1974 the number of cases pending rose by almost 50 percent (see Table 5-2).

Finally, to provide a general context for the subsequent analysis of each issue, we show in Figures 5-1 and 5-2 what happens to robbery and burglary arrestees at the various stages between arrest and final disposition for the two years (1973 figures in italics and 1974 figures in regular typeface). Our focus is on the flow of those defendants who are originally arrested on these charges, then charged by the prosecutor with at least one count of these offenses, and arraigned in the Circuit Court.

Prosecutorial Screening

Here we apply the performance measures to the two prosecutorial issues discussed in Chapter 4—the charging threshold[1] and charging accuracy.

Charging Threshold

In Tables 5-7 and 5-8 we present performance measures relevant to gauging changes in prosecutorial charging threshold. Table 5-7 shows the screening actions taken in 1973 and 1974 by the prosecutor's office on cases booked by the police in which the highest police booking charge was robbery I (an Impact offense in 1974). Some cases contained only one robbery I count, others contained multiple robbery I counts, and still others had one or more robbery I counts plus one or more lesser charges. Table 5-8 shows similar data for cases booked by the police in which the highest booking charge was burglary I. (In Oregon, burglary I includes all dwelling burglaries as well as some nondwelling burglaries.) As mentioned above, the no-plea-negotiation experiment focused on dwelling burglaries in 1974. However, because police booking records do not distinguish between dwelling burglary I and nondwelling burglary I, we could not present screening actions for each suboffense category separately. The data are based on samples for each year and each offense taken from police booking records. Data on prosecutorial screening actions on cases in which any information was filed was gathered from card files in the District Attorney's Office. If a card was missing, our interpretation was that the case had been rejected outright by the prosecutor.

---

[1] That is, the case strength that suffices for the filing of felony charges.

81

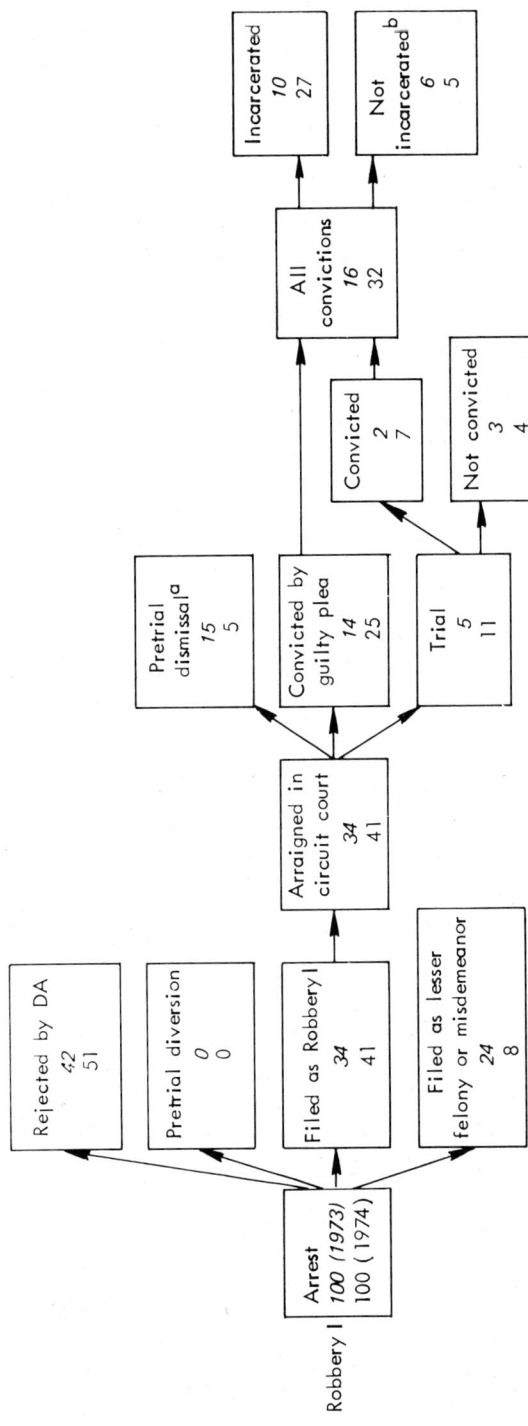

Notes:

ᵃIncludes cases charged as robbery I that are dismissed in lower court or in Circuit Court before trial on a motion by the prosecutor or after a hearing on a motion by the defense.

ᵇIncludes suspended sentences.

Figure 5-1. Movement of Robbery I Cases from Arrest through Final Disposition in the Circuit Court of Multnomah County, 1973 and 1974 (in Percent of Arrests).

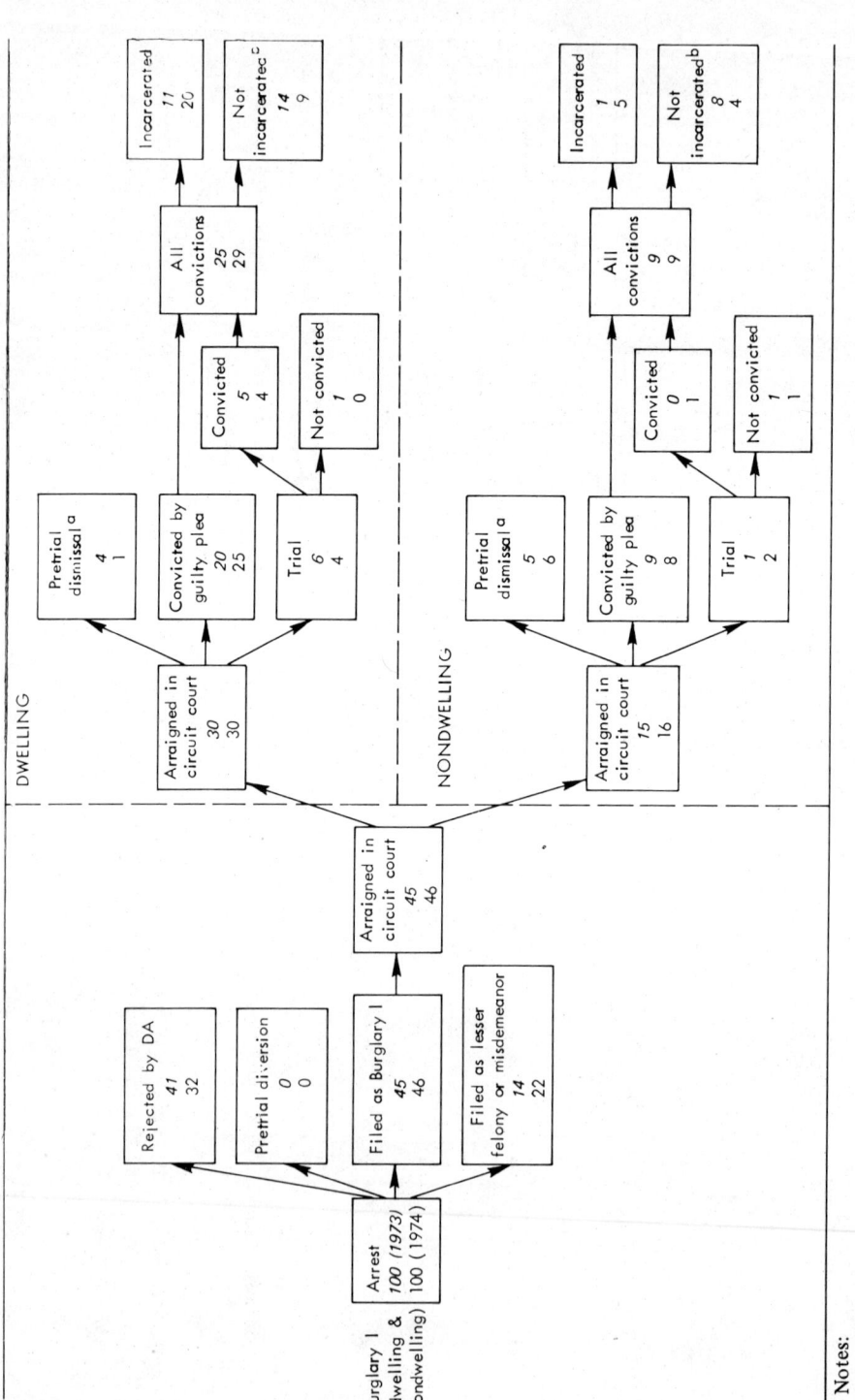

Notes:

aIncludes cases charged as burglary I that are dismissed in lower court or in Circuit Court before trial on a motion by the prosecutor or after a hearing on a motion by the defense.

bIncludes suspended sentences.

Figure 5-2. Movement of Burglary I Cases from Arrest through Final Disposition in the Circuit Court of Multnomah County,

Table 5-7
Prosecutorial Case Screening for Robbery I Bookings in Multnomah County, 1973-1974

	Percent of All Police Bookings	
Charging Threshold	*1973*	*1974*
Rejected outright	42	51
Pretrial diversion[a]	–	–
Filed on (at least) the most serious charge (felony A)	34	41
Filed on lesser felony charge(s) (felony B or C)	21	5
Filed as a misdemeanor	3 24	3 8
All police bookings (*N*)	100 (58)	100 (100)

[a]There are no pretrial diversion programs in Multnomah County.

Turning first to police-booked robbery I cases, we see that between 1973 and 1974, there was no substantial change in either the outright rejection rate or in the filing rate on the most serious charge. Taken alone, these two performance measures suggest that no major changes in prosecutorial charging policies and standards for robbery occurred as a result of the no-plea-negotiation experiment.

Given one of the objectives of the experiment—to reduce dramatically the rate of guilty pleas in which charges are reduced in Impact cases—it has been

Table 5-8
Prosecutorial Case Screening for Burglary I Bookings in Multnomah County, 1973-1974

	Percent of All Police Bookings	
Charging Threshold	*1973*	*1974*
Rejected outright	41	32
Pretrial diversion[a]	–	–
Filed on (at least) the most serious charge (felony A)	45	46
Filed on lesser felony charge(s) (felony B or C)	8	16
Filed as a misdemeanor	6 14	6 22
All police bookings (*N*)	100 (112)	100 (112)

[a]There are no pretrial diversion programs in Multnomah County.

suggested that an improper way of furthering this objective is for the prosecutor to screen out potential Impact cases at the charging stage by reducing the booking charge from a robbery I to some lesser charge. These cases then enter the system as non-Impact cases, and even if they were subsequently charge bargained, they would not be counted as Impact cases that were charge bargained. The fact that the filing rate on lesser charges (i.e., felony B, felony C, or misdemeanor) decreased significantly (from 24 percent in 1973 to 8 percent in 1974) suggests, at the very least, that there was no attempt by the prosecutor's office to use this subterfuge.

Turning next to burglary I bookings, we see that no salient changes occurred in any of the prosecutorial filing actions over the two-year period. Based on these performance measures alone, we infer that the charging threshold for burglary I as a whole did not shift materially. (But since the data could not be estimated separately for dwelling and nondwelling burglaries, we cannot infer from these data about whether the Impact experiment affected charging standards in dwelling burglaries differently from nondwelling burglaries.) However, the results of the case auditing exercise (see Chapter 7), in which small samples of dwelling and nondwelling burglaries were examined, revealed that for both years and both types of burglaries there was no discernible change in the strength of the average case. The audit suggested that almost all the filed cases were strong. However, the case audit was designed primarily to illuminate plea bargaining, and since no rejected cases were audited, it cannot be used to assess adherence to charging standards.

Recall that we argued in Chapter 4 that to illuminate the charging threshold issue one should examine the changes in the relative frequency of reasons for rejection. If, for example, the relative proportion of outright rejections by reason of evidence deficiency declines while the overall rejection rate remains relatively constant between two periods of time, it is fair to infer that the police investigations have improved and that the prosecutor has raised his charging threshold. Had the prosecutor not raised it, he would have rejected outright a smaller proportion of cases in the latter time period, other things equal.

In Table 5-9 we display the relative frequency of rejection reasons for robbery I and dwelling burglary I in the two time periods. These data were gathered and classified (by study team members) from narratives in "prosecution declined" memorandums on file in the prosecutor's office. Notice first that the percent of rejections calling for more investigation declined for both Impact crimes in 1974. This is a strong indicator that one of the experiment's goals was being achieved—improving the quality of cases presented by the police by providing legal advice and assistance to police investigators. Notice further that robbery rejections for evidence deficiencies declined dramatically, from 84 percent in 1973 to 55 percent in 1974.

Proper nonevidentiary reasons were more frequent in 1974 as was the pure excuse of discretion by the prosecutor, but the latter rose only from 8 to 26

Table 5-9

Frequency of Reasons Given for Rejection of Police-Booked Robbery I and Dwelling Burglary I Cases, Multnomah County, 1973-1974

Reason	Robbery I		Burglary I (Dwelling Only)	
	1973	1974	1973	1974
Evidence deficiency				
Insufficient evidence and absence of indispensable parties	53	40	59	60
No *corpus* of crime	0	0	0	2
Evidence inadmissible	0	0	0	1
Good case but needs more investigation	31	15	30	20
Total	84	55	89	83
Proper reasons other than evidence deficiency	8	19	7	7
Interests of justice (discretionary refusal to prosecute)	8	26	4	10
All rejections (*N*)	100 (13)	100 (48)	100 (27)	100 (80)

percent between years—much less than the decline in evidence deficiency rejections. This coupled with the fact that overall rejection rates and filing rates at the most serious charge level remained relatively consistent indicates that the charging threshold for Impact robberies was raised as well. For dwelling burglary I the evidence is more ambiguous: since rejections for evidence deficiencies declined only slightly in 1974, this one indicator seems to suggest that the charging threshold is not noticeably higher under the experiment. But as we noted above, the data were not available to estimate overall rejection and filing rates for dwelling burglaries separately, so we cannot tell whether they have risen, declined, or remained unchanged over the time period. All we know is that such performance measures showed little change for all burglary I's. However, as we noted above, the case audit conclusions support the inference that the charging threshold for both dwelling and nondwelling burglaries was high but did not change materially over the two years.

We have drawn inferences about changes in charging standards from our observations of year-to-year changes in the performance measures. But some of the observed changes in the performance measures might be explained by changes in factors other than charging standards, such as arrestee-related characteristics. For example, if it is thought that the arrestee's prior record or age might affect the prosecutor's screening actions and if these characteristics change from one year to the next for the average burglary or robbery arrestee, not all the observed changes in the performance measures could be attributed to charging threshold differences. It is here that one needs statistical tools such as multivariate analysis to reveal any such effects. Although we apply such statistical tools (see Appendix C for results and a methodological discussion) in attempting to explain conviction probability, sentence severity, and elapsed time, we were not able to apply them to the analysis of prosecutorial screening actions. The reason is that little, if any, data are collected by the court or prosecutorial agencies on background characteristics of arrestees whose cases are rejected by the prosecutor.

Charging Accuracy

Turning next to the issue of charging accuracy, we display in Table 5-10 a set of performance measures discussed in Chapter 4 as being relevant to this issue. The measures (dispositions subsequent to screening actions) were calculated from samples of data collected from Circuit Court felony case files and other court, prosecutor, and public defender agency records. Approximately 100 cases in which the highest charge of burglary I was filed by the prosecutor were selected for each year; similar samples were collected for cases in which the highest charge was robbery I. Measures for dwelling and nondwelling burglaries are shown separately, because the former is an Impact crime in 1974, whereas the latter is not.

What inferences can we draw as to changes in charging accuracy? One ambiguous measure is the proportion of defendants not convicted. For the Impact crimes of Robbery I and dwelling burglary I there was a dramatic reduction in nonconvictions, particularly in the robbery pretrial dismissal rate; for the non-Impact crime of nondwelling burglary I there was no such decline. This is one indicator that the case quality of Impact crimes improved markedly in 1974 compared with 1973, whereas no such change seems to have occurred in nondwelling burglaries. To what extent better case quality is a result of better police investigative work or improved charging accuracy cannot be ascertained from these data. From an examination of the reasons for rejection we concluded above that police investigation did improve. But whether charging accuracy improved also is unclear. The case audit exercise (see Chapter 7) suggests at least that the strength of both dwelling and nondwelling burglary cases did not fall from year to year. To the extent that subjective judgments by practitioners regarding the strength of cases is a measure of charging accuracy, we can at least conclude that charging accuracy did not decline in 1974.

The fact that robbery I and dwelling burglary I convictions on original charges rose markedly in 1974 and, concomitantly, convictions on reduced charges declined must be attributed to the policy ground rules of the no-plea-

Table 5-10

Performance Measures Related to Charging Accuracy: Multnomah County Burglary I and Robbery I Cases, 1973-1974

	Percent of All Dispositions					
	Robbery I		*Dwelling Burglary I*		*Nondwelling Burglary I*	
Disposition of Cases	*1973*	*1974*	*1973*	*1974*	*1973*	*1974*
Not convicted						
Pretrial dismissal	44	12	14	5	33	38
Trial acquittal, dismissal, hung jury	9	12	3	0	9	6
	53	24	17	5	42	44
Convicted on all original charges						
By guilty plea	10	54	19	67	6	23
By trial	6	13	11	12	0	3
	16	67	30	79	6	26
Convicted on at least one most serious original charge (with other charges and/or counts reduced						
By guilty plea	7	4	11	2	3	0
By trial	0	0	3	0	0	0
	7	4	14	2	3	0
Convicted on lesser charge(s)						
By guilty plea	24	4	39	12	49	27
By trial	0	1	0	2	0	3
	24	5	39	14	49	30
All dispositions (*N*)	100 (95)	100 (86)	100 (64)	100 (56)	100 (33)	100 (32)
Trial conviction rate[a]	36	52	82	100	0	50
Trial acquittal, dismissal, mistrial rate[a]	64	48	18	0	50	50

[a]Based on number of trials.

negotiation experiment and not to improved charging accuracy. (On the other hand, if the same year-to-year changes in all of these performance measures had occurred without introducing such an experiment, one could conclude that charging accuracy had indeed improved dramatically.)

Of some note also is the fact that nondwelling burglary convictions on original charges also rose in 1974 but not as greatly as for dwelling burglaries. And convictions on reduced charges also declined in 1974. This pattern seems to suggest that some spillover effect was at work in non-Impact crime cases, even though the nondwelling and dwelling burglary cases are handled by two different units within the prosecutor's office.

As discussed in Appendix C, we attempted to explain and predict conviction probabilities (no conviction, i.e., dismissals; conviction on original charges; conviction on fewer counts, with no level reduction; and conviction at reduced charge level) as related to nonaccuracy factors, such as defendant-related characteristics, number and level of original charges, and so on. But the attempt was unsuccessful in that none of the factors we chose seems to be related to conviction probability. If our technical approach was correct, this suggests that variables or factors other than the ones we hypothesized may be related to the probability of conviction and that future research be directed along these lines.

Plea Bargaining

We turn now to the measurement of the effects of plea bargaining. Before we display the sets of performance measures (discussed in the previous chapter) for gauging the extent of concessions to defendants on the one hand and the effects ("gains" or other impacts) on the system on the other hand, it is instructive to show in some detail the changes in the nature of plea bargaining as affected by the no-plea-negotiation experiment. In other words, we must first show to what extent the major policy objectives of the experiment have been achieved—reducing the frequency of charge bargains to virtually zero and increasing dramatically the frequency of guilty pleas to the highest original charge. Recall that the experiment's goals were silent on other types of plea bargains, such as reduction in the number of counts of lesser charges and the reduction in number of counts of (highest) original charges, sentence agreements, or agreements not to prosecute other cases.

In Table 5-11 we display how guilty plea rates by type of plea changed between 1973 and 1974 for the two Impact offenses (robbery I and dwelling burglary I) and the non-Impact offense of nondwelling burglary I. The most striking change is that negotiated pleas in Impact cases in which the charge was reduced from the original level (with or without other bargain types such as sentence agreements or agreements to drop other charges) dropped dramatically in 1974. In the case of robbery, the charge reduction rate dropped from 59 percent in 1973 to only 6 percent—essentially meeting the experiment's target of 5 percent. In the case of dwelling burglary the rate declined from a similar level in 1973 to 16 percent—somewhat in excess of the 5 percent target, but a dramatic decline nevertheless. For the non-Impact offense of nondwelling burglary there seemed to be a spillover effect; whereas 85 percent of pleas were

Table 5-11
Results of Plea Bargaining in Multnomah County, 1973-1974

Level of Plea and Disposition	Robbery I 1973	Robbery I 1974	Dwelling Burglary I 1973	Dwelling Burglary I 1974	Nondwelling Burglary I 1973	Nondwelling Burglary I 1974
No plea bargain of any kind						
Straight plea (to all original charges and counts)	5	43	11	30	5	27
Straight plea with other plea bargain types						
Sentence agreement	0	11	5	28	0	0
Agreement to drop other cases	18	28	9	22	5	20
Combination of the above	0	6	2	2	0	0
	23	45	16	52	5	20
Plea to at least one count of most serious charge with other charges and/or counts reduced						
With no additional plea bargain types	5	2	0	0	0	0
With sentence agreement and/or agreement to drop other cases	13	4	6	2	5	0
	18	6	6	2	5	0
Plea to lesser charge(s)						
With no additional plea bargain types	13	4	16	8	21	20
With sentence agreement and/or agreement to drop other cases	46	2	41	8	64	33
	59	6	57	16	85	53
Total guilty pleas (N)	100 (39)	100 (53)	100 (44)	100 (46)	100 (19)	100 (16)
Gross plea rate (N ÷ number of dispositions)	41	61	69	82	58	50

charge-bargained in 1973, only 53 percent were so disposed of in 1974, and all the decline was in charge bargains with other types of plea bargains.

Concomitantly, straight-plea rates with or without the plea bargains rose considerably in 1974, not only for the Impact offenses but also for the non-Impact offense as well. In 1973 straight pleas with or without other plea bargains accounted for roughly 25 percent of robbery or dwelling burglary guilty pleas. In 1974 they accounted for over 80 percent, and roughly 50 percent involved sentence agreeements or agreements to drop other cases. A similar, but less pronounced, increase occurred in 1974 in nondwelling burglary guilty pleas as well, indicating the presence of a spillover effect to non-Impact offenses. Incidence of count bargaining—a guilty plea to at least one count of the highest original charge, but with the number of counts of highest original and/or original lesser charges reduced—was low for all three offense categories and showed little year-to-year change.

In summary, implementation of the new no-plea-negotiation policy resulted in a much lower incidence of charge bargaining, a much higher incidence of pleas to at least one count of the highest original charge, and a sizeable increase in other forms of plea bargaining for Impact offenses. In comparison, one non-Impact offense showed similar spillover tendencies.

Given this changed pattern of plea bargaining, what was the pattern of systemwide concessions and "gains"? Tables 5-12 and 5-13 summarize these impacts in gross terms. In Table 5-12 we display a set of performance measures of the systemwide impacts or gains; these include dispositional, imposed sentence severity, and delay measures. The experiment's effect was to substantially reduce dismissal rates and increase overall guilty plea and conviction rates for Impact offenses, whereas these measures showed little year-to-year changes for other felony offenses. Only robbery trial rates increased notably, whereas other Impact or non-Impact offenses showed little change. We cannot explain why only robbery trial rates increased except to speculate that if 1974 defendants were aware that robbery sentences had risen considerably (see below), they were more willing to go to trial on the chance that they would be acquitted.

We have displayed five measures of sentence severity imposed: the percent incarcerated (in jail or in state prison) and the Sentence Severity Index scores for all four sets of weights described in the previous chapter (but sentence severity values are not shown separately for dwelling and nondwelling burglaries). A greater proportion of defendants pleading guilty to robbery charges were incarcerated in the later period and received stiffer sentences. Defendants pleading guilty to either dwelling or nondwelling burglary charges also were more likely to be incarcerated (notice that the year-to-year rate of increase in percent incarcertaion is greater for nondwelling burglary) and receive more severe sentences. Even though a greater proportion of dwelling, as compared with nondwelling, burglars were incarcerated in the later period, the multivariate regression analysis using Sentence Severity Index A (see Appendix C) showed that the independent effect of burglary in a dwelling on Sentence Severity Index score was not significant.

The experiment's goals were silent on sentence severity. That is, no explicit policy was enunciated calling for more severe or less severe sentencing in Impact

Table 5-12

Measures Reflecting the Operational Effects of Plea Bargaining in Multnomah County, 1973-1974

Dispositions, Sentences, and Delays	Robbery I		Dwelling Burglary I		Nondwelling Burglary I		All Burglary I		All Felonies	
	1973	1974	1973	1974	1973	1974	1973	1974	1973	1974
Dispositional measures (%)										
Dismissal rate	44	12	14	5	33	38	20	17	35	38
Trial rate	15	27	17	13	9	13	14	13	13	7
Guilty plea rate	41	61	69	82	58	50	65	70	52	53
Overall conviction rate	47	77	83	95	58	56	75	80	62	58
Sentence severity measures										
Percent incarcerated	67	87	36	67	15	53	33	64	32	39
Sentence severity imposed										
(Index A score)	16.7	26.5	—	—	—	—	11.4	16.9	—	—
(Index B score)	20.9	43.9	—	—	—	—	10.4	20.4	—	—
(Index C score)	25.0	61.2	—	—	—	—	9.4	23.9	—	—
(Index D score)	43.8	116.5	—	—	—	—	19.0	47.0	—	—
Median elapsed time (days)										
Arraignment to guilty plea	37	21	33	31	29	21	31	29	23	29
Arraignment to trial	35	52	30	79	25	72	30	76	30	49
Arraignment to final disposition	71	64	68	68	61	61	58	66	34	63
Continuances and witness appearances										
Number days continued/total cases										
Per uncontexted case	—	—	—	—	—	—	—	—	7	9
Per trial	—	—	—	—	—	—	—	—	14	13

Table 5-13

Concessions as a Result of Plea Bargaining in Multnomah County, 1973-1974

Sentence Severity Index	Type of Defendant	Reductions in Sentence Severity Index Score from Straight Plea Score			
		Burglary I		Robbery I	
		1973[a]	1974[b]	1973[c]	1974[d]
A	Per convicted defendant (including those tried)	5.2	2.1	9.1	1.3
	Per defendant with charge bargain	9.3	9.3	12.4	10.7
	Per defendant with count bargain	NS	NS	16.8	22.2
B	Per convicted defendant (including those tried)	6.8	15.1	23.0	1.9
	Per defendant with charge bargain	12.2	18.0	31.2	31.3
	Per defendant with count bargain	NS	34.9	43.8	NS
C	Per convicted defendant (including those tried)	8.5	23.4	41.0	3.1
	Per defendant with charge bargain	15.1	26.8	49.9	51.9
	Per defendant with count bargain	NS	57.3	70.9	NS
D	Per convicted defendant (including those tried)	17.0	37.7	57.8	NS
	Per defendant with charge bargain	30.2	50.7	72.6	NS
	Per defendant with count bargain	NS	86.7	126.2	NS

Note: NS = not significantly different from zero at the 90 percent confidence level.

[a]56 percent of those convicted pled to reduced charges; 15 percent pled to reduced counts at same level.

[b]23 percent of those convicted pled to reduced charges; 30 percent pled to reduced counts at same level.

[c]51 percent of those convicted pled to reduced charges; 17 percent pled to reduced counts at same level.

[d]6 percent of those convicted pled to reduced charges; 3 percent pled to reduced counts at same level.

offenses. Nevertheless, it is of interest to ask whether or not there was a discernible effect on sentence severity that could be associated with the experiment—that is, did judges appear to be sentencing like defendants more harshly during the experiment? To answer this question requires that we adjust for year-to-year random sampling errors in the population characteristics of defendants and cases. Using Sentence Severity Index A, which is closest to the weighting scheme devised by the California Bureau of Criminal Statistics, we can estimate what the mean Sentence Severity Index score would have been had there been no plea bargaining or sentence policy change and no other changes. To do this, we apply the 1973 sentence severity equations (shown in Appendix

C) in conjunction with the 1973 average charge bargaining rate (no policy change), the 1973 time trend proxy variable, and the average of the 1973 and 1974 means for defendant and case characteristics to estimate the average 1974 score had there been no change. We hypothesize that the 1974 estimate will be lower than the 1974 observed score—the difference being associated with the experiment or other factors.[2]

Table 5-14 summarizes these results. For robbery I it appears that the observed increase in Sentence Severity Index score was 9.8 (or 37 percent of the 1974 observed value), but after adjusting for random sampling errors in defendant and case characteristics, the increase associated with the experimental period was 13.8 (or about 50 percent of the 1974 observed value). For burglary I as a whole the observed increase was 5.5 (or 33 percent of the 1974 observed value), but after adjusting for sampling errors in population characteristics, the increase attributable to the policy change is 3.3 (or about 29 percent of the 1974 observed value). Thus our hypothesis that the experiment did indeed (albeit perhaps unintentionally) induce more severe sentences is not rejected. However, we cannot rule out the possibility that more severe sentencing judges presided in 1974.

Table 5-14
Differences in Sentence Severity Imposed Associated with the No-Plea-Negotiation Experiment in Multnomah County, 1973-1974

Average Score of Sentence Severity Index A for Defendants Pleading Guilty	Robbery I	Burglary I
1973 observed score	16.7	11.4
1974 observed score	26.5	16.9
1974 predicted score, assuming no policy change and no other changes, with adjustments for sampling errors	12.7	13.6
1973 to 1974 total observed increased	9.8	5.5
1973 to 1974 increase associated with the experiment	13.8	3.3

[2] Other factors that could influence sentence severity between the two years include changes in crowding in correctional facilities and changes in individual sentencing judges. However, our procedure adjusts for the former by utilizing the 1973 mean value for the proxy variable that reflects crowding. (In any case, crowding in both state and local correctional facilities increased in 1974, which ought to have resulted in lower average sentence severity.) Most of the sentences upon which our analysis is based were imposed by the Chief Criminal Judge, since most defendants are convicted through pleas of guilty. In Multnomah, this position rotates every two to three months among Circuit Court judges. It is possible, therefore, that the 1974 Chief Criminal Judges simply sentenced more severely than those in 1973 for reasons having nothing to do with the experiment.

Returning to other effects of plea bargaining on the system, Table 5-12 also indicates that, by and large, the experiment had little effect on median elapsed times from arraignment to guilty plea or from arraignment to final disposition for Impact offenses. But for felony cases as a whole, the period to final disposition almost doubled, probably as a consequence of the growing caseload and backlog pressures noted above. This suggests that Impact cases (and nondwelling burglary I cases as well) were treated more expeditiously than the average felony case. The arrest-to-trial period, however, increased by 50 to 100 percent for offense categories shown, but the estimates are based on very small samples.

Some rise in continuance-induced delay was apparent in uncontested cases (from 7 days per average case in 1973 to 9 days in 1974), but for the few trials such delay declined slightly between these two years.

Turning next to plea bargaining concessions, Table 5-13 displays three different concessions measures, all expressed in terms of sentence severity score reductions from straight-plea scores. (Our statistical analysis using Index A revealed that electing a court or jury trial did not generally affect sentence severity when compared with that received on a straight plea. However, our trial sample was very small and we cannot make accurate estimates of this hypothesized effect.) Using each of the sentencing severity indices, we show in each year and for both robbery I and burglary I, the average amount of sentence severity score conceded per convicted defendant (those who plead guilty and those who were convicted at trial), per defendant who pled guilty to lesser charges, and per defendant with a count bargain (i.e., a plea to at least one highest original charge, but where one (or more) count of any original charges is dismissed in return for a guilty plea). (Concession values are shown only if they differed from zero at the 90 percent confidence level.)

It is very clear that in robbery I offenses the amount of sentence severity conceded per convicted defendant (measured by any of the Indices) fell dramatically in 1974. In any given year it is also clear that a robbery defendant who is successful in obtaining a reduction in charge level in return for a plea of guilty receives more of a concession than does the average convicted defendant.

For reasons we cannot explain, count bargaining in robbery I seems to produce even greater concessions than charge bargaining. There also seems to be a little year-to-year change in concessions per defendant who enters a charge bargain or count bargain, which suggests that the effect of the experiment was not to change the concession for any specific type of plea bargain but to change the proportion of defendants pleading within each type. We note further that compared with pure straight pleas, our statistical analysis revealed no significant independent effect of other plea bargain types (sentence agreement or agreement to drop pending cases) on sentence severity.[3] This is perhaps to be expected for

---

[3] In discussing the independent effects of other types of plea bargains, number of original charges at each level of seriousness, etc., on sentence severity, we use the estimates based on Sentence Severity Index A as being illustrative of the others.

the latter but not for the former, for the very nature of a sentence agreement plea bargain should be to reduce the expected severity. But in our data collection we could capture only the fact that sentence agreements were reached or that the prosecutor agreed not to oppose a defense recommendation, not the actual sentence discussed by the practitioners involved (since these were never recorded). This suggests that such data must be recorded routinely in court files if their effects are to be analyzed and interpreted.

In our statistical analysis we also found that the independent effect of the number of original robbery I charges (or other charges of equivalent level) was positively related to sentence severity score, but that the number of additional charges at lesser levels was not. (The independent effects of other variables, such as defendant background characteristics, prior record, custody status, and type of defense attorney, on sentence severity score are discussed later in the chapter when we address the issues of sentence disparity and evenhandedness.)

The sentence concession results for burglary I are somewhat different. We noted above that the independent effect of burglary in a dwelling on the sentence severity score was not significant. It is apparent from Table 5-13 that the amount of concessions per convicted defendant as measured by Index A fell significantly in 1974 compared to 1973 but rose when measured by the other three indices. Index A weights nonincarceration sentences (years of probation, dollars of fine) relatively higher compared to jail or prison sentences than the other three indices. Apparently more burglars who obtained a charge bargain or a count bargain in 1974 were receiving nonincarceration sentences; since these receive less (or zero) weight in Indices B, C, and D, the amount of concession measured against straight pleaders (who are receiving incarceration sentences more frequently) rose. As with robbers who pled guilty, burglars who obtained a charge bargain or a count bargain received less severe sentences than straight pleaders. And the same pattern existed, in that count bargaining in burglars seemed to produce even greater sentence concessions than charge bargaining. As with robbery, the sentences of burglars who pled guilty and were able to have other cases dropped or to make sentence agreements were not significantly different from those of straight pleaders. Unlike robbers, the number of counts of original felony charges (at any level) did not affect sentence severity score.

Sentence Variation

Addressing the issue of sentencing variation, Tables 5-15 and 5-16 display the frequency of sentence type and amount imposed by conviction level for robbery I and burglary I cases in both periods. For clarity, sentence categories have been aggregated into two nonincarceration categories (probation alone and probation plus other—i.e., fine, restitution, community service, or rehabilitation program) and two incarceration categories (jail alone or with any nonincarceration sentence and prison alone or with any nonincarceration sentence). In addition,

Table 5-15
Distribution of Convictees in Multnomah County Robbery I Cases, by Charge Level and Type of Punishment, 1973-1974

	Probation Only			Probation + Other			Jail Alone and Jail + Other			Prison Alone and Prison + Other					Sentence Severity Score (Index A)	
							Percent of All Convictions at a Given Level[a]									
Charge Level	<2 yr	2-4 yr	≥5 yr	<2 yr	2-4 yr	≥5 yr	<6 mo	6-11 mo	≥12 mo	<2 yr	3-4 yr	5-10 yr	11-20 yr	≥21 yr	Mean	Standard Deviation
Felon A																
1973 (N = 19)	–	–	–	–	–	16	–	–	11	–	21	47	–	5	20.8	11.0
1974 (N = 59)	–	–	–	–	2	5	–	2	9	–	2	44	32	2	26.8	10.9
Felony B																
1973 (N = 9)	–	–	–	11	–	22	–	–	33	–	11	22	–	–	16.8	8.9
1974 (N = 2)	–	–	–	–	–	100	–	–	–	–	–	–	–	–	10.0	–
Felony C																
1973 (N = 10)	–	–	10	–	20	20	–	–	20	10	20	–	–	–	12.3	8.4
1974 (N = 2)	–	–	–	–	–	–	–	–	50	–	–	50	–	–	22.5	0.7
Misdemeanor																
1973 (N = 2)	–	–	–	–	–	–	100	–	–	–	–	–	–	–	5.5	6.4
1974 (N = 0)	–	–	–	–	–	–	–	–	–	–	–	–	–	–	–	–

Note: Total number of convictions: 1973, N = 40; 1974, N = 63.
[a]A dash (–) denotes zero.

we show the average sentence severity score for Index A and a measure of its variability (the standard deviation).

For robbery I cases, in which all defendants were initially charged with at least one count at the felony A level, notice that about half the defendants were convicted at the felony A level in 1973, whereas in 1974 almost all were so convicted. In 1973 16 percent of those convicted were given nonincarceration sentences, whereas in 1974 this category decreased to 7 percent. Concomitantly, sentences with some prison time for felony A level convictees rose from 73 percent in 1973 to 80 percent in 1974. The average sentence severity score increased about 30 percent from year to year, but the standard deviation showed little change over that period. In 1973, 33 percent and 50 percent of defendants convicted at the felony B and C levels, respectively, received nonincarceration sentences.

For dwelling burglary cases, in which all defendants were initially charged with at least one count at the felony A level, about 55 percent were convicted at the felony A level, but in 1974 almost 90 percent were so convicted. At the felony A conviction level the percent nonincarcerated fell from 36 percent in 1973 to 20 percent in 1974; there was a corresponding increase over the two-year period in percent prison sentences imposed. But the average sentence severity score rose only 15 percent over the time period, with some increase in variability (as measured by the standard deviation).

Different trends in average sentence severity and sentence variability were apparent in nondwelling burglaries. Most 1973 nondwelling burglars were convicted at lesser charge levels; in 1974 most were convicted at the higher charge levels. At the higher conviction levels, year-to-year average sentence severity score decreased or remained relatively constant, whereas at the lesser conviction levels it increased.

For dwelling and nondwelling burglaries together, conviction at the highest level rose from 45 percent in 1973 to almost 80 percent in 1974, with an accompanying rise in average sentence severity score and variability.

Essentially, Tables 5-15 and 5-16 display what happened in sentencing. Now we turn to why, i.e., how much of the observed variation in severity is accounted for by various legitimate and illegitimate factors? Table 5-17 summarizes these results, which are taken from Appendix C. (In this discussion we focus only on how much of the variation is accounted for by each factor;[4] when we discuss the evenhandedness issue we will show the direction (i.e., more or less severity) of the effect as well.)

---

[4] The reader will note that in Table 5-17 we have employed rather weak standards for gauging statistical significance of the factors affecting sentencing variation. We have included effects that are statistically significant at the 50 percent level or higher (i.e., the chances are better than even that a particular factor has an effect that is not zero). Had we applied stricter standards, such as a 95 percent level of confidence (i.e., the chances are 95 percent or higher that the effect is not zero), more of the entries would be shown as not statistically significant (NS).

Table 5-16
Distribution of Convictees in Multnomah County Burglary I Cases, by Charge Level and Type of Punishment, 1973-1974

| | Percent of All Convictions at a Given Level[a] | | | | | | | | | | | | | | Sentence Severity Score (Index A) | |
| Charge Level | Probation Only | | | Probation + Other | | | Jail Alone and Jail + Other | | | Prison Alone and Prison + Other | | | | | | |
	< 2 yr	2-4 yr	≥ 5 yr	< 2 yr	2-4 yr	5 ≥ yr	< 6 mo	6-11 mo	≥ 12 mo	< 2 yr	3-4 yr	5-10 yr	11-20 yr	≥ 21 yr	Mean	Standard Deviation
Dwelling Burglary I																
Convicted felony A																
1973 (N = 28)	—	3	11	—	4	18	4	7	21	—	—	28	4	—	17.7	7.6
1974 (N = 45)	—	2	7	—	—	11	2	—	22	—	11	41	4	—	20.4	8.1
Convicted felony B																
1973 (N = 2)	—	—	—	—	—	50	50	—	—	—	—	—	—	—	13.0	4.2
1974 (N = 0)	—	—	—	—	—	—	—	—	—	—	—	—	—	—	—	—
Convicted felony C																
1973 (N = 13)	—	23	—	8	23	15	8	—	23	—	—	—	—	—	9.4	6.8
1974 (N = 5)	—	20	—	—	40	—	40	—	—	—	—	—	—	—	8.4	3.0
Convicted misdemeanor																
1973 (N = 8)	13	12	—	63	—	12	—	—	—	—	—	—	—	—	3.7	2.9
1974 (N = 1)	—	—	—	—	100	—	—	—	—	—	—	—	—	—	4.0	0
Nondwelling Burglary I																
Convicted felony A																
1973 (N = 3)	—	—	33	—	—	33	—	—	—	—	—	33	—	—	16.0	10.4
1974 (N = 7)	—	—	14	—	—	14	30	—	14	—	—	14	14	—	13.5	11.7
Convicted felony B																
1973 (N = 2)	—	—	—	—	—	100	—	—	—	—	—	—	—	—	10.0	0
1974 (N = 3)	—	—	—	—	—	33	33	—	33	—	—	—	—	—	9.6	9.3

	1	2	3	4	5	6	7	8	9	10	11	12	13	14
Convicted felony C														
1973 (*N* = 9)	22	–	–	33	22	11	–	11	–	–	–	–	7.6	5.9
1974 (*N* = 2)	–	–	–	50	–	50	–	–	–	–	–	–	11.1	6.9
Convicted misdemeanor														
1973 (*N* = 4)	25	–	50	25	–	–	–	–	–	–	–	–	3.6	1.9
1974 (*N* = 3)	–	–	–	67	–	33	–	–	–	–	–	–	4.3	2.9
All Burglary I														
Convicted felony A														
1973 (*N* = 31)	3	13	–	3	19	3	7	19	–	–	30	3	17.5	7.7
1974 (*N* = 52)	2	8	–	–	11	6	–	21	10	–	36	6	19.3	9.0
Convicted felony B														
1973 (*N* = 4)	–	–	–	–	75	25	–	–	–	–	–	–	11.5	3.0
1974 (*N* = 3)	–	–	–	–	33	33	–	33	–	–	–	–	9.6	9.3
Convicted felony C														
1973 (*N* = 22)	23	–	5	27	18	9	–	18	–	–	–	–	8.6	6.4
1974 (*N* = 7)	–	14	–	43	–	43	–	–	–	–	–	–	9.2	4.0
Convicted misdemeanor														
1973 (*N* = 12)	17	–	49	8	8	–	–	–	–	–	–	–	3.7	2.6
1974 (*N* = 4)	–	–	25	50	–	25	–	–	–	–	–	–	4.3	2.4

Note: Total number of convictions:
Dwelling burglary I: 1973, *N* = 51; 1974, *N* = 51
Nondwelling burglary I: 1973, *N* = 18, 1974, *N* = 15
All burglary I: 1973, *N* = 69, 1974, *N* = 66.
[a]A dash (–) denotes zero.

Table 5-17

Effects of Selected Factors on Sentence Severity in Multnomah County Burglary I and Robbery I Cases, 1973-1974

	Percent of Accountable Variance in Sentence Severity Score (Index A)[a]			
	Burglary I		Robbery I	
Factors Influencing Sentencing	1973	1974	1973	1974
Legitimate factors				
Age	1	3	3	6
Prior criminal record				
Minor	1	1	1	NS
Major	1	NS	1	11
Prison	2	5	11	9
Community ties	0	4	2	4
Nature of charges and counts	20	15	30	18
Aggregate variance explained	25	28	48	48
Illegitimate factors				
Minority status				
Black	1	NS	1	NS
Other	NS	–	1	NS
Pretrial custody status				
In jail	2	NS	3	5
On bail or OR	0	NS	9	3
Defended by private attorney				
Defendant-retained counsel	NS	NS	1	NS
Court-appointed counsel	NS	NS	1	NS
Convicted at trial				
Court	NS	1	11	NS
Jury	NS	0	0	NS
Proxy for correctional facilities crowding	NS	6	2	3
Aggregate variance explained	3	7	29	11
Total variance explained[b]	31	38	79	61

Note: NS = not significant.

[a]Entries are only for variables in regression equations that were statistically significant at the 95 percent level and in which the regression coefficient on that variable was statistically significant at the 50 percent level; entry reads NS otherwise.

[b]Including variance from NS variables and the constant term.

Our statistical analysis of sentencing variation in robbery I cases shows that a very large percentage of the total variation (79 percent in 1973 and 61 percent in 1974) is accounted for by all the factors that we included. About 48 percent is accounted for by legitimate factors in both years. The nature and number of original charges and the nature of plea bargaining were the most important of these legitimate factors in 1973, accounting for 30 percent; in 1974 they accounted for 18 percent. Prior criminal record (compared with no prior record) explained 13 percent of the variation in 1973, but it explained 24 percent in 1974. Apparently prior criminal record contributed more to sentencing disparity in the later period. This was also true for the factor of age.

Illegitimate factors as a whole accounted for less of the variation in robbery sentences than did legitimate factors, and their effect decreased over time (falling from 29 percent in 1973 to 11 percent in 1974). Minority status, or the fact that a defendant had a private attorney (either retained or court appointed) accounted for little or none of the disparity. Compared with defendants whose pretrial custody status included both time in jail and time out on bail or own recognizance (OR), being in jail or on bail or on own recognizance exclusively accounted for a significant proportion of the variation explained by illegitimate factors. Compared with straight pleas, electing a jury trial had no significant effect on disparity. But electing a court trial did account for 11 percent of the variation in 1973, whereas in 1974 it had no effect. Our proxy for crowding of the correctional facilities accounted for a small amount of the sentence variation.

The results of our analysis of burglary I cases were quite different. The factors used in the statistical analysis were able to explain a smaller percent of the total variation in sentencing (31 and 38 percent in the two years, respectively) than in our analysis of robbery I cases. (This indicates that factors excluded from the burglary analysis account for more of the variation.) But most of the accounted-for variation is explained by legitimate factors (25 and 28 percent in two years) and the effect of illegitimate factors is either small or not significant at all. The nature of the charges and counts explains almost all the legitimate variation accounted for in 1973 and over half of it in 1974; but prior criminal record also accounts for a significant portion in 1974.

In summary, we feel that sentencing variation performance measures are useful and that appropriate statistical analysis helps to reveal the extent to which various factors account for that variation. In Multnomah County, we found that illegitimate factors accounted for little or none of the sentence disparity in burglary cases in both years—indicating evenhandedness in sentencing. In robbery cases, however, illegitimate factors (particularly, pretrial custody status and election of court trials) accounted for a large, but decreasing over time, portion of the sentence variation; such outcomes should trigger judges' attention. If these effects persist, it may be an indication of inconsistency or lack of evenhandedness in sentencing over the long term.

Evenhandedness

In this discussion we focus exclusively on the effects on dispositional outcomes and sentences imposed that are attributable or related to illegitimate factors.[5] If illegitimate factors are influential in affecting these performance measures, one can conclude that defendants in similar circumstances are not being treated consistently or evenhandedly.

Dispositional Measures

We turn first to dispositional measures, such as rejection rate at screening, felony-charging rate, dismissal rate, trial rate, straight-plea rate, charge-bargain rate, acquittal rate, etc. For these measures we postulate that the following are illegitimate factors: ethnicity (or minority status), pretrial custody status, and type of defense counsel. Few would argue that ethnicity alone should be a legitimate influence on dispositional outcomes under our system of justice. Most would agree that pretrial custody status should not affect whether an arrestee is charged or rejected or whether a defendant is dismissed, pleads guilty, or is convicted or acquitted at trial. However, the fact that a defendant is in jail or out on bail or his own recognizance may actually be related to dispositional outcome. One argument holds that defendants out on bail or on own recognizance can help build a better defense by seeking out witnesses. Another contends that defendants in custody have more incentive to plea bargain rather than demand a trial, especially in cases for which the probability of receiving a nonincarceration sentence is high—since this is a way of spending less total time in jail (pretrial and postconviction). Also, the failure to obtain pretrial release may be a proxy for the viciousness of the offense or the bad character of the defendant (in ways not fully reflected by the defendant's actual original charges, convicted charges, and prior criminal record).

Most would also agree that whether a defendant has the services of a public

---

[5]We do not here consider the "evenhandedness" of delay, since delay (or elapsed time between important stages in adjudication) is jointly determined by court system characteristics (e.g., calendar crowding and management), by prosecutorial readiness, and by defendant-influenced factors (e.g., number of continuances requested by the defense in a case). The latter sometimes are deliberate attempts to slow down proceedings in the belief that it would redound to the defendant's advantage (e.g., the hope that a prosecution witness would be unavailable after the case has been continued several times). Thus, one could not say whether the court system is or is not evenhanded in the speediness of justice, if much of the variation in delay is defendant-induced. (And as we will show in the discussion of the delay issue, a large proportion of continuances granted are requested by the defense.)

defender, a court-appointed attorney, or retains counsel himself should not influence his disposition. Again, the type of defense attorney may actually influence outcomes. One argument is that a wealthier defendant who retains private counsel may be able to provide more resources in building a defense. Another is that public defenders may be able to achieve better results for the defendant because they know the court system and its practitioners better. Whichever views one holds, it is clearly useful to test whether these effects are present in a jurisdiction and, if so, how they are changing over time.

As we mentioned previously, our multivariate regression analysis was not successful in revealing the independent effects of various legitimate and illegitimate factors on the probability of dismissal or conviction (at various levels). Thus we must turn to cross tabulations as an analytical device for disclosing the presence or absence of such effects, keeping in mind the caveat that any such observed effects may, in fact, be partially due to other factors. In Table 5-18 we show dispositional measures by pretrial custody status.[6] In cases of robbery, most defendants were held in jail during both years. First we note that there seem to be some differences in disposition rates associated with jail or nonjail status, but differences between nonjail categories (bail or OR) are small, except for trial conviction rates. (The latter are based on very small trial sample sizes, however, so we cannot place much confidence in these estimates.) There are year-to-year differences in straight-plea rates; in 1973 jailed defendants were more likely to plead guilty than nonjailed defendants, whereas in 1974 the differences were small. In 1973 jailed defendants were more likely to have their case dismissed, whereas in 1974 the reverse was true. And in 1973 jailed defendants were less likely to be convicted (by any means), whereas in 1974 they were more likely to be convicted.

Table 5-19 shows similar dispositional measures by type of attorney. Public defenders seem to be able to do better for defendants at burglary or robbery trials (in terms of fraction of dispositions that are acquittals) than either type of private attorney, but again, most differences are not impressive. Public defenders seem to do marginally better for their clients than retained counsel (in terms of lower overall robbery conviction rates) in both time periods; in burglary cases this seems to hold in 1974 but not in 1973. However, the differences are generally not large. In general, overall conviction rates for court-appointed attorneys are somewhere in between. As to overall trial rates (i.e., the sum of trial convictions and trial acquittals, dismissals, and mistrial cases in Table 5-19, no consistent differences are observed among types of defense counsel, implying that attorney-fee compensation systems (described in Appendix A) do not seem to influence dispositional outcomes. But one cannot make high-confidence

---

[6]Table 5-18, as well as Tables 5-19 and 5-20, do not include rejection rate by any of the illegitimate factors. Ethnicity and pretrial custody status are usually not recorded in court or prosecution agency files for rejectees, and often a suspect may not have an attorney at the time when the screening decision to reject is made.

Table 5-18

Evenhandedness: The Relationship between Pretrial Custody Status and Dispositional Measures in Multnomah County Robbery and Burglary Cases, 1973-1974

	Percent of All Defendants in a Given Pretrial Custody Status											
	Robbery I						All Burglary I					
	1973			1974			1973			1974		
Dispositional Measure	Jail	Bail	OR	Jail	Bail	OR	Jail	Bail	OR	Jail	Bail	OR
Not convicted												
Pretrial dismissal	46	23	35	7	14	20	24	29	15	17	25	14
Trial acquittal, dismissal, mistrial	9	15	10	10	14	13	9	0	2	2	13	0
Total	55	38	45	17	28	33	33	29	17	19	38	14
Convicted												
Straight plea	19	0	0	59	58	47	20	0	13	46	50	58
Received plea bargain (reduced charges and/or counts)	22	47	50	9	14	0	36	71	63	25	0	17
Gross plea rate (pleas ÷ N)	41	47	50	68	72	47	56	71	76	71	50	75
At trial	4	15	5	15	0	20	11	0	7	10	12	11
Conviction rate (conv. ÷ N)	45	62	55	83	72	67	67	71	83	81	62	86
All dispositions (N)	100 (54)	100 (13)	100 (20)	100 (58)	100 (7)	100 (15)	100 (45)	100 (7)	100 (40)	100 (40)	100 (8)	100 (36)
Trial conviction rate (trial convictions ÷ trials)	29	50	33	60	0	60	55	0	78	83	48	100

Table 5-19

Evenhandedness: The Relationship between Type of Defense Attorney and Dispositional Measures in Multnomah County Robbery I and Burglary I Cases, 1973-1974

	Percent of All Defendants with a Given Type of Defense Attorney											
	Robbery I						All Burglary I					
	1973			1974			1973			1974		
Dispositional Measure	PD[a]	CA	DR	PD[a]	CA	DR	PD[a]	CA	DR	PD[a]	CA	DR
Not convicted												
Pretrial dismissal	45	44	38	12	13	12	17	18	30	22	15	10
Trial acquittal, dismissal, hung jury	7	17	0	18	7	0	4	9	7	5	0	0
Total	52	61	38	30	20	12	21	27	37	27	15	10
Convicted												
Straight plea	13	4	0	51	60	38	20	0	7	49	49	60
Received plea bargain (reduced charges and/or counts)	35	26	39	5	7	25	57	27	48	19	18	20
Gross plea rate (pleas ÷ N)	48	30	39	56	67	63	77	27	55	68	67	80
At trial	0	9	23	14	13	25	2	46	8	5	18	10
Conviction rate (conv. ÷ N)	48	39	62	70	80	88	79	73	63	73	85	90
All dispositions (N)	100 (54)	100 (23)	100 (13)	100 (43)	100 (30)	100 (8)	100 (54)	100 (11)	100 (27)	100 (41)	100 (33)	100 (10)
Trial conviction rate (trial convictions ÷ trials)	0	35	100	44	65	100	33	83	50	50	100	100

[a]PD = public defender; CA = court-appointed; DR = defendant-retained.

inferences from such small samples. (The number of trials in our samples varied between 2 and 11 for a given combination of offense type, year, and type of attorney.[7]) There are also no consistent differences between straight-plea or plea-bargaining rates that can be associated with attorney type.

Table 5-20 shows the effect of minority status on dispositional outcomes. Since in Multnomah County over half the case files do not identify defendant ethnicity, sample sizes are quite small. This means that only very large differences in dispositional rates among ethnicity groups will be statistically significant, compared with nonminority defendants. Black defendants tend to have higher pretrial dismissal rates, are somewhat less likely to plead guilty, and are less likely to be ultimately convicted in such cases. However, the differences generally are weak. Year-to-year changes in these disparities for robbery are small; but in 1974 burglaries, the effect of minority status disappears. To the extent that such small samples permit any inferences, these findings suggest either that cases against blacks tended to be weaker, reflecting over-arrests by the police or over-prosecution by the District Attorney's Office, or that a double standard is applied to black defendants. Given the data at our disposal we could not resolve the question of which hypothesis best explains the observed differences. Moreover, one must keep in mind the caveat that whatever differences are revealed by cross-tabulating disposition rates by ethnic group, some of the observed differences may be due to other factors.

Sentence Severity Measures

In the previous discussion of sentencing disparity we showed (among other things) how much of the total variation explained in our statistical analysis was attributable to each of the illegitimate factors. (These factors included the three examined above under dispositional evenhandedness—ethnicity, custody status, and type of defense attorney, as well as method of conviction.) Here we try to show, in addition, the magnitude and direction of each significant effect. That is, we address the question: What is the magnitude and direction of the change in average sentence severity score (for Index A) associated with a given illegitimate factor? Table 5-21 summarizes the results of the multivariate statistical analysis for both offenses and both time periods. This procedure makes it possible to hold constant the influence on sentence severity (as measured by Index A) of all

---

[7] It is worth mentioning that manual data collection for rare events that would illuminate, say, the effect of attorney type on trial rate, or the effect of trial convictions (compared with straight-plea convictions) on sentence severity (discussed below), or the effect of trials on any other performance measure is very expensive. For example, if one wanted to be certain to obtain a sample of at least 20 burglars in 1973 who were defended at trial by court-appointed attorneys, and if burglaries represented 20 percent of all felonies, court-appointed attorneys represented 20 percent of all burglars, and only 10 percent of all burglary cases went to trial, one would need to examine 5,000 case records for felonies occurring in a one-year period, on the average.

Table 5-20

Evenhandedness: The Relationship between Ethnicity and Dispositional Measures in Multnomah County Robbery I and Burglary Cases, 1973-1974

	Percent of All Defendants in a Given Ethnic Group[a]											
	Robbery I						All Burglary I					
	1973			1974			1973			1974		
Dispositional Measure	NM	B	OM	NM	B	OM	NM	B	OM	NM	B	OM
Not convicted												
Pretrial dismissal	36	63	25	5	50	0	9	42	0	25	25	100
Trial acquittal, dismissal, hung jury	21	6	25	23	0	0	9	8	0	0	0	0
Total	57	68	50	28	50	0	18	50	0	25	25	100
Convicted												
Straight plea	29	19	0	58	50	50	18	17	0	50	37	0
Received plea bargain (reduced charges and/or counts)	14	13	50	5	0	0	46	16	100	8	25	0
Gross plea rate (pleas ÷ N)	43	32	50	63	50	50	64	33	100	58	62	0
At trial	0	0	0	9	0	50	18	17	0	17	13	0
Conviction rate (conv. ÷ N)	43	32	50	72	50	100	82	50	100	75	75	0
All dispositions (N)	100 (14)	100 (16)	100 (4)	100 (22)	100 (6)	100 (2)	100 (11)	100 (12)	100 (1)	100 (12)	100 (8)	100 (1)
Trial conviction rate (trial convictions ÷ trials)	0	0	0	28	0	100	67	67	–	100	–	–

Note: In Multnomah County, well over half of the case files and other records do not identify defendant ethnicity.

[a] NM = nonminority; B = black; OM = other minorities.

Table 5-21

Evenhandedness: The Independent Effect of Illegitimate Factors on Sentence Severity Imposed in Multinomah County Burglary and Robbery Cases, 1973-1974

	Percent Change in Average Sentence Severity Score (Index A) with a Change in a Given Factor[a]			
	Burglary I		Robbery I	
Illegitimate Factor	1973	1974	1973	1974
Ethnicity[b]				
Black	+24 (57%)	NS	−24 (71%)	NS
Other	NS	–	+40 (71%)	NS
Pretrial custody status[c]				
In jail	+50 (86%)	NS	+111 (93%)	+39 (96%)
On bail or OR	NS	NS	+250 (90%)	+50 (72%)
Defended by private attorney[d]				
Defendant-retained	NS	NS	+37 (85%)	NS
Court-appointed	NS	NS	+20 (61%)	NS
Convicted at trial[e]				
Court	+18	+8	–	−9
Jury				

Note: NS = not significant. + = sentence severity score increased; − = score decreased. Entries in parentheses are the levels of statistical significance of the regression coefficient.

[a]Entries are only for variables in regression equations which were statistically significant at the 95 percent level of confidence and in which the regression coefficient on that variable was statistically significant at the 50 percent level; entry NS (not significant) otherwise.

[b]Measured against white (majority) status.

[c]Measured against mixed pretrial custody status.

[d]Measured against defense by public defender.

[e]Measured against straight-plea conviction. Entries are computed from matching pairs of defendants and cases that are similar in most respects; however, one was convicted at trial and the other pled guilty to all original charges (see discussion in text).

specified factors other than the factor being examined. That is, we can estimate the independent effect on sentence severity score imposed, for example, for having obtained a pretrial release, while holding constant the influences of other potential causative factors—such as charges and counts, age, prior record, type of counsel, method of conviction, etc. For each independent causative factor, Table 5-21 indicates both the direction of influence and its magnitude, expressed as a proportion of the average sentence severity score (Index A) imposed in the given offense-year combination.

No clear trends emerged on the effect of minority status in 1973, partly because of the small samples. Black burglars fared 24 percent worse than white burglars in 1973, but black robbers fared 21 percent better, in terms of the average Sentence Severity Index A score. Other minorities (mainly Oriental and American Indian in Multnomah County) were treated the same as whites in 1973 burglary cases but fared 40 percent worse in robbery cases. However, in 1974 minority status was not significantly related to sentence severity in either offense, suggesting more evenhanded treatment of offenders.

Independent effects of pretrial custody status are also mixed. Compared with defendants who spent part of their pretrial time in jail and part out on their own recognizance or bail, burglars in 1973 who were in jail all the time fared 50 percent worse, whereas defendants who were never jailed fared no better or worse. For burglaries in 1974, custody status had no significant effect. For robberies, jailees fared worse in both years, but inexplicably, those on bail or own recognizance all the time fared even worse. These data must be interpreted as being inconclusive in gauging trends in evenhandedness in sentencing as affected by custody status.

Compared with burglars defended by the Public Defender's Office, those defended by either type of private attorney fared no better or worse in both years. This was also true for robbery defendants in 1974. But robbery defendants in 1973 had sentences imposed that were 20 or 37 percent more severe if they were defended by court-appointed or court-retained counsel, respectively. From these data we can conclude that the type of defense attorney had little independent effect on sentence severity score.

Unfortunately the number of trial convictions included in our yearly random samples of 100 burglaries and 100 robberies was very small; therefore, we cannot rely on the regression results reported in Appendix C. Alternatively, we attempted to select matched pairs of convictees in each sample, differing only in whether they were convicted at trial or pleaded guilty to all original counts and charges. These cases were matched exactly on the following characteristics: year, offense (burglary, whether dwelling or nondwelling), number and level of original and convicted charges, and prior criminal record category. In addition, if possible, the cases were also matched on defendant custody status and age. We then computed the percentage difference in mean sentence severity score for the group convicted at trial and the group who made straight pleas of guilty. These results are shown in Table 5-21. Note that because of too few trials, we could not make meaningful estimates for robberies in 1973. For the other three entries, numbers of trials (both court and jury) varied between six to eight. From these small samples it would seem that convictions at trial result in an increase in sentence severity of about 8 to 18 percent over those imposed on straight pleaders. However, this "penalty" imposed by the court system does not account for the probability that a defendant will be acquitted at trial or have the charges reduced (presumably resulting in a lesser sentence). For 1974 robberies, the trial effect is to slightly reduce sentence severity. Thus, to the limited extent that we can conclude *anything* from these small samples, it would seem that trials have little effect on sentence severity compared with straight pleas.

In summary, therefore, our findings regarding evenhandedness of dispositional and sentencing outcomes as affected by minority status, pretrial custody status, type of attorney, and choice of trial versus straight plea are as follows.

Minority Status. Because ethnicity data were not recorded in well over half of the cases examined, sample sizes by ethnic group were quite small and statistically reliable inferences are difficult to draw. For these small samples, black robbery defendants in both years tended to have higher dismissal rates and lower guilty plea and overall conviction rates, suggesting either over-arrests by the police or over-prosecution by the District Attorney's Office or the application of a double standard. Given these data, we could not resolve the question of which hypothesis best explains the observed differences. These same ethnic differences were also present in burglaries in 1973 but disappeared in 1974, indicating a trend toward more evenhandedness in dispositions. Imposed sentence severity differences associated with ethnic group were mixed in both offenses in 1973, but these differences disappeared in 1974, indicating a trend toward more evenhandedness in sentencing.

Pretrial Custody Status. Some differences in dispositional rates associated with being in custody or not (out on bail or on own recognizance) were observed in burglaries and robberies in 1973. But these differences generally disappeared in 1974, indicating a movement toward more evenhandedness in dispositions. Jailed burglars and robbers tended to have more severe sentences imposed in 1973, but pretrial custody status had no effect in 1974 burglaries. However, custody status effects were mixed in 1974 robberies. Consequently, these data must be interpreted as being inconclusive in gauging custody status effects on the evenhandedness of sentencing.

Type of Defense Attorney. Compared to private attorneys, public defenders seemed to achieve higher dismissal rates for burglary and robbery defendants in both years and a somewhat lower likelihood of overall conviction in robbery cases, but little differences associated with type of attorney were observed in trial or straight guilty plea or plea-bargaining rates. As to sentence severity score, no differences between type of attorney were present in burglary cases in both years and in 1974 robberies, but 1974 robbery defendants defended by private attorneys received somewhat more severe sentences. In short, although there were some dispositional and sentencing outcomes that were somewhat more favorable for defendants having public defender representation, our general conclusion is that type of defense attorney had little effect.

Trial versus Straight Pleas. To the limited extent that we can conclude *anything* from our small samples of defendants convicted at trial, it would seem that conviction at trial imposed little or no penalty in terms of sentence severity imposed compared with similar defendants making straight pleas of guilty. A more statistically reliable analysis would require larger sample sizes of defendants who choose a trial.

How the Court System Treats Defendants with
Prior Criminal Records

Although not an issue that fits neatly into one of the several issue categories we have addressed in this study, it seems useful to examine how a jurisdiction treats defendants with prior criminal records as compared with those with no prior record. National concern with the broader issue of the "habitual offender" or the "career criminal" is evidenced by recent LEAA action grants aimed at focusing special prosecutorial resources on the career criminal in several jurisdictions and by at least one LEAA research grant aimed at examining the nature and number of habitual offenders, their impact on criminal behavior, their contacts with public agencies, the impact of public agencies on their behavior, and alternative programs for dealing with segments of the habitual offender population.

Dispositional Measures

In Table 5-22 we show dispositional measures by the four criminal record categories (none, minor, major, prison) employed by the California Bureau of Criminal Statistics.[8] As indicated in the discussion of the evenhandedness issue, we show only dispositional measures for defendants arraigned in Circuit Court. Prosecutorial rejection rate by prior record is not shown because data on the suspect's prior criminal record are generally not present in the prosecutor's files for those who are rejected. Again, one must keep in mind the caveat that observed differences shown in cross tabulations of performance measures by prior record may, in fact, be partially due to other factors.

From Table 5-23 it appears that the only prominent difference associated with prior record is that 1974 robbery defendants with more serious prior records were not convicted more often than those with less serious records. Otherwise, observed differences were insubstantial. From Table 5-23, then, it is fair to conclude that no special attention was focused on burglary or robbery defendants with prior criminal records and no improvements in conviction rate or conviction level of these defendants resulted in either year. It is true that higher conviction rates and higher conviction levels resulted for *all* burglary and robbery defendants in 1974 and were associated with the no-plea-negotiation experiment (as we have shown in the above discussion of the issues of screening

[8] See Chapter 4 for simplified definitions of these categories.

Table 5-22

The Relationship between Prior Record and Dispositional Measures in Multnomah County Robbery I and Burglary I Cases, 1973-1974

Percent of All Defendants with a Given Prior Record Category

	Robbery I								All Burglary I							
	1973				1974				1973				1974			
Dispositional Measure	None	Minor	Major	Prison	None	Minor	Major	Prison	None	Minor	Major	Prison	None	Minor	Major	Prison
Not convicted																
Pretrial dismissal	39	47	32	31	12	21	9	6	17	28	7	33	17	14	11	27
Trial acquittal, dismissal, mistrial	4	20	16	0	5	21	9	11	0	11	14	9	2	0	0	9
Total	43	67	48	31	17	42	18	17	17	39	21	42	19	14	11	36
Convicted																
Straight plea	7	6	15	23	65	37	82	55	15	6	36	8	52	43	66	28
Received plea bargain (reduced charges and/or counts)	46	27	37	31	6	7	0	11	62	44	36	42	21	14	17	27
Gross plea rate (pleas ÷ N)	53	33	52	54	71	44	82	66	77	50	72	50	73	57	83	55
At trial	4	0	0	15	12	14	0	17	6	11	7	8	8	29	6	9
Conviction rate (conv. ÷ N)	57	33	52	69	83	58	82	83	83	61	79	58	81	86	89	64
All dispositions (N)	100 (26)	100 (15)	100 (19)	100 (13)	100 (34)	100 (14)	100 (11)	100 (18)	100 (47)	100 (18)	100 (14)	100 (12)	100 (48)	100 (7)	100 (18)	100 (11)
Trial conviction rate (trial convictions ÷ trials)	50	—	0	100	67	40	—	60	100	50	33	50	80	100	100	50

Table 5-23

The Independent Effect of Prior Criminal Record on Sentence Severity in Multnomah County Burglary I and Robbery I Cases, 1973-1974

| | Percent Change in Sentence Severity Score (Index A) Associated with a Given Category of Prior Record[a] | | | |
| | Burglary I | | Robbery I | |
Prior Record[b]	1973	1974	1973	1975
Minor	+20	+19	+39	NS
Major	−33	NS	+30	+54
Prison	−44	+59	+69	+45

[a]Entries are only for variables in regression equations that were statistically significant at the 95 percent level and in which the regression coefficient on that variable was statistically significant at the 50 percent level; entry NS (not significant) otherwise.
[b]Measured against no prior record.

accuracy and plea bargaining). But the experiment did not set out to focus special attention on defendants with heavy prior criminal records, and thus one should not have expected differential treatment by prior record to result.

Sentence Severity Measures

Table 5-17 showed the percentage of total variation in sentence severity score (Index A) accounted for by the defendant having a prior criminal record. In Table 5-23 we show the size and direction of the independent effect of prior record, in terms of the percent change in the sentence severity score (Index A) associated with a minor, major, or prison record. The change in sentence severity score is measured against defendants with no prior criminal record.

In robbery cases in both years, the effect of prior record was to increase the sentence severity score by 30 to 69 percent, depending on year and category of prior record. Although there were some inconsistencies, the more serious prior records tended to be associated with higher sentence severity score. This observation also held for 1974 burglary defendants. Compared with defendants with no prior record, 1973 burglary defendants with a minor prior record received somewhat more severe sentences, but defendants with more serious prior records received less severe sentences. This latter anomalous result is not explainable in terms of the gross data we collected, but one may speculate that for 1973 burglary defendants with prior major or prison records there may have been other mitigating circumstances associated with their background, case, or behavior that would account for their lower sentences.

In summary, then, dispositional outcomes in burglary and robbery cases were generally not affected by defendant prior record in either year. In terms of sentence severity imposed, there was a trend toward more severe sentences for defendants with some prior criminal record; and, in general, the more serious the prior record, the more severe the sentence. This kind of analysis is useful in establishing "current practice" with regard to treatment of habitual offenders in a jurisdiction. If a special program were introduced that focused on offenders with serious prior record, dispositional and sentence outcomes under the program could be evaluated by comparing them with current practices outcomes.

Delay

Here we apply several performance measures to illuminate the speediness of justice from a variety of viewpoints. First we illustrate what happened in Multnomah County in terms of three measures of elapsed time between major events—median number of days, minimum number of days for the longest 10 percent of cases, and the percent of cases exceeding some elapsed time standard—and in terms of continuances. Then we attempt to analyze *why*—that is, we estimate the magnitude and direction of the change in one elapsed time measure associated with selected factors that we hypothesized would influence the speediness of justice.

Table 5-24 displays the several measures of delay for four offense categories (a random sample of all felonies, robberies, dwelling burglaries, and nondwelling burglaries) in both years. For all felonies, the median number of days from arrest or arraignment to dismissal, or to guilty plea, or to final disposition[9] showed fairly consistent year-to-year increases. Very large year-to-year increases in time between conviction and sentencing are also apparent, probably largely because of the more frequent use of presentence investigation reports in 1974, particularly in the more serious offenses. Median number of days between arrest and trial and between arraignment and trial also rose consistently from year to year. And the minimum time for the longest 10 percent of cases also showed fairly consistent year-to-year increases between major events, although the small sample size (e.g., the longest 10 percent of 20 cases dismissed in a given offense-year sample equal to 2 cases) makes for low confidence in this statistic.

For the two Impact offenses of robbery and dwelling burglaries, year-to-year trends were mixed. Some elapsed time measures showed year-to-year decreases or no change (e.g., median time between arrest and dismissal, from arrest or arraignment to final disposition or to guilty plea for robberies; from arrest or arraignment to guilty plea and from arraignment to final disposition for dwelling burglaries). Still others rose in 1974, such as arrest or arraignment-to-trial periods. Dwelling burglary elapsed time measures behaved in a similar way to elapsed time measures for all felonies.

---

[9] Final disposition is taken as the date of dismissal, nonconviction at trial, or sentencing as a result of a guilty plea or a conviction at trial.

Table 5-24
Measures of Elapsed Time in Multnomah County Felony Cases, 1973-1974

Type of Disposition	All Felonies 1973	All Felonies 1974	Robbery I[a] 1973	Robbery I[a] 1974	Dwelling Burglary I[a] 1973	Dwelling Burglary I[a] 1974	Nondwelling Burglary I[a] 1973	Nondwelling Burglary I[a] 1974
	Median Number of Days							
From arrest to—								
Dismissal	29	41	63	26	42	47	17	71
Guilty plea	57	51	65	54	65	51	66	82
Trial	56	84	51	81	52	93	61	118
Final disposition	62	77	86	86	85	97	61	97
	Minimum Number of Days for Longest 10 Percent of Cases							
From arrest to—								
Dismissal	197	154	—	—	—	—	—	—
Guilty plea	90	93	—	—	—	—	—	—
Trial	107	149	—	—	—	—	—	—
Final disposition	159	151	—	—	—	—	—	—
	Percent of Cases Exceeding 60-Day Standard							
From arrest to—								
Dismissal	31	38	51	38	40	—	25	55
Guilty plea	48	44	66	34	52	44	58	63
Trial	50	100	36	69	38	83	—	—
All cases[b]	42	46	57	42	50	46	46	61
	Median Number of Days							
From arraignment to—								
Dismissal	29	46	79	—	78	—	69	84
Guilty plea	23	29	37	21	33	31	29	21
Trial	30	49	35	52	30	79	25	72
Final disposition	34	63	71	64	68	68	32	61
	Minimum Number of Days for Longest 10 Percent of Cases							
From arraignment to—								
Dismissal	184	110	—	—	—	—	—	—
Guilty plea	85	82	—	—	—	—	—	—
Trial	53	92	—	—	—	—	—	—
Final disposition	145	130	—	—	—	—	—	—
	Median Number of Days							
From conviction to—								
Sentencing	2	34	41	35	19	33	2	31

[a]Entries for minimum number of days for longest 10 percent of cases are omitted because of the small size of the sample.
[b]Excluding elapsed time between conviction and sentencing.

The major point to note here is that Impact offenses did not generally contribute to year-to-year increases in delay experienced for the felony caseload as a whole, suggesting that Impact cases were expedited consciously or unconsciously.

In Table 5-24 we have also included a measure of the extent to which the 60-day time standard is being met. The standard actually applies only to the arrest-to-trial period (of individual cases); however, it is useful to show separately the percent of cases exceeding 60 days from arrest to dismissal, to guilty plea, to trial, and to "final adjudication" (i.e., dismissals, guilty pleas, and trials together, excluding the time between conviction and sentencing). Notice that although the median number of days from arrest to dismissal, guilty plea, or trial was less than 60 days for all felonies in 1973, in fact, 31, 48, and 50 percent of those dispositions, respectively, exceeded the 60-day standard. And in 1974 larger fractions of those dispositions exceeded the 60-day standard.

In general, a greater fraction of 1973 robbery and burglary dispositions exceeded the standard compared with all felonies taken together. In 1974 fewer robbery dispositions exceeded the time standard. One point of interest is that in 1974, most trials for robbery, dwelling burglaries, and all felonies exceeded the standard, whereas half or less did so in 1973. The main points are that a very large proportion of adjudicated cases exceeded the time standard and that, in general, delay was worse during 1974.

Although they provide only indirect measures of overall delay, continuance measures provide additional insight, particularly with regard to which classes of practitioners are responsible for delay and how continuance policy is being applied. Table 5-25 displays a number of continuance measures, by contested (trials) and uncontested disposition, for all felony cases in both periods. For uncontested cases about one-third were continued in both periods, but the average number of continuances per case rose in 1974. Since the average continuance involved 15 to 16 days in both periods, this meant that the average number of continued days per uncontested case (continued and noncontinued) rose from 7 in 1973 to 9 in 1974. Although half or more of the continuances were attributed to the defense in both periods, those attributed to the prosecution declined in 1974.

For contested cases the picture was somewhat different. Compared with uncontested cases, a greater fraction of contested cases were continued and more continuances were granted during the average case; moreover, both measures rose in 1974 over 1973. But since the average continuance declined from 14 to 9 days over the two years, the number of continued days per average contested case remained relatively constant. Unlike uncontested cases, only about 25 to 30 percent of trial case continuances were attributable to the defense; those attributable to the prosecution declined over time. In contested cases a large proportion of continuances were attributable to the court and jointly to the prosecution and defense in both periods.

Table 5-25

Continuance Measures in Multnomah County, 1973-1974

(Based on a 100-Case Sample of All Felony Cases in Each Period)

Continuance Measure	1973	1974
For uncontested cases		
Number of cases continued ÷ all cases (%)	33	31
Number of continuances ÷ all cases	0.46	0.59
Number of days continued ÷ number continuances	15	16
Number of days continued ÷ all cases	7	9
Percent of total number of continuances attributed to—		
Defense	57	49
Prosecution	26	15
Court and other, including unidentified cases[a]	17	36
(N)	(73)	(80)
For contested cases		
Number of cases continued ÷ all cases (%)	45	60
Number of continuances ÷ all cases	1.00	1.40
Number of days continued ÷ number of continuances	14	9
Number of days continued ÷ all cases	14	13
Percent of total number of continuances attributed to—		
Defense	25	29
Prosecution	35	19
Court and other, including unidentified cases[a]	40	52
(N)	(20)	(15)

[a]Attributed to court alone, defense and prosecution jointly, and unidentified attribution.

We turn next to an analysis of what affects delay. We selected average elapsed time between arraignment and final disposition as a reasonable overall measure of the delay introduced into felony proceedings in Circuit Court. We hypothesized that four factors could influence this measure of delay.[10] Pretrial

---

[10] Since we had no prior hypotheses as to why factors other than the four selected should influence delay, we do not show their effect. The results of the statistical analysis displayed in Appendix C does, however, include the effects of other (control) variables on elapsed times.

custody status could affect elapsed time; defendants on bail or their own recognizance might seek to delay proceedings for their advantage, whereas defendants in jail might be less inclined to ask for continuances so as to minimize pretrial jail time. The type of defense attorney could affect delay, especially if one category of attorney tended to know the system better than another; however, we had no prior hypothesis as to which type of attorney would be associated with longer or shorter elapsed times. A trend over time toward heavier caseloads (or court calendar crowding), we hypothesized, should result in increased delay. Finally, the type of disposition—dismissal, plea bargain, or trial—could affect delay. Compared with straight pleas, we hypothesized that dismissed cases should be shorter, and cases disposed by plea bargain and trial should be longer on the average.

Table 5-26 shows these results for all felonies and robberies for both periods. Pretrial custody status had little or no effect on court delay overall (i.e., for the entire felony caseload) in either year. Compared with robbery defendants

Table 5-26
The Independent Effect of Hypothesized Influences on Elapsed Time from Arraignment to Final Disposition for All Felonies and for Robbery I in Multnomah County, 1973-1974

| | Percent of Change in Average Elapsed Time[a] | | | |
| | All Felonies | | Robbery I | |
Influence on Elapsed Time	1973	1974	1973	1974
Pretrial custody status[b]				
Jail	−13	NS	+95	+44
Bail or OR	NS	NS	+74	+88
Defended by private attorney[c]	+76	+48	+84	−37
Type of disposition[d]				
Dismissed	NS	−93	NS	−66
Plea bargained	NS	−68	+98	+110
Tried	−60	+51	−67	+98
Proxy for court calendar crowding	+9	+5	+7	+2
Percent of variance explained by all factors considered	(12)	(18)	(26)	(33)

[a]Entries are only for variables in regression equations which were statistically significant at the 95 percent level and in which the regression coefficient on that variable was statistically significant at the 50 percent level; entry NS (not significant) otherwise.

[b]Measured against mixed custody status.

[c]Measured against defense by public defender.

[d]Measured against straight plea conviction.

who spent part of their pretrial time in jail and part out on bail or their own recognizance, defendants in jail exclusively or out of jail exclusively tended to suffer more delay, and the relative effect varies from year to year. In 1974 being out on bail or own recognizance introduced more delay than being held in jail. In 1973 the effects were inexplicably reversed, but the difference in magnitude was small.

The independent effect of being represented by a private attorney (whether retained or court-appointed) compared with public defender representation was to lengthen the arraignment to final disposition period by approximately 50 to 75 percent (depending on year) in all felony cases. In robbery cases this effect was present in 1973 but was reversed in 1974. In general, though, we can conclude that private attorneys introduce more delay in felony proceedings. Two hypotheses come to mind to explain these findings: either private attorneys deliberately ask for, and are granted, more continuances in the hopes of more favorable (to the defendant) sentences or they ask for, and are granted, continuances because of more calendar conflicts among the cases they handle. Given these data, we cannot choose between these hypotheses.

We found that there was a small, but a highly (statistically) significant, positive effect of court calendar crowding on elapsed time. This effect varied between 2 and 9 percent depending on year and type of offense. Since backlog and filings steadily increased over this 2-year period (see Table 5-2 above), our hypothesis is confirmed. However, the small size of the effect is somewhat surprising.

Having a case dismissed, compared with a straight plea, had no effect in 1973 for either robbery cases or all felony cases, but in 1974 there was a large decrease in delay associated with this type of disposition, confirming our hypothesis. Plea bargaining was associated with more delay in robbery cases in both periods, but in the average felony case the effects were mixed (no effect in 1973, but less delay in 1974). Inexplicably, for both offense categories going to trial was associated with less delay in 1973, but more delay in 1974. Overall, therefore, these data must be viewed as inconclusive with respect to the independent influence of type of disposition on delay.

Use of Victims, Witnesses, and Jurors

As indicated in Appendix B, essentially no data were recorded in available court records that would allow us to estimate measures of the use of victims, other witnesses, and jurors. The sole exception was data on the number of victims and witnesses called per trial[11]—only one ingredient necessary for estimating number of witnesses and victim appearances per disposition. Consequently, we used

---

[11] Data were not recorded on the number of witnesses or victims called per uncontested case.

responses from these lay participants to our mail survey questionnaires as a basis for making rough estimates of such measures.[12]

Table 5-27 displays the resulting measures of the use of victims and other witnesses. The data reflect cases that were active during March through August of 1974. We selected older cases to be certain that they would have been closed by the time the mail surveys were administered (early fall of 1975), since we were interested in the victims' and witnesses' knowledge of the case outcome, among other things.

Table 5-27
Measures of the Use of Victims and Witnesses in Multnomah County, March-August 1974

Type of Response from Lay Participants	Victims	Other Witnesses[a]
Cooperativeness		
Cooperative (%)	89	93
Not cooperative (%)	6	3
Not asked (%)	5	4
Total responses (N)	100 (105)	100 (89)
Average number of appearances by lay participants	2.5	1.9
Average number of appearances by lay participants per disposition	2.5[b]	2.9[c]
Duration of appearances by lay participants		
Less than 1 hour (%)	24	14
One to two hours (%)	50	48
Three hours (all morning or afternoon) (%)	21	34
Six hours (all day) (%)	5	4
Total responses (N)	100 (93)	100 (85)
Average duration of appearance (hr)	1.8	1.9

Source: Responses of victims and other witnesses to Rand mail surveys, except for number of victims or other witnesses called per trial (see below).

[a]Primarily witnesses for the prosecution.

[b]Assumes one victim per disposition times 2.5 victim appearances per victim = 2.5 victim appearances per disposition.

[c]1.5 witnesses per trial disposition (calculated from trial court records) times 1.9 witness appearances per witness = 2.9 witness appearances per disposition.

[12]Since the mail surveys rely on the memories of victims, witnesses, and jurors, the measures must of necessity be viewed as very rough approximations that cannot be checked for accuracy. (See Section X and Appendices F through H of the Rand study report, R-1918-DOJ, for a description and the results of these surveys.)

The survey responses indicated that the overwhelming proportion of victims and other witnesses were cooperative in the proceeding (about 90 percent) and only a few percent indicated that they were not asked for their cooperation. The average number of appearances per victim (2.5) was slightly higher than for other witnesses (1.9). But since the number of victims called per trial (about 1.0) was less than the number of other witnesses called per trial (2.5), the resulting numbers of victim or witness appearances per disposition were 2.5 and 2.9 respectively. And average victim time per appearance (1.8 hours) was about the same as that of other witnesses (1.9 hours).

Table 5-28 displays measures of the use of juror time; jurors who served during the month of June 1975 were queried. The major finding is that about 40 percent of juror time on the average was spent unproductively waiting in the jury room or elsewhere. About half their time was spent on criminal cases, split fairly evenly between *voir dire* and in trial. And about 40 percent of their time, split evenly between *voir dire* and in trial, was spent on civil cases. (Notice that the average time per activity when summed over all activities is in excess of 100 percent; apparently responding jurors neglected to allocate their time accurately across activity categories.) Thus, ratios between categories is a more meaningful measure. If we take time in civil trial as an index of 100 percent, jurors tend to spend about the same time in *voir dire* for civil trials, about 220 percent as much time in *voir dire* for criminal trials, 280 percent as much time in criminal trials, and about 400 percent as much time waiting unproductively.

The Use of Judicial Time: The Weighted-Caseload Approach

One objective of our study was to analyze the use of judicial time in various court activities occurring in felony criminal proceedings. Although the analysis is

Table 5-28
Measures of the Use of Juror Time in Multnomah County, June 1975

| Activity | Percent of Jurors Responding | | | | | Average Percent of Time Spent |
	None	Less Than 25	25-49	50-74	75-100	
Waiting in jury room or elsewhere (N = 163)	0	29	37	26	8	41
Jury selection: criminal cases (N = 159)	0	70	24	3	3	22
In trial: criminal cases (N = 173)	6	46	31	12	5	28
Jury selection: civil cases (N = 155)	3	71	20	3	3	20
In trial: civil cases (N = 168)	18	50	23	5	4	19

described below, we rejected the results because of deficiencies in the available raw data. These problems will be explained after the analytical approach has been described. Our experience illustrates how difficulties can be encountered in working with court data generated for another purpose. Our failure to obtain acceptable results does not imply that the objective was infeasible, but rather that its implementation required data collection efforts beyond the means of our study.

The vehicle of analysis was the so-called weighted-caseload approach (described in Chapter 4), a procedure in which various activities comprising a criminal proceeding are measured by their respective average durations and frequencies of occurrence per proceeding. These in turn are combined into a performance measure termed the average time (judge-time in this study) required to process a case to disposition.

One use of a weighted-caseload analysis is to determine the impact of policies that alter the relative mix of activities within the proceeding (e.g., the impact of a change in plea bargaining policies and a consequent change in the frequency of related activities). Another use is to translate a projection of future case loads into requirements for practitioners and other court personnel. And a third use is to estimate the impact of procedural changes (e.g., the adoption of omnibus hearings) that may alter the average time consumed in affected court activities.

Weighted-caseload analyses have been and are being performed in a number of jurisdictions.[13] We planned to go a step further than prior applications of this approach by separating the calculations into broad offense classes. These more detailed results could then be used to deal directly with changes in the mix of offense types.

Data Collection

The Circuit Court of Multnomah County does not routinely collect data of the type required for weighted-caseload analysis. Nevertheless, we hoped to collect data ourselves from at least a sample of judges for a period of one or two months. It turned out that a logging procedure for court clerks had been initiated in June 1975 to collect data that would help to resist county efforts to reduce (clerk) personnel. This procedure required clerks to log their workday activities both in and out of the court room, to record the time for each activity, and to indicate whether the activity was related to a civil or a criminal matter. Since the court clerk must be present when the judge is on the bench and since we knew the kinds of activities that the judge must preside over, it was possible to infer from the clerk logs how judges used their courtroom time. It was

---

[13]The Judicial Council of California, for example, has implemented regular judicial weighted-caseload analyses for the past 10 years or more.

possible also to infer the amount of judicial time consumed off the bench, presumably in chambers, but its allocation to various matters could not be ascertained. At best, the off-bench time could be prorated between criminal and civil matters on the basis of the corresponding division of time on the bench.

The Chief Criminal Court, which handles all pretrial matters, as well as guilty pleas and sentencing flowing from guilty pleas, was not included in the clerk logging program. However, a daily schedule routinely prepared for that courtroom showed for each activity the scheduled time, defendant's name, case number, type of activity, and defense counsel.

Offense type, an item of information that we needed, was absent both from the clerk's logs and the schedule of the Chief Criminal Court. But we could obtain this information indirectly from a daily schedule of court appearances routinely prepared by the Office of the District Attorney. This schedule could be matched with the Chief Criminal Court schedule on the basis of defendant's names. The match with the trial court clerk logs could be made on the basis of the type of activity, but ambiguities would sometimes arise when a day's activities in a single courtroom were numerous.

Difficulties in using these reports notwithstanding, copies of the Chief Criminal Court schedule and the prosecutor's court appearance schedule were obtained for each judicial day in July 1975. Trial court clerk logs were available for only 119 of the 185 judge-days during that month. Weighted-caseload calculations were made separately for the Chief Criminal Court and the trial courts, both because of the missing data problems and because of differences in activities between the two.

The gross number of dispositions for the entire Circuit Court during the month of July 1975 was taken from the monthly criminal statistics prepared by the Chief Criminal Clerk. Bench warrants, which are included among dispositions for the Court's reporting purposes, were excluded for our purposes.

Analysis

We aggregated court activities into seven types: arraignments, motion hearings, plea hearings, other hearings, court trials, jury trials, and sentencing hearings. The average duration of each type of activity in each of the two types of courts was calculated. The relative frequency of each type of activity per disposition was also calculated. The product of these two measures—that is, the average bench time per specified activity type multiplied by the average frequencies per disposition for a specified activity type—provided the total bench time per disposition for that activity type. Summing these bench times over all activity types then provided the total judge-time consumed in the courtroom (i.e., the bench time) per disposition. Total time in chambers for trial judges was prorated between civil and criminal matters on the basis of the identifiable split of bench time on civil and criminal matters. Time in chambers for the Chief Criminal Judge was estimated to be 10 percent of bench time.

The results of these calculations for felonies as a whole are displayed in Table 5-29. Similar results, not displayed, were obtained for four felony types. Some of the entries in Table 5-29 have questionable magnitudes. The rates of occurrence of plea hearings and sentencing hearings seem unduly low, for example. The combined judicial time per disposition of 118 minutes is less than one-half of the average time reported for Superior Courts in California.[14] These questionable results underscore our doubts about the adequacy of the available data.

Data Deficiencies

The most serious shortcoming in the data sources was the substitution of the clerks' logs for direct records of the use of judicial time. While clerks' logs enabled us to infer how judges' bench time was distributed, they gave no indication as to how the judges employed their off-bench time. And even for the

Table 5-29
Weighted Criminal Caseload Analysis, Circuit Court, Multnomah County, July 1975
(Felonies plus Misdemeanor Appeals)

Activity	Average Bench Time per Activity (min)		Average Frequency per Disposition		Average Bench Time per Disposition (min)		
	CCC[a]	TC[b]	CCC	TC	CCC	TC	Total
Arraignments	11	–	.88	–	10	–	10
Motion hearings	23	58	.09	.02	2	1	3
Plea hearings	17	–	.48	–	8	–	8
Other hearings	20	24	.14	.16	3	4	7
Court trials	–	101	–	.03	–	3	3
Jury trials	–	394	–	.07	–	28	28
Sentencing hearings	20	20	.15	.16	3	3	6
Total bench time per disposition					26	39	65
Estimated off-bench time per disposition					3	50	53
Estimated total of judge's time per disposition					29	89	118

[a]CCC = Chief Criminal Court.
[b]TC = Trial courts.

[14]Final Report, *Judicial Weighted Caseload System Project for the Judicial Council of California*, Arthur Young & Company, Sacramento, May 1974.

purpose of estimating the use of bench time, the clerks' logs were of uneven quality. Some appeared to be complete, to the point of explicitly identifying the parties in both civil and criminal cases; others, however, contained only a few cryptic entries per day. (We did not use the latter logs, since the inference was strong that some courtroom activities had simply not been recorded.) Between these two extremes, some clerks failed to designate whether the noted activity was a civil or criminal matter. It was usually possible for us to make this identification by using the District Attorney's schedule of court appearances, but even so, over 20 percent of total bench time remained unidentified. This data defect could have produced a significant undercounting of criminal case activities, which in turn could have caused a substantial underestimate of judge-time consumed per criminal disposition. Also, some clerk logs for some courtrooms were missing. These data gaps might have biased the mix of bench activities in our data base, since we observed that types of cases and types of activities within cases tended not to be uniformly distributed among judges.

Our estimates of the frequencies of some types of courtroom activities could not, unfortunately, be compared with similar items reported in the court's monthly criminal statistics since their definitions of these activities differed from those used in the logging procedure.

The Chief Criminal Court schedules were deficient for our purposes because they contained scheduled times for activities rather than actual times consumed. In some instances, we elected to use standard time factors prepared by the chief criminal clerk rather than using scheduled times.

We took the count of dispositions directly from the Circuit Court's monthly criminal statistics summary. Since the Court does not report dispositions by offense type, we estimated the distributions for July by offense type by means of a sample of 400 dispositions selected from all dispositions occurring during the first 10 months of 1975. (The sampling was made by means of the Cumulative Status Report, which specified the type of offense but not the date of disposition.)

Other data shortcomings would have been avoidable if our resources had permitted us to collect data over a longer period (or over several periods). One month's data were too few to permit analyses of relatively uncommon offense types or to make reliable estimates of the duration of such a relatively infrequent activity as a trial. Also, more extended data collection facilitates the statistical analysis of courtroom activities that tend to be cyclical. For example, when a trial judge takes his turn as Chief Criminal Judge, his case disposition rate immediately increases about twentyfold, but the increase in his sentencing hearings lags because of the period of time required to prepare presentence investigation reports. Thus one would expect sentencing hearings to be relatively infrequent during the first month of a new Chief Criminal Judge's term. The month that we studied, July 1975, was the first month of this term.

Concluding Remarks

Most of the data barriers that we encountered could be readily overcome in a future weighted-caseload analysis effort. Modest changes in logging procedures and their supervision would markedly enhance the quality of those data sources for weighted-caseload analyses. While the data collection period should be lengthened to at least several months, the relatively frequent activities need not be exhaustively reported. For example, 10 percent of the arraignments over a period of three months should probably suffice. On the other hand, trials should be completely reported because of their infrequency.

The principal open question is how to obtain reliable data on the amount of off-bench time judges devote to various matters, given their sensitivity to "monitoring." Their cooperation probably hinges on being persuaded beforehand of the value of weighted-caseload information. It could be helpful if a data collection scheme were devised to preserve anonymity of information about individual judges.

Gauging Overall Performance: Summary and Comments

Here we summarize our findings in qualitative terms. Each major finding or inference is stated, together with a discussion noting the year-to-year changes (or lack of change) in the relevant set of performance measures. Where appropriate, we also indicate to what extent and why each finding must be qualified, given the nature and sample size of the data and the success of the supporting statistical analysis described in Appendix C.

Findings Relevant to Whether the No-Negotiation Experiment
Achieved its Objectives

I. Case Quality in Impact Crimes Improved Significantly.

Rationale: For Impact crimes, the experiment resulted in relatively little change in overall rejection rates and felony filing rates on the most serious charge but much less frequent rejections by reason of evidence deficiency. Moreover, within this broad rejection reason category, the frequency of cases rejected because they needed more police investigation declined; this was not so for a comparable non-Impact crime. Also, nonconviction rates (dismissals and trial acquittals or mistrials) declined importantly for Impact crimes but not for a comparable non-Impact offense. From these indicators we can conclude that both the quality of individual cases (better police investigation) and the relative frequency of good cases (tightened charging standards) improved.

Qualification: From these indicators it is not possible to separate the improvement in better police investigations from the elevation of the screening threshold.

II. Plea Bargaining Objectives of the Experiment Were Achieved.

Rationale: Guilty plea convictions on reduced charges were virtually eliminated and plea convictions at the highest original level increased markedly for Impact offenses. But one comparable non-Impact offense showed weaker, but similar, changes—indicating some spillover effects of the experiment. Moreover, the District Attorney achieved the plea bargaining objectives of the experiment without resorting to the subterfuge of reducing the booking charge of a potential Impact case to a lesser charge, thereby making it a non-Impact case on which plea bargaining was not constrained by the experiment. This is supported by the fact that filing rates (of Impact-defined cases at booking) on lesser charges decreased markedly during the experiment.

Findings Relevant to the Major Issue Areas Considered

III. Charging Standards Were Tightened for Impact Cases.

Rationale: Since overall rejection rates for one Impact offense remained unchanged and the relative frequency of rejection by reason of evidence deficiency declined, it is reasonable to conclude that the charging threshold was raised and that police investigations improved. (This assumes that the proportion of cases rejected on nonevidentiary (purely) discretionary grounds did not change materially; in fact, this proportion did increase somewhat, but relatively little compared to the decrease in rejections by reason of evidentiary deficiency.) Had the prosecutor not tightened his standards, he would have rejected a smaller proportion of cases during the experiment, *ceteris paribus.*

IV. Charging Accuracy Did Not Lessen for Impact Cases.

Rationale: One ambiguous indicator of possible improvement in charging accuracy or police investigation is that nonconviction rates (dismissals, trial acquittals, mistrials) fell markedly for Impact crimes but not for one comparable non-Impact crime. But this indicator alone cannot disclose whether one or both are responsible. (From the case audit of burglary guilty plea cases we concluded that case strength was high both before and during the experiment.) Changes in other measures normally relevant to charging accuracy (charge-bargaining and straight-plea rates) must be attributed to the policy ground rules of the experiment. Thus we can conclude only that charging accuracy did not lessen.

V. There Was a Year-to-Year Shift in the Plea Bargaining Balance: System Gains Increased and Concessions Decreased.

Rationale: Gains and other operational impacts included the following: lower dismissal rates and higher plea and overall conviction rates for Impact crimes; a large rise occurred in the proportion of defendants incarcerated and in sentence severity imposed for Impact crimes (and some non-Impact crimes as well); most of the observed increase in the sentence severity score of robbery I cases and all the observed increase for burglary I cases are mainly associated with the experiment[15] (perhaps resulting unintentionally); and although delay for felony cases as a whole showed a year-to-year increase, Impact crimes were moved more expeditiously. Compared with straight pleaders, concessions per convicted defendant fell markedly for both Impact crimes. (Convicted defendants here include those convicted at trial as well as those who received a plea bargain.) Concessions granted robbery defendants who entered a charge-bargain or count-bargain showed little year-to-year change, no matter which sentence severity index is applied; the direction of year-to-year changes in concessions granted burglary plea bargainers depends on which index is used, because the frequency of nonincarceration sentences were relatively greater in the latter year and the different indices apply different relative weights to nonincarceration as opposed to incarceration sentence components.

VI. Sentencing Variation Remained Relatively Constant from Year to Year, with Illegitimate Factors Having Little Effect in One Crime and Decreasing Effects in Another.

Rationale: In burglary I cases, illegitimate factors contributed little to sentence variation in both years, indicating evenhandedness in sentencing. In robbery I cases, illegitimate factors, particularly pretrial custody status and the choice of a bench or jury trial (compared with a straight plea) accounted for a large, but decreasing over time, portion of the variation of the sentence severity score explained in our analysis. In both crimes the nature of charges and counts accounts for a large portion of the total variation explained, and prior record is next in importance in explaining that variation due to legitimate factors.

VII. Disposition and Sentencing Were Rather Evenhanded and Becoming More So.

Rationale: Minority Status: Black burglars or robbers in the early year had higher dismissal rates and lower plea and overall conviction rates, suggesting

---

[15]The increase may well be associated with the experiment, even though sentence policy was presumably not part of the experiment's ground rules. After adjusting for random sampling errors in case and defendant characteristics between 1973 and 1974 and for crowding in correctional facilities for the two years, we observed an escalation in average sentence severity in the latter year. However, the customary rotation of sentencing judges could have also contributed to the escalation in sentences.

either over-arrests, over-prosecution, or the application of a double standard. (Our data could not discern which hypothesis best explained the observed differences.) These differences disappeared in 1974 burglary I cases. Mixed effects of minority status on the sentence severity score existed in 1973, depending on offense, but these differences disappeared in 1974.

Pretrial Custody Status: Some mixed effects of custody status (in jail or not) on dispositions existed in 1973, but these differences were reduced or disappeared in 1974, depending on the offense. There were mixed effects of custody status on the sentence severity score, depending on the offense and year; hence, these data must be interpreted as being inconclusive.

Type of Defense Attorney: Although there were some dispositional and sentencing outcomes that were somewhat more favorable for defendants having public defender representation (higher dismissal rate, lower overall conviction probability in robbery, less severe sentences in robbery), our general conclusion is that the type of defense attorney had little effect. We have no reason to believe that taken as a group, public defenders, retained counsel, and court-appointed attorneys were not equally "good."

Trial versus Straight Plea: Compared with straight pleas, conviction by trial seems to result in little or no penalty in the sentence severity score.

Qualifications: The observed differences attributable to minority status and conviction by trial are based on small sample sizes, and inferences cannot be confidently drawn. The "trial effect," especially, needs to be analyzed in more depth, using a large sample of defendants who go to trial.

VIII. Defendants with More Serious Prior Criminal Records Fared No Worse in the Adjudication Phase, but Once Convicted, They Were Sentenced More Severely.

Rationale: No consistent differences in dispositional measures associated with prior criminal record appeared in either year, suggesting little or no effect of prior record either before or during the experiment. More serious prior records, however, tended to be associated with a higher sentence severity score in both years, suggesting that no special effect was associated with the experiment.

IX. Elapsed Time Measures Showed Year-to-Year Increases for the General Caseload, but Impact Cases Were Expedited. Only Type of Attorney and Court Calendar Crowding Showed Consistent Effects on Delay.

Rationale: Most elapsed time and continuance measures exhibited year-to-year increases and a significant fraction of cases exceeded the 60-day standard for the felony caseload in general. However, most delay measures for Impact offenses showed little or no year-to-year change, indicating that special efforts were made to expedite Impact cases. There were either no effects or mixed effects on delay associated with pretrial custody status and type of disposition (dismissal, plea, trial), indicating that these effects on delay are inconclusive. Representation by private attorneys and the increasingly crowded court calendar generally introduced more delay.

X. **Based on Their Mail Survey Responses, the Use of Victims and Other Witnesses Seemed to be Reasonable. On the Other Hand, Juror Idleness Was Excessive.**

Rationale: Almost all victims and other witnesses indicated that they cooperated with the prosecutor when requested. The average number of appearances per disposition were between 2.5 and 3.0 for victims and other witnesses, and each appearance averages about 1.8 to 1.9 hours. Although jurors' time seemed to be relatively equally split between civil matters, criminal matters, and simply waiting, during the period of duty surveyed, they spent a significant proportion of their time in idleness.

XI. **On the Whole, Performance Improved from Year-to-Year: Only Delay for the Entire Felony Caseload is Somewhat Worse, but Performance on All Other Issues (for which Data Were Available) Was Either Better or No Worse. Additional System Costs Incurred Were Modest.**

Rationale: Given findings I through IX, it seems reasonable to conclude that, on the whole, performance improved between 1973 and 1974; that the no-plea-negotiation experiment's goals were largely achieved; and that this experiment was associated with improving overall performance. These overall performance gains were achieved at a cost increase of about 25 percent in prosecutorial staff assigned to felony cases, or about a 13 percent increase in staff for the entire office. There was no evidence that any additional costs were incurred in the Court or in the Public Defender's Office as a result of the experiment.

6 Comparing the Demonstration Jurisdictions

In the previous chapter we attempted to show primarily by statistical measures how the performance in each selected issue area of felony proceedings may have changed between two periods of operations in Multnomah County. In the present chapter, drawing upon information that we collected in Multnomah and Dade and then analyzed, we offer a number of quantitative comparisons of the two jurisdictions in 1974. The comparisons are guided by the views expressed in Chapter 4 about interjurisdictional comparisons in terms of statistical performance measures. This chapter thus extends the summary descriptions given in Appendix A of the two demonstration jurisdictions and their felony proceedings. We begin by presenting additional background information to increase our understanding of the circumstances in which their criminal court systems function.

Background Data on Population, Arrests, and Police Manpower

Table 6-1 presents readily available data (for 1972) on population, arrests, offenses, and police manpower for the principal city and its police force, for the county areas served by the sheriff's department, and for the two combined. The total population of Multnomah County given by the 1970 census was 557,000; Dade County's population was given to be 1,268,000. Thus the Circuit Court in Dade served a population roughly twice that served by the Circuit Court in Multnomah.[1]

We observe in Table 6-1 that arrests per offense are quite similar between Multnomah and Dade. Offenses per 100,000 population for robbery only seems significantly higher in Dade. And while arrests per policeman are higher for all Part I offenses and for burglary only in Multnomah, this measure favors Dade for robbery only.

Selected Comparisons from the Statistical Overviews

For brevity we do not attempt exhaustively to catalogue similarities and differences between Multnomah and Dade Counties viewed as the contexts for

---

[1] Note that the "combined" entries in Table 6-1 for Dade cover a population of only 586,000—there being nine incorporated cities other than Miami which are not included. But we know of no reason why the rates shown in Table 6-1 are not representative of the entire population of Dade.

Table 6-1
Population, Arrests, Offenses, and Police Manpower

| | Multnomah | | | | | | Dade | | | | | |
| | Portland | | Multnomah County[a] | | Combined[b] | | Miami | | Dade County[a] | | Combined[b] | |
Category	1972	Change Since 1971 (%)	1972[c]	Change Since 1971 (%)	1972	Change Since 1971 (%)	1972	Change Since 1971 (%)	1972[c]	Change Since 1971 (%)	1972	Change Since 1971 (%)
Population (000)	384		163[c]		547		343		243[c]		586	
Offenses												
Number reported												
Part I[d]	35,848		9,558		45,406		28,644		35,555		64,199	
Robbery only	1,715		191		1,906		2,555		1,829		4,384	
Burglary only	1,134		3,031		4,165		8,294		10,062		18,356	
Per 100,000 population												
Part I	9,335	−6	5,874	−4	8,217	−5	8,349	−10	6,068	−11	6,910	−11
Robbery only	447	−5	117	+20	349	−2	745	−10	312	−2	504	−5
Burglary only	2,873	+2	1,863	+6	2,572	+3	2,417	−11	1,717	−9	1,975	−10
Arrests												
Total number												
Part I	5,246		1,600		6,846		3,634		5,847		9,481	
Robbery only	307		39		346		451		400		851	
Burglary only	816		832		1,198		633		1,637		2,270	
Police manpower												
Police officers	723		224		947		734		1,199		1,933	
Total employees	933		832		1,315		936		1,597		2,533	

Arrests per offense						
Part I	0.14	0.17	0.15	0.13	0.16	0.15
Robbery only	0.18	0.20	0.18	0.18	0.22	0.19
Burglary only	0.07	0.13	0.11	0.08	0.16	0.12
Arrests per policeman						
Part I	7.26	7.14	7.23	4.95	4.88	4.91
Robbery only	0.42	0.17	0.36	0.61	0.33	0.44
Burglary only	1.13	1.71	1.26	0.86	1.37	1.18

Sources: Federal Bureau of Investigation/Uniform Crime Reports data and the U.S. Census.

aEntries apply to the sheriff's department only.

bEntries are the sums of numbers or the weighted average of ratios in the city and county columns.

cPopulation entry obtained by subtracting the population of the principal city and of all incorporated places known to have police departments from the total population of the county.

dPart I (UCR) offenses are homicide, rape, robbery, felonious assault, burglary, larceny, and auto theft.

our demonstration analyses but merely present selected information in a comparison format. The remainder of this chapter will be devoted to comparisons related to the issue areas for which analyses were performed in our study.

To begin with, Table 6-2 compares the number of felony cases filed and pending in the Circuit Courts of the two jurisdictions in the recent past. Table 6-2 discloses the greater severity of the backlog problem in Dade, where the number of cases pending approximates an entire year's filings. By comparison, the number pending in Multnomah, which has been rising, still does not exceed 3 to 4 months' filings.

Next, in Table 6-3, we compare the distribution of felony cases by offense type in the two jurisdictions, based on random samples of 100 cases processed in 1974. The differences between the two jurisdictions in Table 6-3 that are of a statistically significant magnitude do not include robbery and burglary (or breaking and entering), the exemplary offenses of this study.

When the selected characteristics of felony defendants are compared, as in Table 6-4, we find the age distribution to be similar in the two jurisdictions; a significantly higher proportion of blacks present among Dade defendants; roughly the same proportion of transient defendants occurring in the two locales; a significantly larger fraction of defendants with less than high school education being prosecuted in Dade; a significantly greater proportion of defendants having no prior record in Multnomah, but also a greater proportion of defendants having prison records in that jurisdiction;[2] a greater proportion of defendants being represented by the public defender in Dade (because the Dade

Table 6-2

Comparison of Number of Criminal Cases Filed and Pending in Circuit Court

Caseload Measures	Multnomah County[a]	Dade County
Number of filings		
FY 1973-74	3,250	
FY 1974-75	3,657	
CY 1974		10,552
CY 1975		12,200 (est.)
Number of cases pending ("backlog")		
December 1974	774	9,202
November 1975	1,008	10,512

[a]Includes criminal appeals from the lower court in addition to felony filings.

[2] Note that if the categories "none" and "minor" are combined and similarly the categories "major" and "prison," then the distribution of defendants is nearly the same in the two jurisdictions.

Table 6-3

Distribution of Felony Cases by Type of Offense, 1974

(Percent of All Cases)[a]

Offense Type	Multnomah County	Dade County
Offenses against persons	20	30
Robbery	11	8
Other	9	22+
Offenses against property	37	48
Burglary (breaking and entering)	16	18
Theft	13	22
Other	8	18+
Drug offenses	38	21+
All other felony offenses	5	1

[a]The symbol + denotes, here and in the following tables, a difference between the two counties of a statistically significant magnitude—i.e., the likelihood is 5 percent that a difference of this size (positive or negative) or greater would occur by chance if there is actually no difference between the counties.

Public Defender's Office handles virtually all the indigent cases whereas in Multnomah the Public Defender's Office handles only a portion); and about the same proportion of defendants benefiting from pretrial release in the two counties.

Table 6-5 compares some gross attributes of felony proceedings in Multnomah and Dade Counties.

The significant or nearly significant differences between the two jurisdictions shown in Table 6-5 are in the pretrial dismissal rate, the plea rates (both to original charges and to lesser charges), the proportions receiving jail incarceration and the proportions receiving prison incarceration, and the median elapsed times. (While differences in the trial measures are large, they are not statistically significant because of the small number of trials in the cases comprising our general samples.) The differences in gross dispositional measures undoubtedly reflect the contrasting nature of the proceedings in the two systems, particularly as to screening and plea bargaining, but possibly reflect other factors as well. But we must look to more detailed analyses for explanations. The differences in the proportions given one type of incarceration as against another may devolve from the respective correctional situations in the two counties and states, as well as from disparities in judicial views toward sentencing. The differences in median elapsed times are a palpable product of the more serious caseload situation in Dade.

Finally, Table 6-6 assesses the two jurisdictions in terms of a list of

Table 6-4
Selected Characteristics of Felony Defendants, 1974
(Percent of All Defendants)

Defendant Characteristics	Multnomah County	Dade County
Age[a]		
Under 21	46	47
21-29	39	41
30 and over	15	12
Ethnic group[a]		
Blacks	30	54+
Spanish surname	0	12
Other minorities	13	0
nonminority	57	34+
Transient (less than 2 years in county)[a]	11	15
Less than high school education[a]	50	73+
Prior record[a]		
None	52	30+
Minor	12	32+
Major	19	28+
Prison	17	10+
Type of defense attorney[b]		
Public defender	33	67+
Private (court-appointed and defendant-retained)	67	33+
Pretrial custody status[b]		
In jail (or combination of jail and nonjail status)	30	28
Free on bail or OR	70	72

Note: + denotes statistically significant difference between counties.
[a]From exemplary offense samples, totaling approximately 400 cases.
[b]From general samples, totaling approximately 200 cases.

"comparability features" relevant to the selected issue areas in felony proceedings. (The purpose and use of this list is explained in Chapter 4, where the validity of interjurisdictional comparisons of performance measures is addressed.) Here we employ the list simply to enrich our presentation of background information characterizing and distinguishing Multnomah and Dade Counties.

Table 6-5

Dispositions, Sentences, and Delays in Felony Proceedings, 1974

(Disposition and Sentence Entries in Percent)

Type of Disposition, Sentence, and Delay	Multnomah County	Dade County
Dispositions[a]		
Pretrial dismissal rate	38	9+
For insufficient evidence	8	3
For other reasons	30	6+
Nol-pros plus diversion rate	–	6
Trial rate	7	12
Court	2	5
Jury	5	7
Trial conviction rate[b]	12	59
Trial acquittal rate[b]	14	34
Other trial outcome rate[b]	14	7
Pretrial plea of guilty rate	53	63
To original charges	19	53
To lesser charges	34	10
Overall conviction rate	58	69
Sentences[c]		
Suspended	0	2
No incarceration imposed	61	60
Incarceration imposed	39	40
Jail (plus any other punishment)	28	13+
Prison (plus any other punishment)	11	27+
Median elapsed time (days)		
From arrest to trial	84	119
From arrest to final disposition	77	109
From arraignment to final disposition	63	83

Note: + denotes statistically significant difference between counties.
[a]Based on a sample of 94 dispositions in Multnomah County and 98 in Dade County.
[b]Based on a sample of 7 trials in Multnomah County and 12 in Dade County.
[c]Based on a sample of 57 sentencings in Multnomah County and 70 in Dade County.

Case Screening

The discussion given in Chapter 4 about interjurisdictional comparisons by means of statistical performance measures distinguishes between two purposes of these comparisons. On the one hand, we may be interested in certain products of

Table 6-6

Assessment of Comparability Features for Multnomah and Dade Counties

I. Case processing efficiency and delay

    A. Practitioner productivity

1. Difference in procedural steps	1.	x
2. Pretrial motion practices	2.	√
3. Conduct of jury *voir dire*	3.	u
4. Use of commissioners for judicial functions	4.	√
5. Method of assigning prosecutors or public defenders to cases	5.	x
6. Court calendaring system	6.	x
7. Caseload mix (by offense category)	7.	x
8. Use of court coordinators	8.	√

    B. Witness use

1. Court calendaring system	1.	x
2. Continuance policy and procedure	2.	x
3. Availability rules (e.g., "on call" system)	3.	√

    C. Juror use

1. Conduct of jury *voir dire*	1.	u
2. Policy on jury pool size	2.	x

    D. Delay

1. Court calendaring system	1.	x
2. Continuance policy and procedure	2.	x
3. Differences in procedural steps	3.	x
4. Availability of interlocutory appeals	4.	u
5. Liberality of pretrial discovery	5.	√
6. Existence and nature of time-limit standards; power to refile	6.	x
7. Caseload mix (by offense category)	7.	x
8. Scale of court system (i.e., size relative to load)	8.	x

II. Evenhandedness

1. Police arrest and screening policies	1.	u
2. Bail and OR policies	2.	x
3. Jury selection and composition	3.	u
4. Judicial selection and composition	4.	√
5. Payment system for defense counsel	5.	√

III. Prosecutorial screening[a]

1. Charging or filing standards	1.	x
2. Police arrest and screening practices	2.	u
3. Procedure for *nolle prosequi*	3.	x
4. Existence and nature of time-limit standards; power to refile	4.	x
5. Availability and nature of pretrial diversion programs	5.	x

Table 6-6 (cont.)

III. Prosecutorial screening *(continued)*
      6. Availability of precharging conference   6.   x
      7. Organization of prosecutor's office   7.   x

IV. Plea bargaining
    1-7. As above in III.
      8. Statutory sentencing structure   8.   x
      9. Liberality of pretrial discovery   9.   x
    10. Availability and nature of preliminary hearing   10.   x
    11. Probation policy   11.   x
    12. Judicial involvement   12.   x
    13. Jury or judge sentencing   13.   √
    14. Method of providing defense counsel   14.   √
    15. Jail conditions   15.   x
    16. Caseload and backlog   16.   x

V. Sentencing variation
    1. Statutory sentencing structure   1.   x
    2. Probation policy   2.   x
    3. Plea bargaining practices   3.   x
    4. Charging or filing standards   4.   x
    5. Parole eligibility and practice   5.   x
    6. Public attitudes toward gravity of various offenses and appropriate sentences   6.   u
    7. Availability of sentence review   7.   √
    8. Method of filling judgeships   8.   √
    9. Postsentencing powers of trial judge   9.   √
    10. Availability of presentence reports   10.   x
    11. Overcrowding of correctional facilities   11.   x
    12. Jury or judge sentencing   12.   √
    13. Availability of alternatives to sentencing   13.   x

Note: √ denotes similarity between the two jurisdictions; x denotes dissimilarity; u means undetermined by us.

aCase screening in Dade County is largely a judicial function.

court systems that are important to the community without regard to the institutional machinery that produced them. For example, the number of felony suspects whose cases are not prosecuted after arrest and booking seems to have this independent significance. On the other hand, we may be interested in direct comparisons of the operations per se of criminal court systems in different jurisdictions, assessed in terms of the outputs, both intermediate and final, of felony proceedings. Given the latter purpose, the following question arises: Do the jurisdictions to be compared differ so fundamentally that using statistical performance measures to make these comparisons is misleading. As mentioned above, a set of "comparability features" displayed in Chapter 4 can help to assess how severe the "apples and oranges" problem is in a particular interjurisdictional application of performance measures. This list is applied to Multnomah and Dade Counties in Table 6-6.

As applied to case screening, the list of comparability factors in Table 6-6 underscores the differences between Multnomah and Dade Counties. The scope of our study did not include the first features, police arrest policies; also, we cannot readily compare detailed charge filing standards, the second feature, since neither jurisdiction documents them systematically. These two features aside, the two demonstration jurisdictions differ markedly in how and by whom case screening is accomplished (see especially Appendix A). These differences should not be determinative of outcome in cases that are clearly strong or clearly weak. But in cases where the evidence is marginal (as well as the cases in which nonevidentiary policy factors are prominent), they may have considerable impact. The dependence of screening results on the "quality" of the case flow should be kept in mind when one considers how noncomparability in the screening function may vitiate comparisons of screening performance measures.

The Charging Threshold

As mentioned in the example above, comparisons of the effect of the charging threshold seem meaningful despite profound differences in screening procedures between Multnomah and Dade Counties. Table 6-7 gives a gross portrayal of the operation of the screening threshold in the two jurisdictions in 1974.

This table presents a statistically significant difference between the two jurisdictions in the proportion of robbery prosecutions rejected (as well as in the

Table 6-7
Comparison of Case Screening for Exemplary-Offense Bookings, 1974
(Entries in Percent)

Gross Screening Outcome	Multnomah County		Dade County	
	Burglary I	*Robbery I*	*B&E Offenses*	*Robbery*
Not held to answer	32	51	30	38+
Reduced to misdemeanor and so filed	6	3	1	2
Filed on felony charges	62	46	69	60+

Notes: Based on exemplary offense samples numbering roughly 100 cases for each offense in each jurisdiction. + denotes statistically significant difference between counties.

corresponding proportion of robbery cases filed as felonies). We shall not speculate on the possible explanation for differences between the jurisdictions because we were unable to collect adequate data on "rejection reasons" in Dade.

Charging Accuracy

Criminal proceedings tend to be self-correcting when charging inaccuracies are initially present—dismissals, amendments, *nolle prosequi*, plea agreements, acquittals, convictions at lesser levels, etc., all may serve to redress charging inaccuracy. But how and when these events occur in the proceedings depend on features of the court system that may differ markedly, as many do between Multnomah and Dade Counties. Furthermore, when using dispositional measures as bases for inferences about charging accuracy, we must bear in mind that they are more or less ambiguous for this purpose, as we have discussed in Chapter 4. For simplicity, therefore, we confine ourselves to the two clearest dispositional measures that best reveal charging accuracy performance; namely, the proportion of defendants convicted of all charges as originally filed and the proportion of defendants not convicted (excluding those diverted). These two types of dispositions are less affected by plea bargaining, which tends to obscure the statistical effects of inaccurate charging.

Table 6-8 displays these two dispositional measures for the two demonstration jurisdictions in 1974, again applying only to the exemplary offenses on which this study focuses.

Assuming that a relatively high rate of conviction on charges as originally filed and a relatively low rate of failure to convict imply relatively high accuracy of charging, then Multnomah performance in charging the Impact offenses of dwelling burglary I and robbery I was superior in 1974 to Dade for the comparable offenses. At the same time, Multnomah did significantly worse in terms of these measures for the non-Impact offenses of non-dwelling burglary I than did Dade for non-dwelling breaking and entering offenses. Thus these results seem to reflect the special handling that Multnomah gave Impact crimes involved in the District Attorney's experiment, beginning with arrest and screening and continuing throughout the proceeding. We should not, however, draw inferences about the relative overall screening performance between the two jurisdctions without considering other classes of dispositions at a level of detail sufficient to reveal the dependence of dispositions on screening accuracy. As discussed elsewhere (see, for example, Appendix B), we failed to collect adequate "reasons" data to enable this more complete dispositional analysis to be performed.

Plea Bargaining

We are unable to make enlightening comparisons of plea bargaining between Multnomah and Dade Counties by means of statistical performance measures.

Table 6-8

Comparison of Selected Dispositional Measures Related to Charging Accuracy, 1974

(Percent of All Dispositions)

	Multnomah County			Dade County		
	Burglary I			B&E Offenses		
Disposition	Dwelling	Non-dwelling	Robbery I	Dwelling	Non-dwelling	Robbery
Convicted of all charges as filed	79	26	67	46+	54+	33+
By plea	67	23	54	42+	45+	41+
By trial	12	3	13	4	9	3+
Not convicted	5	44	24	26+[a]	21+	32[a]
Pretrial dismissal	5	38	12	11	7+	16
Other[b]	0	6	12	15	14	16
Sample size (number of dispositions)	56	32	86	55	44	98

Note: + denotes statistically significant difference between counties.

[a]Excludes 2 percent of dispositions involving pretrial intervention.

[b]Includes acquittal, *nolle prosequi* (Dade), mistrial.

Although our demonstration analysis in Multnomah County was quite revealing in the area of plea bargaining, we could not statistically demonstrate the nature and effects of plea bargaining to any great extent in Dade.

This failure devolved from the Dade plea bargaining situation itself. Except for sentence agreements (or assurance), plea agreements were uncommon. But sentence agreements, which were said to be quite frequent, were not recorded in case folders or other available files.

To the extent that we could calculate plea bargaining performance measures for the plea agreements in Dade, we shall here display comparisons with overall Multnomah results. But it must be remembered that the Dade results do not fairly characterize the full plea bargaining situation in that jurisdiction. Furthermore, if one reviews the list of 16 comparability factors given in Table 6-6 for the plea bargaining area, one finds that many differ markedly for Multnomah and Dade Counties. These disparities impose further constraints on statistically based inferences about the relative plea bargaining performance.

Table 6-9 compares gross results of plea bargaining for the exemplary offenses between the two jurisdictions in 1974. Since we could not ascertain whether a Dade straight plea was "pure" or involved a sentence agreement (or perhaps an agreement to drop another pending case), it seems appropriate to compare the Multnomah combined straight-plea and straight-plea plus agreement

Table 6-9

Comparison of Gross Results of Plea Bargaining, 1974

(Percent of All Pleas in Case Sample)

	Multnomah County			Dade County[a]		
		Burglary I			B&E Offenses	
Level of Plea	Robbery I	Dwelling	Non-dwelling	Robbery	Dwelling	Non-dwelling
Straight plea (to all original charges and multiple counts)	43	30	27			
Straight plea plus sentence or other sentence or other agreements	45	52	20	80	68+	69+
Total	88	82	47			
Plea to at least one count of most serious charge but with charge or count reductions	6	2	0	20+	26+	27+
Plea to charges less serious than original	6	16	53	0	6	4+
Total number of guilty pleas in sample (N)	50	34	29	53	46	16
Gross plea rate (N ÷ number of dispositions)	61	82	50	61	65+	70+

Note: + denotes statistically significant difference between counties.

[a]Sentence agreement data not available.

levels with the Dade straight-plea entries. For robbery the result is similar (88 percent versus 80 percent) for the two counties. The Multnomah combined straight-plea rate for dwelling burglary I, an Impact offense, is significantly larger than Dade's straight-plea rate for dwelling breaking and entering offenses (82 percent versus 68 percent). This may be attributable to the District Attorney's experiment in Multnomah. This inference is strengthened by the observation that the nondwelling breaking and entering straight-plea rate in Dade is significantly larger (69 percent versus 47 percent) than the nondwelling burglary I (a non-Impact offense) combined straight-plea rate in Multnomah. At the next lower plea level, the relatively large entries for Dade (20 to 27 percent) compared with those for Multnomah (0 to 20 percent) for burglary-type offenses might be related to a greater propensity to file related charges (e.g., loitering, malicious destruction, possession of burglary tools, larceny). The differences between jurisdictions at the lowest plea level shown in Table 6-9 are readily interpreted. They attest both to the strong policy in Dade opposing charge-reduction plea agreements irrespective of offense type and to the limited policy in Multnomah against such agreements in Impact offenses covered by the District Attorney's experiment.

Elements on the other side of the plea-bargain exchange (or balance) are shown in Table 6-10. These measures of operational impacts on the court system are illustrative of many that help to capture the effects of the plea negotiation process.

The entries for the dispositional measures in Table 6-10, which are based on our exemplary-offenses samples, disclose no significant differences between the two jurisdictions, notwithstanding the contrasts in the plea bargaining picture. And while the percent incarcerated is also not significantly different between the two systems for the exemplary offenses, sentences are moderately less severe in Dade. One may speculate that sentence bargaining in Dade (upon which we were unable to collect data) helps to explain the difference in sentence severity, especially in robbery cases for which statutory maximums are higher in Dade. Finally, the substantial differences in median elapsed times shown by our case samples from the two counties could be interpreted as evidence of operational

Table 6-10

Comparison of Measures Reflecting the Effects of Plea Bargaining in Exemplary Offenses, 1974

Dispositions, Sentences, and Delays	Multnomah County		Dade County	
	Robbery I	Burglary I	Robbery	B&E Offenses
Dispositional measures (%)				
Dismissal rate[a]	12	17	18	19
Trial rate	27	13	20	12
Guilty plea rate	61	70	62	69
Overall conviction rate	77	80	67	76
Sentence severity measures				
Percent incarcerated	87	64	80	61
Sentence severity imposed				
(Index A score)	26.5	16.9	19.3	13.1
(Index B score)	43.9	20.4	32.1	14.6
(Index C score)	61.2	23.9	44.8	16.2
(Index D score)	116.5	47.0	86.3	23.4
Median elapsed time measures (days)				
Arraignment to guilty plea	21	29	116	73
Arraignment to trial	52	76	124	73
Arraignment to final disposition	64	66	126	90

[a]Includes, in Dade, nolle prossed and diverted cases.

"penalties" incurred by Dade for its reluctance to use plea bargaining more frequently to alleviate its serious case congestion.

Sentence Variation

Viewed specifically in terms of the comparability factors listed in Table 6-6 for sentence variation, Multnomah and Dade Counties are dissimilar. One expects to find that the nature and the variability of imposed sentences were observably different between them—in particular, that they differed for the exemplary offenses of this study, whose statutory definitions and punishment structure are not the same in Oregon and Florida.[2] The dissimilarities of Multnomah and Dade felony proceedings further imply that differences in sentence variation shown by statistical performance measures must be cautiously interpreted.

Tables 6-11 and 6-12 indicate (for robbery and burglary offenses, respectively) how sentences in the two jurisdictions varied in type and severity at different levels of conviction in the 1974 exemplary-offenses samples of our study. Table 6-11 reveals that most robbery convictions in either jurisdiction were at the highest level and produced substantial (upwards of 5 years incarceration imposed) prison terms. At the dominant level of conviction, the sentence severity score for Index A is modestly higher for Multnomah, by a statistically significant amount. Table 6-12 shows that breaking and entering convictions in our Dade sample were predominately at the second most serious level (2d degree felony, 15-year maximum prison term), with roughly one-third of these 2d degree felony convictions receiving prison terms. In Multnomah, convictions were predominantly at the highest level (felony A), with roughly one-half receiving prison terms. Again, the sentence severity score (which is dominated by cases at a single level of conviction in each county) is higher for Multnomah by a statistically significant amount. The relatively greater use of probation in Dade in these case samples helps to explain this difference in Index A scores, which weights probation relatively higher than Indices B, C, and D (see Chapter 4).

Table 6-13 exhibits results from our analytical attempt to account for sentence variation by means of selected legitimate and illegitimate factors. The equations used to estimate the sentence severity score for Index A succeeded in explaining over 60 percent of the variance in Multnomah robbery I sentences, nearly 40 percent in Multnomah burglary I sentences, nearly 40 percent in Dade breaking and entering sentences, but essentially none in Dade robbery sentences. In the three instances where this analysis was productive, we observe the illegitimate factors selected were only minor contributors to sentence variation in both jurisdictions. The nature of the criminal conduct (as reflected in the charges and counts) was the strongest explanatory factor in both jurisdictions,

[2] See Appendix A and Chapter 5 for statutory definitions and punishment limits applying to the exemplary offenses.

Table 6-11

Comparison of the Distribution of Imposed Sentence Type and Amount of Punishment by Level of Conviction for Robbery Cases, 1974 *(Percent of All Convicted at Given Level)*

| | Level of Conviction | | | | | | | |
| | Multnomah County | | | | Dade County | | | |
Sentence Type / Amount of Punishment	Felony A (N=59)	Felony B (N=2)	Felony C (N=2)	Misdemeanor (N=0)	1° Felony (N=48)	2° Felony (N=3)	3° Felony (N=3)	Misdemeanor (N=5)
Probation only								
<2 yr	—	—	—	—	—	33	—	—
2-4 yr	—	—	—	—	—	—	—	—
>5 yr	—	—	—	—	8	—	—	—
Probation and other								
<2 yr	2	—	—	—	—	—	—	—
2-4 yr	2	—	—	—	2	—	50	—
>5 yr	5	100	—	—	—	—	—	—
Jail alone and jail + other								
<6 mo	2	—	—	—	—	—	—	80
7-11 mo	2	—	—	—	2	—	—	—
>12 mo	9	—	50	—	13	33	50	20
Prison alone and prison + other								
<2 yr	—	—	—	—	2	—	—	—
3-4 yr	2	—	—	—	12	33	—	—
5-10 yr	44	—	50	—	27	—	—	—
11-20 yr	32	—	—	—	19	—	—	—
>21 yr	2	—	—	—	15	—	—	—
Sentence severity score—Index A								
Mean	26.8	10.0	22.5	—	22.0	11.9	9.0	4.5
Standard deviation	10.9	—	0.7	—	13.9	3.9	7.1	5.0

Table 6-12

Comparison of the Distribution of Imposed Sentence Type and Amount of Punishment by Level of Conviction for Burglary and B&E Cases, 1974 *(Percent of All Convicted at Given Level)*

| | | Level of Conviction | | | | | | | |
| | | Multnomah County | | | | Dade County | | | |
Sentence Type	Amount of Punishment	Felony A (N=52)	Felony B (N=3)	Felony C (N=7)	Misdemeanor (N=4)	1° Felony (N=2)	2° Felony (N=54)	3° Felony (N=14)	Misdemeanor (N=3)
Probation only	<2 yr	—	—	—	—	—	2	14	—
	2-4 yr	2	—	—	—	50	25	21	—
	≥5 yr	8	—	14	—	—	9	14	—
Probation and other	<2 yr	—	—	—	25	—	—	—	—
	2-4 yr	11	33	43	50	—	4	—	—
	≥5 yr	—	—	—	—	—	2	7	—
Jail alone and jail + other	<6 mo	6	33	43	25	—	9	—	100
	6-11 mo	—	—	—	—	—	—	—	—
	≥12 mo	21	33	—	—	—	15	15	—
Prison alone and prison + other	<2 yr	—	—	—	—	—	6	15	—
	3-4 yr	10	—	—	—	—	8	7	—
	5-10 yr	36	—	—	—	—	18	7	—
	11-20 yr	6	—	—	—	—	2	—	—
	≥21 yr	—	—	—	—	50	—	—	—
Sentence severity score—Index A	Mean	10.3	9.6	9.2	4.3	25.7	13.4	12.6	2.0
	Standard deviation	9.0	9.3	4.0	2.4	27.9	8.5	8.2	1.7

148

Table 6-13

Comparison of Effects of Selected Factors on Sentence Severity, Exemplary Offenses, 1974 *(Percent of Accountable Variance in Sentence Score (Index A))*[a]

Factors Influencing Sentencing	Multnomah County		Dade County	
	Robbery I	Burglary I	Robbery	B&E Offenses
Legitimate factors				
Age	6	3	NS	NS
Prior criminal record				
Minor	NS	1	NS	2
Major	11	NS	NS	9
Prison	9	5	NS	3
Community ties (index)	4	4	NS	NS
Nature of charges or counts	18	15	NS	13
Total variance explained	48	28	–	27
Illegitimate factors				
Minority status				
Black	NS	NS	NS	2
Other	NS	–	NS	3
Pretrial custody status				
In jail	5	NS	NS	1
Released (bail, OR)	3	NS	NS	NS
Defended by private counsel				
Defendant-retained	NS	NS	NS	1
Court-appointed	NS	NS	NS	1
Convicted at trial				
Court	NS	1	NS	NS
Jury	NS	0	NS	NS
Proxy for calendar crowding or corrections crowding	3	6	NS	(b)
Total variance explained	11	7	–	8
Total variance explained (including that from nonsignificant variables and the constant term)	61	38	–	38

[a]Entries made only for variables in regression equations that were statistically significant at the 95 percent level and in which the regression coefficient on that variable was statistically significant at the 50 percent level; otherwise, NS (not significant) is indicated.
[b]Significant, but very small ($\leqslant$ 1 percent).

with prior criminal record also tending to be consequential in both jurisdictions. Overall, to the extent that our case samples permitted this more refined statistical analysis, highly unusual differences in explanatory factors between Multnomah and Dade Counties were not disclosed.

Evenhandedness

Our conceptual approach to the measurement of evenhandedness performance has been presented in Chapter 4, and its application to Multnomah County was given in Chapter 5. Our analysis was primarily concerned with the effects that ethnicity, pretrial custody status, and type of defense counsel (the illegitimate factors) have on dispositions and on the severity of sentences imposed. (The term *illegitimate* connotes that these factors ought significantly affect neither the outcome of a felony proceeding nor the severity of the sentence if the defendant is convicted.) Selected results from Multnomah County are juxtaposed with those from Dade County below as a basis for comparing the two jurisdictions in this issue area.

Dispositional Measures

Tables 6-14, 6-15, and 6-16 are cross tabulations that exhibit the dependence of various dispositional measures upon pretrial custody status, type of defense counsel, and ethnicity, respectively. The entries are based upon the 1974 exemplary-offenses samples from the two counties, containing roughly 400 cases.

The distribution of dispositions by jail, bail, and own recognizance pretrial custody status, as shown in Table 6-14 (note the magnitudes of N in the final row), generally preclude clear findings about the relative impact of pretrial custody status between the two jurisdictions. For robbery, the conviction by bargained plea rate in Multnomah was significantly lower than in Dade for defendants who remained incarcerated during their proceedings. In both Multnomah and Dade, the distribution of robbery defendants was skewed, with most sampled cases involving a defendant who was not free during the proceeding. There is a (not statistically significant) reduction in the conviction rate between defendants in jail and those freed on bail. In both jurisdictions, the less gross measures tend to show that robbery defendants at liberty fared better than those who remained in jail, but the results are not statistically significant because of the small samples involved.

For burglary, the conviction rate in Multnomah shows no consistent dependence on pretrial custody status, and the differences that are present are not statistically significant. On the other hand, a difference in the Dade straight-plea rate for breaking and entering offenses between jailed defendants and those on bail (55 percent versus 35 percent) leads to a difference in the overall conviction rate (85 percent versus 70 percent). But the other measures do not reinforce this indication of a lack of evenhandedness in Dade for breaking and entering defendants, related to their pretrial custody status.

In sum, we cannot infer any clear distinction between Multnomah and Dade Counties on the basis of Table 6-14. If pretrial custody status had an important impact on disposition of defendants charged with the exemplary offenses, our samples were not sufficiently large to reliably reveal this effect.

Table 6-15, which concerns the effect of type of defense counsel on disposition, reveals that public defenders appear to defend their clients slightly more effectively in Multnomah County for both exemplary offenses. No such

Table 6-14

Evenhandedness: Comparison of the Relationship Between Pretrial Custody Status and Dispositional Measures in Robbery and Burglary (or B&E) Cases, 1974 (Percent of All Defendants in a Given Pretrial Custody Status)

| | Multnomah County | | | | | | Dade County | | | | | |
| | Robbery I | | | All Burglary I | | | Robbery | | | B&E Offenses | | |
Dispositional Measure	Jail	Bail	OR	Jail	Bail	OR	Jail	Bail	OR	Jail	Bail	OR
Not convicted	17	28	33	19	38	14	30	62	0	15	30	25
Pretrial dismissal	7	14	20	17	25	14	6	12	0	6	13	6
Nolle pros., diversion	NA	NA	NA	NA	NA	NA	10	12	0	6	13	19
Trial acquittal, mistrial, dismissal	10	14	13	2	13	0	14	38	0	3	4	0
Convicted (conviction rate)[a]	83	72	67	81	62	86	70	38	100	85	70	75
By straight plea	59	58	47	46	50	58	45	25	0	55	35	44
By bargained plea[b]	9	14	0	25	0	17	22+	0	100	24	27	19
Gross plea rate[c]	68	72	47	71	50	75	67	25	100	79	62	63
At trial	15	0	20	10	12	11	3	13	0	6	8	12
Trial conviction rate[d]	60	0	60	83	48	100	20	25	0	67	67	100
Number of dispositions (N)	58	7	15	40	8	36	83	8	2	33	48	16

Note: + denotes statistically significant difference between counties.

[a]Number of convictions ÷ number of dispositions.

[b]Charges or counts reduced.

[c]Number of pleas ÷ number of dispositions.

[d]Number of convictions at trial ÷ number of trials (no tests of significance).

Table 6-15

Evenhandedness: Comparison of the Relationship Between Type of Defense Counsel and Dispositional Measures in Robbery and Burglary (OR B&E) Cases, 1974 *(Percent of All Defendants with a Given Type of Defense Counsel)*

Dispositional Measure	Multnomah County						Dade County					
	Robbery I			All Burglary I			Robbery			B&E Offenses		
	PD	CA	DR	PD	CA	DR	PD	CA	DR	PD	CA	DR
Not convicted	30	20	12	27	15	10	30	83	25	22	0	35
Pretrial dismissal	12	13	12	22	15	10	6	0	8	12	0	0
Nolle pros., diversion	NA	NA	NA	NA	NA	NA	9	33	17	9	0	25
Trial acquittal, mistrial, dismissal	18	7	0	5	0	0	15	50	0	1	0	10
Convicted (conviction rate)[a]	70	80	88	73	85	90	70	17	75	78	100	65
By straight plea	51	60	38	49	49	60	42	17	42	46	50	30
By bargained plea[b]	5	7	25	19	18	20	23+	0	25	24	50	25
Gross plea rate[c]	56	67	63	68	67	80	65	17	67	70	100	55
At trial	14	13	25	5	18	10	5	0	8	8	0	10
Trial conviction rate[d]	44	65	100	50	100	100	25	0	100	86	0	50
Number of dispositions (N)	43	30	8	41	33	10	79	6	12	76	2	20

Notes: + denotes statistically significant difference between counties. Key: PD = public defender; CA = court-appointed private counsel; DR = defendant-retained private counsel.

[a]Number of convictions ÷ number of dispositions.

[b]Charges or counts reduced.

[c]Number of pleas ÷ number of dispositions.

[d]Number of convictions at trial ÷ number of trials (no tests of significance).

Table 6-16
Evenhandedness: Comparison of the Relationship between Ethnicity and Dispositional Measures in Robbery and Burglary (or B&E) Cases, 1974

(Percent of All Defendants in a Given Ethnic Group)

	Multnomah County						Dade County					
	Robbery I			All Burglary I			Robbery			B&E Offenses		
Dispositional Measure	Maj.	Black	Other Minor.	Maj.	Black	Other Minor.	Maj.	Black	Other Minor.	Maj.	Black	Other Minor.
Not convicted	28	50	0	25	25	100	33	33	37	20	26	31
Pretrial dismissal	5	50	0	25	25	100	5	4	25	3	16	0
Nolle pros., diversion	NA	NA	NA	NA	NA	NA	19	12	0	14	8	23
Trial acquittal, mistrial, dismissal	23	0	0	0	0	0	9	17	12	3	2	8
Convicted (conviction rate)[a]	72	59	100	75	75	0	67	67	63	80	74	69
By straight plea	58	50	50	50	37	0	57	36	38	41	43	46
By bargained plea[b]	5	0	0	8	25	0	5	25	25	28	25	15
Gross plea rate[c]	63	50	50	58	62	0	62	61	63	69	68	61
At trial	9	0	50	17	13	0	5	6	0	11	6	8
Trial conviction rate[d]	28	0	100	100	0	0	50	25	0	80	75	50
Number of dispositions (N)	22	6	2	12	8	1	21	69	8	36	49	13

[a] Number of convictions ÷ number of dispositions.
[b] Charges or counts reduced.
[c] Number of pleas ÷ number of dispositions.
[d] Number of convictions at trial ÷ number of trials.

effect is observed in the Dade measures. We may infer that a slight distinction between the two counties exists as to the advantage gained by the defendant in being represented by the Dade defender.

Our attempt to compare Multnomah and Dade on the basis of Table 6-16 which relates dispositions to defendant ethnicity, is hamstrung by the small number of cases in our Multnomah samples that gave ethnic information. We cannot rely on the differences among ethnic categories, as shown by Table 6-16, as being indicative of any concrete relationships between outcomes and race in Multnomah. For Dade, Table 6-16 shows differences between the black and majority categories in the two types of plea rates for robbery and the pretrial dismissal rate for breaking and entering offenses. This is at most a very limited indication that blacks may, in some circumstances, fare better than others in Dade proceedings. But the sparseness of the Multnomah data precludes our contrasting this Dade effect of ethnicity.

Sentence Severity Measures

In Chapter 5 we address the question: What is the magnitude and direction of the change in average sentence severity score (for Index A) associated with a change in each of the specified illegitimate factors? Table 6-17 compares the results of our analysis of the 1974 sentence severity scores for Index A in both jurisdictions based on the exemplary-offenses samples. Are the two counties revealed to be different in evenhandedness performance by these results? We observe in Table 6-17 that no significant independent effects are shown in sentence severity scores for robbery convictions in Dade, and none are shown for burglary I convictions in Multnomah, save for a relatively slight increase as the result of being convicted at trial rather than pleading. By contrast, pretrial custody status has a marked effect on Index A sentence severity score for 1974 robbery I convictions in Multnomah; inexplicably, both those defendants who remained in jail and those who remained at liberty received significantly heavier sentences than those with mixed pretrial custody status. The only other notable effect on Multnomah robbery I defendants was a slight easing of punishment for those convicted at trial rather than pleading, an unexpected direction of change. Finally, we see that the strongest evidence of a lack of evenhandedness is in the sentences of Dade defendants of breaking and entering offenses, where, for example, sentence severity score increased by over 50 percent for other minorities (mainly Cuban) relative to majority defendants.

Viewing Table 6-17 as a whole, we cannot conclude that a consistent pattern of lack of evenhandedness is presented in either jurisdiction in 1974. The contrast between the two with respect to sentencing severity for the exemplary offenses is at best inconclusive.

Table 6-17

Evenhandedness: The Independent Effect of Illegitimate Factors on Sentence Severity Imposed, 1974 *(Percent Change in Average Sentence Severity Score (Index A) with a Change in a Given Factor[a])*

	Multnomah County		Dade County	
Illegitimate Factor	*Robbery I*	*Burglary I*	*Robbery*	*B&E Offenses*
Ethnicity[b]				
Black	NS[c]	NS	NS	+22
Other minorities	NS	NS	NS	+51
Pretrial custody status[d]				
In jail	+39	NS	NS	+26
Freed on bail or OR	+50	NS	NS	NS
Defended by private attorney[e]				
Defendant-retained	NS	NS	NS	+26
Court-appointed	NS	NS	NS	([f])
Convicted at trial[g]	−9	+8	NS	([f])

[a]See Table 5-21 for additional notes.
[b]Measured against majority status.
[c]Not significant (NS). See note to Table 5-21 for definitions of significance.
[d]Measured against mixed pretrial custody status.
[e]Measured against representation by the public defender.
[f]Omitted because of the rarity of the event in the case samples.
[g]Measured against straight-plea conviction. Entries computed from matching pairs of defendants and cases are similar in essential respects, except that one defendant was convicted at trial and the other of the matched pair pled guilty to all original charges.

How the Court System Treats Defendants with Pior Records

The fact that a defendant has a prior criminal record may impinge in various ways at a number of points in a felony proceeding. The police may be prompted to make a more thorough investigation of the offense; the charging may be performed with greater care; the defendant may be more likely to remain in jail during the proceeding because of ineligibility for release on own recognizance or inability to meet a higher bail requirement; the defendant may elect not to testify because of his vulnerability to impeachment by evidence of his prior record; or the sentencing judge may be strongly influenced by the defendant's history of criminal conduct: all these and other effects could lead to an outcome significantly different from that for a defendant with no prior record.

Table 6-18 compares the role of prior record in the exemplary-offenses samples in the demonstration jurisdictions. The 1974 dispositional measures for both Multnomah and Dade Counties, as displayed in Table 6-18, indicate no consistent relationship between the degree of prior record and the defendant's

Table 6-18
Evenhandedness: Comparison of the Relationship Between Prior Record and Dispositional Measures in Robbery and Burglary (or B&E) Cases, 1974

(Percent of All Defendants in a Prior Record Category)

	Multnomah County								Dade County							
	Robbery I				All Burglary I				Robbery				B&E Offenses			
Dispositional Measure	No Record	Minor	Major	Prison	No Record	Minor	Major	Prison	No Record	Minor	Major	Prison	No Record	Minor	Major	Prison
Not convicted	17	42	18	17	19	14	11	36	45	25	18	43	14	20	6	18
Pretrial dismissal	12	21	9	6	17	14	11	27	9	11	0	0	0	13	0	33
Nolle pros., diversion	NA	NA	NA	NA	NA	NA	NA	NA	9	3	18	0	9	7	5	0
Trial acquittal, mistrial, dismissal	5	21	9	11	2	0	0	9	27	11	0	43	5	0	0	0
Convicted (conviction rate)[a]	83	58	82	83	81	86	89	64	55	75	82	57	86	79	94	67
By straight plea	65	37	82	55	52	43	66	28	9+	54+	55+	43+	49+	33+	78+	50+
By bargained plea[b]	6	7	0	11	21	14	17	27	27	21	27	14	24	33	16	17
Gross plea rate[c]	71	44	82	66	73	57	83	55	36	75	82	57	72	66	94	67
At trial	12	14	0	17	8	29	6	9	19	0	0	0	14	13	0	0
Trial conviction rate[d]	67	40	–	60	80	100	–	50	40	0	–	0	75	0	–	–
Number of dispositions (N)	34	14	11	18	48	7	18	11	11	28	11	7	21	15	18	6

Notes: + indicates that the difference between counties of the weighted average of the straight-plea conviction rate in the No Record and Minor categories is significant at the 95 percent level for robbery and also for burglary (or B&E). The same is true for the weighted average of the straight-plea conviction rate in the Major and Prison categories. In addition, the difference between the straight-plea conviction rates in the two counties for the Minor category is significant.

[a]Number of convictions ÷ number of dispositions.
[b]Charges or counts reduced.
[c]Number of pleas ÷ number of dispositions.
[d]Number of convictions at trial ÷ number of trials.

disposition; this was true for all of the exemplary offenses. Where a difference
between entries is significant—for example, 83 percent versus 58 percent for the
conviction rate in Multnomah applying to robbery I defendants with no or
minor records, respectively—it strengthens the impression that past record was
not a governing factor in the pattern of dispositions in either county, where the
expected relationship would be just the reverse. So we are unable to usefully
distinguish between the performance of these two court systems by the results in
Table 6-18.

Table 6-19 explores the relationship between Index A scores and the degree
of prior record, again for 1974 exemplary offenses. Multnomah County in both
offenses and Dade County in breaking and entering offenses show roughly the
expected trend of increasing sentence severity score as the degree of prior record
increases. We have no information to explain the failure or the robbery cases in
our 1974 Dade sample to exhibit the same dependence.

Delay

The contrast between Multnomah and Dade Counties with respect to the
duration of felony proceedings is so marked that we need comment little about
the specific differences shown in Table 6-20. The median number of days from
arrest to various points in the proceeding tended to be 1.5 to 2.0 times as large
in Dade as in Multnomah, with some exceptions for nondwelling burglary (or
breaking and entering) cases. The most time-consuming cases in Dade were
roughly twice as long in Dade as in Multnomah. The same story obtains when
the consumption of time is measured from arraignment rather than arrest. These
results simply underscore the more serious problem of court congestion in Dade.
However, if we refer speediness performance in Multnomah Circuit Court to the
statutory standard that the period from arrest to initiation of trial (if any)

Table 6-19
**Comparison of the Independent Effect of Prior Criminal Record on Sentence
Severity Score, 1974**

*(Percent Change in Sentence Severity Score (Index A) Associated with a Given Category of
Prior Record)*

	Multnomah County		Dade County	
Prior Record	Robbery I	Burglary I	Robbery	B&E Offenses
Minor	NS	+19	NS	+30
Major	+54	NS	NS	+65
Prison	+45	+59	NS	+65

aNot significant (NS). See note to Table 5-23 for definition of significance.

should not exceed 60 days and performance in Dade Circuit Court to the court-imposed rule that this period should not exceed 180 days, Table 6-20 indicates that in 1974 Dade met its standard in a greater proportion of cases than Multnomah met its standard.

Continuances are both a cause and a result of delays in felony proceedings. Table 6-21 discloses gross differences in continuance practices between the two jurisdictions. Whether a case is contested (i.e., involves a trial) or uncontested, the frequency of continuance in Multnomah proceedings is sharply less than in Dade, and the average length of Multnomah continuances is much shorter than those of Dade. To the extent that the movant for a continuance could be identified in our case samples, it was the defense alone and the prosecution alone in a greater proportion of cases in Multnomah than in Dade.

Table 6-22 presents a comparison of the results of our effort to identify the magnitude and direction of the independent effect of various hypothesized factors on the duration of proceedings. We observe that there is more consistency than not in the pattern of effects shown for the two jurisdictions. The change in elapsed time associated with a change in pretrial custody status is remarkably similar between Multnomah and Dade. In Multnomah having private attorney representation tended to introduce more delay in felony cases in general but less delay in robbery cases; in Dade type of counsel had no effect on delay. The direction of effects associated with the type of disposition is generally consistent between the two jurisdictions, but the magnitude of the effects is usually greater in Multnomah. We have no explanation for the disparity between the two court systems concerning the change in average elapsed time when robbery conviction was by bargained plea rather than by straight plea— +110 percent in Multnomah versus −42 percent in Dade. And it is noteworthy that the hypothesized factors explained considerably more of the variability (i.e., variance) of elapsed time in Dade than in Multnomah.

Utilization of Victims, Other Witnesses, and Jurors

As explained in Chapter 5 and Appendix B, we were largely unable to obtain the data sought on lay participants directly from court records in either jurisdiction. As an expedient, we used the responses to our mail surveys of lay participants in the two counties as the primary data source. Our comparison of Multnomah and Dade in their use of lay participants reflects the self-recalled experiences of the surveyed participants.

Table 6-23 applies to the use of victims and other witnesses. The assessment of the participants as to their own cooperativeness seems reasonably alike in the two locales. We observe that the average number of appearances made by a witness other than a victim is twice as large in Dade as in Multnomah. Given the nature of the continuance practices in Dade, as shown above, this difference is

Table 6-20
Comparison of Measures of Elapsed Time in Felony Proceedings, 1974[a]

Type of Disposition	Multnomah County				Dade County			
	All Felonies	Robbery I	Dwelling Burglary I	Non-dwelling Burglary I	All Felonies	Robbery	Dwelling B&E	Non-dwelling B&E
Median number of days from arrest to:								
Dismissal	41	26	47	71	88	119	116	118
Guilty plea	51	54	51	82	109	123	76	95
Trial	84	81	93	118	131	119	109	72
Final disposition	77	86	97	97	109	124	90	103
Minimum number of days in longest 10 percent of cases from arrest to:								
Dismissal	154	—	—	—	214	—	—	—
Guilty plea	93	—	—	—	299	—	—	—
Trial	149	—	—	—	246	—	—	—
Final disposition	151	—	—	—	270	—	—	—
Percent of cases exceeding 60 days (Multnomah) or 180 days (Dade) from arrest to:								
Dismissal	38	38	—	55	12	23	0	50
Guilty plea	44	34	44	63	17	23	3	17
Trial	100	69	83	—	8	33	0	0
All cases[b]	46	42	46	61	15	23	2	18

Median number of days from arraignment to:							
Dismissal	46	—	—	84	58	100	89	171
Guilty plea	29	21	31	21	67	91	47	57
Trial	49	52	79	72	106	103	91	45
Final disposition	63	64	68	61	83	99	62	74
Minimum number of days in longest 10 percent of cases from arraignment to:							
Dismissal	110	—	—	—	187	—	—	—
Guilty plea	82	—	—	—	237	—	—	—
Trial	92	—	—	—	198	—	—	—
Final disposition	130	—	—	—	205	—	—	—
Median number of days from conviction to sentencing	34	35	33	31	4	4	4	1

[a]Some entries are omitted because of the smallness of sample.

[b]Time between conviction and sentencing excluded.

Table 6-21
Comparison of Measures of Continuance Practices, 1974

Continuance Measure	Multnomah County	Dade County
For uncontested cases:		
Number of cases continued ÷ number of cases	31%	67%
Number of continuances ÷ number of cases (number of continuances per case)	0.59	2.3
Number of days continued ÷ number of continuances (number of days per continuance)	16	42
Number of days continued ÷ number of cases (number of days continued per case)	9	97
Number of cases (N)	80	86
Percent of the number of continuances attributed to:		
defense	49%	9%
prosecution	15%	7%
court and other[a]	36%	84%
For contested cases:		
Number of cases continued ÷ number of cases	60%	92%
Number of continuances ÷ number of cases	1.4	4.3
Number of days continued ÷ number of continuances	9	42
Number of days continued ÷ number of cases	13	149
Number of cases (N)	15	12
Percent of the number of continuances attributed to:		
defense	29%	12%
prosecution	19%	5%
court and other[a]	52%	83%

[a]Attributed to the court alone, defense and prosecution jointly, and unidentified attribution.

expected. In consequence, the average number of appearances of other witnesses per disposition is also much larger in Dade. It is not clear why victim appearances fail to follow this pattern. There is fairly good agreement shown in Table 6-23 for the distribution of appearance duration and its average, given the crude data.

Table 6-24, which applies to the use of jurors, reflects a surprising degree of agreement between the two jurisdictions, given the significant differences between the court systems and the crude data. It is noteworthy that in both jurisdictions, jurors spend nearly half their time waiting to perform their duties.

Table 6-22

Comparison of the Independent Effect of Hypothesized Influences on Average Elapsed Time from Arraignment to Final Disposition, 1974

(Percent Change in Average Elapsed Time Associated with a Change in a Given Factor, Measured Against Reference Condition)

Influence on Elapsed Time	Multnomah County		Dade County	
	All Felonies	Robbery I	All Felonies	Robbery
Pretrial custody status[a]				
In jail	NS[b]	+44	NS	+39
Freed on bail or OR	NS	+88	NS	+39
Defended by private attorney[c]	+48	−37	NS	NS
Type of disposition[d]				
Dismissal	−93	−66	−18	−30
Conviction by bargained plea	−68	+110	−33	−42
Conviction by trial	+51	+98	+54	+32
Proxy for court calendar crowding	+5	+98	+54	+32
Percent of variance explained by above factors	18	33	37	52

[a]Measured against mixed pretrial custody status.
[b]See Table 5-26 for notes on the definition of statistical significance.
[c]Measured against representation by the public defender.
[d]Measured against conviction by straight plea.

Summarizing the Comparisons

Multnomah and Dade Counties and their respective Circuit Courts differ in many essential respects. This is the thrust of the descriptive information we have presented in Appendix A, in this chapter, and at various other points in this book. It is clear that the comparison of these two jurisdictions ought not to be approached as if one were assessing a competition between two similar entities operating in like environments and seeking to achieve well-defined, common goals. When we observe differences in the results of applying the same performance measures to the two jurisdictions, our interpretation of these differences must necessarily be cautious, for the differences may reflect disparities in the nature of the two systems and not their relative effectiveness.

The comparisons that have been made in this section were based largely on data obtained from the 1974 exemplary-offenses case samples—that is, from four

Table 6-23

Comparison of Measures of the Use of Victims and Other Witnesses

Type of Response from Lay Participants	Multnomah County		Dade County	
	Victim	Other Witness[a]	Victim	Other Witness[a]
Cooperativeness (%)				
Cooperative	89	93	90	88
Uncooperative	6	3	6	10
Not asked for cooperation	5	4	4	2
Number of responses (N)	(105)	(89)	(101)	(100)
Average number of appearances per victim or other witness (per disposition)	2.5	1.9	2.2	4.0
Average number of victim or other witness appearances per disposition (estimated)	2.5[b]	2.9[c]	2.2[d]	5.6[e]
Length of appearance of victim or other witness (%)				
Less than one hour	24	14	10	6
Two-three hours	50	48	45	44
Three hours (half-day)	21	34	43	41
Six hours (full-day)	5	4	2	9
Number of responses (N)	(93)	(85)	(88)	(79)
Average time per appearance (hr)	1.8	1.9	2.1	2.5

Source: Responses of victims and other witnesses to Rand mail surveys except for number of witnesses appearing per trial.

[a]Nearly all witnesses surveyed were called by the prosecution.

[b]Calculated as the product of one victim per disposition and 2.5 victim appearances per disposition.

[c]Calculated as the product of 1.5 other witnesses per disposition (estimated from case records) and 1.9 appearances per other witness.

[d]Calculated as the product of one victim per disposition and 2.2 victim appearances per disposition.

[e]Calculated as the product of 1.4 other witnesses per disposition (estimated from case records) and 4.0 appearances per other witness.

samples each roughly numbering 100 cases that involve the two exemplary offenses in the two jurisdictions respectively. In summary, drawing upon the analyses described in Chapter 5 and Appendix C, we observed the following.

The Statistical Overview

1. Felony case input is several times as large in Dade as in Multnomah, and the case backlog problem in Dade is correspondingly more severe. Annual felony

Table 6-24

Comparison of Measures of the Use of Jurors Time

(Percent of Jurors Responding, Except for "Average" Columns)

	Percent of Time Spent											
	Multnomah County						Dade County					
Activity	None	Less Than 25%	25%-49%	50%-74%	75%-100%	Average	None	Less Than 25%	25%-49%	50%-74%	75%-100%	Average
Waiting in jury room or elsewhere												
(N = 163)[a]	0	29	37	26	8	41						
(N = 160)[b]							1	23	31	26	19	47
Criminal jury selection												
(N = 159)	0	70	24	3	3	22						
(N = 161)							3	60	27	5	4	25
In criminal trial												
(N = 173)	6	46	31	12	5	28						
(N = 154)							9	29	30	20	12	38

[a]Upper N is number of responses in Multnomah County.
[b]Lower N is number of responses in Dade County.

caseload per prosecutor assigned to felonies in Dade is more than twice that of Multnomah; the comparable caseload ratio for public defenders is slightly higher in Dade than in Multnomah. (This gross type of comparison cannot be made for judges, since we were unable to allocate the time for Multnomah trial judges accurately between civil and criminal matters.)

2. There were significant differences in the distribution of felony cases by offense type between the two counties, but the incidence of the exemplary offenses was fairly similar (in 1974).

3. Among the characteristics of felony defendants examined, the most significant differences between Dade and Multnomah Counties were the higher proportion of ethnic minorities, the lower educational level, and the higher proportion represented by the public defender among the Dade defendants in the cases sampled.

Case Screening

1. The operation of the charging threshold in the two court systems gave rise to a mixed comparison for the 1974 exemplary-offenses bookings. On the one hand, comparing burglary I cases in Multnomah (some of which were Impact offense cases and some not) and breaking and entering cases in Dade, we found the gross screening output to be similar. On the other hand, the screening results of robbery bookings were significantly different between the two jurisdictions, with the rejection rate being markedly higher in Multnomah.

2. Since charging accuracy could not be fully assessed by means of dispositional measures (see discussion in Chapter 5), we were able to gain only fragmentary impressions of this aspect of case screening. Cases involving Impact offenses (robbery I and dwelling burglary I) seemed to be more accurately charged in Multnomah than were cases involving similar offenses in Dade. At the same time, we found indications that this would not be the general finding for other types of cases.

Plea Bargaining

1. Only limited comparisons of plea bargaining performance were possible, primarily because sentence agreements are the predominant type of bargain in Dade and no written record of such agreements was contained in the case files. In particular, it was not possible to make adequate comparisons of the sentence severity concessions embodied in the plea agreements of the two jurisdictions.

2. A high rate of straight pleas (i.e., to all charges and counts as originally filed, but possibly with tacit sentence agreements) characterized both counties in the cases involving the Impact offenses in Multnomah and the comparable

offenses in Dade. But for cases in which the other offense type (nondwelling burglary or breaking and entering) analyzed in this study was charged, there was a significant difference between the two counties—Multnomah engaged in charge and count bargains far more frequently.

Sentence Variation

1. The pattern of sentencing for robbery convictions was similar in the two jurisdictions—conviction usually being at the highest level, and a substantial prison term then being imposed. On the average, the sentence severity score was moderately higher in Multnomah for robbery convictions.

2. By contrast, the pattern of sentencing differed between the counties for convictions on burglary I or breaking and entering charges. In Multnomah convictions were predominantly at the highest level (felony A), and prison terms were imposed in roughly one-half of the sampled cases. In Dade convictions were mostly at the second most serious level (2d degree felony), and roughly one-third of the defendants were given prison terms. Again the average sentence severity score turned out to be higher in Multnomah.

3. Little of the sentence variation in exemplary-offenses cases in either jurisdiction was accounted for by the set of illegitimate factors we hypothesized. But the legitimate factors of the nature of the defendant's criminal conduct and his prior record did account for most of the sentence variation that we could explain statistically.

Evenhandedness

1. To distinguish the evenhandedness of dispositions between Multnomah and Dade Counties, we attempted to relate the nature of a defendant's disposition to his pretrial custody status, type of defense counsel, and ethnic group, but we found no clear distinctions on this basis (except that the defendant appeared to gain a small advantage in being represented by the public defender in Multnomah but not in Dade).

2. Sentence severity scores also manifested no consistent patterns that enabled us to distinguish between the two jurisdictions. But there was evidence of a lack of evenhandedness in specific circumstances in both court systems—more severe sentences for breaking and entering convictions in Dade were associated with minority status, retained counsel, and pretrial jail confinement; pretrial custody status was correlated with the severity of robbery sentences in Multnomah.

The Role of Prior Record

1. Judged by comparison of dispositional measures, prior criminal record did not turn out to be a governing factor in the dispositions of the 1974 exemplary-offenses cases either in Multnomah or Dade.

2. Prior criminal record appeared to affect sentence severity scores consistently in both robbery I and burglary I cases in Multnomah and in breaking and entering cases in Dade, but it did not significantly affect these scores in Dade robbery cases. We cannot explain the latter difference, and therefore we cannot infer that it reflects an essential distinction between the two counties.

Delay

1. The clearest distinction between the two jurisdictions appeared to be in the duration of felony proceedings. Much less time generally elapsed between stages of the proceedings in the Multnomah court system.

2. However, a smaller proportion of cases in Dade exceeded the court-imposed 180-day standard for the maximum time between arrest and trial than exceeded the statutory 90-day standard for this maximum time in Multnomah. (This was also true for the periods from arrest to dismissal, to guilty plea, or to final disposition.)

3. Statistical performance measures attested to the marked difference in continuance practices between the two jurisdictions (e.g., the average number of continuance days per case was over 10 times greater in Dade than in Multnomah.

4. There was no significant difference between Multnomah and Dade in the pattern of effects on case processing time attributable to the factors we hypothesized as being influential. However, these factors accounted for substantially more of the variation in case processing time in Dade than they did in Multnomah.

Use of Victims, Other Witnesses, and Jurors

1. The average number of appearances per witness, the average number of appearances by all witnesses per disposition, and the average time per witness appearance all tended to be higher in Dade—most likely a by-product of the differences observed in the length of proceedings and in the continuance practices in the two counties. On the average, victims devoted about 4.5 hours of their time per disposition in both jurisdictions, but other witnesses spent about 14 hours per disposition in Dade compared with 5.5 hours in Multnomah.

2. The pattern of juror activities appeared not to differ materially between the two counties. Jurors were idle somewhat less than half of their tour of duty in both systems.

Overall Performance

1. We find it infeasible to compare overall performance between the two court systems for a variety of reasons. Even if it were possible to devise an acceptable composite performance measure that would reflect the importance of one activity (say, screening) relative to another (say, case processing delay), we would be defeated here by the inadequacy of the data available in Dade.

2. We do have a "collective" impression of the relative performance in the several issue areas. In some—e.g., sentence variation, or evenhandedness in disposition and sentencing—the two jurisdictions performed similarly. In others—e.g., charging accuracy, or case processing delay—one jurisdiction seemed to do better than the other. In still others—e.g., applying the charging threshold, or the plea bargaining balance—our data do not suffice for a judgment.

7

The Role of Criminal Case Auditing in Performance Measurement

Background

Case Auditing Characterized

In the context of this performance measures study, the term *case auditing* designates a procedure in which an experienced criminal justice practitioner or a team of such individuals closely examines the records of a selected sample of cases that have entered the court system being analyzed and have undergone (or are undergoing) disposition. The auditors may be internal personnel—i.e., participants in the regular operations of the system, with or without substantial management or policymaking responsibilities, or they may be external and more or less independent in their relationship to the system. How the sample of cases should be chosen for auditing would properly depend upon the purposes of this review. For example, the appropriate sampling might be fully random over a period of system activities, or be random within a stratified or clustered design, or even be confined to (and possibly exhaust) a specified class of cases—for example, those with multiple defendants, filed within a stated period, and not reaching trial within 270 days from date of initial arrest.

Whatever the designated purposes of the audit, those conducting it would seek:

1. To assemble the full documentation on the selected cases.
2. To assess the state of the evidence at various points during the proceedings.
3. To discern departures from normally prevailing policies of the agencies involved.
4. To comprehend the reasons why events occurred as they did.

For completeness, case auditing might include interviews with some of the participants in the selected cases, not only with some of the practitioners but also possibly with some of the lay persons who were involved. Indeed, where the auditors are external to the system and are likely to lack first-hand knowledge of local rules and policy, they may be compelled to interview senior system officials to obtain a proper foundation for their work. Normally, materials pertaining to each of the selected cases would be drawn from various case files, including those of the police, the prosecutor's office, the court, the public defender's office, the probation authorities, etc. While the coverage of these

169

several sources tends to overlap on some aspects of a case, the appearance of disparities among them on the same item could be especially revealing to an auditor.

Case auditing might be conducted at regular intervals, say, quarterly or semiannually, serving to continually monitor the operations of the court system or a component agency; for this purpose it may stand alone (especially if the system is a small one) or be an adjunct to other management information devices. Alternatively, case auditing could be an occasional activity within the jurisdiction, to illuminate the causes of and remedies for operational problems.

Case Auditing Related to Statistical Performance Measures

We are interested in the case-auditing approach for at least three reasons:

1. As a performance assessment system in itself. Some court systems, particularly the smaller ones, may want to install case-audit procedures as an alternative to statistical performance measures for evaluating operations and programs.
2. As substantiation to the statistical approach. Case auditing can provide another perspective into the processes of a court system and thus be used as a check on the insights derived from statistical performance measures.
3. As a source of new hypotheses on how court systems work. By delving behind quantitative data, case auditing of even a relatively small sample of cases may reveal explanations not made apparent by statistical performance measures.

For this discussion, let us assume that a court system employs statistical performance measures. It may not possess a formal information system, but nevertheless it systematically collects some data on various aspects of its operation and uses them to provide quantitative indices of performance. These measures may be few in number and gross in texture—for example, a complaint rejection rate, a felony case filing rate, a plea of guilty rate, a trial rate, a trial conviction rate, an average time between arrest and trial, and possibly others. Or they may be numerous and richly detailed, as typified by a measure such as proportion of jury trials producing convictions, where the defendant was a black, represented by a public defender, and held in custody throughout the proceeding. But whatever the extent of the performance measures that the court system presently employs and the uses it makes of them, an appropriate question to raise is What value would case auditing have in this context? Answers to this question should reflect the essential distinction between the two information approaches. On the one hand, statistical performance measures purport to capture a relatively limited amount of information about each of a relatively large body of events; by enlarging the set of such measures, one gains completeness in describing system performance. By contrast, case auditing offers a deeply detailed view of how a relatively small sample of cases is processed by the system from entry to disposition and why events turned out as they did.

To begin with, one value of the case-auditing approach is that it goes behind numerical rates to uncover true causes of events. It can help establish the degree of confidence that may be placed on inferences from a set of performance measures about a population of cases that has been processed by the system. If the audit findings from a sample of cases are consistent with the statistical inferences concerning the parent population, then confidence in the latter would be enhanced. For example, suppose that one observed the following magnitudes in a given set of measures relative to an earlier period or perhaps by comparison with those in a closely similar jurisdiction:

Complaint rejection rate—lower.

Pretrial dismissal rate—higher.

Guilty plea rate with charges as originally filed—lower.

Trial rate with charges as originally filed—lower.

Trial conviction rate on charges as originally filed—lower.

Guilty plea rate with lesser charges—higher.

One inference that might be drawn from the magnitudes of these measures is that the prosecutor's office has increased its propensity to "over-charge." Confidence in this inference, as against alternative explanations, would be enhanced by a showing that cases were indeed being filed at levels of charge severity and multiplicity not sufficiently supported by the evidence available at the time of screening. Within the limitations of sample size, case auditing could provide such a showing, or alternatively help to discredit the inference.

Another way of expressing this potential value of case audits conducted as an adjunct to the use of statistical performance measures is to say that they are means of increasing the reliability of the entire performance information system. To this end, auditors should scrutinize the sample cases as if prompted by the question What significant details of performance are being concealed by the statistical nature of the calculated measures?

One shortcoming of statistical performance measures is that in some circumstances the inferences desired from them are ambiguous. To illustrate, consider the difficult problem of assessing the accuracy of prosecutorial charging—that is, on the basis of information available at the time of complaint screening, does the prosecutor file those charges for which the available admissible evidence will support a conviction? This question may be illuminated, if imperfectly, by collecting data and calculating performance measures to show what happens to defendants in terms of the original charges and the ultimate disposition. One asks: What is the bindover rate? What is the overall pretrial dismissal rate? At what rate are cases disposed of as a result of a plea to lesser charges? With what relative frequency are defendants tried on charges less severe than those originally filed? On the average, how large a reduction in sentence severity occurs when cases are disposed of by pleas of guilty to reduced charges? At what rate do trial convictions result on charges less serious than those originally filed? And so on. The more extensive the set of relevant measures, the less ambiguous could be inferences concerning prosecutorial charging accuracy. Yet, the outcome of each event in a criminal proceeding is a product of many factors, only one of which might be charging inaccuracy. Pretrial dismissals occur for various reasons other than inaccurate charging. Plea bargains reflect many considerations in addition to the possibility of inaccurate charging. In a practical sense, some degree of ambiguity is unavoidable in assessing the accuracy of prosecutorial charging by means of statistical performance measures alone. Case auditing affords a means of reducing the imprecision of such inferences; its impact will depend upon the scope and frequency of the auditing efforts.

Case auditing, in other words, can aid in locating the "missing variables" that help explain the outcome in question. And a major advantage of the auditing approach is that such illusive variables may come to light in the very process of close-range personal observation of the workings of the system.

Many events in a criminal proceeding are the outcome of the legitimate exercise of prosecutorial or judicial discretion. For example, ought prosecution be deferred in favor of diverting the defendant into a rehabilitation program? Do "the interests of justice" justify filing no charges against the suspect? How much expert assistance at public expense should be provided the indigent defendant in preparing his defense? Should sentencing be suspended in favor of unsupervised probation? Inevitably, questions are raised about possible abuses of discretion. Sometimes these issues are properly presented to higher courts in the course of appeals. Often they are not and cannot be so reviewed, as in the instance of prosecutorial discretion to reject a complaint. Statistical performance measures may serve to give a gross indication of the presence of abuse when they attest to an anomalously high frequency of a particular action, but case audits (combined with appropriate interviews) would then be necessary to expose the problem more fully.

Our concluding comment on the value of case auditing in relation to the use of statistical performance measures touches upon what may have the richest potential of all. Case audits, even of modest dimensions, can reveal overlooked ways of interpreting the calculated magnitudes of performance measures. That is, case audits can produce insights about criminal proceedings that escape an unimaginative consideration of statistical performance measures.[1] And case audits may suggest new hypotheses about what's going on in the court system to be tested, by, among other ways, inspecting the past and current magnitudes of the statistical measures.

Practitioner Viewpoints on the Role of Case Auditing

As one phase of our study of statistical performance measures, we conducted a set of interviews aimed at eliciting the views and attitudes of criminal justice practitioners (judges, court administrators, defense counsel, prosecutors, and academicians) toward the value and use of performance measures.[2] Thirty-three professionals were queried in the course of 26 interviews, which ranged from an hour and a half to a full day. The interviews were conducted in more than a dozen jurisdictions located in major metropolitan areas throughout the country. Case auditing was one of many topics on which these practitioners expressed their opinions.

Current professional views about the relative roles of case auditing and statistical performance measures seemed strongly divided. Some of our interviewees felt that reliable monitoring of the performance of a court system required case auditing. To them, this role was dominant. Others were not so extreme, but if compelled to a choice between case auditing and statistical performance measures, they would tend to opt for the former as their information source. Still others put a relatively higher value on statistical measures, but chiefly as a means of internal management control. Others advocated a broader role for statistical measures—the assessment of progress toward the external goals of the court system and the comparison of one jurisdiction's system with that of another. Generally, they expressed no opposition to case audits per se; rather, the divergence of views related to how much and how regularly case auditing should be performed, given its costliness and the alternatives available in other information sources.

Case Auditing in This Study

Scope and Design

Prompted by our appreciation of the relevance of case audits to the use of performance measures, as discussed above, and by the comments made in the

---

[1] For example, as discussed in Chapter 5, an experiment to limit the use of plea bargaining in one of our pilot demonstrations resulted in a much higher rate of conviction at original charge level; case auditing revealed that improved preparation of cases by the local police was, along with increased prosecutorial size, contributing to the desired outcome.

[2] This survey is described in Chapter 3.

174

interviews, we included a modest case-auditing effort in the demonstration phase of this study. Case audits were conducted in the Circuit Court systems of both Multnomah County, Oregon, and Dade County, Florida. The auditing team was composed of two Rand consultants—one a highly experienced prosecutor and supervisor from the Office of the District Attorney, Los Angeles County (the largest and generally regarded as one of the most professional in the country) and the other a professor of criminal law and a state-certified specialist in the field, who had substantial experience as both a criminal defense counsel and a federal prosecutor.

The scope of this undertaking was dictated mainly by the resource limitations on our study. Its design derived from our specific interests, as described below, and from the constraints on scope.

The auditing team was able to devote three to four working days in each of the two demonstration jurisdictions. Given this limitation, it was estimated that the appropriate sample size at each location would be roughly 20 to 25 cases.[3]

The samples, as finally selected, comprised 20 cases in Multnomah County and 23 cases in Dade County, drawn (subject to a sampling guide described below) from the much larger collection of cases subjected to statistical analysis during the demonstration phase of our study. However, the case auditing effort was conducted and assessed before preliminary notions as to what the statistical analysis would show were available. In a real sense, therefore, this limited case-audit effort can be viewed as an independent check of some of the inferences that we subsequently drew from our central statistical approach to measuring performance.

Our case-auditing effort focused primarily on plea bargaining. The small samples necessarily limited the potential of the audits to illuminate prosecutorial screening and sentencing variations. The audits proved even less useful for examining evenhandedness and case processing efficiency, the other selected issue areas. In Multnomah County we sought to assess the effects of an important no-plea-bargaining experiment involving three types of offenses (namely, dwelling burglaries, armed robberies, and receiving stolen property), under Portland's High Impact Anti-Crime Program, supported by LEAA funding. We were prompted to tailor the Multnomah case-audit sample to reflect this special interest (which extended to our statistical performance analysis as well). To select our samples we used the following guides:

1. Only cases whose disposition was by pretrial pleas of guilty would be chosen.
2. Approximately one-half the cases would be sampled from a period of months preceding the initiation of the District Attorney's no-plea-bargaining experiment; one-half the cases, from a period following its initiation. The

[3] It should be noted that the sample sizes used to calculate statistical performance measures averaged over 600 cases in each jurisdiction.

effect of defendants' characteristics would be controlled by matching (insofar as possible) each sampled case in the first period with one in the second period, the matching being in terms of the age and prior record of the defendants, the two most accessible items of personal information.

3. Approximately one-half the cases from each time period would be chosen to contain at least one count of dwelling burglary I as the most serious charged offense, this being one of the Impact crime types subjected to the no-plea-bargaining experiment; for purposes of comparison (i.e., as a control), one-half would be cases of nondwelling burglary I, which were not Impact offenses and were therefore processed differently.

The planned Multnomah County case-audit sample is displayed in Table 7-1.

The Dade County case-audit sample was in large measure shaped by the earlier Multnomah design, because we wanted to enhance interjurisdictional consistency and thus make comparison easier. Again, the sample was divided between two periods of time, namely, before and after the initiation of a master calendar experiment in the Circuit Court. This basis for a division in time was convenient and definite, but otherwise had little significance to the case-auditing activity, which involved too few cases to shed light on the calendaring experiment. Once again we concentrated on burglary offenses, notwithstanding differences between Oregon and Florida statutes in the definitions of these offenses and their penalties. Matching of the defendant's age and prior record in paired cases from the two time periods was also attempted here. Table 7-2 shows the planned Dade County case-audit sample.

Findings from the Multnomah County Case Audit

Data drawn from the files of the 20 cases audited by the Rand team in Multnomah County are summarized in Table 7-3. Observations and inferences made by the auditors are given below, broadly grouped by issue area. It is to be remembered, however, that the primary focus of this auditing activity was on plea bargaining, with the sample designed accordingly.

Prosecutorial Screening

Nondwelling Burglaries. The sample contained nine nondwelling burglary cases, four from the first (1973) period and five from the second (1974). All these cases were strong, with the suspect being apprehended at the scene, generally as the result of a police response to a silent alarm. Furthermore, legally admissible confessions were obtained from five of the nine defendants. There appeared to be a form of over-charging in the screening of nondwelling burglaries in both

Table 7-1

Planned Case-Audit Sample for Multnomah County, Oregon

(Burglaries[a] with Dispositions Only by Plea of Guilty)

Case No.	Dwelling	Period[b]	Defendant's Age	Defendant's Prior Record[c]
1	Yes	1	20-24	None
2	Yes	1	24+	Prison
3	Yes	1	24+	Minor
4	Yes	1	24+	Major
5	Yes	1	24+	Major
6	Yes	1	20−	None
7[d]	Yes	2	20−	None
8[d]	Yes	2	20-24	Minor
9[d]	Yes	2	20-24	Major
10[d]	Yes	2	24+	Major
11	Yes	2	20−	None
12	No	1	24+	Prison
13	No	2	20-24	None
14	No	1	20-24	None
15	No	1	24+	Major
16	No	2	24+	Prison
17	No	2	20−	None
18	No	2	20-24	None
19	No	2	24+	Prison
20	No	1	24+	Prison

[a]Entering and remaining unlawfully in a dwelling with intent to commit a crime in the dwelling is burglary in the first degree, a class A felony; if the building involved is not a dwelling and the perpetrator is not armed either with a burglar's tool or a deadly weapon and does not cause or attempt to cause physical injury, the offense is burglary in the second degree, a class C felony (ORS 164.225).

[b]Period 1 comprises the first 11 months in 1973; period 2, the first 11 months in 1974.

[c]The four categories of prior record are defined in Chapter 4. Definitions are based on the work of the California Bureau of Criminal Statistics.

[d]Impact cases.

time periods, that is, they were routinely charged as burglary I whenever any type of implement was used that could be characterized as a "burglary tool," even if it was only a screwdriver. Five of these nine cases originally charged as burglary I were disposed of by a plea to a reduced charge. In only two cases were multiple charges filed originally; in both, conviction was on a single charge. The

Table 7-2

Planned Case-Audit Sample for Dade County, Florida

(Burglaries[a] with Dispositions Only by Plea of Guilty)

Case No.	Dwelling	Period[b]	Defendant's Age	Defendant's Prior Record[c]
1	Yes	1	20–	None
2	Yes	1	20–	Major
3	Yes	1	20-24	None
4	Yes	1	20–	Prison
5	Yes	1	24+	Major
6	Yes	2	20–	None
7	Yes	2	20–	Major
8	Yes	2	20-24	Minor
9	Yes	2	20-24	Prison
10	Yes	2	20-24	Major
11	Yes	1	20-24	Minor
12	Yes	1	24+	Prison
13	No[d]	2	20–	None
14	No[d]	1	20–	None
15	No[d]	2	20-24	None
16	No[d]	1	24+	Prison
17	No[e]	2	24+	Major
18	No[d]	2	20–	None
19	No[e]	2	24+	Prison
20	No[d]	2	20-24	None
21	No[d]	2	20-24	Prison
22	No[d]	1	20-24	Prison
23	No[d]	2	20–	None

[a]Breaking and entering a dwelling house, when armed with a dangerous weapon or if an occupant is assaulted, is a felony of the first degree; without such arming or assault, it is a second-degree felony (SS 810.01).

[b]Period 1 spans 6 months from December 1973 through May 1974; period 2, 6 months from December 1974 through May 1975.

[c]The four categories of prior record are defined in Chapter 4. Definitions are based on the work of the California Bureau of Criminal Statistics.

[d]Refers to the offense defined in SS 810.02, breaking and entering a building other than a dwelling (or a ship or vessel) with intent to commit a felony—a burglary offense that is a second-degree felony.

[e]Refers to SS 810.05, breaking and entering any building (or ship, vessel, aircraft, or railroad car) with intent to commit a misdemeanor—a third-degree felony.

Table 7-3
Multnomah County Case-Audit Information

Case No.	Age	Prior Record	Custody Status	Type of Counsel[a]	Days (Arrest to Sentence)	Original Charge[b]	Convicted Charge	Sentence	Sentencing Judge	Caught at Scene	Admission	Affirmative Defense	Physical Evidence	Weapon	Theft	Victim Present	Mode of Entry	Number of Co-Defendants	PSR[c]
		Defendant's Background								*Strength of Case*				*Severity of Offense*					
1st Period, Dwelling																			
1	20	No	OR	PD	33	B-I	Theft-I	2-yr-prb $500 fine	1	Yes	No	No	Poss prpty	No	Yes, stereo	No	?	0	No
2	25	Prison	Jail	PD	113	B-I Theft-I	Theft-I	1-yr jail 5-yr prb	1	No 1 EW[d]	No (Denial)	No	Poss prpty	No	Yes, TV	No	?	0	Yes
3	26	Minor	OR	DR	170	B-I	B-II	18-mo prb $85 fine	2	Yes	Yes	No	Poss prpty	No	Yes, food	No	?	2	No
4	29	Major	Jail	PD	149	B-I CAID Hars	B-I	5-yr prb	1	Yes	Yes	No	Poss prpty	No	Yes, purse, clothes	Yes	?	0	Yes
5	32	Major	Jail	PD	56	B-I	B-I	5-yr prb $200 fine	3	No	No	No	Poss prpty	No	Yes, TV	No	?	0	Yes
6	19	No	OR	PD	23	B-I Theft-I	Attempted B-II	18-mo prb $250 fine	2	No	Yes	No	Poss prpty	No	Yes, TV	?	Forced	1	No
2d Period, Dwelling (Impact Offenses)																			
7	18	No	OR	PD	205	B-I Escape	B-I	5-yr prb 1-yr jail	4	No	Yes	No	No	No	Yes, rifles	No	Window	1	Yes
8	23	Minor	OR	CA	137	B-I	B-I	10-yr prison	5	Yes EWs	No	No	Poss prpty	No	Yes, $4, purse	No	Back door	0	Yes
9	24	Major	Jail	CA	89	B-I	B-I	1-yr jail 5-yr prb $216 fine	4	No	No	No	Fpe[e] & poss prpty	No	Yes, checks, stereo	No	?	0	Yes
10	34	Major	Jail	CA	107	B-I B-II	B-I	5-yr prb	3	No	No (Denial)	No	Poss prpty	No	Yes	No	?	0	Yes
11	18	No	OR	PD	96	B-I	B-I	5-yr prb 1-yr jail	3	Yes	?	No	No	No	Yes, liquor	Yes	Back door	0	Yes
1st Period, Nondwelling																			
12	32	Prison	Jail	PD	34	B-I	B-II	3-yr prison	6	Yes	Yes	No	No	Knife	No	No	Roof	0	No

Case																			
13	21	No	OR	CA	58	B-I	B-II	3-yr prb	2	Yes	?	No	Tool	No	No	No	Door	1	No
14	21	No	OR	PD	71	B-I Mschf	Crim. Mschf-II	3-yr prb	4	Yes	No	Yes	No	No	No	No	Forced	0	No
15	33	Major	Jail	PD	87	B-I	B-I	10-yr prison	3	Yes	Yes	No	No	No	Yes, money	No	Picked lock	0	Yes
2d Period, Nondwelling																			
16	60	Prison	Jail	PD	97	B-I	B-II	3-yr prb	7	Yes	No	No	Prpty tools	No	Attempt-ed	No	Forced	0	No
17	19	No	OR	CA	74	B-I	B-II	3-yr prb $100 fine	8	Yes	Yes	No	No	Gun in car	Yes, TV	No	Back door	2	Yes
18	21	No	OR	PD	165	B-I	Attempt-ed B-I	5-yr prb $505 fine	8	Yes	Yes	No	FP	No	Yes, food	No	Roof hole	4	Yes
19	28	Prison	Jail OR	PD	175 (350)	B-I	B-I	5-yr prb	3	Yes	No	No	Master key	No	Yes, drugs	No	Key	1	Yes
20	35	Prison	Jail	PD	147	B-I Ex-convict w/gun	B-I	15-yr prison	4	Yes	Yes	No	Tools	Gun	Attempt-ed, money	No	Window	0	Yes

[a] PD = public defender; DR = defendant-retained private attorney; CA = court-appointed private attorney.

[b] CAID = criminal activity in drugs; Hars = harassment (Class B misdemeanor); Mschf = criminal mischief (Class A misdemeanor if in the 2d degree); B = Burglary

[c] PSR = pre-sentence report.

[d] EW = eye witness.

[e] FP = fingerprints.

Case Notes:

Case 5: Federal charges pending (defendant received 5-yr commitment to federal program); defendant has drug problem.

Case 7: Escape was from juvenile facility; defendant has extensive juvenile record; implicated by co-defendant.

Case 8: DA agreed to take no position on sentence.

Case 9: Defendant has drug problem.

Case 10: B-1 charge based on residence, B-2 on dentist's office; defendant has 15-yr drug problem.

Case 11: DA agreed to take no position on sentence; probation suspended after 3 mo with 3-yr sentence then imposed.

Case 12: Escapee at time of offense.

Case 13: School building burglarized.

Case 14: Entered office of rubber co. for alleged purpose of using phone; DA agreed not to oppose probation.

Case 15: Had served five years in San Quentin.

Case 17: Burglarized golf-course clubhouse.

Case 18: Arrested while on O.R.; stolen shotgun in car; theft charge dismissed (bargain).

Case 19: Skipped after arrest; failure-to-appear charge dismissed (bargain); drug problem; accomplice sentenced to 7 yrs after trial.

Case 20: Two additional burglary charges dismissed.

screening of these cases was performed by the specialized Intake Unit of the District Attorney's office, located separately in a police facility. The unit's filing policy was not standardized but wàs purported to be "somewhere between a *prima facie* case and beyond a reasonable doubt."

Dwelling Burglaries. Taken as a whole, the eleven dwelling burglary cases in the audit sample—six in the first period prior to the initiation of the no-plea-bargaining experiment and the formation of the Impact Unit in the District Attorney's office, and five subsequent cases—appeared to be strong. Two cases from each period involved arrests at the scene, with admissions coming from the two such 1973 cases. Case strength derived generally (nine of eleven cases) from the existence of physical evidence, usually stolen property found in the defendant's possession, coupled with his being linked to the scene by eyewitnesses or prior acquaintance with the victim. But in only one case was a positive fingerprint identification made. Taken separately for the two periods, the case audit revealed no significant difference in the strength of the residential burglary cases for the two periods.

All eleven cases were charged as burglary I offenses. Four of the six 1973 cases were disposed of on reduced charges. The five 1974 cases, consonant with Impact policy, were disposed of by a plea to the original charge of burglary I.

The sample presented no indication of an increase in the use of multiple charges in the second period. In three of the six 1973 cases, charges in addition to burglary I were included. In two of the 1974 (Impact) cases, additional charges were filed, but these arose from separate incidents.

Impact cases are filed by the Impact unit, with the filing deputy retaining responsibility for the prosecution of the case. Filing standards for these cases appear to be both tougher and more explicit than for cases that enter by way of the Intake Unit. The audit as a whole, but not the particular cases audited, revealed no evidence that residential burglaries, if weak, were charged as some offense other than burglary I to shunt them from the Impact Unit.

Plea Bargaining

We shall discuss in succession three types of plea bargains—namely, charge reduction, dismissal of unrelated charges, and sentence concessions—first for the nondwelling burglary cases in both periods and then for the dwelling burglary cases, both non-Impact and Impact.

Nondwelling Burglaries. In the nine nondwelling burglary cases audited from the 1973 and 1974 periods, only three defendants pled guilty to the original burglary I charge, which carries a 20-year maximum sentence, and all three had prior prison records. These results suggest that the District Attorney's bargaining posture was to employ charge reduction as a means of "giving a break" to some defendants, but not those with heavy prior records. In the six cases in which charges were reduced, the audit sample reveals no pattern that explains the depth of concession. The substantial reduction in one case clearly derived from its weakness; that is, given the defendant's affirmative defense wherein his claim of necessity was strongly corroborated, the misdemeanor charge of criminal mischief II was more accurate than burglary I, but the remaining cases present scant clues as to the determination of the pled charge.

In three of the nine nondwelling burglaries, the plea was accompanied by the dismissal of unrelated charges. Only one nondwelling burglary case among the nine could be said to reflect a sentencing concession.

Dwelling Burglaries—1973. Turning next to dwelling burglary cases from the first (1973) period before the no-negotiation experiment, we find that four of the six were disposed of by pleas to reduced charges, but no rationale for observed disparity was evidenced by the audit information. But the Impact cases from 1974 reflect an entirely different appearance. Consistent with the avowed policy of handling these dwelling burglaries, none of the five defendants charged with burglary I were offered reduced charges; all pled to the charge as originally filed.

The pattern observed above for nondwelling burglaries concerning concessions in unrelated cases does appear in two dwelling burglary cases drawn from the first period. The remaining 1973 dwelling burglary cases, all of which contained charge reductions, involved no dismissal of unrelated charges. Finally, none of the 1973 dwelling burglaries presented any indications of sentence concessions.

Dwelling Burglaries—1974. We have already noted that none of the five Impact cases (1974 residential burglaries) revealed charge reductions. However, two of these five pleas of guilty to an original burglary I charge were accompanied by dismissal of unrelated charges were accompanied by a specific agreement by the prosecutor to take no position on sentencing.

Interpretation. In brief, what did the Rand case-audit effort show about plea bargaining in Multnomah County for burglary offenses in the time periods addressed? To begin with, we observed that the different types of prosecutorial concessions tended to be mutually exclusive—either a charge reduction, a dismissal of unrelated charges, or a sentence concession might be given, but rarely two of them in the same case. For the non-Impact cases, the most common concession was a charge reduction, but we perceived no consistent policy governing the depth of reduction. While the policies for dealing with the Impact cases have eliminated charge reductions as plea inducements, such cases may often involve the other two types of concessions. And our background

182

interviews indiated that still another type of concession—namely, not to proceed with unrelated cases that have not yet been filed—was not uncommon, even in Impact cases.[4]

The case audit revealed other useful and interesting information. We observed, for example, that there was an effort to dispose of cases at the pretrial conference; this meeting provides the usual context for plea bargaining. The court took no part in the pretrial conference. Furthermore, there was little "judge shopping" in connection with pleas of guilty. In the face of a strong judicial policy against it, few defense attorneys risk court disapproval by the use of such tactics. There were a number of inducements for defendants to plead guilty. The District Attorney's office had a reputation of willingness to go to trial, despite the contrary indication of a low overall trial rate. If a case is tried and the defendant convicted, the prosecutor would not be constrained in making sentence recommendations. And at least some judges were thought to be more severe in sentencing convicted defendants who have insisted on going to trial.

Sentencing Variation

A sample of only 20 cases is, of itself, not a sound basis for inferences that observed sentencing disparities are or are not justified. Nonetheless, we discuss briefly what we observed in this area and comment on possible explanatory circumstances in the Multinomah context.

The 15 non-Impact cases, both dwelling and nondwelling burglaries drawn from both periods, reflect an appearance of leniency. Only four defendants were incarcerated; their common denominator was that all had previously served prison sentences, The one with the heaviest prior record drew a 15-year sentence. This factor seemed more influential than the gravity of the charge to which the defendant pled.

The other 11 defendants in the non-Impact cases were given straight probation, for periods ranging from 18 months to 5 years, with the length of the probationary period being roughly proportional to the defendant's prior record. Many of the sentences appeared unduly lenient to our auditors.

As a whole, the sentences meted out in the five Impact cases were much more severe than for the other group, with incarceration being imposed in four of the cases, even in two cases for 18-year-olds with no prior adult record. The one prison sentence imposed in an Impact case, a 10-year period of incarceration, seemed unusually harsh for the facts of the case.

One cannot attribute the greater severity of sentencing in the Impact cases to the fact that these defendants pled guilty to burglary I. Rather, it appears that the identification of these cases as "Impact" had some effect on the court's sentencing decisions. Other considerations are that a more extensive presentence

---

[4] We found no reference to this practice in the audited files.

report was prepared for Impact cases than for routine cases, that nearly half the non-Impact cases audited had no presentence report prepared, and that the prosecutors were said to have been more actively concerned about sentencing in the Impact cases, even though in two of the Impact cases the prosecutor expressly agreed to take no position on sentencing as part of the plea agreement. The limited information that the case audits revealed about how the defendant's pretrial custody status affected his treatment and disposition seemed consistent with the conventional wisdom; in this small sample we found on evidence that the type of defense counsel influenced case outcomes.

Findings from the Dade County Case Audit

Twenty-three cases whose disposition was by plea of guilty were audited in Dade County. Information pertaining to these cases is summarized in Table 7-4. Again, the comments and inferences by the two auditors are presented within the framework of the issues.

In Appendix A, we discussed the unusual nature of complaint screening in Dade County. Observation of these procedures led us to expect that the cases bound over to Circuit Court for felony prosecution would include many relatively weak ones. Yet the 23 audited burglary cases, both dwelling and nondwelling, were sufficiently strong and did not demonstrate inadequacy of screening. In nine of them (nearly 40 percent of the sample), positive fingerprint identifications linked the defendant to the scene of the burglary. Confessions were given in six cases, only two of which contained the fingerprint identifications. The defendant was caught at the scene in six of the twelve dwelling cases and in eight of the nondwelling cases. Only three cases of the sample had neither apprehension at the scene, nor a confession, nor a positive fingerprint identification. It appears, then, that this sample of audited cases—because it was designed primarily to illuminate plea bargaining—is poorly suited to reveal deficiencies in screening.

Some inconsistency of charging is shown by the nondwelling cases of the audited sample. Six of these eleven cases were filed as multiple-count cases. Yet the same evidentiary basis appeared, more or less, in most of the other nondwelling cases charged only as single-count burglaries. The dwelling burglaries, by contrast, presented a consistent pattern of charging. The cases that were filed with multiple counts almost invariably involved a charge of grand larceny, seemingly justified by the evidence. Absent such evidence, the case was filed as a single-count burglary.

In sum, the audited cases do not reflect significant prosecutorial screening effect. Ill-fitted as our particular sample may be to illuminate this issue area, the result is, nonetheless, consistent with the policy of the State Attorney's office (and with a longstanding tradition in Dade County) that the court have the primary responsibility to exercise the screening function.

Table 7-4
Dade County Case-Audit Information

	Defendant's Background					Days (Arrest to Sentence)	Original Charge	Conviction Charge	Sentence	Sentencing Judge	Strength of Case			Gun	Theft	Severity of Offense			
Case No.	Race	Age	Prior Record	Custody Status	Type of Counsel[a]						Caught at Scene	Admission	FP[b]			Victim Present	Mode of Entry	Number of Co-Defendants	PSR[c]
1st Period, Dwelling																			
1	B	17	No	OR	PD	86	B/E Dw[d] Gr Lrc	Same	5-yr prb	1	No	Yes	No	Yes	Yes, guns	No	Window	1	Yes
2	B	19	Major	Jail	PD	51	B/E Dw (4 cts) Gr Lrc (4 cts)	B/E Dw (1 ct)	12-yr prison	1	No	No	Yes	No	Yes, TV, $$, stereo	No	Window	0	No
3	B	21	No	OR	PD	113	B/E Dw	Trespass	24-days jail	2	Yes	No	Yes	No	No	No	Forced	0	No
4	B	19	Prison	OR	PD	215	B/E Dw Rcving	Same	10-yr prb	3	Yes	Yes	No	No	No	Yes	?	0	No
5	W	58	Major	Jail	PD	?	B/E Dw Gr Lrc	Same	1-yr jail	4	No	No	Yes	No	Yes, valuables	No	Door	0	No
11	PR	20	Minor	Bail	PD	93	B/E Dw	Same	5-yr prb	4	Yes	No	Yes	No	No	No	?	2	No
12	B	38	Prison	Jail	PD	43	B/E Dw	Same	2-yr prison	5	Yes	No	No	No	No	Yes	?	0	No
2d Period, Dwelling																			
6	B	16	No	Jail	PD	?	B/E Dw Att GL	Same	5-yr prison	5	Yes	No	No	No	Yes, TV	No	Back door	2	No
7	B	18	Major	Bail	PD	31	B/E Dw Obs Jus	Same	5-yr prison	6	Yes	No	No	No	No	No	Ladder	1	No
8	B	22	Minor	Jail	PD	91	B/E Dw Gr Lrc	Same	1-yr jail	7	No	No	No	No	Yes, TV	No	Window	1	No
9	PR	21	Prison	Jail	PD	?	B/E Dw Gr Lrc	Same	10-yr prison	7	No	No	Yes	Yes	Yes, guns, $	No	Back door	0	No
10	Cuban	21	Major	Bail	DR	95	B/E Dw	Same	3-yr prison	4	No	No	No	No	No	No	Back door	2	No
1st Period, Nondwelling																			
14	W	17	No	Bail	DR	?	B/E Bld Mal Dest	Same	3-yr prb	7	No	Yes	Yes	No	Yes	No	Window	1	No

Case	Race	Age	Prior	Release	Atty	No.	Charge	Conviction	Sentence					Property		Entry		
22	W	21	Prison	OR	DR	144	B/E Bld Gr Lrc	Same	3-yr prison	1	No	No	No	Yes, drugs	No	Window	0	No

2d Period, Nondwelling

Case	Race	Age	Prior	Release	Atty	No.	Charge	Conviction	Sentence					Property		Entry		
13	B	18	No	Jail	PD	186	B/E Bld	Same	2-yr prb	8	Yes	No	Yes	No	No	Window	1	No
15	B	22	No	OR	PD	92	B/E Bld Gr Lrc Mal Dest A & B	All but A & B	3-yr prb	5	Yes	No	No	Yes, $, food, cigs	No	Door	1	No (w/d)
17	W	59	Major	Jail	PD	67	B/E Bld	B/E w/ intent misdm.[d]	3-yr prison	9	Yes	No	No	No	No	Window	0	No
18	W	19	No	Jail	PD	79	B/E Bld Gr Lrc Bg Tools	Same	18-mo prb	10 (master cal.)	Yes	Yes	No	Yes, drugs	No	A/C vent	1	No (w/rl)
19	Cuban	36	Prison	Bail	PD	132	B/E Bld	B/E w/ intent misdm.[e]	6-12 mo jail	8	Yes	Yes	No	Yes, paint	No	Window	1	Yes
20	B	24	No	OR	PD	165	B/E Bld Gr Lrc	B/E Bld	6-mo jail 2-yr prb	8	Yes	No	No	Yes, $$	No	Door	0	Yes
21	B	23	Prison	Bail	PD	?	B/E Bld Gr Lrc Loiter	Same	3½-yr prison	11	No	No	Yes	Yes, clothes	No	?	0	No
23	W	19	No	OR	PD	71	B/E Bld	Same	5-yr prb	7	Yes	Yes	No	Yes, drugs	No	Window	1	No

aPD = public defender; DR = defendant-retained private attorney.

bFP = fingerprints.

cPSR = pre-sentence report.

dSee footnote a, Table 7-2.

eSee footnote d, Table 7-2.

Case Notes:

Case 1: Codefendant not apprehended.
Case 2: Conc. to another B/E dwelling case; probation revoked.
Case 3: Found guilty on stipulated facts; skipped; rearrested.
Case 4: Sentence consec. to another B/E dwelling and GL case with 2-yr prison and 2-yr probation; skipped.
Case 5: Same defendant as case 17.
Case 7: Conc. to two prior cases; probation revoked; codefendant acquitted.
Case 8: Identified by two neighbors. Consec. to another B/E case.
Case 9: Consec. to another B/E dwelling case.
Case 10: Codefendant who testified received 2-yr probation.
Case 11: Defendant shot fleeing scene; sentence consec. to another.

Case 12: Defendant served 3 yrs in prison on prior B/Es.
Case 13: Probation later revoked; sentenced to 1-yr jail.
Case 14: Conc. to another B/E of theater, same night.
Case 15: Codefendant assaulted food store manager.
Case 16: Three prison priors in three states for burglary.
Case 17: Same defendant as case 5.
Case 18: Used crowbar; both defendants "cooperated" after arrest.
Case 21: Conc. with three other burglary cases.
Case 22: Doctor's office; conc. to attempted B/E bld case.
Case 23: Doctor's office; defendant waited in car while codefendant entered; codefendant received 1-yr jail sentence.

Plea Bargaining

As a preliminary to the discussion of the plea negotiation aspects of the audited burglary cases, we note the posture of the principal involved agencies toward such bargaining. The State Attorney is a vociferous public critic of plea bargaining. He has recently stated that negotiated pleas are not in the best interest of either the community or the individual, that his policy is not to permit a plea agreement without the approval of the victim and the police, and never to invade the court's province by bargaining over sentences.[5] The position of the Public Defender is said to be that his office will not enter a plea of guilty without advance assurance of what sentence would be meted out.[6] The position of the bench may be inferred from the observation that sentence bargains commonly are struck in the trial judge's chambers. The upshot of this melange of policy appears to be, judging from the case audit, that all types of plea bargaining are infrequent save one—sentence bargaining, which is commonplace.

In only two of the audited cases was the plea to a level of charge less than that originally charged. While the auditing team concluded that the great majority of cases disposed of on a plea of guilty involved a sentence assurance or agreement, this cannot readily be shown by the audit case sample since the case files do not normally contain a record of such agreements, if any. Also, the case files usually lacked a presentence investigation report.[7]

It was evident to the auditing team that sentence bargains struck in Dade County would be strongly shaped by the concern of both sentencing judges and the State Attorney's Office for the views of the victim and the police in individual cases, and by crowding in correctional facilities as well. Other sources of discrepancies in sentences are discussed below.

Sentencing Variation

Collectively, the sentences in the audited cases turned out to be quite severe, with incarceration often imposed. Of the eleven defendants convicted of dwelling burglaries, six received prison sentences and two were given jail terms of one year. Three young defendants were given straight probation, but in one of these instances, the term of probation was consecutive to a prison sentence in an unrelated case. The average duration of the prison sentences was roughly six years in length.

The defendants convicted of nondwelling burglaries also did not receive

[5] 17 Criminal Law Rptr. 2438 (August 27, 1975).

[6] Private communication.

[7] Florida law provides a right to a presentence investigation only when the defendant is younger than 18 or has no prior record. Apparently this investigation is frequently waived even when these requirements are met.

patently lenient treatment. Four were given prison terms, averaging nearly four years in length. Jail terms were imposed on two. The remaining five were given straight probation, but they were all young first offenders.

Eleven different judges imposed sentences in the audited cases. Their sentencing patterns seem quite similar, with the defendant's prior record appearing to be a salient consideration. On the face of the audited cases, the effect of sentence agreements in burglary plea-of-guilty cases appears to be diminished by a pervasive inclination toward severity of treatment by judges in all cases except those most deserving of leniency.

Case Processing Efficiency; Evenhandedness

The size and nature of the case sample audited precluded useful inferences about the master calendar experiment or other case processing issues.

Further, we were unable to perceive any pattern of events in the audited cases that could be related to the race, type of counsel, and custody status associated with the defendants.

Recapitulation

Strongly divided views about the relative roles of case auditing and statistical performance measurement, expressed by the experienced criminal justice practitioners interviewed during an early phase of this study, led us to conduct auditing on a modest scale in the two demonstration jurisdictions, Multnomah County and Dade County. We sought to investigate several of the claimed benefits of case auditing used in conjunction with the statistical analysis of court system performance and, in particular, with the calculation of performance measures. Could case auditing enhance confidence in inferences drawn from the statistical analysis of the court system records? Would it be a source of findings not revealed by the statistical treatment of relatively large volumes of operational data from the system. These were general questions at issue.

Since our resources for case auditing were sharply constrained, it was necessary to focus its scope rather narrowly. The sample of cases numbered 20 in Multnomah County and 23 in Dade County, all involving burglary as the principal charge and all disposed of by a plea of guilty. Two principal factors embodied in the design of the case sample were time (i.e., two different periods of operation) and type of burglary (i.e., occurring in a dwelling or a nonresidential building). Within each jurisdiction, the case samples were roughly balanced in terms of the most accessible defendant characteristics, age and prior record. Our particular interest in shaping the Multnomah case-audit sample was to further illuminate a limited no-plea-negotiation experiment undertaken by the

District Attorney in that jurisdiction; the design of the parallel Dade case-audit sample was then largely dictated by our wish to make interjurisdictional comparisons, if appropriate. The Rand case-audit team was composed of two seasoned practitioners.

The Multnomah case audit developed a picture that was consonant with our information, both statistical and qualitative, from other sources and with findings based thereon.

Much the same could be said for the Dade case audit. But the generally poorer state of the case files, coupled with the diffuse nature of case screening and the practice of concealing plea agreements,[8] if any, in that jurisdiction made case auditing generally less fruitful than in Multnomah. Differences in screening, plea bargaining, and sentencing between the two time periods and between types of burglaries perceived by means of the case-audit activity corresponded to differences revealed by the statistical approach. The cases that we audited produced no significant new insights, for example, about how practice relates to policy in this jurisdiction. But this result might be attributed to the character of the selected sample rather than to the auditing process. Perhaps if the sample had been deliberately designed to encompass cases of marginal strength,[9] the audit might have exposed forces at work which were unlikely to be revealed by statistical analysis. What our experience does underscore is the relevance of an elementary guideline; namely, one needs accurate, full, and fairly detailed knowledge about the nature of a court system if he is to make sound and comprehensive inferences about its performance on the basis of statistical analysis of operational data. If he has that knowledge, case auditing is unlikely to produce surprises. If he lacks it, case auditing could be instructive.

Concluding Remarks

Case auditing is an interesting method of generating system knowledge for analysts who can then go about constructing statistical performance measures. This suggests that audits be scheduled early in any exercise to develop the performance-measures auditing approach. Case auditing has more direct benefits as well, as we believe our experience has taught us:

1. It can provide information about important but nonquantifiable variables that, although impossible to integrate into a statistical estimation equation, must inform the interpretation of statistical estimates.

---

[8] That is, the case files in Dade County show only instances of agreements to reduce number or level of charges; sentence concessions or agreements to drop charges in unrelated cases simply are not recorded.

[9] The cases were selected randomly and, as it turned out, all were judged by the audit team to be strong or fairly strong cases.

2. It can be the source of new hypotheses about how the system works, which then can be tested on the basis of data collected in a statistical performance measures enterprise.

3. It can give assurance that the causal sequence uncovered in a statistical exercise accords with the perceptions concerning cause and effect of people actually on the scene.

4. It has more validity, on its face, to the average practitioner; that is, it seems more natural and less mysteriously technical. Thus, when there is concurrence between audit and performance-measure results, the conclusions of the statistical enterprise will be more acceptable to the interested professional reader as well as to the lay person.

This last point is not to argue that case audits should be used primarily to confirm or validate results derived from well-executed statistical analyses. The audit samples are inevitably so small that any discrepancy in findings must be considered inconclusive. The best source of technical confirmation for the statistical results is a better sample than the original, or a better formulation of the hypothesis, or better measurement of variables, none of which a case audit can guarantee.

Taken together, the two audits intensify our appreciation of the dramatic differences between the two jurisdictions in felony proceedings. In fact, interjurisdictional comparisons in the absence of case audits seem to us rather risky. And the findings emphasize that comparisons between these two jurisdictions are best made in terms of output measures (e.g., incarceration rate, diversion rate, cost per disposition, etc.) that show impacts on the community, rather in terms of internal performance measures (e.g., rate of dismissal at preliminary hearings).

Although we generally believe that case audits would best be conducted in the initial phases of a project to measure court performances, there is one factor that operates in the other direction. Sudden departures from trends or normal patterns will often show up in the statistical indicators. When that happens, on-the-scene investigation by experienced practitioners can reveal the reason, and this ferreting activity can be fruitfully combined with a case audit.

Case audits are by their nature much more expensive per case included than the data collection required to develop performance measures. That is obvious; they require all the information that one has to collect for performance measures plus more. So as the sample size for the case audit expands, it begins to approach that typically utilized for generating statistical performance measures, but of course at much greater cost.[10] Obviously, case-audit samples must be

---

[10] We should also observe the existence of trends toward PROMIS-type information systems, which not only facilitate the use of statistical performance measures, but also provide a depth of detail that resembles case-auditing results in many respects. For example, such systems typically collect and process a number of information elements on case strength. Consequently, they can show how case strength tends to explain observed events in the criminal proceeding, not only as a statistical effect in a large number of cases but also as separate observations pertaining to individual cases (as does a case audit). PROMIS-type systems may thus be regarded as a bridge between the two (polar) performance-measure approaches discussed above.

much smaller. We trade off comprehensiveness of information against depth of information, or extensity for intensity. The question becomes: Is that more intensive information worth the extra cost? Our experience indicates that the costs are worth paying if a modest, well-designed audit undertaking is performed early in the course of events by experienced and thoughtful practitioners who consciously seek ways to improve the subsequent development of statistical performance measures.

8 General Findings and Implications of the Study

A number of (general) findings and implications emerged from this study. They involve the potential benefits of an integrated performance measurement program, the problems of data availability and case sampling, the need for extensions to our demonstration work, and, most important, the relationships between the potential capabilities of existing or planned information systems and the more comprehensive approach outlined in this study for measuring the performance of prosecution, defense, and court agencies. In addition, we present very gross cost estimates that bound the range of alternatives discussed in this study.

The Desirability of an Integrated Performance Measurement Program (IPMP)

Our study has shown that there is a richness of court system performance information that, if the jurisdictions in which we worked are representative, is largely untapped. (We say this with the full understanding that the data elements recorded in the various agencies' files were by no means complete.) The careful collection of specified data elements, the computation, grouping, and cross-tabulation of performance measures, and the analysis (using multivariate statistical techniques) of what factors account for the variation in key performance measures can provide greatly strengthened informational bases for officials in court, prosecution, and public defender agencies to improve criminal proceedings.

The actions to be taken jointly by the court, prosecution, and public defender agencies in a jurisdiction to strengthen the informational and analytical base for measuring their performance may be visualized as an integrated performance measurement program (IPMP). A fairly comprehensive IPMP would consist of:

1. An enumeration of required data elements (or categories) and performance measures.
2. Standardized data collection and output forms for each policy issue area of interest (charging, plea bargaining, sentence variation, evenhandedness, delay, case processing efficiency (separately for each of the three agencies), or others of interest to particular jurisdictions).

3. Flexible, modular, software packages (i.e., computer programs) for computing, displaying, and analyzing performance measures within each issue area—for example, for performing cross tabulations and for applying multivariate regression models that help to explain conviction probability, delay, and sentence severity imposed.
4. Guidelines for conducting case audits at each major decision point (screening, guilty plea, trial, sentencing) in the proceeding—using either outside practitioner/consultants or inhouse supervisory personnel.
5. The administration of sampling plans and standard mail survey questionnaires, and the analysis of responses of victims, other witnesses, and jurors (using appropriate software packages).
6. The administration of sampling plans and standard personal interview questionnaires, and the analysis of responses of defendants (using appropriate software packages).

An IPMP can be designed for several uses: the routine retrospective monitoring of performance within a jurisdiction; the retrospective evaluation of policy, organizational, and procedural innovations within a jurisdiction;[1] and (to a lesser extent) the retrospective comparison of performance between jurisdictions. To the extent that the statistical models succeed in explaining and predicting conviction probability, delay, and sentence severity imposed, it may be possible to use them in a limited way to do (prospective) performance analysis, that is, to forecast some effects of planned policy on organizational changes or of anticipated changes in agency workloads. As visualized here, an IPMP would not be designed to track pending cases; other existing or planned information systems perform this function.

If data collection procedures and software packages were flexible and modular in design, the scale and scope of an IPMP could be tailored to individual jurisdictions. For example, the three agencies in a using jurisdiction could decide whether to embrace all elements (e.g., to include case auditing and defendant interviews) and whether to measure performance in all the listed issue areas (e.g., to include the measurement of case processing efficiency in the prosecutor's and public defender's office, as well as in the court). What would be vital to proper tailoring is a clear enunciation by agency officials of the management and policy issues on which performance measurement should focus.

This study is a first step toward the design of an IPMP. We have enumerated required data elements and performance measures and, with varying degrees of success, have devised and applied statistical models to explain key performance measures. We have also designed and applied mail and personal interview

---

[1] Examples of such innovations include the plea bargaining policy, shifting the charging threshold, introducing a program for the special handling of habitual offenders, changing the policy of case assignments to the public defender's office, modifying the court calendar system, and instituting arrangements for lessening unwarranted sentence variation.

questionnaires to the four classes of lay participants. More work needs to be done, however, and its nature is discussed below.

In this study we have not made a serious attempt to analyze the resource implications of inaugurating an IPMP. Later in this chapter, however, we make very rough cost estimates for two bounding cases, based on actual costs incurred in this study and on rough guesses of costs of activities not covered in this study. Actual costs would vary from jurisdiction to jurisdiction and would depend on the scale of performance measurement desired and the extent to which existing or planned information systems were used to measure performance, as opposed to inaugurating a new and more comprehensive information system designed solely for an IPMP. In any event, the statistical analysis necessary (developing statistical models and applying techniques such as multivariate regression) for more fully explaining the factors associated with performance changes would require a competent statistician or econometrician (at least part-time) who has acquired detailed knowledge of criminal court systems.

In this study we have demonstrated that it was feasible to apply statistical performance measures in two jurisdictions. This demonstration was more successful in applying performance measures to certain policy issues than to others because of inherent differences in the precision of the performance measures (e.g., in those which measure charging threshold compared with those which measure delay) or because of differences in the availability of data (e.g., the availability of data on sentence agreements in Multnomah compared with its unavailability in Dade for measuring plea bargaining effects). Whether the institutionalization of an IPMP is practical and has utility (i.e., whether its benefits outweigh its incremental costs) is as yet undetermined. It would require a pilot demonstration in at least one jurisdiction over some period of time, after which officials in the using agencies would have to make their own judgments about practicality and utility.

Data Availability and Methodology

Case Audits

Our pilot case-auditing exercises (of cases in which there was a plea of guilty) in the demonstration jurisdictions strongly suggest that case auditing provides complementary information about qualitative factors that aid in the interpretations of the statistical performance measures. (By their very nature, case audits are much more expensive per case included than the data collection required to develop statistical performance measures. Thus, with limited resources, audit samples are inevitably too small to stand alone as a substitute for statistical performance measures.)

We believe that the average practitioner regards case auditing to be a natural and nontechnical way of revealing performance. His confidence in the correctness of what is shown by statistical performance measures is undoubtedly increased when the results of (even quite limited) case auditing confirm the statistical story. Another possible benefit of case auditing is that it may help reveal the explanations for the "behavior" of statistical indices. And, finally, it may considerably strengthen the credibility of interjurisdictional comparisons by means of statistical measures. It would appear that, in general, case audits would best be conducted in the initial phases of a project to measure court performance. (Our suggestions for broadening case auditing to test its value more fully are discussed below.)

Data Availability and Sampling Problems

A salient lesson in our attempt to demonstrate the application of performance measures in two selected jurisdictions was that many necessary or desirable data elements normally recorded in various files were missing from the customary records, and some were simply not recorded at all. And this is likely to be the situation in other jurisdictions as well.

Among the data elements that had been (at best) incompletely recorded and preserved were defendant-related characteristics such as ethnicity, prior criminal record, occupation and employment, family status, income, and transiency; the number of appearances per victim or other witness in the course of a proceeding; data describing how judges apportion their time among judicial tasks; and attribution of continuances to the responsible movant(s).

Among the data elements that were not recorded at all were the apportionment of time among the principal activities of prosecutors, public defenders, and jurors; background characteristics of suspects whose cases were screened out before arraignment on felony charges; full information on the outcome of plea bargaining, including the nature of any sentence agreement reached; judicial statements of the rationale for sentences in individual cases; detailed reasons for case dismissals in lower court; duration of appearances of victims and other witnesses; and information on the attitudes of lay participants and defendants toward their experiences and toward the performance of the court agencies.

Our demonstration work also imbued us with a deeper appreciation of the need to tailor case sampling to the type of the data element sought. Events of interest in the performance measurement of criminal proceedings differ dramatically in their expected frequency of occurrence. When data on rare events are required (e.g., data on the outcomes of jury trials for a specified offense wherein a minority defendant is represented by retained defense counsel), one must employ well-planned "oversampling." Fortunately, many key events in court proceedings occur frequently enough that moderate (on the order of 100) case sample sizes suffice as a basis for reliable inferences.

Desirable Extensions

We feel that a fuller foundation for the design of an operational IPMP would be provided by the following extensions in scope and in refinement in methodology to our demonstration work.

1. Classes of data that were not recorded or were incompletely recorded in Multnomah and Dade counties should be collected and analyzed elsewhere. Evenhandedness in screening should be analyzed with a proper body of data containing appropriate defendant-related characteristics. The allocation of prosecutors' and public defenders' time to their various activities is another performance area warranting examination and would need a proper body of data.

2. The assessment of case auditing should be broadened in the screening area (to include rejected cases) and also extended to the trial area, so that our inferences as to the value of case auditing as a complement to statistical performance measurement can be tested more fully.

3. Improved statistical models should be constructed to help explain performance outcomes in criminal proceedings. Those we developed for explaining sentence outcomes and delay in proceedings worked fairly well but need further refinement. Because we were unsuccessful in explaining the determinants of conviction probability, we believe much more theoretical and empirical work is necessary. We speculate that data on the seriousness of the crime incident, on mitigating and exacerbating circumstances of the defendant and the crime incident, and on factors describing the strength of the case at the time of screening are relevant for constructing better conviction probability models.

**Potential Capabilities of Other Information Systems
for Performance Measurement**

A number of state and local agency level information systems already exist or will be installed soon in a number of state and local jurisdictions. Given the considerable resources that will be devoted to these systems, it is clearly important to indicate their potential capabilities for the kind of performance measurement envisaged for an IPMP. In particular, it is important to compare their potential performance measurement capabilities (e.g., how many issue areas can be analyzed and in what depth) with an IPMP under two conditions: (1) if only those data elements already collected by these information systems are available; and (2) if a modest, inexpensive extension in data collection is added.

Examples of current or planned information systems are:

1. CCH (Computerized Criminal Histories): a component of the LEAA's Comprehensive Data System (CDS) Plan.
2. OBTS (Offender-Based Transaction Statistics System): a component of LEAA's CDS Plan.

3. SJIS (State Judicial Information System).
4. PROMIS (Prosecutor's Management Information System).

All these systems are designed to track defendants or cases through that part of the criminal justice system with which they are concerned, and all rely on the local criminal justice agencies for input data. The first three are state-level or multistate systems, whereas the fourth is intended for use by local prosecutors' offices. CCH focuses on information concerning the identity, location, characteristics, and description of the known criminal offender. OBTS is a statistical system describing the aggregate experiences of arrested individuals from their encounter with the police through court processing and entry into, and exit from, the correctional system. CCH and OBTS are components of LEAA's Comprehensive Data System Program. The relevant part of SJIS (i.e., the entry and passage of people and cases through courts of general jurisdiction) is designed to evaluate the organization, practice, and procedures of the courts in a state; assist with dispatch of judicial business; and facilitate technical assistance and long-range planning activities. The conditions for a state's participation in SJIS include a commitment for the state judicial system to provide the information needed for a "comprehensive criminal justice data system." As defined by LEAA guidelines, such a system must include a CCH file, an OBTS file, and a statistical analysis center.

PROMIS is designed to aid local prosecutors in identifying the more serious criminal cases to which prosecutorial priority should be given, to aid in controlling or eliminating impediments to effective prosecution, to aid in regulating the exercise of prosecutorial discretion so as to maintain evenhandedness and consistency, and to aid in conducting relevant analyses of screening and prosecution of criminal cases. PROMIS tracks the arrested person from arrest through processing and disposition in the lower and felony courts. As indicated at the outset, an IPMP would not track open cases, but is designed to do retrospective performance analysis.

Table 8-1 displays the data elements or categories collected by these four information systems that are relevant to the kind of performance measurement and analysis demonstrated in this study. For purposes of comparison, we also display those data elements or data categories collected in our demonstration work, as well as those that would be collected if the desirable extensions to an IPMP, discussed above, were implemented. From Table 8-1 we observe that none of the existing or planned systems obtains data on lay participant attitudes and experiences, on how practitioner or lay participant time is used, or on all potentially relevant characteristics of defendants (e.g., CCH/OBTS and SJIS omit data on education, employment, transiency, family status, and income level, and PROMIS omits data on education, income, and family status). However, PROMIS is designed to collect data on all filed and final charges and counts and on other aspects of plea bargaining, such as sentence bargaining.

CCH/OBTS and SJIS do not collect data on rejection actions and their reasons, nor on the fact and nature of sentence bargaining.

Given these differences and similarities in data categories to be collected, what are the implications for performance measurement?[2] To answer this question, we consider four options for each of the following: the combined CCH/OBT, SJIS (with CCH/OBTS), and PROMIS.

Option I: The basic system with existing data elements, assuming that a simple software package is available that can compute the values or performance measures and produce summaries and cross tabulations.

Option II: Option I plus a few added data elements that can be collected inexpensively.

Option III: Option I plus few added data elements (e.g., statistical models and standard multivariate statistical analysis routines) for estimating the independent effect of important factors on delay and sentence severity. Additional research is needed to develop a similar package for explaining conviction probability.

Option IV: Option II plus Option III.

To our knowledge, more sophisticated statistical software packages (as in Options III and IV) are not planned for any of these systems; at best, simpler software packages of the Option I variety will be available.

Potential Capabilities of CCH/OBTS

Table 8-2 compares the potential capabilities of the four CCH/OBTS options with two versions of an IPMP. For a specified issue area, an entry of "No" indicates that the option cannot measure performance: an entry of "partial" indicates that certain relevant data items are still needed or that cross tabulations are the best available tool, or both; and an entry of "Yes" indicates that the available data elements and the software packages are adequate for performance measurement.

This table is a means of showing that adding a few more data elements (listed at the bottom of Table 8-2) without adding a more sophisticated software package (Option II) would not appreciably improve the performance measurement capability. Adding both (Option IV) would (by design) clearly provide the most benefits. Option IV would enable better analysis of the plea bargaining

---

[2] The following comparisons of performance measurement capabilities of the various systems are viewed only in terms of the ensemble of issue areas we considered for an IPMP. There may be other issue areas (e.g., bail and OR policy) of interest to a jurisdiction, too; thus, comparisons among the systems might look different, depending on whether or not an IPMP was designed to address these issues.

Table 8-1

A Comparison of Data Elements and Categories Collected that Are Relevant to Performance Measurement[a]

Data Element or Category	Information System					
	CCH	OBTS	SJIS (with CCH/OBTS)	PROMIS	IPMP (as illustrated in this study)	Improved IPMP (with extensions)
Defendant-related characteristics:				(For filings and rejections)	(For filings only)	(For filings and rejections)
Age	Yes	Yes	Yes	Yes	Yes	Yes
Ethnicity	Yes	Yes	Yes	Yes	Yes	Yes
Prior record	Yes	Yes	Yes	Yes[b]	Yes	Yes
Education	No	No	No	No	Yes	Yes
Income	No	No	No	No	Yes	Yes
Employment	No	No	No	Yes	Yes	Yes
Family status	No	No	No	No	Yes	Yes
Transiency (years living in jurisdiction)	No	No	No	Yes	Yes	Yes
Pretrial custody status	No	Yes	Yes	Yes	Yes	Yes
Type of defense counsel	Yes	Yes	Yes	Yes	Yes	Yes
Date and nature of each major event from arrest through disposition (including sentencing, if applicable)	Yes	Yes	Yes	Yes	Yes	Yes
Most serious arrest offense	Yes	Yes	Yes	Yes	Yes	Yes
Full specification of arrest offenses	Yes	No	Yes	Yes	Yes	Yes
Factors describing the seriousness of the crime incident	No	No	No	Yes	No	Yes
Mitigating/exacerbating circumstances of defendant or crime	No	No	No	Yes	No	Yes
Strength of case at screening	No	No	No	Yes	No	Yes

Screening actions:					
Rejection	No	No	Yes	Yes	Yes
Reasons for rejection	No	No	Yes	Yes	Yes
Most serious charge filed	Yes	Yes	Yes	Yes	Yes
Full specifications of filed charges and counts	No	Yes	Yes	Yes	Yes
Final most serious charge	Yes	Yes	Yes	Yes	Yes
Full specifications of final charges and counts	No	Yes	Yes	Yes	Yes
Other types of bargain agreements:					
Fact of sentence assurance or agreement	No	No	Yes	Yes	Yes
Nature of sentence agreement	No	No	Yes	No	Yes
Agreement to drop other pending cases	No	No	Yes	Yes	Yes
Full specifications of sentence elements imposed	Yes, but fine excluded	Yes	Yes	Yes	Yes
Continuances:					
Number per case	No	No	Yes	Yes	Yes
Duration of each continuance	No	No	Yes	Yes	Yes
Attribution to defense, prosecution, court, or joint	No	No	Yes	Yes	Yes
Data elements required to estimate weighted-caseload performance measures:					
Judge[c]	No	Yes (gross information only)	Partial[d]	Yes	Yes
Prosecutors	No	No	Partial[d]	No	Yes
Public defenders	No	No	Partial[d]	No	Yes

Table 8-1(cont.)

Data Element or Category	Information System					
	CCH	OBTS	SJIS (with CCH/OBTS)	PROMIS	IPMP (as illustrated in this study)	Improved IPMP (with extensions)
Defendant-related characteristics:				(For filings and rejections)	(For filings only)	(For filings and rejections)
Use of lay participant time:						
Number of victim/witness appearances per disposition[e]	No	No	No	No	Yes[f]	Yes[g]
Duration of victim/witness appearance[e]	No	No	No	No	Yes[f]	Yes[g]
Proportion of juror time spent:						
In idleness	No	No	No	No	Yes[f]	Yes[g]
In voir dire, criminal	No	No	No	No	Yes[f]	Yes[g]
In trial, criminal	No	No	No	No	Yes[f]	Yes[g]
In voir dire, civil	No	No	No	No	Yes[f]	Yes[g]
In trial, civil	No	No	No	No	Yes[f]	Yes[g]
Questions asked in defendant personal interview questionnaire and mail survey questionnaires for victims, other witnesses, and jurors[h]	No	No	No	No	Yes	Yes

Sources: We draw descriptive information and information on data elements collected by CCH, OBTS, and PROMIS from the National Advisory Commission on Criminal Justice Standards and Goals, *Criminal Justice System*, U.S. Government Printing Office, Washington, D.C., 1973, pp. 100-101; *PROMIS Briefing Series*, Institute for Law and Social Research, Washington, D.C., October 1974, especially No. 1, "Management Overview of PROMIS", and No. 17, "Interface with Other CJIS", and "Data Base and Data Element Dictionary" (App. D to Vol. I of the six volumes of PROMIS software documentation). Information on data elements to be collected by SJIS is drawn from *State Judicial Information System Project, Requirements Analysis Subcommittee Final Report*, The Institute of Judicial Administration, Inc., New York, April 1975.

[a]The entry indicates whether the data element is recorded.

[b]Arrests and convictions only, not sentences imposed.

[c]See Chapter 4.

[d]PROMIS contains the data elements associated with the computation of weighted caseload *except* for time data, that is, the time associated with each activity or proceeding connected with a case (letter from William Hamilton, President, Institute of Law and Social Research, April 30, 1976).

[e]Separately for victims and other lay witnesses.

[f]Based on memories of victims, other witnesses, and jurors who responded to mail surveys.

[g]These data elements would be collected by personnel in prosecution, defense, and court agencies at the time when these lay participants appear.

[h]See the questionnaires in Apps. G and I of Rand Corporation report R-1918-DOJ, Op. Cit.

Potential Performance Measurement Capabilities of CCH/OBTS[a]

Issue Areas	Option, Data Elements Collected, Software Packages				Reference IPMP Options	
	I Existing Cross-Tabs Only	II Improved[b] Cross-Tabs Only	III Existing Cross-Tabs and Regression Models	IV Improved[b] Cross-Tabs and Regression Models	As Demonstrated in This Study	Improved with Extensions Specified Above
Charging threshold	No	No	No	No	Yes	Yes
Charging accuracy	Yes	Yes	Yes	Yes	Yes	Yes
Evenhandedness in screening	No	No	No	No	No	Yes
Effects and concessions in plea bargaining	Partial	Partial	Partial	*Yes*[c]	Yes	Yes
Determinants of conviction probability:						
Legitimate factors	No	No	No	No	No	Yes
Illegitimate factors (evenhandedness)	Partial	Partial	Partial	Partial	Partial	Yes
Estimation of sentence variation	Yes	Yes	Yes	Yes	Yes	Yes
Determinants of sentence variation:						
Legitimate factors	Partial	Partial	Partial	*Yes*	Yes	Yes
Illegitimate factors (evenhandedness)	Partial	Partial	Partial	*Yes*	Yes	Yes
Estimation of delay	Yes	Yes	Yes	Yes	Yes	Yes
Determinants of delay	Partial	Partial	*Yes*	*Yes*	Yes	Yes
Analysis of continuances	No	No	No	No	Yes	Yes
The use of jurors' time	No	No	No	No	Yes	Yes
Duration and number of appearances of victims and witnesses	No	No	No	No	Yes	Yes
The use of practitioners' time:						
Judges	No	No	No	No	Partial	Yes
Prosecutors and public defenders	No	No	No	No	No	Yes
Attitudes of lay participants and their determinants	No	No	No	No	Yes	Yes

[a]The entries indicate the extent to which the specified option can measure performance in the indicated issue areas.

[b]Additional data elements that can be added inexpensively to those already specified in the existing system are:

1. Defendant community ties (education, income, employment, family status, transiency).
2. Other types of plea bargains: the fact and nature of sentence agreements; agreement to drop other pending cases.
3. Time trend of inmate population in local jails and state prisons.

[c]An italicized entry indicates that the specified option improves performance measurement capability over Option I for the indicated issue area.

balance, the independent effects of important factors on delay, and the independent effects of legitimate and illegitimate factors on sentence severity imposed. However, compared with an improved IPMP, none of the four options are capable of performance measurement in the following issue areas: charging threshold, evenhandedness in screening, the effect of legitimate factors on conviction probability, continuances, the use of practitioner and lay participant time, and the attitudes (and their determinants) of lay participants.

Potential Capabilities of SJIS

Because SJIS must include CCH/OBTS files, an inspection of Table 8-2 reveals that the capabilities of the various SJIS options (assuming the same added data elements for Options II and IV) would be nearly identical with the corresponding CCH/OBTS options, with only one major difference: the basic SJIS is capable of very gross estimates of the use of judicial time.

Potential Capabilities of PROMIS

The basic system (Option I) will have better potentialities for performance measurement than the basic CCH/OBTS (Option I), as shown in Table 8-3. In addition to all the CCH/OBTS Option I capabilities, PROMIS Option I has a good capability in the charging threshold area and a partial capability in analyzing evenhandedness in screening and the effects of legitimate factors on conviction probability. Adding only the additional data elements (Option II) listed at the bottom of Table 8-3 leads to no significant improvement. However, adding both additional data elements and software (Option IV) provides the most benefits. Option IV would improve the capability to analyze evenhandedness in screening, the plea bargaining balance, the independent effects of important factors on delay, and the independent effects of legitimate and illegitimate factors on conviction probability and sentence severity imposed. However, compared with an improved IPMP, none of the four options are capable of performance measurement in the following issue areas: the use of practitioner and lay participant time and the attitudes (and their determinants) of lay participants. However, because PROMIS already collects much of the data needed for estimating practitioners' weighted caseload, if practitioner time data associated with various activities and proceedings in each case were sampled outside PROMIS, any of the PROMIS options would be able to measure the use of practitioner time.

In summary, none of the existing or planned information systems would have the breadth and depth in performance measurement capabilities of an improved IPMP for two reasons. (1) Many data elements are not collected and,

Potential Performance Measurement Capabilities of PROMIS (with or without CCH/OBTS, SJIS)[a]

Issue Areas	Option, Data Elements Collected, Software Packages				Reference IPMP Options	
	I Existing Cross-Tabs Only	II Improved[b] Cross-Tabs Only	III Existing Cross-Tabs and Regression Models	IV Improved[b] Cross-Tabs and Regression Models	As Demonstrated in This Study	Improved with Extensions Specified Above
Charging threshold	Yes	Yes	Yes	Yes	Yes	Yes
Charging accuracy	Yes	Yes	Yes	Yes	Yes	Yes
Evenhandedness in screening	Partial	Partial	*Yes*[c]	*Yes*	No	Yes
Effects and concessions in plea bargaining	Partial	Partial	Partial	*Yes*	Yes	Yes
Determinants of conviction probability:						
Legitimate factors	Partial	Partial	Yes	*Yes*	No	Yes
Illegitimate factors (evenhandedness)	Partial	Partial	*Yes*	*Yes*	Partial	Yes
Estimation of sentence variation	Yes	Yes	Yes	Yes	Yes	Yes
Determinants of sentence variation:						
Legitimate factors	Partial	Partial	Partial	*Yes*	Yes	Yes
Illegitimate factors (evenhandedness)	Partial	Partial	Partial	*Yes*	Yes	Yes
Estimation of delay	Yes	Yes	Yes	Yes	Yes	Yes
Determinants of delay	Partial	Partial	*Yes*	*Yes*	Yes	Yes
Analysis of continuances	Yes	Yes	Yes	Yes	Yes	Yes
The use of jurors' time	No	No	No	No	Yes	Yes
Duration and number of appearances of victims and witnesses	No	No	No	No	Yes	Yes
The use of practitioners' time:						
Judges	No	No	No	No	Partial	Yes
Prosecutors and public defenders	No	No	No	No	No	Yes
Attitudes of lay participants and their determinants	No	No	No	No	Yes	Yes

[a]The entries indicate the extent to which the specified option can measure performance in the indicated issue areas.

[b]Additional data elements that can be added inexpensively to those already specified in the existing system are:

1. Sentences associated with prior convictions of defendant (if CCH unavailable).

2. Data elements comprising the defendant community ties index that are not already collected in PROMIS, that is, education, income, and family status.

3. Time trend of inmate population in local jails and state prisons.

[c]An italicized entry indicates that the specified option improves performance measurement capability over Option I for the indicated issue area.

(2) to our knowledge, none of the existing and planned systems will have the full array of statistical models and software packages required for analyzing the independent effects of important parameters on delay, dispositional, and sentence outcomes. Each basic system could function as a partial IPMP as is, and if upgraded (i.e., a few data elements are added for routine collection as well as the required software packages), their performance measurement capability could be substantially improved. In this connection, it appears that among the planned systems considered in this report (CCH/OBTS, SJIS, PROMIS) an upgraded PROMIS would have the most comprehensive performance measurement capability, primarily because it can address case screening issues as well as the issues that can be addressed by CCH/OBTS and SJIS.

Some Final Comments on Benefits, Costs, and
Utility of Performance Measurement Systems

Given the preceding discussion of the potential capabilities of existing or planned systems, of planned systems that are upgraded in the ways we specified, and of an improved IPMP, how is a jurisdiction to decide which alternative to choose? The decision would depend on a variety of considerations: the availability of (and which) a computerized information system and whether it is already installed or planned; the issue areas or policy issues of interest to the court, prosecution, and public defender agencies; and the incremental costs and benefits of installing and operating CCH/OBTS, SJIS, and PROMIS, and of upgrading these systems as we indicated, and of moving toward an improved IPMP.

Issue Areas of Interest to Agencies

We cannot generalize about which issue areas would be of greatest interest. However, in Chapter 3 we noted that the practitioner interviews confirmed their importance, and we can indicate how the agencies reacted in the two demonstration jurisdictions in which we worked. Officials there received early drafts of our reports and then were briefed and interviewed by a Rand team. In general, officials were enthusiastic and felt that there was great value in the application of performance measures, primarily as an objective way of demonstrating what was going on, how well certain well-defined objectives were being met (e.g., arrest to trial standards), and in explaining why performance measures varied. The chief judge and the court administrator in one of the jurisdictions were particularly interested in the applications to charging accuracy, plea bargaining, sentence variation and evenhandedness, the use of lay participant time, and the relationships between lay participant attitudes and the problems they faced (that could be manipulated by policy changes). The court administrator in the other jurisdiction was particularly interested in delay, but indicated that almost all the findings in our pilot application of performance measures were "new," since the few statistics they did produce had to be manually estimated (due to the lack of computerization). The prosecutors in both jurisdictions were particularly interested in applications to screening, plea bargaining, sentence variation, evenhandedness, treatment of habitual or "career" offenders, and the attitudes and problems of lay participants. The public defenders in both jurisdictions were particularly interested in their performance relative to private attorneys, defendant attitudes, evenhandedness, delay, and the tentative finding that trials seemed to involve little or no sentence penalty compared with straight pleas. (In one jurisdiction, the public defender's office was also very interested in other issue areas not demonstrated in our work, such as the use of public defender time, the attitudes of judges toward public defenders as opposed to retained counsel, and the utility of support staff.)

Incremental Costs

We stated at the outset the careful estimates of the incremental cost implications of upgrading the capabilities of existing or planned information systems or of implementing an improved IPMP from scratch were beyond the scope of this study. However, it may be useful to provide the reader with a breakdown of the resources we used in manual data collection (from agency case files), in computer processing and analysis of these data, in the administration of mail surveys (of victims, witnesses, jurors) and personal interviews (of defendants), and in the computer processing and analysis of these survey responses. Assuming that jurisdictions would be provided with the necessary standardized data collection forms, lay participant questionnaires, and the necessary software packages at no cost, the resources we allocated to the data acquisition, processing, and analysis can be viewed as a rough starting point for estimating the range of incremental costs that might be incurred by interested jurisdictions. We also include very approximate cost estimates for collecting and analyzing data necessary for examining weighted caseloads in the court, the prosecutor's office, and the public defender's office; these estimates are based on telephone conversations with personnel from consulting firms that have implemented weighted-caseload measurement systems in such local agencies, since we did not ourselves collect these data in this study.

We consider two bounding cases: (1) jurisdictions with access to a computer, but no existing or planned information system, wishing to measure performance in all issue areas covered by an improved IPMP, and (2) jurisdictions with a CCH/OBTS, SJIS, or PROMIS system wishing only to upgrade to Option IV. In both cases, the rough estimates are annual costs for measuring performance (once) per year, although the data collection may be intermittment or continuous over the year.[3]

Rough cost estimates are shown in Table 8-4 for these two cases. For a jurisdiction without an existing information system, but with access to a computer, Case I might cost on the order of $50,000 per year to operate a full IPMP once it is set up. (First-year costs should be considerably higher, perhaps by 25 to 50 percent, because of nonrecurring set-up costs.) This assumes that the software is made available without cost, that practitioner time devoted to data collection (e.g., having prosecutors fill out data sheets at each stage of the felony proceeding) is essentially "free,"[4] and that the number and size of data samples collected and analyzed are similar to those we collected in this study. If a jurisdiction wished to draw additional case file samples (e.g., for more offense types and/or for over-sampling trials), total costs for analyzing the case file data should not increase very much, because most of the additional cost would be in data collection (a small part of the total) and not in data processing, analysis, and interpretation. Costs would also rise if larger samples of defendants were interviewed, or if larger samples of victims, witnesses, and jurors were surveyed. The largest fraction of the total operating costs of an IPMP may well be attributed to the analysis of the use of judicial, prosecutorial, and public defender time. However, we have listed limited confidence in the estimates shown in the table, because we did not have first-hand experience in gathering and analyzing such data in this study.

For a jurisdiction with one of the information systems discussed, incremental annual costs of about $10,000 might be incurred if it were upgraded to Option IV. Whichever alternative a jurisdiction chooses, a competent statistician or econometrician, who has acquired a detailed knowledge of criminal court systems, would be required (at least part-time) to perform the statistical analysis and interpretation.

We should emphasize that all the estimated costs displayed in Table 8-4 are quite uncertain predictors of what jurisdictions would actually incur. Readers should view them only as very gross approximations. Given the probable low marginal costs associated with upgrading an existing or planned information system and its major benefits (an increased understanding of the independent effects of important factors on major performance measures or outcome), it is probably cost-effective for a jurisdiction to pursue this alternative. Whether a full IPMP is cost-effective is a judgment that can only be made by an implementing jurisdiction after such a system is installed and operated over several years and when its actual costs and benefits are assessed.

---

[3] The issue of how often performance should be measured cannot be resolved in general terms. It would depend on the resources available to each agency, the issue area or policy issue under consideration, the agency's perceptions about the acuteness of their problems, and perceptions about the public's interests and attitudes toward the performance of the court system.

[4] Experience with collecting PROMIS and judicial weighted-caseload data suggests that a judge or prosecutor might spend only a small fraction of an hour per day (approximately 15 minutes) filling out data sheets.

Table 8-4
Rough Cost Estimates for Performance Measurement

Case I: Implementing an IPMP from scratch (assumes that software packages are provided free and that practitioners' time devoted to data collection is "free")	*Approximate Range of Man-Months Required*	*Approximate Range of Direct[a] Dollar Cost*
Case file data (three 100 case samples of filed cases, two 100-case samples of screening actions, two 100-case samples of rejection reasons, one 100-case sample of continuances and victim/witness appearances):		
Manual data collection (at $3-$5/hr)	1.5-2.0	1,000-2,000
Data cleaning, keypunching, and computer processing	–	10,000
Statistical analysis and interpretation (at $10/hr)	2.0-3.0	3,000-5,000
Subtotal		14,000-17,000
Weighted-caseload use of practitioner time (assumes 3 man-months of a coordinator-analyst required in each agency and that practitioner time for data input, coordination, etc., is "free"):		
Court (10-15 judge sample; 4-6 weeks each/year)	3	5,000-10,000
Prosecution (10-15 prosecutor sample; 4-6 weeks each/year)	3	5,000-10,000
Public defender (10-15 defender sample; 4-6 weeks each/year)	3	5,000-10,000
Subtotal		15,000-30,000
Mail surveys of 150-200 samples each of victims, witnesses, and jurors (assuming questionnaires are free):		
Administration (initial mailing, follow-up mailing, and telephoning)	2.5	5,000
Data cleaning, keypunching, and computer processing	1-2	1,500
Statistical analysis and interpretation	1-2	2,000-3,000
Subtotal		8,500-9,500
Defendant interviews (45 interviews) (assuming questionnaires are free):		
Administration		1,000-1,500
Computer processing		500
Subtotal		1,500-2,000
Report writing (one month per agency)	3	5,000
Grand total		44,000-64,000 (approx.)

Table 8-4 (cont.)

Case II: Upgrading Existing or Planned Systems (CCH/OBTS, SJIS, PROMIS) to Option IV	Incremental[b] Man-Months Required	Incremental[b] Direct[a] Costs
Case file data (same data samples as case I (assumes that software packages are free and practitioners' time devoted to data collection is "free"):		
Data collection	Negligible	Negligible
Data cleaning and key punching	Negligible	Negligible
Computer processing	–	2,000
Statistical analysis and interpretation	1-2	2,000-3,000
Report writing (one month per agency)	3	5,000
Grand total		9,000-10,000 (approx.)

[a]Excludes overhead and fringe benefit costs.

[b]Over and above Option I costs or existing or planned systems.

Appendix A
The Demonstration
Jurisdictions

The Selection Criteria

Our study, even at its earliest formulation, was not envisaged as a purely theoretical investigation of the subject of statistical performance measures. Rather, it has sought a fuller understanding of how the improved application of performance measures might contribute to the betterment of criminal proceedings, as well as a deeper appreciation of practical impediments to such use. Given this study orientation, our analyses seem to be most appropriately performed in the context of actual criminal court systems. Our judgment was that a single jurisdiction would not suffice for this purpose, for criminal court systems were far too variable from one jurisdiction to another. But resource limitations on our study program limited field work of substantial depth to only two jurisdictions.

If we were to work in only two jurisdictions, we felt that they should be widely separated geographically and markedly contrasting in the way that criminal proceedings were handled. Also, it was desirable that neither jurisdiction be so large nor so overburdened by its caseload as to be highly atypical. Nor was it thought desirable to select a small jurisdiction with a very light caseload, since the small number of cases would then make less interesting the application of statistical techniques. Small jurisdictions also inevitably generate small case samples that would make it difficult to explain why certain performance measures vary and which factors most importantly affect that variation. Within these bounds we sought to select two jurisdictions that were more typical of medium to large (in terms of population, crime rate, and court caseload) urbanized felony court systems.

A further, exceedingly vital criterion was the quality of the data sources at our disposal. Since we would be drawing most of our data from closed case files and related records, it was essential that these materials be reasonably complete, accurate, and consistent. Still another consideration was that the existence of a recent court experiment or substantial policy change would facilitate our demonstration objectives, namely, to show how performance measures could help to illuminate the consequences of system changes. Finally, a necessary, but not sufficient, selection factor was simply the receptiveness of the jurisdiction to our presence—would the bench, the office of the prosecutor, and the office of the public defender all join in extending permission and assistance to our delving into their case-related files?

Given these criteria, the soundest approach to selecting two demonstration jurisdictions would have entailed *in situ* investigations of a number of candidates (including various possibilities suggested by our Advisory Group). But such preliminaries were plainly too costly. Instead, we conducted the practitioner interviews described in Chapter 3 with the additional objective in mind of exploring the choice of two from among the 13 jurisdictions visited. As it turned out, Multnomah County, Oregon (containing the City of Portland) and Dade County, Florida (containing the City of Miami) together appeared to meet our selection criteria, and we subsequently arranged for them to be the subjects of our demonstration analyses.

Below we present concise overviews of the criminal justice process in the two counties, emphasizing the aspects most related to our studies.[1] These overviews will serve to contrast the two jurisdictions without comparing their performance per se in criminal proceedings. Statistical overviews based on data samples that we ourselves collected from case files are not included in this appendix; they are presented in Chapters 5 and 6.

The Felony Court System in Multnomah County, Oregon

The Flow and Timing in Felony Cases

Arrests in Multnomah County are made primarily by the Police Bureau of the City of Portland, a force of 700-plus officers, and the Sheriff's Office, a 250-officer force. A small proportion of the felony arrests in the county are produced by the State Police and the Police Department of the City of Gresham. A felony suspect, within 24 hours after his arrest (unless a weekend intervenes) makes his first appearance in District Court, the lower court of a two-tiered system. Within five days of arrest, a preliminary hearing[2] and bindover (if any) will have occurred in District Court. Until recently, all but the most routine cases would then have proceeded by way of grand jury indictment (if any) to arraignment in the Circuit Court. In 1975, however, a markedly increased use of informations began,[3] whereby the case moved into Circuit Court without indictment. On the first-mentioned route the defendant would, by approximately the twenty-fifth day after arrest, have been arraigned in Circuit Court, have entered a plea of not guilty, and have been assigned dates for a pretrial conference and a trial; on the second route, which omits the grand jury hearing, a Circuit Court arraignment would generally ensue without two weeks of arrest. Another alternative involves the return of an (secret) indictment by the grand jury prior to an arrest, which is then under warrant. In this sequence of events,

---

[1] This background information was provided by personnel of the two systems, by internal and external publications of their various agencies, and by our observations during data collection and case auditing.

[2] In Multnomah County the preliminary hearing is relatively informal. No court reporter is present, but the use of a cassette recorder has recently been initiated.

[3] As a result of a recent change in the Oregon Constitution and Statutes.

the Circuit Court arraignment usually comes within three days after the defendant has entered custody. A pretrial conference would customarily be held within two weeks after arraignment and important pretrial motions would be filed and heard a few (3 to 5) days later. Elapsed time between conference and beginning of trial would be roughly 3 to 4 weeks; between end of trial and sentencing, about 30 days.

There is no formal pretrial intervention (diversion) program in Multnomah County.

Oregon has a statutory requirement that a defendant be tried no more than 60 days after his arrest if he is in custody.[4] Motions for setover (continuance) of the trial date are readily granted provided the new date requested is within this statutory period and does not cause a loss of witnesses to the nonmoving side. Otherwise, a full-scale hearing is required by the court to rule on the motion. If defense counsel is the moving party, he must show that the defendant's rights will be prejudiced unless the setover is granted. If the prosecutor is the moving party, he must justify his request by showing that it is necessitated by unforeseeable events beyond his control. That the two sides join in asking the delay is of itself given no weight. For the past several years, the time from first arrest to beginning of trial for felony cases in the Circuit Court has generally been meeting the statutory standard, but not all individual cases do so[5] (see Table A-1).

The Multnomah County Circuit Court

Organization and Calendaring. Judges are elected for six-year terms on a nonpartisan basis. The Presiding Judge is chosen by the judges of the court and serves two successive one-year terms. He hears all pretrial civil matters and assigns all civil and criminal trials. The Chief Criminal Court, presided over by a Circuit Court judge for a term of three to four months, was established in its present form in 1972. The Chief Criminal Judge conducts recognizance and bail hearings, hears motions to dismiss and all dispositive motions, conducts trials on stipulated facts, receives all pleas except those taken in the course of a trial, and generally sentences on the pleas of guilty taken. The 11 trial judges conduct both civil and criminal trials, hearings on trial motions, and sentencing hearings after a judgment of guilty in a trial or a plea of guilty taken in the course of trial. A trial judge is assigned to a criminal case on the day preceding the trial date by a random-assignment method that virtually precludes "judge shopping."[6] And

[4] In Multnomah County, the Circuit Court judges, by philosophy and policy, attempt to meet this requirement in all felony cases, whether or not the defendant is in custody.

[5] A marked increase in case intake in 1975 may significantly elevate the percent of cases failing to meet the 60-day standard in the current year.

[6] Either defense counsel or the prosecutor could cause the transfer of a case (but no more than twice) by "affidaviting" the judge for prejudice—thus, there is potential for "judge shopping" by this means. It is infrequently done because of its abrasive nature.

212

Table A-1
Statistical Information Provided by the Circuit Court of Multnomah County
(Criminal Proceedings)

Item	1972	1973	1974	January-April 1975	April 1975
Total criminal case intake	2897	2730	2869	1341	369
Felony arraignments	2412	2037	2317	1144	303
District Court appeals	485	693	552	197	66
Average monthly case intake	241	227	239	335	369
Felony arraignments	201	170	193	286	303
District Court appeals	40	57	46	49	66
Average monthly pleas of guilty	183	197	224	248	262
Average monthly trials (verdict)	60	50	38	40	33
Circuit Court cases	42	29	25	25	18
District Court appeal cases	18	21	13	15	15
Elapsed days from arrest to beginning of trial, Circuit Court cases					
Average	58	46	54	–	61
Median	44	41	52	–	60

Source: May 15, 1975 internal memorandum from the Chief Criminal Judge.

there is a judicial policy in opposition to allowing a defendant to appear in trial court for the purpose of pleading guilty and being sentenced there rather than in Chief Criminal Court. Table A-1 conveys an impression of the scale of criminal case activity in the Circuit Court.

Juror Handling. The term of jury duty is 4 to 5 weeks. A pool of 200 veniremen is created by calling about 800 candidates. A panel of 20 veniremen is sent from the pool to a criminal courtroom for the *voir dire* examination. In the selection of the 12-person jury, defense counsel is accorded 6 preemptory challenges and the prosecutor has 3, except in capital cases wherein each side has double this allowance.

Witness Handling. Each side is responsible for the service of subpoenas on its own witnesses, who are directed to appear at a specified date and time. Typically, the attorneys in criminal cases require their witnesses to appear at the beginning of either a morning or an afternoon session and then wait for their case to be called. It is felt that this procedure does not unduly extend a witness's commitment of time.

Court Involvement in Plea Bargaining. As a matter of judicial policy current in mid-1975, the Chief Criminal Judge eschews involvement in plea negotiation. Infrequently the parties may confer with the court to obtain his views on possible sentencing solutions in a specific case, but no sentencing commitment will be made. A negotiated plea of guilty tends to be the object of judicial inquiry where a very serious crime or a very substantial reduction in charges are involved; otherwise, the court is mainly concerned with the voluntariness of the plea. Plea agreements must be committed to writing.

Sentencing. Statutory maximums for imprisonment and fines are set under the Oregon Criminal Code, revised in 1971. Nearly all felonies are now classified as one of three types (A, B, or C) with corresponding maxima being specified.[7] (At the court's discretion, class C felonies may be regarded as an alternate felony/misdemeanor type.) The sentencing judge may impose a maximum sentence less than the statutory limit. The choice between consecutive and concurrent sentences in the event of multiple convictions rests within his discretion, with a presumption of concurrency if not otherwise specified. Written presentence reports are not prepared for all defendants, so sentencing without this report does occur. An informal, advisory-only sentencing panel consisting of the current, past, and prospective Chief Criminal Judges has been used in Multnomah County for plea-of-guilty cases, which comprise 75 to 78 percent of the total to be sentenced. Sentencing in Impact Crime cases has been a particular focus of the panels.[8] But at least one judge who presided over the Chief Criminal Court did not elect to use the panel arrangement.

Bail and Own Recognizance. Subsequent to January 1974, an arrestee may gain release from custody by posting with the court 10 percent of the bail set for this case. He ultimately recovers 90 percent of the posted amount by making his required appearances.[9] This procedure has virtually eliminated bondsmen. A prefixed bail schedule applies to some felonies (and to misdemeanors in general). Most pretrial release is, however, on the basis of own recognizance (OR). The arrested suspect is interviewed in jail by the OR staff. If he does not qualify for OR release, he is so informed at his first appearance in District Court, where his bail is set or reviewed. Some arrestees avoid OR interviews by posting bail at the time of police booking, provided the prefixed bail schedule is applicable.

---

[7] Class A felonies incur a maximum prison term of 20 years and a maximum fine of $2,500; class B, 10 years and $2,500; class C, 5 years and $2,500.

[8] Within the Impact program, the District Attorney's office has received a grant to implement a "no-negotiation" experiment for three crimes—dwelling burglaries, serious robberies, and "fencing."

[9] The Court Administrator estimates the current "skip" rate to be in the neighborhood of 5 percent, lower than it was before January 1974.

Office of the Multnomah County District Attorney

Size and Workload. The office serves as the prosecutor of both felony and misdemeanor cases arising in Multnomah County, which comprise about 45 percent of the state's criminal cases. Currently, its caseload is composed of roughly 2,500 felonies and upwards of 6,000 misdemeanors per year, DUIL (drunk driving) and domestic relations cases each numbering into the thousands, District Court appeals and extradition cases each numbering into the hundreds, and a variety of Juvenile Court, consumer protection, and negligent homicide matters. This caseload is borne by a staff of nearly 50 attorneys, 4 interns, and 75 support personnel.

Organization. To handle its felony caseload, which is our concern here, the Office of the District Attorney divides its duties broadly as follows. The responsibilities of a District Court (lower court) prosecutorial staff include the preliminary hearings to which felony cases move after they are initially screened and a complaint issued.[10] An Intake Unit, attached to the District Court Unit, draws up complaints, obtains arrest warrants, reviews search warrants, prepares evidence in direct presentation cases, deals with citizen's complaints, and so on. A Pretrial Unit has the task of presenting evidence to grand juries, both for direct cases and those moving from preliminary hearing along the grand jury indictment route rather than the information route. This unit also argues in opposition to pretrial motions by defense counsel and handles extradition and appeals. There are four trial teams in the Circuit Court Trial Unit, which take cases as they move from the Intake and Pretrial Units, each being assigned a broad offense category; namely, team A is assigned homicides, rapes, and serious assaults; B, felony drug and vice cases; D, the non-Impact burglaries and robberies; and E, fraud, bad check, and welfare offenses. These teams are involved in the pretrial conference, plea negotiations, motion hearings, and trial. However, only the team heads have authority to enter into a plea agreement.

The fifth team, team C, is unique, for it has responsibility for cases from intake to disposition when they involve the three (Impact) crimes of residential burglary, serious robbery, or "fencing." This team is the core of the District Attorney's no-negotiation experiment begun in December 1973 (see Chapter 5 for a description of this project).

The scale of the felony (and District Court appeals) case activity of the District Attorney's office is suggested by the data provided by them and presented in Table A-2.

[10]Felony cases in which the suspect is not in custody may be presented directly to the grand jury for indictment. If an indictment is returned, an arrest warrant will issue. Once the defendant is in custody, he is arraigned immediately in the Circuit Court; thus, no preliminary hearing occurs in these cases.

Table A-2

Statistical Information Provided by the District Attorney's Office of Multnomah County

Type of Activity	1971	1972	1973	1974
Number of indictments	2264	2340	2247	2428
Number of defendants indicted	2313	2429	2280	2368
Number of informations	221	86	169	127
Number of District Court appeals	178	405	459	401
Number of defendants convicted either by trial or plea of guilty	2164	1982	1765	1711
Total number of defendants tried	445	650	428	429
Number tried by jury	236	294	194	215
Number tried by court	209	356	234	214
Total number of defendants convicted by trial	336	485	316	339
Number convicted by jury trial	180	207	130	153
Number convicted by court trial	156	278	186	186
Percent judgments of guilty after trial	75.5	74.9	73.3	79.0
Defendants convicted, as percent of defendants who were tried or pled guilty[a]	95.2	92.4	94.0	95.0
Defendants disposed of by trial, as percent of defendants who were tried or pled guilty	19.6	30.3	23.0	24.0

Felony Case Screening				
Type of Activity	Jan. 75	Feb. 75	Mar. 75	Apr. 75	May 75
Number of complaints issued	182	142	167	154	144
Number of cases with "No Complaint"	93	81	97	87	58
Percent rejected	33.4	36.3	36.7	36.1	28.7
Direct presentations to grand jury:					
Number of cases logged in	69	81	83	112	103
Number of cases sent to GJ	59	55	51	62	58
Number of cases referred back	–	26	34	50	35
Number of cases pending	20	20	19	20	28
Cases referred back, as percent of cases either sent to GJ or referred back to source	0	32.1	40.0	44.6	37.6

High Impact Project: Dec. 1973 to Dec. 1974 (13 months)	
Cases tried	56
Guilty	39
Not guilty	12
Not guilty/insanity	5
Cases pending (Dec. 1974)	51
Cases pled to charge	172

Table A-2 (cont.)

Cases pled to lesser charge	4
Cases returned to police	149
Cases dismissed	46
Cases not indicted by grand jury	14

Source: Office of the District Attorney, internal memoranda and 1974 year-end report.
aDoes not reflect dismissals or other terminations of prosecution.

Policy Considerations. Prosecutorial policy about the intake and prosecution of cases related to the no-negotiation experiment is discussed elsewhere (Chapter 5). For other cases, no standard filing policies guide the Intake Unit.[11] Nevertheless, it is impractical for the police to exploit the absence of standardized filing standards to their advantage, since one deputy has a nearly exclusive assignment of the felony screening function.

Three types of concessions are made in return for pleas of guilty, namely, to reduce charges (the most frequent type), to dismiss pending charges in other unrelated cases or not to file these other charges, or to recommend a (relatively favorable) sentence or not to oppose a defense-recommended one. No standard policy governs how much will be afforded to effect an agreement. The office seeks to dispose of cases at the pretrial conference but also remains "willing to try cases."

With one exception, there is no uniform policy concerning whether or not a deputy should make a sentencing recommendation after obtaining a conviction.[12] It is generally left to his discretion to make a recommendation at the probation and sentencing hearing.

The office posture toward cooperation with defense counsel is substantially shaped by Oregon's liberal discovery statutes, which give the defendant full access to police reports, witnesses, physical evidence, etc.

The Public Defender's Office: The Metropolitan
Public Defender

Size and Workload. The Metropolitan Public Defender, a private nonprofit corporation, provides (under contract) legel defense services to indigent defendants in Multnomah County and, to a lesser extent, in neighboring Washington County and in the Federal District Court. The county funds defense counsel

[11] One exception is the consistent policy of discouraging domestic-relations-type complaints.
[12] There is now a policy of recommending restitution to the victim in every case where appropriate.

(public defenders plus court-appointed counsel) in roughly 60 percent of the felony cases and 20 percent of the misdemeanor cases (plus a small percentage of the traffic cases). The Metropolitan Public Defender handles about 45 percent of all felony cases and about 10 percent of all misdemeanors (excluding traffic). Twelve attorneys are assigned to Multnomah cases. Eight are assigned to felonies, three to misdemeanors and one to both plus other duties. The annual total of felony cases handled by these eight attorneys is about 1,600 (i.e., 200 cases per attorney) of which approximately 5 percent go to trial. (The misdemeanor caseload per attorney is about twice as large.) The public defenders take cases on a first-come-first-served basis up to the point where the quota is fulfilled each month.

Organization. The eight attorneys assigned to Multnomah felony cases are divided into four two-man teams, each consisting of a senior and a junior attorney. A team defends a case from appointment to disposition.[13] A blind case assignment system is used, with each team drawing appointment that are made initially in Circuit Court one week a month, appointments that are made initially in District Court two weeks a month, and no new cases during the fourth week. An unusually important case appointment might be assigned by the Public Defender himself outside of the regular assignment system. A defender team has the support of an "alternatives" staff, which is familiar with existing community programs for offenders and which helps to organize new ones; of trial assistants, who perform initial interviews with defendants, retrieve their property from police, handle subpoenas, and maintain trial books; and of an investigations unit. Table A-3 shows the nature of the felony case activities of the Metropolitan Public Defender's Office.

Defense Counsel Compensation. Attorneys of the Metropolitan Public Defender are compensated by salary. By contrast, court-appointed private attorneys are paid a fee per appearance, the amount of which depends upon the type of appearance. Defendant-retained private attorneys are generally remunerated by a fee per case.

Oregon Corrections Background

A felon, if not classified as a dangerous offender, is eligible for parole six months after admission to prison. The parole authorities set reviews at a time slightly before one-third of the imposed maximum time has been served. Consequently,

---

[13] If the defendant appeals, the Oregon State Public Defender's Office assumes responsibility for his representation. On the other hand, if the District Attorney appeals a dismissal (say, after a successful defense motion to suppress essential evidence), then the Metropolitan Public Defender team will continue its representation.

Table A-3

Statistical Information on Felony Cases Provided by the Metropolitan Public Defender, Multnomah County[a]

Type of Activity	May 1975		July 1974 to May 1975	
Case Flow	Number		Number	
Open at start	363		274	
Refiled	10		66	
Appointed during period	193		1796	
Total open during period	566		2136	
Closed during period	207		1777	
Open at end	359		359	
Case Closings	Number	Percent	Number	Percent
Total closed	207	100.0	1777	100.0
Adjudicated	155	74.9	1272	71.6
To probation/extradition	31	15.0	281	15.8
To other defense counsel	11	5.3	142	8.0
Retained private counsel	3	1.4	35	2.0
Appointed private counsel	8	3.9	107	6.0
Bench warrant issued	10	4.8	82	4.6
Adjudications	Number	Percent	Number	Percent
Total cases adjudicated	155	100.0	1272	100.0
Total not convicted	56	36.1	543	42.7
Dismissed	48	31.0	504	39.6
Not guilty/jury trial	1	0.6	14	1.1
Not guilty/bench trial	–	–	1	0.7
Not guilty/insane	7	4.5	24	1.9
Total convicted	99	63.9	729	57.3
Plea as charged	43	27.7	308	24.2
Plea to lesser felony	43	27.7	207	16.3
Plea to misdemeanor	10	6.4	151	11.9
Guilty/jury trial	2	1.3	51	4.0
Guilty/bench trial	1	0.6	12	0.9
Trials	Number	Percent	Number	Percent
Total number of trials	11		102	
Percent of adjudications by trial		7.1		8.0
Win rate (not guilty/guilty)				
Jury trials		33.3		21.5
Bench trials		–		7.7

Table A-3 (cont.)

Sentences	Number	Percent	Number	Percent
Total number of sentences	99	100.0	729	100.0
No jail after sentence	72	72.7	489	67.1
Jail after sentence	27	27.3	240	32.9
Penitentiary	11	11.1	114	15.6

Source: Office of the Metropolitan Public Defender, internal statistical reports.

parole is frequently granted after the felon has served one-third of the imposed maximum term. According to the State Department of Corrections, the typical Oregon felon actually serves roughly 33 percent of the maximum prison sentence imposed by the court.

The State Department of Corrections provides local probation and parole services. Probation could be either under court supervision or state supervision, at the discretion of the sentencing judge. Incarceration for younger offenders is generally at the Oregon Correctional Institution; for older offenders and the most serious offenders regardless of age, it is at the State Prison.

Dade County, Florida

The Flow and Timing in Felony Cases

The bulk of felony arrests in Dade County are made by officers of the Police Department of the City of Miami and the Public Safety Department of the county, which respectively number about 750 and 1,200 sworn personnel. Provided the arrestee does not immediately post bond (according to a prefixed schedule that does not include capital offenses, which are nonbailable), he is given a bond hearing in the Magistrate's Division of the County Court, generally within 24 hours. This is a nonadversarial hearing in which the magistrate purports to make a probable-cause determination on the basis of the police affidavit and sometimes, if necessary, the arresting officer's testimony. The affidavit may be prepared after arrest or, in some instances, before arrest to enable the issuance of an arrest warrant.

Most felony cases (perhaps 80 percent) then have a second lower-court hearing to determine whether or not the suspect should be bound over to the Circuit Court. Prior to April 1975, this was in the nature of an adversarial (though informal) preliminary hearing. Currently, as one of the procedural changes engendered by *Gerstein* v. *Pugh*, US, 43 L ED 2d54 (1975), a nonadversarial probable-cause hearing is conducted.[14] If the suspect is bound over to Circuit Court, he is arraigned in that forum within one week if in custody, within two weeks otherwise. In other cases (roughly 5 percent of the total), the State Attorney's office may directly file an information in Circuit Court without further proceedings in County Court (other than the bail hearing, if any). In the remaining cases, the grand jury will be used, either to return an indictment after the arrest and bail hearing, followed by arraignment in Circuit Court if the indictment is returned, or to indict prior to arrest, whereupon the defendant is arrested pursuant to a warrant and then directly arraigned in Circuit Court. The State Attorney has authority to "no action" a case before the probable-cause (preliminary) hearing or to "no information" it after a bindover. Furthermore, he can file an information even though the magistrate does not hold the suspect to answer. However, these powers are not frequently exercised.

There is considerable employment of *nolle prosequi* (perhaps 15 to 20 percent of the cases) once felony cases have been filed in Circuit Court.[15] Continuances of trial date are common, usually justified by schedule conflicts and discovery needs. Most cases are set for trial from 30 days to 6 weeks after arraignment, but trials do not often occur before 60 days. A court-imposed speedy-trial rule of 180 days between arrest and trial applies in Florida. In addition, a defendant may demand a trial within 60 days after the information is filed in Circuit Court. Both these rules can be waived by the defendant or, under exceptional circumstances, disregarded by the Court.

The Criminal Division of the Circuit Court

Organization and Calendaring. Judges sit in the Circuit Court by virtue of nonpartisan election to 6-year terms. Prior to October 1974, a system of individual calendaring applied to all 10 criminal trial courts. Subsequent to that date, five trial courts retained individual calendaring with "blind" assignment of cases to them and from then continuing responsibility for all aspects of a case; and five courts were organized into an experimental master calendar system, with a Master Calendar Court presiding over arraignments, pretrial motions, and other pretrial matters, and with four trial courts to whom trials are assigned on a "blind" basis. Currently two normally civil courts have been added to the

[14]Under the revised procedures, an adversarial preliminary hearing is available before the Administrative Judge of the Magistrate's Division but only after bindover and on defense motion. On the other hand, the magistrate has discretion to permit the probable-cause hearing to be adversarial.

[15]We were informed that most *nolle prosequi* occur as a result of restitution made in worthless check cases in which the complainant no longer wished to prosecute, and that another frequent reason is the admission of the defendant into the Pre-Trial Intervention Program. (In October 1975, 174 cases were *nolle pros.*, of which 72 were worthless check cases and 42 were diversions.)

criminal division to help alleviate caseload pressures, and the total number may soon further rise to fourteen. Further experimentation with master calendar arrangements is planned. Table A-4 displays descriptive statistics that suggest the scale of felony proceedings in Dade County.

Juror Handling. Except for capital cases, criminal juries in Florida have six members (plus an alternate). In the Circuit Court, the practice is to call a panel of 15 veniremen to the courtroom for jury selection, each side being allowed six preemptory challenges. Twelve-person juries sit on capital cases, with each side being given ten peremptory challenges to apply. Initial panels of 25 to 30 veniremen are subjected to *voir dire* examinations in these cases. The term of jury duty is one week. Each week 400 candidates are notified to appear; roughly 250 appear; and about 150 to 160 are empaneled.

Witness Handling. Subpoenas for witnesses (including victims) are prepared by a computer system and then are served either personally or by mail. The witness is

Table A-4
Statistical Information Provided by the Criminal Division of Dade County Circuit Court

Felony Proceedings	1974			January-July 1975		
Felonies filed	11,000			7,000		
Cases closed	9,600			5,000		
Cases open at end of period	3,400			3,000		
Disposition of closed cases:						
Probation without adjudication	2,150	(22%)		1,200	(24%)	
Convicted	3,450	(36%)		1,650	(33%)	
Acquitted	650	(7%)		400	(8%)	
Nolle pros.	1,350	(14%)		650	(13%)	
Dismissed	1,300	(14%)		650	(13%)	
Other (including pretrial diversion)	700	(7%)		450	(9%)	
Total	9,600	(100%)		5,000	(100%)	
How cases closed:						
Guilty plea	4,400	(72%)	(47%)	2,400	(72%)	(48%)
Nolo contendere plea	500	(8%)	(5%)	300	(9%)	(6%)
Nonjury trial	600	(10%)	(6%)	450	(13%)	(9%)
Jury trial	600	(10%)	(6%)	200	(6%)	(4%)
Subtotal	6,100	(100%)	(64%)	3,350	(100%)	(67%)
Other (dismissals, *nolle pros.* transfer, etc.)	3,500	(36%)		1,650	(33%)	
Total	9,600	(100%)		5,000	(100%)	

Source: Criminal Division of Dade County Circuit Court, internal statistical reports.

usually required to appear in court by 9 A.M. on a specified date. In some instances, witnesses are placed in a standby, on-call status. The Greater Miami Crime Commission is currently sponsoring a witness control project whose purpose is to maintain liaison between witnesses and the Offices of the State Attorney and the Public Defender, as well as to provide liaison police officers on location in the court building. The latter assure the timely appearance of individual police witnesses.

Court Involvement in Plea Bargaining. The degree of court involvement in plea bargaining is discretionary with the individual court, given the absence of general court policy. Occasionally, to deal with caseload emergencies, the Chief Judge has directed that intensified plea negotiation be utilized to dispose of appropriate cases. The type of plea agreement is overwhelmingly a sentence bargain rather than a charge bargain. Where court involvement occurs, it is often in chambers, where the court will or will not ratify a sentence agreed to by the attorneys or will state what his sentence will be when there is no attorney agreement. Obtaining sentence commitments from judges appears to be facilitated by the practice in Dade County of not ordering a presentence investigation report, which might reveal information that would preclude judicial commitment to a sentence in return for a plea. The views of both the victim and the police are an important ingredient in Dade County plea bargains.

Sentencing. Florida sentencing may be characterized as indeterminate in nature, with a statutory general minimum of six months for a noncapital felony. The judge may impose a maximum sentence less than the maximum prescribed for the offense. Sentences for multiple convictions may be concurrent or consecutive at the sentencing court's discretion; absent designation, these sentences are rendered concurrent. In addition to capital felonies, for which (in the absence of the death penalty) the punishment is life imprisonment with parole eligibility after 25 years, the other classes of felonies are the following: life, for which the imprisonment is a life term or a term of years not less than 30; first degree, for which the prison term shall not exceed 30 years and the fine, $10,000, unless the statute specifically provides greater punishment; second degree, for which the maxima are 15 years and $10,000; and third degree, 5 years and $5,000. Sentencing advisory panels are not used in Circuit Court, nor are sentences reviewable by appeal. Florida law provides a right to presentence investigation only for first offenders or for those younger than 18 years. In Dade County, even when these conditions are met, the PSI report is commonly waived. Overall, perhaps 5 percent of the sentences are based, in part at least, on the PSI report. Sentencing alternatives include supervised and unsupervised probation (where either the judgment or the sentence may be suspended), jail, fines, combinations of jail, probation, and fines, and state prison. "Probation without adjudication"—i.e., probation granted under suspension of judgment—is a prominent category of disposition.

Bail and Own Recognizance. Dade County provides a standard bail schedule for felonies other than those punishable by life sentence, which are denied bail under the Florida Constitution. Standard commercial bail bondsmen procedures are available to arrestees who do not meet the standards for release on recognizance. If the suspect is not released on his own recognizance or in the custody of another person, or fails to meet the scheduled bail, then he remains in custody for his first appearance in the Magistrate's Division of County Court, namely, a bail hearing where the probable cause for arrest is reviewed by a magistrate on the basis of a police affidavit and bail is set specifically for this case. One estimate (by a judge) is that 40 to 45 percent of arrestees are released on own recognizance or in the custody of another, 30 percent released by means of bail bond, and the remainder continue in custody.

Office of the State Attorney of Dade County

Size and Caseload. The State Attorney has responsibility for the prosecution of all felony and misdemeanor cases arising in Dade County. The staff numbers 80 attorneys, of whom 12 are assigned to misdemeanor cases, 4 to consumer protection cases, 1 to obscenity matters, 5 to Juvenile Court, 3 to organized crime prosecutions, 5 to appellate activities, and 46 to adult felony cases (exclusive of organized crime prosecutions). There are approximately 11,000 felony cases arraigned in Circuit Court per year and roughly 1,200 felony trials. Some felony cases (perhaps 20 to 25 percent of the total felony arrests) do not survive to arraignment, and these too involve the State Attorney's staff at the county court level. There are 15 investigators and a large secretarial staff to aid the attorneys in carrying their caseload.

Organization. The 46 attorneys committed to adult felony cases are assigned as follows: 5 to each of the 5 courts with individual calendars, 16 to the courts within the master calendar system, and 5 to comprise an intake group that screens cases wherein the arrest is preceded by the preparation of a police affidavit and by the issuance of a warrant. The only significant specialization by crime type in the State Attorney's office is the Major Crimes Unit, which handles all capital cases and other aggravated and serious offenses. Beyond this specialization and the intake assignments, the deputies committed to adult felony cases are generalists. Cases are assigned to them in advance of the probable-cause (or preliminary) hearing. They then have authority to "no action" a case, to offer a misdemeanor disposition, or to offer a plea to a lesser felony; but some deputies exercise this power infrequently. Should a case be bound over and an information filed, the initially assigned deputy then becomes the trial deputy, responsible for all aspects of the proceeding. But the State Attorney can elect not to file an information even if the defendant is bound over (or can file an information if the defendant is not held to answer). Table A-5

Table A-5
Selected Statistics on Felony Prosecutions in Dade County

Average number of felony arraignments per year	11,000
Average number of felony trials per year	1,200
Conviction rate (percent of disposed cases)	60
Plea rate (percent of cases disposed by trial or plea)	80
Trial rate (percent of cases disposed by trial or plea)	15-20
Nolle prosequi rate (percent of disposed cases)	20

Source: Office of the State Attorney of Dade County, internal statistical reports.

presents some gross statistics on prosecutorial activity and performance based on data supplied by system personnel.

Policy Considerations. In two major prosecutorial areas, namely, screening and plea bargaining, the policies of the State Attorney uniquely shape the activities of his office. Traditional prosecutorial screening is not conducted. That is, the prosecutor does not (with some exceptions) exercise discretion to file or not to file an accusatory pleading before judicial involvement in a prosecution. In the ordinary case, where a police officer has arrested a suspect, the officer initiates the prosecution by filing an arrest affidavit with the court.[16] The prosecutor has a screening role in noncustody cases, in citizen complaints, and in (complicated and unusual) cases where the police seek prosecutorial counsel. The State Attorney does not feel a responsibility to systematically exercise the screening function, since it is the magistrate who formally makes the bindover decision in the bulk of felony cases. His power to "no action" cases before the preliminary hearing or to "no information" them afterwards is not commonly exercised. While the county court magistrates typically discharge 20 to 25 percent of the felony suspects, the State Attorney does eliminate an additional 15 to 20 percent after arraignment by the use of *nolle pros.*

The present State Attorney, who has directed the office for 19 years, is a vociferous public critic of plea bargaining and his announced policy is not to permit plea bargaining without the approval of the victim and the police and never to invade the court's province by bargaining over sentences.[17] By contrast, no such opposition is evidenced by the courts and, of course, the Public Defender. In practice, charge bargaining seems indeed to be rare, but sentencing agreements or assurances appear to be frequently present. Often a prosecutor

[16] All misdemeanor arrest affidavits are screened in the State Attorney's office and approximately 20 to 25 percent are rejected at this time for failure of the arrest affidavit to state probable cause.

[17] See 17 Criminal Law Rptr. 2438, August 27, 1975.

and a defense attorney will have an understanding ratified in chambers by the trial judge or will be told what his sentence will be if the attorneys are in disagreement. The court and the prosecutor continue to regard the punishment views of the victim and the police as central.

The Pretrial Intervention (Diversion) Program

Initiated by means of LEAA funding in 1972, the pretrial intervention program is now county-funded under the Administrative Office of the Courts. The diversion decision is made jointly by the program director and the State Attorney's office. The latter then agrees to defer prosecution at the arraignment hearing in Circuit Court. The defendant waives only his right to a speedy trial and enters the three- to six-month program.[18] Upon successful completion of the program, the State Attorney will *nolle pros.* the information if one has been filed or will file a "no information" if an information has not been filed. Restitution is a condition of the program if property was taken from the victim.

The original criteria for entrance into the diversion program were that the defendant be a first offender, a resident of Dade County, between 17 and 25 years of age, and charged with a nonviolent offense (including drug possession, breaking and entering an auto, carrying a concealed weapon, and grand larceny). The success of the program has prompted changes in the criteria for admission: defendants may now be older than 25, need not be residents of Dade County, and are not precluded by a juvenile record. Furthermore, given the concurrence of the victim and the police, defendants charged with robbery, aggravated assault, or drug sale may be admitted. And the program has been expanded to include some misdemeanants.

About 7 percent of all felony defendants are currently being diverted. The program claims an 80 percent rate of successful completion. The rate of recidivism (any rearrest) for those completing the program is estimated to be under 10 percent. Among the 20 percent failures to complete the program, the recidivism rate has been found to be about 38 percent; among a control group of eligible, but nonparticipating, defendants (who were granted probation instead), the recidivism rate was 32 percent. The relatively low rate of recidivism of those completing the program is regarded by observers as a persuasive indication of its value.

Office of the Public Defender

Size and Caseload. The Public Defender is an elected public official whose office is funded by a state appropriation. The staff contains 46 attorneys assigned as

---

[18]Twice-a-week counseling sessions are conducted by professional counselors, who also provide social service assistance to the participants. Their individual caseload is approximately 30 offenders.

follows: 2 to misdemeanor cases, 2 to traffic, 4 to juvenile, 1 to bond hearings, 6 to appeals, 3 to mental incompetence hearings and administrative work, and 27 to the felony division. The Public Defender is appointed to roughly 5,000 felony cases per year (about half the total but most of the indigent cases) and an even larger number of misdemeanor cases.

Organization. The 27 attorneys in the felony division are assigned as follows: 14 to the master calendar system, including two senior attorneys, and the remaining 13 to the courts that are individually calendared, again including two senior attorneys who supervise the defenders in three and two courts, respectively. All attorneys are generalists and handle cases from assignment to disposition. Case assignments are generally "blind"; but in the master calendar system, one defender may take an entire week of cases as a single assignment. Florida has a recoupment statute, but recovery of incurred defender costs is slight.

The Public Defender estimates that approximately 20 percent of his cases are disposed of by a dismissal or *nolle prosequi*, 60 percent by a plea of guilty, and 15 to 20 percent by trial. (His policy is never to enter a plea of guilty for a client without advance assurance of the sentence that would be imposed.) Table A-6 provides further statistical insights by means of data supplied by the public defender.

Defense Counsel Compensation. Public defenders are remunerated by salary. Compensation for court-appointed or defendant-retained private counsel is

Table A-6
Selected Statistics Provided by the Dade County Public Defender's Office

Type of Case and Disposition	In Process July 1, 1974	Cases Added by Information and Indictments in Quarter Ending –	
		September 30, 1974	December 31, 1974
Capital offenses	16	22	65
Other felonies	1383	1253	1191
Misdemeanors	821	1750	1693
Total	2220	3025	2949
Dispositions, all cases			
Nolle pros.	–	331 (17%)	348 (18%)
Public defender relieved	–	130 (7%)	227 (12%)
Plea of guilty	–	1015 (51%)	931 (48%)
Convicted by trial	–	300 (15%)	299 (15%)
Acquittal by trial	–	212 (11%)	154 (8%)
Total	–	1988 (100%)	1959 (100%)

Source: Dade County Public Defender's Office, internal statistical reports.

generally by a fee per case. A maximum of $750 per case, including trial, applies to court-appointed attorneys. This limit is construed by some judges in some cases, especially involving a capital crime, to be $750 per count. Some private attorneys charge defendants a retainer plus a daily fee; others charge a flat fee per appearance, depending on the type of appearance.

Florida Corrections Background

A felon is immediately eligible for parole if his cumulative sentences total at least 12 months; eligibility for felons convicted of capital crime is at the discretion of the parole board. The practice of the parole authorities is to set the initial review at 6 months served and subsequent reviews at intervals of 6 months when the imposed sentence is 5 years or less; for longer sentences, the initial review occurs when 1 year has been served, and subsequent reviews are at intervals of 1 year. On the average, felons are released after serving roughly 40 percent of the imposed maximum term.

The overcrowding of the Dade County Jail in which defendants await trial has impelled emergency court measures from time to time to relieve the trial backlog, including increased and accelerated plea negotiation. Jail terms are served in the Stockade, reputedly an excellent penal institution. The state prison is severely overloaded and inadequate. It is a major source of pressure on the court system and has a substantial effect on the policy toward probationary sentences.

Appendix B
Data Collection in the
Demonstration Jurisdictions:
Methods and Sources

Data Collection Activities in Multnomah County, Oregon

To serve the demonstration purposes of this study, data concerning Multnomah County felony proceedings were collected by a team composed of three law students, two court administration students, and a Rand staff member who supervised their efforts. Major items of information elicited from various source files were the following:

1. Felony case information from samples of case folders as follows:
   a. 200 cases representative of all felony types (the general sample).
   b. 200 cases in which (at least one count of) burglary I, dwelling or nondwelling type, was the most serious initially charged offense.[1]
   c. 200 cases in which (at least one count of) robbery I was the most serious initially charged offense.[2]
2. Defendant-related (biographic and prior record) information, some of which was often missing from the above 400 exemplary-offenses (burglary I and robbery I) case folders.
3. Charges at police booking versus charges at DA filing for 400 cases in which one or more counts of burglary I or robbery I were included in the booked charges.
4. Reasons given for declining to prosecute cases involving (dwelling only) burglary I and robbery I charges (for all such cases within the two periods studied).
5. Number of lay witnesses per trial in a sample of roughly 100 trials among three courtrooms.
6. Frequency and duration of continuances in a sample of 200 felony proceedings.
7. Type and duration of judicial activities.

---

[1] Under Oregon Statutes (ORS 164.225) burglary, which is committed when one enters or remains unlawfully in a building with the intent to commit a crime therein, becomes of the first degree when the building is a dwelling; or the offender is armed with a burglar's tool or a deadly weapon; or the offender causes or attempts to cause physical injury or uses or threatens the use of a dangerous weapon.

[2] Under Oregon Statutes (ORS 164.395, 164.405, 164.415) robbery is committed if one, when committing or attempting a theft, uses or threatens the use of physical force upon another person (with defined types of intent). It is of the first degree if the offender is armed with a deadly weapon, or uses or attempts to use a deadly weapon, or causes or attempts to cause serious physical injury.

229

More detailed descriptions of the nature and sources of each of these bodies of data are given below, concluding with a recapitulation of the available data.

Felony Case Information

Multnomah Circuit Court case folders are filed in a criminal records office in numerical (roughly chronological) order for each calendar year. A registration card is completed for each case, and these cards, which identify the charges and important dates in the cases, are maintained as a separate file. For purposes of our demonstration phase, six samples (each numbering 100 registration cards) were drawn, viz.:

1. The first-period general sample: drawn from all closed felony cases that were filed February through December 1973.
2. The second-period general sample: drawn from all closed felony cases that were filed February through December 1974.
3. The first-period burglary I sample: drawn from closed cases of the first period in which the most serious charges included at least one count of burglary I.
4. The second-period burglary I sample: as above for the second period.
5. The first-period robbery I sample: drawn from closed cases of the first period in which the most serious charges included at least one count of robbery I.
6. The second-period robbery I sample: as above for the second period.

The General Samples. We sought case samples that were uniformly distributed in time within the two selected periods of court operations. Given that the above-described registration cards were filed in nearly the chronological order of the cases, we obtained the two samples by performing a systematic sampling of the card file, with sampling intervals of 36 and 37 cards, respectively, for the first (1973) and second (1974) periods. A chronologically adjacent case was substituted if the one originally selected had its folder missing, or had not yet been closed, or involved a fugitive arrested on the basis of a warrant from another jurisdiction, or had not advanced to the Circuit Court from the District (lower) Court.

Annexed to this appendix is the recording form that sets forth the items of information we desired to obtain from the case folders of the general samples.[3]

---

[3] Of the four unspecified auxiliary spaces (items 9 to 12) in the form, one (12) was used to report the following disposition information:

(1) Plea of "no contest," with conviction indicated in item 3.
(2) Plea of not guilty by reason of insanity, with conviction indicated in item 3.
(3) Mistrial.

One of these items, date of arrest, had to be derived frequently by inference, since Multnomah case folders did not show this date except for cases initiated by secret indictment. Our assumption was that the arrest date could be taken as two days prior to the date of first appearance, for first appearances were almost invariably made within 24 hours of arrest on weekdays and within, at most, 72 hours of arrest on weekends or holidays.

The collection team maintained sampling forms that contained the following information for each selected case: its sample sequence number, its docket number, the docket number of the substituted case (if any), the identification of the responsible team member, and an indicator for showing that the recording form had been "cleansed"—i.e., reviewed for legibility, completeness, and absence of logical and methodological errors.

The Burglary I Samples. Again, a distribution of sample cases uniform over time within the two selected periods was sought. This was obtained by allocating a quota of case files to each month of the 11-month periods, then scanning the case files for each month in numerical order, and finally selecting those cases containing burglary I charges until the quota was met for the month. Substitutions were sometimes required for selected cases, for reasons described above; the substituted cases were obtained by extending the selection process farther into the case file for that month. Sampling control sheets were maintained as described for the general samples.

The information form used by the data collection team for these (exemplary offense) samples is the second annex to this appendix. (The same form served both for the burglary I and for the robbery I samples.) The four auxiliary response items at the end of the information form were used in Multnomah as follows:

Item 33: What was the nature of sentence suspension, if any?[4]

(01) Entire sentence suspended.
(02) Only incarceration suspended.
(03) Only fines suspended.
(04) Both incarceration and fines suspended.
(05) Suspensions other than above.

Item 34: Were the following prosecutorial concessions contained in the plea agreement?

(01) DA agreed not to prosecute other pending cases against this defendant.
(02) DA agreed to make sentence recommendation or not to oppose defense's sentence recommendation.
(03) Both the above.

---

[4] Information given in items 19 through 32, which relate to elements of the imposed sentence, applies prior to any suspension of punishment.

Item 35: Was burglary of a dwelling charged?

Affirmative shown by entry of symbol *D*.

Item 36: Did the case disposition reflect one of the following?

(01) Plea of "no contest," with conviction indicated in item 15.
(02) Plea of not guilty by reason of insanity, with conviction indicated in item 15.
(03) Mistrial.

The Robbery I Samples. The selection procedures for the robbery I samples were identical to these for the burglary I samples. The sample for the second period is virtually exhaustive because of the relatively few closed 1974 robbery I cases at the time of our data collection. Item 35, given above, was the only inapplicable information item for the robbery I samples.

Defendant Biographic and Prior Record Information. If present in the sampled case folders, the Recognizance Sheet served to provide biographic and prior record information. But this item was frequently missing. If the Public Defender had represented the defendant, the desired information could be obtained from that office.[5] The information could also be derived from a presentence investigation report, provided the defendant had been convicted, a presentence investigation was conducted, and the judge in whose files the report was held was not absent during the period of our data collection.

Charges at Police versus Charges at DA Filing. It would help to illuminate the performance of prosecutorial screening in Multnomah County, we felt, if the charges at police booking were compared with the filed charges in samples of cases appropriate to our study emphases. To this end, we set out to obtain four samples each of 100 cases—one sample for each time period with at least one count of burglary I included in the booking charges of every case and, similarly, one sample for each time period for robbery I charges. The sampling source was the daily summary of police bookings, a storage file that was available at the Rocky Butte Jail. Included in each entry of a daily summary was the defendant's name, race, sex, age, date of booking, and booked offenses. Unfortunately, nearly one-half the 1973 (first period) summaries were missing and, consequently, only 58 cases with robbery I charged at booking were available for this period. For the other three samples, the desired number of 100 cases (distributed uniformly within the time periods) was obtained again by assigning case quotas for each month of the period, scanning the case bookings in order of

---

[5] The Metropolitan Public Defender defends nearly one-half of the felony cases in Multnomah County. Data collectors were required to subscribe to a confidentiality of information release form.

booking date, and selecting appropriate cases until each month's quota was filled.

The District Attorney's Office maintained a case card file in which disposed cases were filed in alphabetical order of defendants' surnames. In addition to the defendant's name, each card contained the filed charges, the dates of important case events, and the ultimate disposition. The cases sampled from the booking summaries could thus be matched, by means of defendant surnames, with a file record containing the results of prosecutorial screening. If no card were present corresponding to a sampled booking, we assumed that the District Attorney had declined to file charges in that arrest.

Reasons for Declining to Prosecute. To further reveal prosecutorial screening performance, we sought to ascertain the reasons for declining to prosecute in all cases within the two selected periods wherein the charges at booking included at least one count of robbery I or (dwelling only) burglary I. When a case submitted by the police was rejected by the District Attorney's office, a "prosecution declined" memorandum was customarily prepared. The reasons for rejection would not always be explicitly articulated in this memorandum but could be inferred by the collection team head (with occasional assistance from DA personnel). These memoranda were available in two locations. For the first period, the file was located in the Prosecution Intake Office, housed in the police headquarters building. The supervising prosecutor provided all rejected cases involving robbery I and (dwelling only) burglary I charges from this file. For the second period, since robbery I and (dwelling only) burglary I were Impact offenses, the rejection memoranda were maintained in a file in the District Attorney's Impact Office in another location. The collection team head drew all relevant memoranda from this file to ascertain the rejection reasons.

Number of Lay Witnesses per Trial. The court clerks in individual trial courtrooms of the Multnomah County Circuit Court maintain "Jury Books," which contain the names of all persons who participate in cases that come before the court. These records were the source of a sample of approximately 100 criminal trials (eventuating in a judgment) from which the number of lay witnesses per trial could be estimated. Three judges of the Circuit Court were selected at random. Counts of witnesses were made for each completed criminal trial conducted by them during the period June 1974 through May 1975—there being approximately 100 such trials during this period. These witnesses included victims, since the latter were not specifically identified in the records. A witness was counted once, regardless of the number of his appearances.

Frequency and Duration of Continuances. Information on continuances is essential to an understanding of the observed duration of criminal proceedings. These data could be obtained from a card file maintained by the Clerk of the

Chief Criminal Court. Using the same monthly case quota procedure described earlier, we obtained a sample of 100 cases distributed uniformly in time within each of two periods selected for our study. These cases reflected both dispositions in the Chief Criminal Court (mostly dismissals and guilty pleas) and dispositions in the trial courts. For each case, we collected the following continuance information: the number of continuances; the duration in days for each continuance; the movant (requestor) for each continuance, identified as defense counsel, prosecutor, both defense counsel and prosecutor, or the court; and whether or not the case went to trial.

Type and Duration of Judicial Activities. The need for data on judicial activities arose from our wish to demonstrate the application of the judicial efficiency measure described in Chapter 4, namely, the so-called weighted-caseload measure (the number of weighted caseloads processed per available judge-year). Calculating this performance measure entails the decomposition of proceedings into elemental judicial activities, estimating the average duration (in judicial time) of each of these activities, and also estimating the frequency with which each activity occurs per proceeding. Each judicial activity generally reflects the consumption of time both on the bench and in chambers.

The problem of collecting data on the use of judicial time markedly differs between the Chief Criminal Court and the trial courts. The Chief Criminal Judge is wholly involved with criminal matters and he has little occasion to work in chambers. Trial judges in the Circuit Court conduct both civil and criminal proceedings and spend a significant amount of time working in chambers. Data of the type needed for weighted-caseload analyses are not routinely collected in Multnomah County, but we hoped that our team might itself collect the requisite data applying to at least a sample of judges for a one- or two-month period. However, the resistance of the judges to our logging their activities compelled us to seek other data sources.

The daily schedule prepared for the Chief Criminal Court reveals each activity occurring in that court. It would be an adequate record of the Chief Criminal Judge's activities (since the court is nearly always in session) but for the fact that it provides scheduled durations of activities rather than actual time. (While it gives defendant and attorney identities and the case number, the schedule does not show the charges in the case before the court. Thus, a further data source must be used if the weighted-caseload measure is to be calculated separately by class of offense. The tentative-court-appearances schedule prepared in the District Attorney's office provides this information on charges, after cases have been matched to the court schedule on the basis of defendant's names).

Inferences about the allocation of trial judges' time while sitting on the bench after June 1975 could be made from court clerk logs kept as part of a current effort by the Circuit Court to justify the need for the current complement of court clerks. The clerks were required daily to log the time consumed in each of their activities and identify whether the time was spent in a civil or criminal matter. One could ascertain from these logs the periods when the judge was on the bench and in what activities engaged. (Again, the DA's tentative-court-appearances schedule could be employed to identify the charges in the criminal matters shown in the court clerks' logs).

As an expedient, we attempted to calculate the weighted-caseload measure for July 1975 on the basis of information available in the schedules of the Chief Criminal Court, the District Attorney's schedules of appearances, the court clerk logs, and the monthly criminal statistics prepared by the Clerk of the Chief Criminal Court (which provided the number of dispositions). The crude assumption was made that trial judges used their time in chambers in proportion to the use of their time on the bench. We obtained the Chief Criminal Court schedule and the DA's appearances schedule for each judicial day of July, but found trial court clerk logs to be available for only 119 of the 185 judge-days during that month. The latter logs were also quite variable in detail and completeness, and despite our follow-up efforts, over 20 percent of the trial judges' courtoom time remained unidentifiable. Nevertheless, we proceeded with calculations of the weighted-caseload measure separately for the Chief Criminal Court and the trial courts, for felonies as a whole, and for each of four felony types.[6]

The results of the calculations are displayed in Chapter 5 and illustrate the serious inconsistencies; they serve mainly to show that the above-described indirect sources of information on judicial activities were too incomplete and inaccurate.

Recapitulation of Data Availability

1. Felony case information (from case folders):
   a. Virtually all dispositional data were present in the case folders of the general and exemplary-offenses samples.
   b. Virtually all sentencing data were available in the case samples.
   c. Dates of proceeding steps were fairly complete, but one or more were missing in some individual cases.
2. Defendant-related data (partly from case folders and partly from other sources)
   a. See Table B-1.
3. Charges at police booking versus charges at DA filing:
   a. Only 58 cases with robbery I booking charges available in the police booking file for first period.
   b. 100-case sample available for robbery I in second period; for burglary I in both periods.

---

[6] Court activities in criminal proceedings were aggregated into seven types: arraignments, motion hearings, plea hearings, other hearings, bench trials, jury trials, and sentencing hearings.

Table B-1

Percentage of Sampled Cases for which Defendant Data Were Available, Burglary I and Robbery I

	1973 Samples		1974 Samples	
Item	Burglary I	Robbery I	Burglary I	Robbery I
Age	97	80	94	94
Ethnicity	25	36	24	36
Transiency	87	72	70	66
Occupation	58	60	45	67
Income	6	5	2	5
Education	71	57	83	69
Marital status	79	69	85	84
No. dependents	80	69	78	78
Prior record	94	77	95	91
Pretrial custody	95	92	97	93
Type of attorney	95	95	95	94
No. in sample	97	95	88	86

  c. Absence of case in DA file, assumed to be due to rejection.

4. Reasons for declining to prosecute:

  a. For robbery I, a sample of 13 rejected cases in the first period and 48 rejected cases in the second period exhausted the District Attorney's file.

  b. For (dwelling only) burglary I, a sample of 27 rejected cases exhausted the file for the first period; a sample of 80 cases was drawn from the second-period file.

5. Frequency of witnesses per trial:

  a. Data available in the sample of approximately 100 trials among three courtrooms.

6. Continuances:

  a. Data on frequency and duration of continuances and the identity of the movant available in a sample of 100 cases from each period.

Data Collection Activities in Dade County, Florida

Data collection in Dade County for the demonstration phase of this study was performed by a team of six, of whom five were local law students and the sixth was a member of the Florida Bar. Their efforts were directed at obtaining the following bodies of data:

1. Felony case information from the following samples:
   a.   200 cases representative of all felony types (the general sample).
   b.   200 cases in which some type of breaking and entering felony offense was initially charged.[7]
   c.   200 cases in which robbery was initially charged.[8]
2. Defendant-related (biographic and prior-record) information in the above 400 cases involving either robbery or breaking and entering charges.
3. Dispositions in the Magistrate's Division of the County Court (the lower court) for a sample of 400 cases involving either robbery of breaking and entering booking charges.
4. Reasons given for "no information" actions by the State Attorney on all available robbery or breaking and entering cases in the two periods studied.
5. Type and duration of judicial activities
   a.   Fragmentary and inaccurate data available from indirect sources only (see above discussion).
6. Number of lay witnesses per case and number of witness (or victim) appearances per case in the general sample of 200 cases.
7. Type and duration of judicial activities.

The nature and sources of these data are described below, followed by a recapitulation of the available data.

Felony Case Information

Felony case folders are filed in the office of the Clerk of the Criminal Division in numerical (roughly chronological) order within each year. Open and closed case folders are filed together. A "control" card, on which is recorded the defendant's name, the charges, and the important case dates, exists for each case folder. Control card files are separate for open and closed cases. For our

---

[7] *Florida Substantive Laws,* Chapter 810, Burglary, defines the following breaking and entering felony offenses (among others):

810.01   Breaking and entering a dwelling house (felony of first degree if armed or assault committed; otherwise, second degree).
810.02   Breaking and entering other buildings, ship, or vessel (generally of second degree unless high explosive used).
810.03   Entering without breaking (generally of third degree).
810.05   Breaking and entering with intent to commit a misdemeanor (a felony of the third degree).
810.051 Breaking and entering or entering without breaking a vehicle (a felony of the third degree).

[8] All robberies fall under FSL 813.011, which defines them to be felonies of the first degree punishable by life imprisonment or any lesser term of years.

purposes, six samples (each numbering 100 control cards) were drawn, as follows:

1. The first-period general sample: drawn from all closed felony cases that were filed during December 1973 through May 1974.
2. The second-period general sample: drawn from all closed felony cases that were filed during December 1974 through May 1975.
3. The first-period breaking and entering sample: drawn from first-period closed cases whose most serious charges included breaking and entering felony offenses.
4. The second-period breaking and entering sample: as above for the second period.
5. The first-period robbery sample: drawn from first-period closed cases whose charges included robbery.
6. The second-period robbery sample: as above for the second period.

The General Samples. Systematic sampling of the control card file, with an interval of 30 cards, was used to provide a sample of case folders distributed uniformly in time over the two selected periods. (For each of the first 5 months, sampling was discontinued after the eighteenth case selection of the month; for the final month (May) of each period, 10 cases were sampled). If the sampled case proved to be open rather than closed, or had a missing case folder, or involved an arrest on a writ, then we substituted a case obtained by searching the file in reverse chronological order for the first appropriate case preceding the inappropriate one. Some selected cases had been combined with another case against the same defendant, in which instance, the latter case entered the sample. Sample control sheets were maintained, as described in the discussion of Multnomah County data collection procedure.

The first annexed Information Form at the end of this appendix served to record case data for the Dade general samples as well as those for Multnomah. The four auxiliary response spaces (items 9 to 12) were employed in Dade as follows: (01) was entered in item 9 if the case was *nolle pros.*—the date for this event being entered in item 8-*H*; the number of lay witness depositions was entered in item 10; the number of defendants was entered in item 11; and (01) was entered in item 12 if the defendant pleaded not guilty for reason of insanity. An alphanumeric code was devised to enable two symbols to suffice for the total number of days consumed in continuances for item 7*E*, which sometimes exceeded two digits.

The Breaking and Entering Samples. The 100-case sample for each of the two periods was obtained by selecting the first 18 cases containing breaking and entering felony charges in each of the first 5 months of a period and 10 cases in the final month (May). Case substitutions were necessary for some of these selections, for reasons noted above; the substituted case was drawn from the same month as the inappropriate case. Sampling control was maintained as described above. The second annexed Information Form at the end of this appendix served to record the case data for the breaking and entering samples. Here the four auxiliary response items were employed as follows:

Item 33: What was the nature of sentence suspension, if any?

(01) Entire sentence suspended.
(02) Only incarceration suspended.
(03) Only fines suspended.
(04) Both incarceration and fines suspended.
(05) Suspensions other than above.

Item 34: What type of case dismissal?

(01) *Nolle prosequi.*
(02) Other.

Item 35: Was breaking and entering of a dwelling charged?

Affirmative shown by entry of symbol "D".

Item 36: How many defendants in the case?

Because little information was found in the case folders pertaining to the defendant's prior record (item 11) and biography (items 1 to 10), a separate sampling effort was made to fill this gap (see below).

The Robbery Samples. The selection procedures for the robbery samples were the same as for the breaking and entering samples. Because of a paucity of closed robbery cases from the latter part of the second period (at the time of the data collection), the second-period robbery sample is more concentrated in the first three months of the period. The optional response items of the second annexed Information Form at the end of this appendix were used as described above, with the exception that item 35 did not apply.

Defendant Biographic and Prior Record Information. Given the lack of biographic and prior-record data in the 400 exemplary-offenses folders sampled from the Court Clerk's files, we sought alternative sources for this information. Biographic data turned out to be obtainable from three sources. For the second period, the Pre-Trial Release Program produced records with (defendant-provided) biographic data on defendants eligible for pretrial release. While this was the most comprehensive source for the second period, it provided no coverage of the first. Another source of biographic data was the Public Defender's Office, which maintained case folders on defendants represented by that office. And a third source was presentence reports (which are prepared for youthful or first-time offenders, unless waived). The most available file of these reports was found in the offices of the Probation and Parole Commission, provided the defendant was not currently on active probation. Some presentence reports were available in the files of the sentencing judges.

Defendant's "rap" sheets would have been the most reliable source of prior-record information, but they proved not to be sufficiently accessible. Contrary to expectations, case folders maintained in the State Attorney's office turned out generally to lack these "rap" sheets. The police department was said to keep a "rap" sheet file on all defendants, but access would have required formal approval by law enforcement agencies. As an expedient, we turned to the sources used for biographic data, although recognizing that these prior-record data are not as accurate as would be found on "rap" sheets.

Dispositions in the Magistrate's Division. To better understand the effect of judicial screening that occurs in the Magistrate's Division of the Dade County Court System, we took four samples of cases to show how suspects fared at that stage of the proceedings, i.e., to show the proportions of cases filed as a felony, filed as a misdemeanor, dismissed (by the Magistrate), or "no information" by the State Attorney. Two samples were composed of breaking and entering cases from the two periods studied, respectively; two were of robbery cases from the two periods, respectively. Each sample numbered about 100 cases, with 18 cases coming from each of the first five months of a period and 10 from the final month. The sampling was performed by means of a computer listing of cases produced by the Court Clerk's office. The listing provided for each case: the offenses charged, the defendant's name, the date of the Magistrate's hearing, and the case disposition as defined above.

Reasons for "No Information." We had anticipated sampling 400 cases to reveal the reasons given by the State Attorney for his decision not to file an information against a breaking and entering or robbery suspect. A convenient source for this data was the monthly summary of cases, prepared by the State Attorney's office. It turned out, however, that only 43 of these breaking and entering and robbery cases arose during the entire span of months from December 1973 to May 1975. And the reasons given for "no information" in a majority of these cases was pretrial intervention (i.e., diversion).

Number of Witnesses per Case and Number of Witness Appearances per Case. We sought to draw data concerning the number of witnesses per case and the number of witness appearances per case from the general sample of 200 case folders (all felony offenses). Unfortunately, a high proportion of these data was not obtainable from the materials within the folders.

Type and Duration of Judicial Activities. Our plans to demonstrate an application of the weighted-caseload measure were preempted by a weighted-caseload study that the Circuit Court had itself recently completed, as part of a statewide effort mandated by the Florida Supreme Court. We have not been able to gain access to this information, so the topic is not included in the coverage of this report on Dade County.

Recapitulation of Data Availability.

1. Felony case information (from case folders):
   a. Virtually all dispositional data were present in the case folders of the general and exemplary-offenses samples.
   b. Virtually all sentencing data were available in the case samples.
   c. Dates of proceeding steps were fairly complete, but one or more were missing in some individual cases.
2. Defendant-related data (generally from sources other than case folders):
   a. See Table B-2.
3. Dispositions in the Magistrate's Division:
   a. Data available for four samples of 100 cases each (respectively for the exemplary offenses, both periods).
4. Reasons for "no information":
   a. The State Attorney elected to "no information" only 43 cases involving

Table B-2
Percentage of Sampled Cases for which Defendant Data Were Available, B&E and Robbery

Item	1974 Samples B&E	Robbery	1975 Samples B&E	Robbery
Age	100	100	99	98
Ethnicity	99	100	97	100
Transiency	58	51	72	70
Occupation	72	72	70	65
Income	24	32	34	40
Education	59	50	55	64
Marital status	66	56	75	78
No. dependents	64	53	74	77
Prior record	61	58	75	75
Pretrial custody	98	95	95	95
Type of attorney	99	99	97	97
No. in sample	99	99	99	100

the exemplary offenses during the two periods study (the majority being for reasons of pretrial intervention). Our sample was of all 43.

5. Number of witnesses per case and number of witness (or victim) appearances per case:

    a. Data were obtainable from only 14 cases (9 trial and 5 nontrial) of the 100-case general sample for the first period.

    b Data were obtainable from only 6 cases (3 trial and 3 nontrial) of the 100-case sample for the second period.

First Annex

Information Form:
General Case Sample — All Offense Types

Jurisdiction _____

Period Covered _____

Recorded by _____

Date Recorded _____

Case Information   01/   02/   03-04/   05-07/

□   □   □   □   □

Site   Period Form   Q. No.

                                                        CARD 01   08-09/

□□□□□□□□□□

Docket No.

1. Indicate most serious original charge (Specify):

_____

_____

_____

                              (Coders Only)   □□□   20-22/

2. Offender's pretrial custody status (Circle One):

    Out on bail or OR 1   23/
    In jail 2
    Combination of above 3

3. Outcome of trial (Circle One):

    Convicted (Circle and Go To Q. 4) 1   24/
    Acquitted (Circle and Go To Q. 5) 2
    Dismissed (Circle and Go To Q. 5) 3
    Other: e.g., mistrial, hung jury (Circle and Go to Q. 5) 4

4. If convicted, indicate on what charge (Circle One):

    Most serious original 1   25/
    Lesser 2

5. Category of sentence imposed (Circle All That Apply):

    Probation 1   26/
    Fine 2   27/
    Jail Term 3   28/
    Prison Term 4   29/
    Suspended 5   30/
    Other 6   31/

6. Lay participant called at hearings and trial: (Enter Totals)

Type of Lay Participant	Tally Sheet	Total No. Called	Tally Sheet	Total No. of Separate Appearances
		32-33/		38-39/
A. Victims				
		34-35/		40-41/
B. Witnesses (Nonexpert)				
		36-37/		42-43/
C. Defendants				

7. Continuances Requested: (Enter Totals)

Requestor	Tally Sheet	Total No. Called	Tally Sheet	Total Days Consumed
		44-45/		54-55/
A. Defense				
		46-47/		56-57/
B. Prosecution				
		48-49/		58-59/
C. Court				
		50-51/		60-61/
D. Reported as Combination				
		52-53/		62-63/
E. Unidentified Requestor				

8. Indicate the dates at which *any* of the following occurred.　　*CARD* 02

A. Arrest . . . .

　　　　　　　　　　　　　　　Mo.　　Day　　Yr.　　　*10-15/*

B. Charging or indictment
(enter earliest) . . . .

　　　　　　　　　　　　　　　Mo.　　Day　　Yr.　　　*16-21/*

If charged, record the name of the prosecutor involved.
(LAST NAME FIRST):

Prosecutor: *22-34/*　　　　　*35-40/*

　　　　　　　　(Last Name)　　　　　　　(First Name)

C. First appearance
(lower court) . . . .

　　　　　　　　　　　　　　　Mo.　　Day　　Yr.　　　*41-46/*

D. Preliminary hearing
(lower court) . . . .

　　　　　　　　　　　　　　　Mo.　　Day　　Yr.　　　*47-52/*

E. Arraignment . . . .

　　　　　　　　　　　　　　　Mo.　　Day　　Yr.　　　*53-58/*

F. Transfer to another
jurisdiction . . . .

　　　　　　　　　　　　　　　Mo.　　Day　　Yr.　　　*59-64/*

G. Diversion . . . .

　　　　　　　　　　　　　　　Mo.　　Day　　Yr.　　　*65-70/*

H. Pre-trial Dismissal . . . .

　　　　　　　　　　　　　　　Mo.　　Day　　Yr.　　　*71-76/*

If dismissed, indicate the reason. (Circle One):　　*CARD* 03

Insufficient evidence . . . . 1　　*13/*
Search and seizure 2
Other (including "interest of justice") or 3
Unspecified 4

I. Pretrial plea of guilty . . . .

　　　　　　　　　　　　　　　Mo.　　Day　　Yr.　　　*14-19/*

If pretrial plea, indicate charge plead to: (Circle One):

Most serious original charge(s)/count(s) . . . . 1　　*20/*
Lesser charge(s)/count(s) 2

J. Indicate type of trial:

Court . . . . 1　　*21/*
Jury 2
Other 3

1. Enter date(s) of trial:

Began: ☐☐☐☐☐☐ *22-27/*
        Mo. Day Yr.

Ended: ☐☐☐☐☐☐ *28-33/*
        Mo. Day Yr.

2. Record the following names (Last Name First):

   a. Judge: *34-46/*   *47-52/*

☐☐☐☐☐☐☐☐☐☐☐☐☐ ☐☐☐☐☐☐
      (Last Name)   (First Name)

   b. Prosecutor at trial or who
      negotiated guilty plea
           53-65/   *66-71/*

☐☐☐☐☐☐☐☐☐☐☐☐☐ ☐☐☐☐☐☐
      (Last Name)   (First Name)

CARD 04

   c. Defense Counsel:
           13-25/   *26-32/*

☐☐☐☐☐☐☐☐☐☐☐☐☐ ☐☐☐☐☐☐
      (Last Name)   (First Name)

Indicate type of defense counsel. (Circle One):

Public Defender 1 *32/*
Private (court-appointed, defendant-retained) 2

K. Sentence imposed: ☐☐☐☐☐☐ *33-38/*
                  Mo. Day Yr.
If sentenced, record the name of the sentencing judge.
(LAST NAME FIRST):

Judge: *39-51/*   *52-57/*

☐☐☐☐☐☐☐☐☐☐☐☐☐ ☐☐☐☐☐☐

L. Was this case appealed?

No 1 *58/*
Yes 2

Additional Information

9.   ☐☐ *59-60/*

248

10. ☐☐ *61-62/*

11. ☐☐ *63-64/*

12. ☐☐ *65-66/*

Second Annex

Information Form:
Specified Offense Case Sample

Jurisdiction _____

Period Covered _____

Offense Type _____

Recorded by _____

Date Recorded _____

Offender Information

1/	2/	3-4/	5-7/

Site   Period   Form   Q. No.

CARD 01   8-9/

Docket No.   10-19/

Biographic Information

1. Age of offender:

   Years   *20-21/*

2. Race/Ethnic (Circle One):

   Black 1   *22/*
   Spanish surname 2
   American Indian 3
   Oriental 4
   Other 5
   Unspecified 6

3. How long living in jurisdiction: Years   *23-24/*

4. Did offender have regular employment?

   No 1   *25/*
   Yes 2

   If Yes: How long last job?   Months   *26-27/*

5. Usual occupation (Specify):

   _____

   _____

       28-29/

6. Estimated annual income. $,   *30-35/*

7. Now attending school?

   No 1   *36/*
   Yes 2

8. Number of school years completed.   Years   □□   *37-38/*

9. Ever married?

   No 1   *39/*
   Yes 2

10. Number of dependent minor children (under 18).   □□   *40-41/*

Prior Record

11. Indicate status of prior record (Circle One).

    No prior record 1   *42/*
        (less than 3 prior arrests and no convictions)

    Minor prior record 2
        (3 or more arrests or some convictions but none carrying more
        than 90 days jail or 2 years probation)

    Major prior record 3
        (any convictions carrying more than 90 days jail or 2 years pro-
        bation but no prison commitments)

    Prison record 4
        (any prison commitments)

Pretrial Custody Status

12. Indicate pre-trial custody status (Circle One):

    In jail 1   *43/*
    Out on bail 2
    Out on OR 3
    Combinations of jail and bail or OR 4

Defense Counsel

13. Indicate type of defense counsel (Circle One):

    Public Defender 1   *44/*
    Court Appointed 2
    Defendent-retained 3
    Other 4

14. Indicate the dates at which any of the following occurred.

A. Arrest . . . .   Mo.   Day   Yr.   *45-50/*

If charged, record the name of the prosecutor involved.
(LAST NAME FIRST)

51-63/   *64-69/*

Last Name   First Name

B. Charging or Indictment (enter   *70-75/*
   earliest) . . . .   Mo.   Day   Yr.

CARD 02

C. First appearance (lower   *13-18/*
   court) . . . . Mo.   Day   Yr.

D. Preliminary hearing (lower   *19-24/*
   court) . . . . Mo.   Day   Yr.

E. Arraignment *25-30/*
                                            Mo.   Day   Yr.

F. Transfer to another   *31-36/*
   jurisdiction . . . .   Mo.   Day   Yr.

G. Diversion *37-42/*
                                            Mo.   Day   Yr.

H. Pretrial dismissal *43-48/*
                                            Mo.   Day   Yr.

If dismissed, indicate the reason: (Circle One):

Insufficient evidence 1   *49/*
Search and seizure 2
Other (including interest of justice) 3

I. Pretrial plea of guilty *50-55/*
                                            Mo.   Day   Yr.

J. 1. Enter date(s) of trial:

   Began: *56-61/*
                                            Mo.   Day   Yr.

   Ended: *62-67/*
                                            Mo.   Day   Yr.

2. Record the following names (Last Name First):

a. Judge: *13-25/*   *26-31/*

Last Name   First Name

b. Prosecutor at trial or who
    negotiated guilty plea

                  32-44/   *45-50/*

Last Name   First Name

c. Defense Counsel   *51-63/*   *64-69/*

Last Name   First Name

K. Sentence handed down *70-75/*

                         Mo.   Day   Yr.

If sentenced, record the name of the judge involved.
(LAST NAME FIRST)

Judge: *13-25/*   *26-31/*

Last Name   First Name

15. Original Charges and dispositions.

	No. Specify	Specifications — Coder Only	Specifications — Enter No. of Counts	Dropped — Enter No. of Counts	Dropped — Charges (Circle One)	Pretrial Plea — Enter No. of Counts	Pretrial Plea — Charges (Circle One)	Court Trial — Enter No. of Counts	Court Trial — Charges (Circle One)	Jury Trial — Enter No. of Counts	Jury Trial — Charges (Circle One)	Other Contested Dispositions Method — Enter No. of Counts	Other Contested Dispositions Method — Charges (Circle One)
C H A R G E S	1	32-33/	34/	36/	35/ No 1 / Yes 2	38/	37/ Guilty 1 / Not Guilty 2	40/	39/ Convict 1 / Acquit 2 / Dismiss 3 / Other 4	42/	41/ Convict 1 / Acquit 2 / Dismiss 3 / Other 4	44/	43/ Convict 1 / Acquit 2 / Dismiss 3 / Other 4
	2	45-46/	47/	49/	48/ No 1 / Yes 2	51/	50/ Guilty 1 / Not Guilty 2	53/	52/ Convict 1 / Acquit 2 / Dismiss 3 / Other 4	55/	54/ Convict 1 / Acquit 2 / Dismiss 3 / Other 4	57/	56/ Convict 1 / Acquit 2 / Dismiss 3 / Other 4
	3	58-59/	60/	62/	61/ No 1 / Yes 2	64/	63/ Guilty 1 / Not Guilty 2	66/	65/ Convict 1 / Acquit 2 / Dismiss 3 / Other 4	68/	67/ Convict 1 / Acquit 2 / Dismiss 3 / Other 4	70/	69/ Convict 1 / Acquit 2 / Dismiss 3 / Other 4
CARD 05													
	4	13-14/	15/	17/	16/ No 1 / Yes 2	19/	18/ Guilty 1 / Not Guilty 2	21/	20/ Convict 1 / Acquit 2 / Dismiss 3 / Other 4	23/	22/ Convict 1 / Acquit 2 / Dismiss 3 / Other 4	25/	24/ Convict 1 / Acquit 2 / Dismiss 3 / Other 4
	5	26-27/	28/	30/	29/ No 1 / Yes 2	32/	31/ Guilty 1 / Not Guilty 2	34/	33/ Convict 1 / Acquit 2 / Dismiss 3 / Other 4	36/	35/ Convict 1 / Acquit 2 / Dismiss 3 / Other 4	38/	37/ Convict 1 / Acquit 2 / Dismiss 3 / Other 4
A L L E G A T I O N S	1	39-40/			41/ No 1 / Yes 2		42/ Guilty 1 / Not Guilty 2		43/ Convict 1 / Acquit 2 / Dismiss 3 / Other 4		44/ Convict 1 / Acquit 2 / Dismiss 3 / Other 4		45/ Convict 1 / Acquit 2 / Dismiss 3 / Other 4

46-47/	2

48/ No 1 Yes 2

49/ Guilty 1 Not Guilty 2

50/
Convict 1
Acquit 2
Dismiss 3
Other 4

51/
Convict 1
Acquit 2
Dismiss 3
Other 4

52/
Convict 1
Acquit 2
Dismiss 3
Other 4

53-54/	3

55/ No 1 Yes 2

56/ Guilty 1 Not Guilty 2

57/
Convict 1
Acquit 2
Dismiss 3
Other 4

58/
Convict 1
Acquit 2
Dismiss 3
Other 4

59/
Convict 1
Acquit 2
Dismiss 3
Other 4

16. Were any charges amended? (Circle One)

No (Go To Q. 18) 1
Yes (Go To Q. 17) 2

CARD 06
13/

17. Amended charges and dispositions.

CHARGES		Specifications			Dropped		Pretrial Plea		Court Trial		Jury Trial		Other Contested Dispositions Method	
	No. Specify	Coder Only	Enter No. of Counts		Charges (Circle One)	Enter No. of Counts	Charges (Circle One)	Enter No. of Counts	Charges (Circle One)	Enter No. of Counts	Charges (Circle One)	Enter No. of Counts	Charges (Circle One)	Enter No. of Counts
1		14-15/	16/		17/ No 1 Yes 2	18/	19/ Guilty 1 Not Guilty 2	20/	21/ Convict 1 Acquit 2 Dismiss 3 Other 4	22/	23/ Convict 1 Acquit 2 Dismiss 3 Other 4	24/	25/ Convict 1 Acquit 2 Dismiss 3 Other 4	26/
2		27-28/	29/		30/ No 1 Yes 2	31/	32/ Guilty 1 Not Guilty 2	33/	34/ Convict 1 Acquit 2 Dismiss 3 Other 4	35/	36/ Convict 1 Acquit 2 Dismiss 3 Other 4	37/	38/ Convict 1 Acquit 2 Dismiss 3 Other 4	39/
3		40-41/	42/		43/ No 1 Yes 2	44/	45/ Guilty 1 Not Guilty 2	46/	47/ Convict 1 Acquit 2 Dismiss 3 Other 4	48/	49/ Convict 1 Acquit 2 Dismiss 3 Other 4	50/	51/ Convict 1 Acquit 2 Dismiss 3 Other 4	52/
4		53-54/	55/		56/ No 1 Yes 2	57/	58/ Guilty 1 Not Guilty 2	59/	60/ Convict 1 Acquit 2 Dismiss 3 Other 4	61/	62/ Convict 1 Acquit 2 Dismiss 3 Other 4	63/	64/ Convict 1 Acquit 2 Dismiss 3 Other 4	65/
5		66-67/	68/		69/ No 1 Yes 2	70/	71/ Guilty 1 Not Guilty 2	72/	73/ Convict 1 Acquit 2 Dismiss 3 Other 4	74/	75/ Convict 1 Acquit 2 Dismiss 3 Other 4	76/	77/ Convict 1 Acquit 2 Dismiss 3 Other 4	78/

257

	13-14/	15/	16/	17/	18/	19/
CARD 07		No 1 Yes 2	Guilty 1 Not Guilty 2	Convict 1 Acquit 2 Dismiss 3 Other 4	Convict 1 Acquit 2 Dismiss 3 Other 4	Convict 1 Acquit 2 Dismiss 3 Other 4
1		15/	16/	17/	18/	19/

ALLEGATIONS	20-21/	22/	23/	24/	25/	26/
2		No 1 Yes 2	Guilty 1 Not Guilty 2	Convict 1 Acquit 2 Dismiss 3 Other 4	Convict 1 Acquit 2 Dismiss 3 Other 4	Convict 1 Acquit 2 Dismiss 3 Other 4

	27-28/	29/	30/	31/	32/	33/
3		No 1 Yes 2	Guilty 1 Not Guilty 2	Convict 1 Acquit 2 Dismiss 3 Other 4	Convict 1 Acquit 2 Dismiss 3 Other 4	Convict 1 Acquit 2 Dismiss 3 Other 4

18. Was the subject convicted on any charge?

    No (End Survey) 1   *34/*

    Yes 2

19. Was a probation sentence imposed?

    No (Go To Q. 22) 1   *35/*

    Yes, One Charge Only 2

    Yes, More Than One Charge, Concurrent 3

    Yes, More Than One Charge, Consecutive 4

20. What was aggregate time on probation?

    If definite probation time imposed, enter same no. in both places.

    A. Minimum No. of Months   ☐☐☐   *36-38/*

    B. Maximum No. of Months   ☐☐☐   *39-41/*

21. Was probation supervised?

    No 1   *42/*

    Yes 2

22. Was a jail sentence imposed?

    No (Go To Q. 25) 1   *43/*

    Yes, One Charge Only 2

    Yes, More Than One Charge, Concurrent 3

    Yes, More Than One Charge, Consecutive 4

23. What was the aggregate time of the jail sentence? If a definite jail sentence was imposed, enter the same number in both places:

    A. Minimum No. of Months   ☐☐☐   *44-46/*

    B. Maximum No. of Months   ☐☐☐   *47-49/*

24. Was the presentence time served credited against the jail sentence?

    No 1   *50/*

    Yes 2

25. Was a prison sentence imposed?

No (Go To Q. 8) 1 *51/*
Yes, One Charge Only 2
Yes, More Than One Charge, Concurrent 3
Yes, More Than One Charge, Consecutive 4

26. What was the aggregate time of the prison sentence?

If a definite prison sentence was imposed, enter the same number in both places.

A. Minimum No. of Years   [ ][ ][ ]   *52-54/*

B. Maximum No. of Years   [ ][ ][ ]   *55-57/*

27. Was the presentence time served credited against the prison sentence?

No 1 *58/*
Yes 2

28. Was a fine imposed?

No (Go To Q. 20) 1 *59/*
Yes, One Charge Only   2
Yes, More Than One Charge 3

29. What was the aggregate amount of the fine?   *60-63/*

$ [ ][ ][ ][ ]

30. Was a sentence of restitution imposed?

No 1 *64/*
Yes 2

31. Was a sentence of community service imposed?

No 1 *65/*
Yes 2

32. Was a sentence of special rehabilitation in an institution or hospital imposed?

No 1   *66/*
Yes 2

Additional Information

33.   *67-68/*

34.   *69-70/*

35.   *71-72/*

36.   *73-74/*

Appendix C
Descriptions of Variables
and Results of Statistical
Analyses

In this appendix we define all the variables used in the multivariate regression equations, present the means and standard deviations for all variables, and indicate the results of the multivariate analysis for conviction probability, sentence severity, and case duration. A final section presents the formulas used to evaluate the statistical significance of differences between means and proportions for tables in the text.

Definition of Variables

Table C-1 describes each of the variables used and indicates how each was constructed. It will be noted that most independent variables were transformed into dichotomous zero/one dummies. We experimented with a community ties index to measure how established a defendant was in the local community, which we hypothesized would influence the sentence imposed on him, and other outcomes as well. Its construction is explained in note 1 to Table C-1. Methods used to collect the samples and definitions of the offense classification are given in Chapter 4.

Means and Standard Deviations of Variables

Tables C-2 through C-5 contain the means (μ) and standard deviations (σ) of all variables utilized in the multivariate analysis by jurisdiction and year. A long dash (−) or a blank indicate that the variable did not apply (e.g., OFF. IN DWELL. for robberies), that information was not available (e.g., SENT. BARG. in Dade County) or was not collected (e.g., ORIG A($1°$) CHGS. for all felonies). A single zero (0) indicates that the event did not occur in that particular sample (e.g., JURY TRIAL in Dade County breaking and entering offenses, 1975). Statistics for a subsample of convictees only (by plea of guilty or by trial) are shown for the exemplary offenses, since the sentence severity equations were estimated for these defendants only.

Results of the Multivariate Analyses

Tables C-6 through C-25 present the results for the multivariate regression equations using ordinary least-squares estimation. All variables were run in their linear forms, since we had no theoretical justification for transforming them.

The column headings indicate the regression coefficient and its *T* value. η is the elasticity, evaluated at the mean, and shows for each variable the percentage change in the dependent variable associated with a 1-percent change in the independent variable.

The values for the dichotomous variables should be interpreted as the effect of the variable listed as compared to a situation in which the excluded variable obtains. For example:

Included Variable	*Excluded Variable*
BLACK	Nonblack
OTHER MINORITY	Black or majority
MIN. P.R. MAJ. P.R. PRIS. P.R.	No prior record
JAIL CUSTODY BAIL O.R.	Combination of jail and bail or own recognizance
CT. APP. COUN. DEF. RET. COUN.	Public defender
OFF. IN DWELL.	Offense not in dwelling
CHG. RED. BARG. COUNT. RED. BARG. DISM. & TRI. ACQ.	Conviction on all charges and counts
SENT. BARG. DROP OTH. CASE BARG.	No such bargain
COURT TRIAL JURY TRIAL	No trial for conviction and duration eqns; straight plea for sentence eqns.
PUB. DEFDR.	Private counsel
PROP. OFF. DRUG OFF. OTH. OFF.	Remaining offense types

R^2's, adjusted R^2's, and the *F* statistic for each equation are given at the foot of the tables. Whether or not the regression equation is significant (i.e., whether the composite of independent variables explains more of the variance in the dependent variable than random chance alone) can be evaluated in terms of the F statistic with the appropriate degrees of freedom (D.F.) For reference, the F value must be at least as high as 1.93 for D.F. = 20, 70 and at least as high as 1.84 for D.F. 25, 50 at the 95 percent level of confidence.

Determinants of Conviction

Our purpose in running these equations was to estimate the effect of the hypothesized independent variables on the probability of conviction at the three alternative levels plus nonconviction, which are indicated in the column headings. The independent variables reflect characteristics of the defendant, his pretrial status and type of counsel, the original charges filed against him, whether he was tried, and the influence of the case backlog (a proxy variable for which is MO. FIN. DISPO.) These regressions are based on samples of all defendants. Adjusted R^2's are mostly under 0.10 and rarely exceed 0.30. The F test was met in only 13 of 32 equations. We therefore tend to place little faith in the model we developed to explain conviction level.

Determinants of Sentence Severity

Our purpose in running these equations was to estimate the contribution of the hypothesized independent variables to a score that indicates the severity of the sentence imposed on the defendant. The sentence score was generated according to four alternative indices (see Chapter 4). In addition to the independent variables employed in the conviction equations, we added the type of bargain (and, therefore, type of disposition) the defendant had.[1] The samples of course contained only defendants who were convicted. R^2's (except for the 1974 Dade robberies) were mostly in excess of 0.40. Six out of 32 equations failed to meet the F test but four of these failures were for 1974 robbery cases in Dade County (Table C-20). There does appear to be a good deal of volatility in the size, signs, and significance of the coefficients on independent variables across indices, years, offenses and jurisdictions; more work on the sentence severity model thus seems indicated.

The Determinants of Case Duration

Our purpose in running these equations was to estimate the contribution of the hypothesized independent variables to case elapsed time measured from arraign-

---

[1] In these equations the variable MO. FIN. DISPO. is best interpreted as a proxy for crowding in county and state correctional facilities that built up steadily over time in both jurisdictions.

ment to final disposition. We used samples of all felonies, for which we had fewer and somewhat different data elements, as well as samples of our exemplary offenses. Adjusted R^2's mostly exceeded 0.20 and never fell below 0.10 for those equations it was possible to estimate. (Time truncation in the sample of all felonies for Dade in 1975 precluded the calculation of meaningful estimates; the estimates for the exemplary offense samples for Dade 1975 should be treated with great caution as well.) The F statistics were acceptable at a 95 percent level of confidence in 7 equations out of 11. Since the estimates do not behave very consistently in magnitude and direction across years, offenses, or jurisdictions, we feel that more work on both model specification and data improvement is necessary.

Test for Significance of Difference Between Statistics

In peforming statistical tests of the difference between two proportions, we used the following formula:[2]

$$T = \frac{P_1 - P_2}{\sqrt{\dfrac{p'q'}{N_1} + \dfrac{p'q'}{N_2}}}$$

where P_1 = the proportion for the first sample

P_2 = the proportion for the second sample

N_1 = the size of the first sample

N_2 = the size of the second sample

$$p' = \frac{P_1 N_1 + P_2 N_2}{N_1 + N_2}$$

$$q' = 1 - p'$$

  In performing statistical tests of the difference between two means, we used the standard formula, i.e.:

---

[2] Adopted from P.G. Hoel, *Introduction to Mathematical Statistics*, New York, Wiley, 1974, pp. 148-151.

$$T = \frac{\mu_1 - \mu_2}{\sqrt{\dfrac{\sigma_1^2}{N_1} + \dfrac{\sigma_2^2}{N_2}}}$$

where μ_1 = the mean for the first sample

μ_2 = the mean for the second sample

σ_1 = the standard deviation of the first sample

σ_2 = the standard deviation of the second sample

N_1 = the size of the first sample

N_2 = the size of the second sample

T statistics were evaluated at the 95 percent level of confidence. Tests of differences between proportions or between means were applied to all year-to-year comparisons and sometimes to other comparisons, such as prior record classes within a given year, or race/ethnic classes within a given year, or to jurisdiction comparisons (e.g., proportion of robbery defendants obtaining pretrial dismissal) within a given year.

Table C-1
Definition of Variables

Abbreviation	Description	Construction
Com. Ties Index	A proxy variable constructed to reflect the strength of the defendant's community ties	Adjusted score based on a principal components analysis of variables reflecting defendant's socioeconomic and family attributes[a]
Age	Age of defendant	Less than 20 yr = 0 20-30 yr = 1 Over 30 yr = 2
Black	Race of defendant	Other = 0 Black = 1
Other Minority	Ethnic category of defendant	Anglo, black = 0 Spanish surname, Asian, American Indian = 1
Min. P.R.[b]	Defendant has minor prior criminal record	No record, major or prison record = 0 Minor record = 1
Maj. P.R.[b]	Defendant has major prior criminal record	No record, minor or prison record = 0 Major record = 1
Pris. P.R.[b]	Defendant has prison prior criminal record	No record, minor or major record = 0 Prison record = 1
Jail Custody	Defendant was confined to jail prior to case disposition	Bail, OR or combination of bail/OR and jail = 0; Jail = 1
Bail[c]	Defendant was out on bail prior to case disposition	OR, jail or combination of bail/OR and jail = 0; OR = 1
O.R.[c]	Defendant was out on own recognizance prior to disposition	Bail, jail or combination of bail/OR and jail = 0; OR = 1
Ct. App. Coun.[d]	Defendant was represented by counsel appointed by the court	Public defender or defendant-retained counsel = 0 Court-appointed counsel = 1
Def. Ret. Coun.[d]	Defendant was represented by counsel he retained himself	Public defender or court-appointed counsel = 0 Defendant-retained counsel = 1
Orig. A(1°) Chgs.	A level (Multnomah) or first degree (Dade) charges originally filed against defendant	Total number of counts at that level

Table C-1 (cont.)

Abbreviation	Description	Construction
Orig. B(2°) Chgs.	B level (Multnomah) or second degree (Dade) charges originally filed against defendant	Total number of counts at that level
Orig. C(3°) Chgs.	C level (Multnomah) or third degree (Dade) charges originally filed against defendant	Total number of counts at that level
Orig. Misd. Chgs.	Misdemeanor charges originally filed against defendant	Total number of misdemeanor counts
Off. in Dwell.	Burglary (Multnomah) or breaking and entering offense (Dade) took place in a dwelling	Not in dwelling = 0 In dwelling = 1
Chg. Red. Barg.	Charge(s) upon which the defendant was convicted by plea (or at trial) was at a level or a degree lower than that at which he was originally charged	Convicted on all charges or at same level (degree) as original charges or not convicted = 0 Convicted at reduced charge level (degree) = 1
Count. Red. Barg.	Defendant was convicted by plea (or at trial) on fewer total counts than originally filed against him but at the same level (degree) as the original charges	Convicted on all charges or at a reduced charge level or not convicted = 0 Convicted on fewer counts, same level (degree) = 1
Sent. Barg.[e]	Defendant negotiated an agreement on or was given an assurance as to his sentence in return for a plea; or prosecutor agreed not to oppose a sentence recommendation made by defense	Did not get sentence bargain = 0 Did get sentence bargain = 1
Drop Oth. Case Barg.[e]	Prosecutor agreed to drop other pending case(s) against defendant in return for a guilty plea in this case	Had no other cases dropped = 0 Had other cases dropped = 1
Court Trial	Defendant was tried by judge (i.e., no jury)	Did not have court trial = 0 Had court trial = 1

Table C-1 (cont.)

Abbreviation	Description	Construction
Jury Trial	Defendant was tried by jury	Did not have jury trial = 0 Had jury trial = 1
Mo. Fin. Dispo.[f]	Month of final disposition of case	Numbered sequentially by month beginning January 1973
Pub. Defdr.[g]	Defendant was represented by the public defender	Was not represented by public defender = 0 Was represented by public defender = 1
No. Defs.[g,h]	Number of defendants involved in case	Total number
Prop. Off.[g]	Felony offenses against property (e.g., theft, larceny, burglary)	Offense against person,[i] involving drugs, or other offense type = 0 Offense against property = 1
Drug Off.[g]	Felony offense involving sale or possession of drugs	Offense against person, property, or other offense type = 0 Offense involving drugs = 1
Oth. Off.[g]	All felony offenses other than against persons, property, or involving drugs (e.g., flight to avoid prosecution, bribery, etc.)	Offense against persons, property, or involving drugs = 0 Other offenses = 1
Conv. on All Chgs. and Counts	Defendant was convicted on all charges and counts originally filed against him	Convicted on reduced charges or fewer counts or not convicted = 0 Convicted on all charges and counts = 1
Conv. on Fewer Counts	See Count Red. Barg. variable	
Conv. on Red. Chgs.	See Chg. Red. Barg. variable	
Dism. and Tri. Acq.	Defendant was dismissed, *nolle pros.*, or diverted before trial; or trial ended in acquittal, mistrial, of dismissal	Defendant was convicted = 0 Defendant was not convicted = 1
SSI A[j]	Score for defendant on Sentence Severity Index A	Value of score
SSI B[j]	Score for defendant on Sentence Severity Index B	Value of score
SSI C[j]	Score for defendant on Sentence Severity Index C	Value of score

Table C-1 (cont.)

Abbreviation	Description	Construction
SSI D[j]	Score for defendant on Sentence Severity Index D	Value of score
ELT:AFD	Duration of case	Number of days elapsed from arraignment in circuit court to final disposition (e.g., dismissal, acquittal, sentencing)

[a]A principal components analysis was performed to devise a variable that would reflect the strength of the defendant's ties to the community in which he lived. The variables included in the analysis were:

Variable	Construction
Transiency	Less than 2 years residence in county = 0 2 or more years residence = 1
Occupation and employment	Unemployed, disabled, ill, out of labor force = 0 Operative, laborer, service worker = 1 Sales, craftsman and foreman, operative, student, armed forces = 2 Professional, technical, manager, official, proprietor = 3
Estimated annual income	0-$4,999 = 0 $5,000-$9,999 = 1 $10,000 and over = 2
Education	Not a high school graduate = 0 High school graduate = 1
Marital status	Never married = 0 Ever married = 1
Number of dependents	None = 0 Some = 1

When no defendant data on these variables were available, the mean value of the variable for the appropriate sample—e.g., 1974 robbery defendants in Dade County—was used for each defendant for whom the information was missing. Only one important component was extracted. An examination of correlations between the variables in that component and the weighting coefficients for the variables indicated that all variables should be retained in computing a score for the component. The simple algebraic sum of the variables scores constituted an adequate estimate of the component. The signs associated with the weighting coefficients were taken into account in computing the component, i.e., variables associated with negative weights were reversed so that a high score reflects strong community ties.

[b]Based on California Bureau of Criminal Statistics criteria for prior record categories. See Chapter 4.

[c]For the samples of all felonies, both categories of pretrial release were combined into a single variable, i.e., "Did not obtain pretrial release" = 0; "Did obtain pretrial release (i.e., bail or OR)" = 1.

[d]For robbery and burglary (B&E) offenses only.

[e]Data on this variable not available in Dade County.

[f]Variable is a proxy introduced to reflect the steady buildup over time in the felony case backlog and the crowding in correctional facilities (county jails and state prisons) that occurred in both jurisdictions.

[g]For all felonies sample only.

[h]Data on this variable were not available in Multnomah County.

[i]Offenses against persons include homicide, rape, assault, robbery, and so forth.

[j]See Chapter 4 especially Table 4-5, for details of formulas for indices.

Table C-2

Means and Standard Deviations of Variables: Multnomah County, 1973

(μ = Mean; σ = Standard Deviation)

	Robberies				Burglaries				All Felonies	
	All Defendants		Convictees		All Defendants		Convictees			
Variable	μ	σ	μ	σ	μ	σ	μ	σ	μ	σ
Independent Variable										
Com. Ties Index	0.01	1.98	0.09	2.36	−0.00	1.84	−0.03	1.80	–	–
Age	1.76	0.63	1.69	0.64	1.72	0.69	1.70	0.68	–	–
Black	0.18	0.39	0.12	0.33	0.13	0.33	0.09	0.29	–	–
Other Minority	0.05	0.22	0.05	0.22	0.01	0.11	0.02	0.12	–	–
Min. P.R.	0.14	0.35	0.12	0.33	0.19	0.40	0.15	0.36	–	–
Maj. P.R.	0.20	0.41	0.22	0.42	0.14	0.35	0.14	0.35	–	–
Pris. P.R.	0.14	0.35	0.20	0.40	0.14	0.35	0.11	0.31	–	–
Jail Custody	0.59	0.49	0.51	0.51	0.41	0.49	0.35	0.48	0.15	0.36
Bail	0.13	0.34	0.20	0.40	0.07	0.25	0.06	0.24 ⎫	0.83	0.38
O.R.	0.24	0.43	0.27	0.45	0.44	0.50	0.49	0.50 ⎭		
Ct. App. Coun.	0.27	0.44	0.22	0.42	0.13	0.33	0.12	0.33	–	–
Def. Ret. Coun.	0.14	0.35	0.17	0.38	0.30	0.46	0.25	0.43	–	–
Orig A(1°) Chgs.	1.34	0.82	0.51	1.05	1.11	0.38	1.12	0.41	–	–
Orig B(2°) Chgs.	0.06	0.24	0.12	0.33	0.08	0.31	0.08	0.27	–	–
Orig C(3°) Chgs.	0.07	0.30	0.09	0.37	0.06	0.23	0.08	0.27	–	–
Orig. Misd. Chgs.	0.04	0.19	0.07	0.26	0.07	0.30	0.09	0.34	–	–
Off. in Dwell	–	–	–	–	0.65	0.48	0.72	0.45	–	–
Chg. Red. Barg.[a]	0.25	0.44	0.51	0.51	0.41	0.49	0.55	0.50 ⎫	0.30	0.46
Count. Red. Barg.[a]	0.08	0.28	0.17	0.38	0.11	0.32	0.15	0.36 ⎭		
Sent. Barg.	0.09	0.30	0.20	0.40	0.14	0.35	0.18	0.39	–	–
Drop Oth. Case Barg.	0.22	0.41	0.44	0.50	0.30	0.46	0.40	0.49	–	–
Court Trial	0.06	0.24	0.05	0.22	0.07	0.25	0.06	0.24	0.06	0.24
Jury Trial	0.06	0.24	0.07	0.26	0.06	0.23	0.06	0.24	0.08	0.27
Mo. Fin. Dispo.	16.78	4.42	17.20	4.86	15.36	4.10	15.65	4.11	13.78	6.03
Pub. Defender									0.50	0.50
Prop. Off.									0.44	0.50
Drug Off.									0.29	0.46
Other Off.									0.01	0.11
Dependent Variable										
(conv. on) All Chgs & Counts	0.16	0.37	0.32	0.47	0.22	0.41	0.29	0.46	0.28	0.45
(conv. on) Fewer Counts[a]	0.08	0.28	0.17	0.38	0.11	0.32	0.15	0.36 ⎫	0.30	0.46
(conv. on) Reduced Chgs.[a]	0.25	0.44	0.51	0.51	0.41	0.49	0.55	0.50 ⎭		
Dism. & Tri. Acq. (i.e., no conv.)	0.51	0.50	0.00	0.00	0.26	0.44	0.00	0.00	0.43	0.50
SSI A	8.26	11.23	16.73	10.65	8.43	8.72	11.41	8.30		

Table C-2 (cont.)

Variable	Robberies All Defendants μ	σ	Convictees μ	σ	Burglaries All Defendants μ	σ	Convictees μ	σ	All Felonies μ	σ
SSI B	10.31	18.59	20.86	21.98	7.70	12.43	10.42	13.46		
SSI C	12.35	27.17	25.00	34.48	6.97	17.49	9.43	19.81		
SSI D	21.64	64.82	43.80	71.87	14.07	31.64	19.04	35.56		
ELT:AFD	61.18	54.41	73.29	55.99	55.01	64.15	63.28	63.30	33.85	50.19

[a]The same variable was used as an independent for sentence and duration equations, and as a dependent for conviction equations, i.e.:

Chg. Red. Barg. ≡ (conv. on) Red. Chgs.

Count Red. Barg. ≡ (conv. on) Fewer Counts

Table C-3
Means and Standard Deviations of Variables: Multnomah County, 1974

(μ = Mean; σ = Standard Deviation)

Variable	Robberies All Defendants μ	σ	Convictees μ	σ	Burglaries All Defendants μ	σ	Convictees μ	σ	All Felonies μ	σ
Independent Variable										
Com. Ties Index	0.00	1.96	−0.18	1.85	0.01	2.21	0.05	1.88	−	−
Age	1.88	0.74	1.88	0.78	1.59	0.68	1.55	0.65	−	−
Black	0.06	0.25	0.03	0.18	0.10	0.30	0.09	0.29	−	−
Other Minority	0.03	0.16	0.03	0.18	0.01	0.11	0.00	0.00	−	−
Min. P.R.	0.18	0.39	0.13	0.34	0.09	0.28	0.09	0.29	−	−
Maj. P.R.	0.10	0.31	0.12	0.32	0.22	0.42	0.24	0.43	−	−
Pris. P.R.	0.21	0.41	0.22	0.42	0.13	0.34	0.11	0.31	−	−
Jail Custody	0.60	0.49	0.65	0.48	0.34	0.48	0.35	0.48	0.29	0.46
Bail	0.09	0.29	0.08	0.28	0.10	0.30	0.08	0.27	0.69	0.46
O.R.	0.19	0.40	0.17	0.38	0.44	0.50	0.47	0.50		
Ct. App. Coun.	0.37	0.49	0.40	0.49	0.40	0.49	0.42	0.50	−	−
Def. Ret. Coun.	0.09	0.29	0.10	0.30	0.11	0.31	0.14	0.35	−	−
Orig. A(1°) Chgs.	1.05	0.36	1.07	0.41	1.02	0.22	1.03	0.25	−	−
Orig. B(2°) Chgs.	0.04	0.19	0.05	0.22	0.02	0.22	0.00	0.00	−	−
Orig. C(3°) Chgs.	0.04	0.19	0.03	0.18	0.06	0.24	0.05	0.21	−	−
Orig. Misd. Chgs	0		0		0.04	0.25	0.05	0.27	−	−
Off. in Dwell.	−	−	−	−	0.63	0.48	0.74	0.44	−	−
Chg. Red. Barg.[a]	0.05	0.22	0.07	0.25	0.18	0.39	0.23	0.42	0.35	0.48
Count. Red. Barg.[a]	0.03	0.16	0.03	0.18	0.02	0.16	0.03	0.17		
Sent. Barg.	0.08	0.27	0.10	0.30	0.20	0.40	0.24	0.43	−	−
Drop Oth. Case Barg.	0.19	0.40	0.25	0.44	0.22	0.42	0.27	0.45	−	−
Court Trial	0.12	0.32	0.05	0.22	0.05	0.22	0.05	0.21	0.09	0.29
Jury Trial	0.15	0.36	0.15	0.36	0.09	0.28	0.09	0.29	0.01	0.11

Table C-3 (cont.)

Variable	Robberies				Burglaries				All Felonies	
	All Defendants		Convictees		All Defendants		Convictees			
	μ	σ	μ	σ	μ	σ	μ	σ	μ	σ
Mo. Fin. Dispo.	24.73	8.87	26.70	5.73	25.32	9.01	25.83	8.84	25.40	8.92
Pub. Defdr.									0.33	0.47
Prop. Off.									0.33	0.47
Drug Off.									0.42	0.50
Other Off.									0.03	0.16
Dependent Variable										
(conv. on) All Chgs. & Counts	0.69	0.46	0.90	0.30	0.60	0.49	0.74	0.44	0.24	0.43
(conv. on) Fewer Counts[a]	0.03	0.16	0.03	0.18	0.02	0.16	0.03	0.17	0.35	0.48
(conv. on) Reduced Chgs.[a]	0.05	0.22	0.07	0.25	0.18	0.39	0.23	0.42		
Dism. & Tri. Acq. (i.e., no conv.)	0.23	0.42	0.00	0.00	0.20	0.40	0.00	0.00	0.41	0.50
SSI A	20.40	14.43	26.52	10.33	13.62	10.95	16.92	9.63		
SSI B	33.74	31.57	43.87	29.14	16.43	18.94	20.41	19.10		
SSI C	47.09	49.59	61.22	48.27	19.23	28.26	23.89	29.69		
SSI D	89.59	103.34	116.87	106.30	37.80	56.75	46.97	59.80		
ELT:AFD	40.92	47.82	50.97	49.45	41.05	48.00	46.55	48.11	44.10	50.79

[a]See note a to Table C-2.

Table C-4
Means and Standard Deviations of Variables: Dade County, 1974

(μ = Mean; σ = Standard Deviation)

Variable	Robberies				B&E Offenses				All Felonies	
	All Defendants		Convictees		All Defendants		Convictees			
	μ	σ	μ	σ	μ	σ	μ	σ	μ	σ
Independent Variable										
Com. Ties Index	0.00	1.65	−0.16	1.69	0.00	2.35	0.07	2.64	—	—
Age	1.66	0.70	1.63	0.68	1.68	0.72	1.73	0.69	—	—
Black	0.70	0.46	0.70	0.46	0.49	0.50	0.49	0.50	—	—
Other Minority	0.09	0.28	0.08	0.27	0.13	0.33	0.11	0.31	—	—
Min. P.R.	0.28	0.45	0.32	0.47	0.16	0.37	0.16	0.37	—	—
Maj. P.R.	0.12	0.32	0.14	0.35	0.17	0.38	0.21	0.41	—	—
Pris. P.R.	0.08	0.27	0.06	0.25	0.06	0.24	0.05	0.23	—	—
Jail Custody	0.84	0.37	0.89	0.32	0.24	0.43	0.26	0.44	0.20	0.40
Bail	0.09	0.28	0.05	0.21	0.51	0.50	0.47	0.50	0.72	0.45
O.R.	0.02	0.15	0.03	0.18	0.16	0.37	0.16	0.37		
Ct. App. Coun.	0.05	0.23	0.02	0.13	0.02	0.14	0.03	0.16	—	—
Def. Ret. Coun.	0.11	0.31	0.13	0.34	0.18	0.39	0.16	0.37	—	—

Table C-4 (cont.)

Variable	Robberies All Defendants μ	σ	Convictees μ	σ	Burglaries All Defendants μ	σ	Convictees μ	σ	All Felonies μ	σ
Orig. A(1°) Chgs.	1.20	0.68	1.30	0.82	0.03	0.23	0.04	0.26	–	–
Orig. B(2°) Chgs.	0.33	0.54	0.35	0.54	0.89	0.54	0.95	0.55	–	–
Orig. C(3°) Chgs.	0.10	0.36	0.08	0.33	0.75	0.73	0.74	0.77	–	–
Orig. Misd. Chgs.	0.02	0.15	0.03	0.18	0.20	0.47	0.19	0.49	–	–
Off. in Dwell.	–	–	–	–	0.55	0.50	0.52	0.50	–	–
Chg. Red. Barg.[a]	0.12	0.32	0.17	0.38	0.08	0.28	0.11	0.31 ⎫	0.11	0.31
Count. Red. Barg.[a]	0.12	0.32	0.17	0.38	0.19	0.39	0.25	0.43 ⎭		
Court Trial	0.09	0.28	0.03	0.18	0.08	0.28	0.08	0.28	0.07	0.25
Jury Trial	0.11	0.31	0.03	0.18	0.03	0.18	0.03	0.16	0.08	0.27
Mo. Fin. Dispo.	21.52	8.93	23.41	6.16	20.57	7.90	22.11	5.36	22.03	8.47
Pub. Defdr.									0.67	0.47
No. Defs.									0.82	0.78
Prop. Off.									0.48	0.50
Drug Off.									0.20	0.40
Other Off.									0.01	0.10
Dependent Variable										
(conv. on) All Chgs. & Counts	0.44	0.50	0.65	0.48	0.49	0.50	0.64	0.48	0.55	0.50
(conv. on) Fewer Counts[a]	0.12	0.32	0.17	0.38	0.08	0.28	0.25	0.43 ⎫	0.11	0.31
(conv. on) Reduced Chgs.[a]	0.12	0.32	0.17	0.38	0.19	0.39	0.11	0.31 ⎭		
Dism. & Tri. Acq. (i.e., no conv.)	0.32	0.47	0.00	0.00	0.23	0.42	0.00	0.00	0.34	0.48
SSI A	13.06	14.75	19.28	14.18	10.04	9.90	13.06	9.38		
SSI B	21.72	29.49	32.06	30.88	11.23	16.25	14.62	17.16		
SSI C	30.38	45.82	44.84	49.57	12.43	23.84	16.18	26.09		
SSI D	58.45	99.54	86.29	110.73	17.94	45.18	23.36	50.36		
ELT:AFD	110.43	93.92	124.83	93.24	78.46	89.92	81.26	94.24	92.63	87.97

[a]See note a to C-2.

Table C-5
Means and Standard Deviations of Variables: Dade County, 1975

(μ = Mean; σ = Standard Deviation)

Variable	Robberies All Defendants μ	σ	Convictees μ	σ	B&E Offenses All Defendants μ	σ	Convictees μ	σ	All Felonies μ	σ
Independent Variable										
Com. Ties Index	0.00	2.29	0.03	2.50	−0.00	2.19	−0.03	2.28	–	–
Age	1.79	0.66	1.71	0.64	1.74	0.64	1.77	0.65	–	–

Table C-5 (cont.)

Variable	Robberies — All Defendants μ	σ	Convictees μ	σ	Burglaries — All Defendants μ	σ	Convictees μ	σ	All Felonies μ	σ
Black	0.66	0.48	0.64	0.48	0.55	0.50	0.55	0.50	–	–
Other Minority	0.05	0.23	0.03	0.17	0.11	0.31	0.11	0.31	–	–
Min. P.R.	0.26	0.44	0.30	0.46	0.23	0.42	0.22	0.42	–	–
Maj. P.R.	0.15	0.36	0.13	0.34	0.18	0.39	0.20	0.40	–	–
Pris. P.R.	0.05	0.23	0.07	0.26	0.09	0.28	0.10	0.30	–	–
Jail Custody	0.05	0.36	0.88	0.32	0.37	0.49	0.40	0.49	0.32	0.47
Bail	0.02	0.15	0.01	0.12	0.37	0.49	0.35	0.48 }	0.64	0.48
O.R.	0.01	0.10	0.14	0.12	0.18	0.39	0.18	0.39 }		
Ct. App. Coun.	0.04	0.20	0.04	0.21	0.03	0.18	0.02	0.16	–	–
Def. Ret. Coun.	0.13	0.34	0.10	0.30	0.07	0.25	0.06	0.24	–	–
Orig. A(1°) Chgs.	1.14	0.38	1.10	0.30	0.02	0.15	0.02	0.16	–	–
Orig. B(2°) Chgs.	0.47	0.67	0.46	0.70	0.83	0.51	0.82	0.52	–	–
Orig. C(3°) Chgs.	0.11	0.34	0.10	0.35	0.95	0.73	0.98	0.74	–	–
Orig. Misd. Chgs.	0.01	0.10	0		0.20	0.43	0.21	0.44	–	–
Off. in Dwell.	–	–	–	–	0.53	0.50	0.52	0.50	–	–
Chg. Red. Barg.[a]	0.13	0.34	0.17	0.38	0.05	0.23	0.06	0.24 }	0.16	0.37
Count. Red. Barg.[a]	0.15	0.36	0.20	0.41	0.27	0.45	0.30	0.46 }		
Court Trial	0.07	0.26	0.03	0.17	0.03	0.18	0.04	0.19	0.03	0.18
Jury Trial	0.03	0.18	0		0		0		0	
Mo. Fin. Dispo.	31.71	9.85	33.65	6.09	33.12	7.24	33.80	5.57	34.18	3.96
Pub. Defdr.									0.63	0.48
No. Defs.									0.68	0.47
Prop. Off.									0.44	0.50
Drug Off.									0.17	0.38
Oth. Off.									0.08	0.28
Dependent Variable										
(conv. on) All Chgs. & Counts	0.46	0.50	0.62	0.49	0.51	0.50	0.63	0.48	0.53	0.50
(conv. on) Fewer Counts[a]	0.15	0.36	0.20	0.41	0.27	0.45	0.30	0.46 }	0.16	0.37
(conv. on) Reduced Chgs.[a]	0.13	0.34	0.17	0.38	0.05	0.23	0.06	0.24 }		
Dism. & Tri. Acq. (i.e., no conv.)	0.27	0.44	0.00	0.00	0.11	0.31	0.00	0.00	0.32	0.47
SSI A	14.75	12.59	20.09	10.39	11.74	9.31	13.17	8.85		
SSI B	19.13	20.20	26.06	19.36	14.04	15.64	15.75	15.73		
SSI C	23.51	29.66	32.03	30.43	16.34	22.81	18.34	23.40		
SSI D	41.71	69.59	56.82	75.84	26.80	42.68	30.07	44.13		
ELT:AFD	66.89	39.06	71.51	30.70	56.86	52.89	54.07	41.06	49.84	43.62

[a]See note a to Table C-2.

The Determinants of Conviction for Burglary Defendants: Multnomah County, 1973

(Multivariate Regression Equation Results, Ordinary Least Squares Estimation)

Variable	All Chgs. & Counts			Fewer Counts			Reduced Chgs.			Dism. & Tri. Acq.		
	Coef	T	η	Coef	T	η	Coef	T	η	Coef	T	η
Com. Ties Index	0.00	0.13	0.00	0.00	0.29	0.00	0.00	0.11	0.00	-0.01	0.37	-0.00
Age	-0.04	0.48	-0.28	0.02	0.62	0.34	0.03	0.37	0.13	-0.02	0.23	-0.12
Black	0.08	0.54	0.04	-0.02	0.30	-0.02	-0.07	0.44	-0.02	0.02	0.11	0.01
Other Minority	-0.06	0.13	-0.00	0.45	1.97	0.04	-0.05	0.09	-0.00	-0.34	0.69	-0.01
Min. P.R.	-0.15	1.14	-0.13	0.06	0.91	0.10	-0.22	1.50	-0.10	0.31	2.20	0.23
Maj. P.R.	0.09	0.61	0.06	-0.01	0.09	-0.01	-0.09	0.50	-0.03	0.00	0.00	0.00
Pris. P.R.	0.02	0.11	0.01	-0.01	0.14	-0.01	-0.15	0.78	-0.05	0.14	0.79	0.07
Jail Custody	-0.15	0.82	-0.28	-0.14	1.54	-0.50	0.12	0.60	0.12	0.16	0.84	0.26
Bail	-0.26	1.00	-0.08	-0.13	0.99	-0.08	0.37	1.26	0.06	0.02	0.06	0.00
O.R.	-0.21	1.03	-0.42	-0.15	1.52	-0.59	0.40	1.73	0.43	-0.04	0.17	-0.06
Ct. App. Coun.	0.06	0.38	0.03	-0.10	1.27	-0.11	-0.02	0.13	-0.01	0.06	0.37	0.03
Def. Ret. Coun.	-0.11	1.06	-0.15	-0.01	0.14	-0.02	-0.12	0.97	-0.08	0.24	2.04	0.27
Orig A(1°) Chgs.	-0.23	1.67	-1.18	0.51	7.40	4.96	-0.16	1.01	-0.43	-0.12	0.81	-0.51
Orig B(2°) Chgs.	-0.08	0.47	-0.03	0.14	1.75	0.10	-0.05	0.30	-0.01	-0.01	0.06	-0.00
Orig C(3°) Chgs.	-0.10	0.50	-0.03	-0.10	1.00	0.05	0.53	2.43	0.07	-0.34	1.62	-0.74
Orig. Misd. Chgs.	-0.10	0.64	-0.03	0.42	5.17	0.25	-0.14	0.75	-0.02	-0.17	1.00	-0.05
Off. in Dwell.	0.22	2.24	0.67	0.02	0.34	0.10	-0.00	0.01	-0.00	-0.24	2.20	-0.59
Court Trial	0.14	0.74	0.04	0.11	1.21	0.07	-0.35	1.63	-0.06	0.01	0.47	0.02
Jury Trial	0.34	1.64	0.09	0.13	1.26	0.06	-0.34	1.46	-0.05	-0.13	0.56	-0.03
Mo. Fin. Dispo.	0.01	1.15	0.93	-0.00	0.26	-0.20	-0.00	0.15	-0.07	-0.01	0.78	-0.56
Constant	0.38	1.07		-0.39	2.23		0.46	1.15		0.55	1.45	
R^2	0.31			0.71			0.38			0.28		
Due to Multicolin.	0.10			0.25			0.16			0.03		
Due to Regressors	0.21			0.46			0.21			0.25		
Adj. R^2	0.11			0.62			0.19			0.07		
Standard Error	0.39			0.20			0.44			0.43		
F statistic (D.F.)	1.51 (20,67)			8.25 (20,67)			2.03 (20,67)			1.33 (20,67)		

Table C-7
The Determinants of Conviction for Burglary Defendants: Multnomah County, 1974

(Multivariate Regression Equation Results, Ordinary Least Squares Estimation)

Variable	All Chgs. & Counts			Fewer Counts			Reduced Chgs.			Dism. & Tri. Acq.		
	Coef	T	η	Coef	T	η	Coef	T	η	Coef	T'	η
Com. Ties Index	0.01	0.49	0.00	-0.02	2.25	-0.01	0.02	0.70	0.00	-0.01	0.55	-0.00
Age	-0.10	1.00	-0.27	0.03	0.94	1.84	0.07	0.75	0.62	0.00	0.01	0.01
Black	-0.03	0.21	-0.01	0.01	0.25	0.05	-0.03	0.16	-0.01	0.05	0.33	0.02
Other Minority	-0.61	1.15	-0.01	-0.11	0.69	-0.05	-0.31	0.63	-0.02	1.03	2.23	0.06
Min. P.R.	0.01	0.06	0.00	0.02	0.46	0.09	-0.07	0.40	-0.03	0.03	0.21	0.01
Maj. P.R.	-0.01	0.42	-0.00	0.03	0.75	0.27	-0.02	0.15	-0.02	-0.01	0.04	-0.01
Pris. P.R.	-0.15	0.78	-0.03	0.11	1.96	0.60	-0.09	0.51	-0.07	0.13	0.77	0.09
Jail Custody	0.08	0.40	0.05	0.03	0.48	0.39	-0.23	1.23	-0.43	0.12	0.71	0.22
Bail	0.28	1.19	0.05	-0.05	0.70	-0.19	-0.39	1.74	-0.21	0.16	0.75	0.08
O.R.	0.03	0.17	0.02	0.25	0.05	0.05	-0.15	0.89	-0.37	0.12	0.75	0.27
Ct. App. Coun.	-0.07	0.61	-0.05	-0.00	0.10	-0.06	0.06	0.59	0.14	0.01	0.09	0.02
Def. Ret. Coun.	0.02	0.14	0.00	-0.04	0.84	-0.19	0.11	0.65	0.06	-0.09	0.58	-0.05
Orig A(1°) Chgs.	0.34	1.48	-0.58	-0.03	0.46	-1.32	0.43	1.98	2.40	-0.06	0.29	-0.31
Orig B(2°) Chgs.	-0.07	0.29	-0.00	-0.05	0.71	-0.05	-0.13	0.60	-0.02	0.25	1.21	0.03
Orig C(3°) Chgs.	-0.50	2.07	-0.05	0.04	0.52	0.09	0.21	0.91	0.07	0.26	1.21	0.08
Orig Misd. Chgs.	-0.15	0.64	-0.01	0.37	5.41	0.55	-0.05	0.22	-0.01	-0.18	0.87	-0.03
Off. in Dwell.	0.54	4.66	0.58	-0.03	0.99	-0.89	-0.12	1.09	-0.42	-0.39	3.81	-1.26
Court Trial	0.24	0.96	0.01	-0.02	0.30	-0.04	-0.06	0.27	-0.02	-0.15	0.71	-0.04
Jury Trial	0.05	0.28	0.01	0.02	0.42	0.08	-0.13	0.76	-0.06	0.06	0.36	0.03
Mo. Fin. Dispo.	-0.00	0.33	-0.08	0.00	1.14	2.07	-0.00	0.14	-0.11	0.00	0.14	0.09
Constant	0.82	2.20		-0.06	0.50		-0.09	0.26		0.33	1.01	
R^2	0.46			0.52			0.21			0.36		
Due to Multicolin.	0.10			0.15			0.02			0.07		
Due to Regressors	0.36			0.36			0.19			0.29		
Adj. R^2	0.28			0.36			-0.04			0.15		
Standard Error	0.42			0.12			0.40			0.37		
F statistic (D.F.)	2.56 (20,61)			3.25 (20,61)			0.83 (20,61)			1.73 (20,61)		

Table C-8

The Determinants of Conviction for Robbery Defendants: Multnomah County, 1973

(Multivariate Regression Equation Results, Ordinary Least Squares Estimation)

Variable	All Chgs. & Counts			Fewer Counts			Reduced Chgs.			Dism. & Tri. Acq.		
	Coef	T	η	Coef	T	η	Coef	T	η	Coef	T	η
Com. Ties Index	0.01	0.57	-0.00	-0.02	1.21	-0.00	0.02	0.58	-0.00	-0.01	0.35	-0.00
Age	-0.01	0.07	-0.07	0.07	1.19	1.43	-0.12	1.11	-0.83	0.06	0.46	0.20
Black	0.01	0.12	0.02	-0.06	0.81	-0.13	-0.10	0.75	-0.07	0.15	0.92	0.05
Other Minority	-0.16	0.71	-0.05	0.07	0.49	0.04	0.07	0.26	0.01	0.02	0.07	0.00
Min. P.R.	-0.00	0.01	-0.00	-0.02	0.25	-0.04	-0.04	0.26	-0.02	0.07	0.35	0.02
Maj. P.R.	0.04	0.35	0.06	-0.06	0.81	-0.15	0.07	0.51	0.06	-0.05	0.32	-0.02
Pris. P.R.	0.17	1.29	0.16	-0.07	0.86	-0.12	-0.07	0.43	-0.04	-0.18	0.96	-0.05
Jail Custody	0.25	0.98	0.92	-0.08	0.49	0.54	-0.13	0.43	-0.30	-0.04	0.12	-0.05
Bail	0.12	0.45	0.10	0.11	0.67	0.17	0.10	0.33	0.05	-0.33	0.92	-0.09
O.R.	0.06	0.24	0.09	0.06	0.38	0.16	-0.05	0.19	-0.05	-0.06	0.18	-0.03
Ct. App. Coun.	-0.08	0.80	-0.14	0.02	0.33	0.07	-0.10	0.83	-0.10	0.16	1.14	0.08
Def. Ret. Coun.	0.15	0.97	0.13	-0.11	1.19	-0.19	-0.01	0.04	-0.00	0.03	0.13	0.01
Orig A(1°) Chgs	0.01	0.23	0.11	0.20	5.83	3.16	-0.05	0.80	-0.27	-0.16	2.15	-0.42
Orig B(2°) Chgs	-0.04	0.19	-0.01	0.06	0.49	0.04	0.38	1.61	0.90	-0.40	1.46	-0.05
Orig C(3°) Chgs	-0.13	0.82	-0.06	-0.08	0.83	-0.07	-0.23	1.28	-0.07	-0.02	0.11	-0.00
Orig Misd. Chgs	-0.17	0.65	-0.04	0.27	1.64	0.12	0.27	0.88	0.04	-0.37	1.03	-0.03
Court Trial	0.27	1.41	0.10	-0.09	0.73	-0.06	-0.32	1.42	-0.08	0.14	0.53	0.02
Jury Trial	0.45	2.48	0.17	-0.13	1.17	-0.10	-0.18	0.85	-0.04	-0.13	0.53	-0.02
Mo. Fin. Dispo.	0.00	0.24	0.27	0.02	2.40	3.11	-0.00	0.26	-0.21	-0.01	1.05	-0.50
Constant	-0.12	0.35		-0.52	2.40		0.68	1.69		0.95	2.02	
R^2	0.26			0.50			0.28			0.25		
Due to Multicolin.	0.09			0.03			0.11			0.04		
Due to Regressors	0.18			0.47			0.17			0.21		
Adj R^2	0.04			0.35			0.07			0.03		
Standard error	0.36			0.23			0.42			0.50		
F statistic (D.F.)	1.17 (19,63)			3.27 (19,63)			1.31 (19,63)			1.13 (19,63)		

Table C-9

The Determinants of Conviction for Robbery Defendants: Multnomah County, 1974

(Multivariate Regression Equation Results, Ordinary Least Squares Estimation)

Variable	All Chgs. & Counts			Fewer Counts			Reduced Chgs.			Dism. & Tri. Acq.		
	Coef	T	η	Coef	T	η	Coef	T	η	Coef	T	η
Com. Ties Index	-0.01	0.23	-0.00	0.00	0.17	0.00	-0.01	0.43	-0.00	-0.01	0.48	-0.00
Age	0.02	0.22	0.06	0.02	1.02	1.50	-0.02	0.51	0.90	-0.02	0.21	-0.14
Black	-0.39	1.69	-0.04	-0.02	0.45	-0.05	-0.05	0.47	-0.07	0.47	2.38	0.13
Other Minority	-0.18	0.50	-0.01	-0.02	0.21	-0.02	0.39	2.16	0.20	-0.19	0.63	-0.02
Min. P.R.	-0.08	0.50	-0.02	0.02	0.69	0.16	-0.05	0.65	-0.18	0.11	0.80	0.08
Maj. P.R.	0.26	1.42	0.04	0.00	0.05	0.01	-0.06	0.66	-0.12	-0.20	1.30	-0.09
Pris. P.R.	0.04	0.22	0.01	0.00	0.11	0.04	-0.12	1.30	-0.48	0.07	0.48	0.07
Jail Custody	0.13	0.71	0.11	-0.00	0.07	-0.06	-0.09	1.02	-1.05	-0.03	0.23	-0.09
Bail	0.09	0.33	0.01	0.01	0.26	0.05	-0.12	0.94	-0.22	0.02	0.09	0.01
O.R.	0.10	0.50	0.03	-0.06	1.35	-0.44	-0.15	1.41	-0.55	0.10	0.57	0.08
Ct. App. Coun.	0.00	0.00	0.00	-0.03	1.30	-0.47	0.02	0.31	0.13	0.01	0.14	0.02
Def. Ret. Coun.	-0.06	0.26	-0.01	0.06	1.26	0.21	-0.06	0.52	-0.10	0.06	0.30	0.02
Orig A(1°) Chgs.	0.09	0.52	0.14	-0.00	0.08	-0.12	0.02	0.23	0.40	-0.11	0.73	-0.48
Orig B(2°) Chgs.	-0.48	1.67	-0.03	0.66	11.05	0.99	0.01	0.07	0.01	-0.19	0.77	-0.03
Orig C(3°) Chgs.	-0.33	0.95	-0.02	0.02	0.22	0.02	0.35	2.03	0.26	-0.03	0.11	-0.01
Orig Misd. Chgs	0			0			0			0		
Court Trial	-0.38	2.10	-0.06	-0.03	0.92	-0.15	-0.08	0.87	-0.17	0.49	3.22	0.24
Jury Trial	-0.00	0.01	-0.00	-0.07	1.87	-0.42	-0.04	0.47	-0.13	0.12	0.75	0.07
Mo. Fin. Dispo.	0.01	1.92	0.45	-0.00	0.22	-0.29	0.00	0.32	0.50	-0.01	2.41	-1.43
Constant	0.23	0.78		0.00	0.03		0.18	1.20		0.59	2.32	
R^2	0.29			0.74			0.24			0.39		
Due to Multicolin.	0.06			0.15			0.00			0.06		
Due to Regressors	0.23			0.59			0.24			0.34		
Adj. R^2	0.08			0.66			0.01			0.21		
Standard Error	0.45			0.09			0.22			0.38		
F statistic (D.F.)	1.35 (18,59)			9.35 (18,59)			1.04 (18,59)			2.13 (18,59)		

The Determinants of Conviction for B&E Defendants: Dade County, 1974

(Multivariate Regression Equation Results, Ordinary Least Squares Estimation)

Variable	All Chgs. & Counts			Fewer Counts			Reduced Chgs.			Dism. & Tri. Acq.		
	Coef	T	η	Coef	T	η	Coef	T	η	Coef	T	η
Com. Ties Index	0.04	1.40	0.00	-0.01	0.53	-0.00	-0.01	0.70	-0.00	-0.02	0.11	-0.00
Age	-0.07	0.88	-0.24	0.10	1.79	0.92	0.04	0.88	0.82	-0.08	1.12	-0.55
Black	-0.09	0.77	-0.09	0.12	1.29	0.30	-0.76	1.06	-0.44	0.05	0.53	0.12
Other Minority	0.05	0.27	0.01	-0.15	1.20	-0.10	-0.02	0.15	-0.02	0.12	0.82	0.07
Min. P.R.	-0.03	0.21	-0.01	-0.06	0.58	-0.05	0.14	1.63	0.27	-0.05	0.37	-0.03
Maj. P.R.	0.30	1.93	0.10	-0.11	0.98	-0.97	-0.08	0.91	-0.16	-0.10	0.79	-0.08
Pris. P.R.	0.05	0.20	0.01	-0.21	1.22	-0.69	-0.05	0.38	-0.04	0.21	1.08	0.06
Jail Custody	0.10	0.50	0.05	-0.13	0.84	-0.16	0.01	0.05	0.02	0.02	1.00	0.02
Bail	-0.12	0.62	-0.12	0.08	0.05	0.02	-0.05	0.40	-0.27	0.16	0.95	0.35
O.R.	-0.04	0.19	-0.01	-0.09	0.56	-0.08	-0.00	0.03	-0.01	0.14	0.73	1.00
Ct. App. Coun.	-0.14	0.37	-0.01	-0.31	1.12	-0.03	0.42	1.91	0.11	0.03	0.09	0.00
Def. Ret. Coun.	-0.24	1.51	-0.09	0.00	0.26	0.00	0.09	1.04	0.20	0.14	1.04	0.11
Orig A(1°) Chgs.	-0.21	0.86	-0.01	0.24	1.34	0.04	0.03	0.18	0.01	-0.06	0.27	-0.00
Orig B(2°) Chgs.	-0.04	0.42	-0.08	0.14	1.91	0.68	0.02	0.41	0.26	-0.13	1.42	-0.48
Orig C(3°) Chgs.	-0.20	2.71	-0.30	0.22	4.08	0.87	-0.01	0.24	-0.09	-0.01	0.16	-0.03
Orig Misd. Chgs.	-0.17	1.47	-0.07	0.21	2.52	0.22	-0.07	1.06	-0.17	0.03	0.29	0.02
Off. in Dwell.	-0.10	0.87	-0.11	-0.09	0.99	-0.25	0.06	0.89	0.40	0.13	1.26	0.30
Court Trial	0.20	1.03	0.03	-0.05	0.36	-0.02	0.03	0.27	0.03	-0.18	1.09	-0.07
Jury Trial	-0.03	0.11	-0.00	-0.01	0.06	-0.00	-0.12	0.67	-0.04	0.17	0.64	0.02
Mon. Fin. Dispo.	0.01	1.50	0.43	0.01	1.29	0.70	0.00	0.45	0.44	-0.02	3.18	-1.65
Constant	0.75	2.41		-0.36	1.58		-0.02	0.14		0.63	2.39	
R^2	0.27			0.36			0.18			0.25		
Due to Multicolin.	0.04			0.03			0.03			0.03		
Due to Regressors	0.30			0.39			0.15			0.29		
Adj. R^2	0.07			0.19			-0.04			0.05		
Standard Error	0.49			0.36			0.28			0.17		
F statistic (D.F.)	1.34 (20,74)			2.08 (20,74)			0.84 (20,74)			1.25 (20,74)		

Table C-11
The Determinants of Conviction for B&E Defendants: Dade County, 1975
(Multivariate Regression Equation Results, Ordinary Least Squares Estimation)

Variable	All Chgs. & Counts			Fewer Counts			Reduced Chgs.			Dism. & Tri.Acq.		
	Coef	T	η	Coef	T	η	Coef	T	η	Coef	T	η
Com. Ties Index	-0.01	0.22	-0.00	0.00	0.00	-0.00	0.00	0.19	-0.00	0.00	0.21	-0.00
Age	0.01	0.11	0.03	-0.44	0.54	-0.28	0.06	1.51	2.07	-0.03	0.55	-0.49
Black	-0.06	0.52	-0.06	0.01	0.12	0.03	0.03	0.55	0.33	0.02	0.25	0.10
Other Minority	-0.21	1.02	-0.04	0.15	0.79	0.06	-0.07	0.68	-0.13	0.13	1.03	0.13
Min. P.R.	0.05	0.35	0.02	0.03	0.27	0.03	-0.06	1.00	-0.27	-0.02	0.18	-0.03
Maj. P.R.	0.01	0.06	0.00	0.10	0.71	0.07	-0.08	1.11	-0.28	-0.03	0.27	-0.04
Pris. P.R.	0.38	1.67	0.06	-0.17	0.85	-0.05	-0.06	0.55	-0.09	-0.15	1.07	-0.12
Jail Custody	0.16	0.69	0.10	0.07	0.36	0.10	0.05	0.46	0.34	-0.28	1.98	-0.97
Bail	0.14	0.63	0.09	-0.03	0.15	-0.04	0.07	0.70	0.49	-0.18	1.34	-0.62
O.R.	-0.04	0.17	-0.01	0.14	0.64	0.09	0.08	0.70	0.27	-0.17	1.17	-0.30
Ct. App. Coun.	-0.22	0.70	-0.01	-0.35	1.29	-0.04	0.27	1.83	0.16	0.31	1.58	0.09
Def. Ret. Coun.	-0.33	1.45	-0.04	0.28	1.41	0.07	-0.07	0.68	-0.09	0.12	0.83	0.07
Orig A(1°) Chgs.	0.07	0.19	0.00	0.01	0.03	0.00	-0.04	0.21	-0.02	-0.04	0.18	-0.01
Orig B(2°) Chgs.	-0.02	0.13	-0.02	0.06	0.61	0.20	-0.02	0.35	-0.30	-0.03	0.39	-0.22
Orig C(3°) Chgs.	-0.15	1.90	-0.25	0.18	2.55	0.62	0.05	1.22	0.78	-0.07	1.49	0.63
Orig Misd. Chgs.	-0.12	0.81	-0.04	0.26	1.99	0.19	-0.05	0.79	-0.20	-0.09	0.94	-0.15
Off. in Dwell.	-0.18	1.54	-0.17	0.10	0.96	0.20	0.06	1.10	0.61	0.02	0.28	0.10
Court Trial	0.07	0.23	0.00	0.07	0.24	0.01	-0.05	0.35	-0.03	-0.09	0.44	0.03
Jury Trial	0			0			0			0		
Mo. Fin. Dispo.	0.01	1.19	0.54	0.00	0.31	0.26	0.00	0.56	1.24	-0.01	2.78	-4.05
Constant	0.45	1.12		-0.13	0.37		-0.21	1.10		0.89	3.52	
R^2	0.21			0.23			0.16			0.23		
Due to Multicolin.	0.02			0.03			-0.02			-0.17		
Due to Regressors	0.19			0.20			0.18			0.39		
Adj. R^2	0.00			0.03			0.06			0.02		
Standard Error	0.50			0.44			0.23			0.31		
F statistic (D.F.)	0.98 (19,72)			1.14 (19,72)			0.74 (19,72)			1.10 (19,72)		

Table C-12

The Determinants of Conviction for Robbery Defendants: Dade County, 1974

(Multivariate Regression Equation Results, Ordinary Least Squares Estimation)

Variable	All Chgs. & Counts			Fewer Counts			Reduced Chgs.			Dism. & Tri. Acq.		
	Coef	T	η	Coef	T	η	Coef	T	η	Coef	T	η
Com. Ties Index	-0.03	0.78	-0.00	-0.01	0.65	-0.00	0.01	0.39	0.00	0.03	1.02	0.00
Age	0.01	0.13	0.04	-0.04	0.76	-0.54	0.09	1.51	1.21	-0.06	0.79	-0.30
Black	-0.33	2.55	-0.52	0.08	0.97	0.46	0.16	1.72	0.92	0.10	0.84	0.21
Other Minority	-0.50	2.17	-0.10	-0.04	0.27	-0.03	0.18	1.11	0.13	0.36	1.76	0.10
Min. P.R.	0.00	0.00	0.00	-0.04	0.60	-0.10	-0.01	0.09	-0.02	0.05	0.48	0.43
Maj. P.R.	0.33	1.93	0.09	-0.00	0.04	-0.00	-0.12	0.97	-0.12	-0.21	1.37	-0.08
Pris. P.R.	0.09	0.43	0.02	-0.01	0.04	-0.00	-0.20	1.38	-0.13	0.12	0.62	0.03
Jail Custody	0.47	2.07	0.90	-0.15	1.05	-1.06	-0.14	0.87	-0.99	-0.19	0.91	-0.48
Bail	0.32	1.21	0.06	-0.21	1.27	-0.15	-0.23	1.52	-0.21	0.17	0.72	0.05
O.R.	0.14	0.35	0.01	0.24	0.94	-0.04	0.76	2.67	0.14	-0.67	1.82	-0.04
Ct. App. Coun.	0.18	0.76	0.02	-0.32	2.17	-0.14	-0.05	0.30	-0.02	0.19	0.89	0.03
Def. Ret. Coun.	0.07	0.36	0.02	0.02	0.21	0.02	0.03	0.19	0.02	-0.12	0.69	-0.05
Orig A(1°) Chgs.	-0.03	0.34	-0.07	0.16	3.34	1.61	-0.04	0.75	-0.40	-0.09	1.35	-0.34
Orig B(2°) Chgs.	-0.14	1.51	-0.11	0.13	2.26	0.38	0.00	0.04	0.01	0.01	0.08	0.01
Orig C(3°) Chgs.	-0.43	2.50	-0.09	0.41	3.86	0.34	0.01	0.11	0.01	0.00	0.03	0.00
Orig Misd. Chgs.	0.48	1.22	0.02	0.06	0.26	0.01	-0.17	0.62	-0.03	-0.37	1.06	-0.02
Court Trial	-0.13	0.66	-0.02	-0.11	0.90	-0.08	-0.10	0.74	-0.07	0.34	1.94	0.09
Jury Trial	-0.29	1.78	-0.07	-0.03	0.34	-0.31	-0.06	0.53	-0.05	0.38	2.65	0.13
Mo. Fin. Dispo.	0.02	3.06	0.94	-0.11	0.32	-0.23	0.00	0.69	0.55	-0.02	3.75	-1.40
Constant	-0.05	0.17		0.07	0.35		0.01	0.02		0.98	3.36	
R^2	0.38			0.43			0.29			0.44		
Due to Multicolin.	-0.01			0.10			0.07			0.04		
Due to Regressors	0.39			0.33			0.21			0.40		
Adj. R^2	0.22			0.29			0.10			0.30		
Standard Error	0.44			0.27			0.31			0.39		
F statistic (D.F.)	2.35 (19,73)			2.94 (19,73)			1.56 (19,73)			3.05 (19,73)		

Table C-13
The Determinants of Conviction for Robbery Defendants: Dade County, 1975
(Multivariate Regression Equation Results, Ordinary Least Squares Estimation)

Variable	All Chgs. & Counts			Fewer Counts			Reduced Chgs.			Dism. & Tri. Acq.		
	Coef	T	η	Coef	T	η	Coef	T	η	Coef	T	η
Com. Ties Index	0.03	1.17	0.00	-0.13	0.85	-0.06	-0.01	0.52	-0.00	-0.00	0.27	-0.00
Age	-0.06	0.67	-0.24	-0.00	0.05	-0.04	-0.05	0.75	-0.67	0.11	1.54	0.75
Black	-0.10	0.81	-0.14	-0.12	1.50	-0.53	0.09	1.05	0.47	0.13	1.31	0.32
Other Minority	-0.53	1.95	-0.06	0.36	2.03	0.13	0.08	0.44	0.03	0.09	0.41	0.02
Min. P.R.	-0.03	0.25	-0.02	-0.08	0.89	-0.13	0.23	2.46	0.45	-0.12	1.12	0.11
Maj. P.R.	-0.14	0.89	-0.05	0.02	0.24	0.02	0.07	0.67	0.09	0.04	0.33	0.02
Pris. P.R.	-0.05	0.19	-0.01	0.35	2.20	0.12	-0.07	0.42	-0.03	-0.23	1.19	-0.05
Jail Custody	0.03	0.15	0.05	0.10	0.81	0.58	-0.05	0.37	-0.33	-0.09	0.52	-0.26
Bail	0.35	0.80	0.02	-0.05	0.19	0.01	-0.06	0.19	-0.01	-0.24	0.69	-0.02
O.R.	0.47	0.89	0.01	0.09	0.26	0.01	-0.36	0.98	-0.03	-0.19	0.47	-0.01
Ct. App. Coun.	0.13	0.43	0.01	0.05	0.24	0.01	-0.20	1.00	-0.07	0.03	0.13	0.01
Def. Ret. Coun.	-0.11	0.63	-0.03	-0.07	0.58	-0.06	0.03	0.28	0.03	0.14	1.02	0.07
Orig. A(1°) Chgs.	-0.10	0.68	-0.26	-0.11	1.16	-0.88	0.18	1.67	1.58	0.04	0.34	0.17
Orig. B(2°) Chgs.	-0.16	1.88	-0.16	0.19	3.59	0.61	-0.01	0.24	-0.05	-0.02	0.36	-0.04
Orig. C(3°) Chgs.	-0.26	1.49	-0.06	0.16	1.36	0.11	0.18	0.51	0.15	-0.08	0.56	-0.03
Orig. Misd. Chgs.	0.23	0.36	0.01	-0.35	0.82	-0.02	0.11	0.24	0.01	0.00	0.00	0.00
Court Trial	-0.24	1.05	-0.04	-0.13	0.85	-0.06	-0.08	0.47	-0.04	0.45	2.42	0.13
Jury Trial	-0.39	1.03	-0.03	-0.07	0.27	-0.01	-0.31	1.16	-0.08	0.76	2.53	0.09
Mo. Fin. Dispo.	0.01	1.01	0.39	0.01	2.20	1.71	0.00	0.83	0.81	-0.02	3.79	-2.02
Constant	0.73	2.26		-0.08	0.40		-0.17	0.75		-0.52	2.03	

R^2	0.27	0.39	0.20	0.41
Due to Multicolin.	0.03	0.01	0.00	0.09
Due to Regressors	0.24	0.30	0.20	0.32
Adj. R^2	0.08	0.24	0.00	0.26
Standard Error	0.48	0.31	0.34	0.38
F statistic (D.F.)	1.44 (19,74)	2.54 (19,74)	1.00 (19,74)	2.73 (19,74)

Table C-14

The Determinants of Sentence Severity for Burglary Convictees: Multnomah County, 1973

(Multivariate Regression Equation Results, Ordinary Least Squares Estimation)

Variable	Sentence Severity Index											
	A			B			C			D		
	Coef	T	η	Coef	T	η	Coef	T	η	Coef	T	η
Com Ties Index	-0.39	0.69	-0.00	-1.71	2.04	-0.01	-3.04	2.47	-0.01	3.40	1.32	0.01
Age	1.65	0.98	0.25	5.56	2.23	0.91	9.48	2.60	1.71	16.62	2.17	1.49
Black	2.77	0.79	0.02	5.87	1.12	0.05	8.96	1.17	0.09	18.24	1.14	0.09
Other Minority	-2.58	0.29	-0.00	-1.44	0.11	-0.00	-0.30	0.02	-0.00	-3.99	0.10	-0.00
Min. P.R.	2.25	0.72	0.03	2.78	0.60	0.04	3.32	0.49	0.05	8.20	0.58	0.07
Maj. P.R.	-3.75	1.04	-0.05	-8.83	1.64	-0.12	-13.91	1.76	-0.20	-25.97	1.57	-0.19
Pris. P.R.	-4.97	1.35	-0.05	-7.48	1.37	-0.08	-10.00	1.25	-0.11	-6.18	0.37	0.03
Jail Custody	5.73	1.50	0.18	12.87	2.26	0.44	20.01	2.39	0.75	32.51	1.86	0.60
Bail	0.42	0.07	0.00	4.62	0.53	0.03	8.83	0.69	0.06	41.78	1.56	0.13
O.R.	1.34	0.33	0.06	6.11	1.00	0.29	10.87	1.22	0.57	24.92	1.34	0.64
Ct. App. Coun.	-1.71	0.45	-0.02	-2.77	0.49	-0.03	-3.83	0.46	-0.05	-12.32	0.71	-0.08
Def. Ret. Coun.	0.49	0.21	0.01	2.22	0.63	0.05	3.95	0.77	0.10	0.69	0.06	0.01
Orig A(1°) Chgs.	-1.30	0.30	-0.13	1.89	0.29	0.20	5.08	0.54	0.60	18.32	0.93	1.08
Orig B(2°) Chgs.	4.44	0.96	0.03	10.90	1.57	0.08	17.35	1.71	0.14	35.28	1.66	0.14
Orig C(3°) Chgs.	4.79	1.28	0.03	2.38	0.43	0.02	-0.04	0.00	-0.00	2.45	0.14	0.01
Orig. Misd. Chgs.	-6.12	1.65	-0.05	-8.74	1.58	-0.08	-11.36	1.40	-0.11	-19.87	1.17	-0.10
Off. in Dwell.	0.58	0.24	0.04	0.05	0.01	0.00	-0.48	0.09	-0.04	-1.37	0.12	-0.05
Chg. Red. Barg.	-9.33	3.66	-0.45	-12.22	3.21	-0.65	-15.10	2.70	-0.89	-30.19	2.59	-0.88
Count Red. Barg.	2.02	0.36	0.03	1.24	0.15	0.02	0.45	0.04	0.01	-8.08	0.31	-0.07
Sent Barg.	0.01	0.00	0.00	0.94	0.22	0.02	1.88	0.29	0.04	-2.28	0.17	-0.02
Drop Oth. Case Barg.	-0.42	0.18	-0.01	-0.05	0.01	-0.00	0.32	0.06	0.01	-11.65	1.08	-0.24
Court Trial	-0.90	0.19	-0.00	3.48	0.49	0.02	7.85	0.76	0.05	5.27	0.24	0.02

Jury Trial	3.08	0.57	0.02	9.93	1.24	0.06	16.79	1.43	0.11	11.83	0.48	0.04
Mo. Fin. Dispo.	0.11	0.45	0.15	-0.27	0.77	-0.41	-0.65	1.26	-1.08	-1.18	1.10	-0.97
Constant	10.60	1.34		1.40	0.12		-7.79	0.45		-13.11	0.36	
R^2	0.58			0.64			0.65			0.52		
Due to Multicolin.	0.27			0.29			0.25			0.12		
Due to Regressors	0.31			0.36			0.39			0.40		
Adj. R^2	0.33			0.43			0.44			0.23		
Standard Error	6.80			10.15			14.88			31.11		
F statistic (D.F.)	2.30 (24,40)			3.03 (24,40)			3.06 (24,40)			1.82 (24,40)		

Table C-15

The Determinants of Sentence Severity for Burglary Convictees: Multnomah County, 1974

(Multivariate Regression Equation Results, Ordinary Least Squares Estimation)

Variable	Sentence Severity Index											
	A			B			C			D		
	Coef	*T*	*η*	*Coef*	*T*	*η*	*Coef*	*T*	*η*	*Coef*	*T*	*η*
Com. Ties Index	1.44	2.11	0.00	2.30	1.73	0.01	3.16	1.51	0.01	-0.31	0.07	-0.00
Age	-3.83	1.76	-0.35	-6.55	1.55	-0.50	-9.27	1.39	-0.60	0.86	0.06	0.03
Black	-0.20	0.05	-0.00	-8.77	1.23	-0.04	17.34	1.54	-0.07	-14.67	0.65	-0.03
Other Minority	0			0			0			0		
Min. P.R.	3.15	0.87	0.02	4.69	0.66	0.02	6.22	0.56	0.02	2.19	0.10	0.00
Maj. P.R.	1.83	0.65	0.03	1.17	0.21	0.01	0.50	0.06	0.01	-8.17	0.46	-0.04
Pris. P.R.	10.02	2.39	0.06	24.58	3.02	0.13	39.14	3.06	0.17	52.04	2.01	0.12
Jail Custody	-0.14	0.03	-0.00	1.52	0.18	0.03	3.17	0.24	0.05	6.39	0.24	0.05
Bail	2.94	0.55	0.01	7.12	0.68	0.03	11.29	0.69	0.04	4.50	0.14	0.01
O.R.	-2.73	0.68	-0.08	-6.56	0.84	-0.15	-10.40	0.84	-0.20	-20.38	0.81	-0.20
Ct. App. Coun.	1.56	0.65	0.04	7.74	1.68	0.16	13.93	1.91	0.25	25.30	1.72	0.23
Def. Ret. Coun.	1.85	0.59	0.01	3.52	0.58	0.02	5.20	0.54	0.03	-8.73	-0.45	-0.03
Orig A(1°) Chgs.	5.49	1.24	0.33	16.22	1.89	0.82	26.94	1.99	1.16	73.32	2.67	1.61
Orig B(2°) Chgs.	0			0			0			0		
Orig C(3°) Chgs.	-3.68	0.58	-0.01	1.72	0.14	0.00	7.12	0.37	0.01	24.21	0.61	0.02
Orig. Misd. Chgs.	1.16	0.22	0.00	3.06	0.30	0.01	4.95	0.31	0.01	92.34	2.85	0.09
Off. in Dwell.	2.69	0.99	0.12	1.52	0.29	0.06	0.35	0.04	0.01	5.63	0.34	0.09
Chg. Red. Barg.	-9.29	3.40	-0.12	-18.03	3.40	-0.20	-26.78	3.21	-0.25	-50.67	3.00	-0.25
Count Red. Barg.	-12.55	1.50	-0.02	-34.90	2.15	-0.05	-57.26	2.24	-0.07	-86.69	1.68	-0.06
Sent. Barg.	-0.88	0.29	-0.01	-2.24	0.38	-0.03	-3.60	0.39	-0.04	-9.00	0.48	-0.05
Drop Oth. Case Barg.	3.02	1.04	0.05	2.73	0.49	0.04	2.43	0.28	0.03	7.36	0.41	0.04

Court Trial	-4.73	0.91	-0.01	-6.24	0.62	-0.01	-7.75	0.49	-0.01	-20.19	0.63	-0.02
Jury Trial	2.61	0.68	0.01	0.83	0.11	0.00	-0.94	0.08	-0.00	-1.58	0.07	-0.00
Mo. Fin. Dispo.	0.30	2.57	0.47	0.45	1.93	0.56	0.59	1.61	0.63	0.70	0.96	0.39
Constant	7.63	1.05		1.75	0.12		-4.12	0.19		-47.11	1.05	
R^2	0.62			0.63			0.62			0.62		
Due to Multicolin.	0.23			0.24			0.24			0.27		
Due to Regressors	0.38			0.39			0.39			0.35		
Adj. R^2	0.42			0.44			0.43			0.42		
Standard Error	7.34			14.24			22.43			45.42		
F statistic (D.F.)	313 (22,43)			3.36 (22,43)			3.22 (22,43)			3.17 (22,43)		

Table C-16

The Determinants of Sentence Severity for Robbery Convictees: Multnomah County, 1973

(Multivariate Regression Equation Results, Ordinary Least Squares Estimation)

	Sentence Severity Index											
	A			B			C			D		
Variable	Coef	T	η	Coef	T	η	Coef	T	η	Coef	T	η
Com. Ties Index	0.99	1.58	0.01	1.67	1.40	0.01	2.35	1.23	0.01	1.28	0.33	0.00
Age	-5.74	1.96	-0.58	-11.10	2.00	-0.90	-16.45	1.85	-1.11	-33.98	1.87	-1.31
Black	-4.03	1.08	-0.03	-6.10	0.87	-0.04	-8.17	0.72	-0.04	-29.81	1.29	-0.08
Other Minority	6.61	1.10	0.02	7.46	0.65	0.02	8.31	0.45	0.02	-37.70	1.01	-0.04
Min. P.R.	6.53	1.17	0.05	11.71	1.10	0.07	16.90	0.99	0.08	48.41	1.39	0.13
Maj. P.R.	5.12	1.31	0.07	15.40	2.08	0.16	25.68	2.16	0.23	74.30	3.06	0.37
Pris. P.R.	11.39	3.59	0.13	22.43	3.73	0.21	33.48	3.46	0.26	92.78	4.70	0.41
Jail Custody	18.58	1.97	0.57	13.93	0.78	0.34	9.28	0.32	0.19	36.73	0.63	0.43
Bail	26.80	3.08	0.31	25.20	1.50	0.24	23.60	0.88	0.18	41.89	0.76	0.19
O.R.	14.65	1.55	0.24	9.79	0.55	0.13	4.93	0.17	0.05	40.89	0.70	0.25
Ct. App. Coun.	3.32	0.89	0.04	3.86	0.55	0.04	4.40	0.39	0.04	-4.06	0.17	-0.02
Def. Ret. Coun.	6.22	1.50	0.06	5.28	0.67	0.04	4.35	0.35	0.03	-15.53	0.60	-0.06
Orig A(1°) Chgs.	4.00	2.38	0.36	10.62	3.34	0.77	17.24	3.37	1.04	47.17	4.52	1.63
Orig B(2°) Chgs.	-0.87	0.20	-0.01	4.11	0.49	0.02	9.09	0.68	0.04	30.22	1.10	0.8
Orig C(3°) Chgs.	2.45	0.68	0.01	3.68	0.54	0.02	4.90	0.45	0.02	-20.29	0.91	-0.05
Orig Misd. Chgs.	-0.34	0.05	-0.00	-1.38	0.11	-0.00	-2.42	0.12	-0.00	-49.03	1.19	-0.08
Chg. Red. Barg.	-12.44	3.31	-0.38	-31.15	4.38	-0.76	-49.86	4.36	-1.02	-72.58	3.11	-0.85
Count Red. Barg.	-16.80	3.11	-0.17	-43.80	4.29	-0.36	-70.86	4.31	-0.48	-126.23	3.76	-0.49
Sent. Barg.	-10.83	2.48	-0.13	-6.17	0.74	-0.06	-1.50	0.11	-0.01	-16.41	0.60	-0.07
Drop Oth. Case Barg.	-5.94	1.84	-0.16	-9.29	1.52	-0.20	-12.64	1.28	-0.22	-45.89	2.28	-0.46

	(1)			(2)			(3)			(4)		
Court Trial	-35.94	3.66	-0.10	-60.67	3.27	-0.14	-85.39	2.86	-0.17	-146.99	2.41	-0.16
Jury Trial	1.49	0.25	0.01	15.40	1.37	0.05	29.32	1.62	0.09	57.86	1.56	0.10
Mo. Fin. Dispo.	0.52	1.63	0.53	0.34	0.56	0.28	0.16	0.16	0.11	-1.75	0.88	-0.69
Constant	2.44	0.19		22.18	0.89		41.92	1.05		77.58	0.95	
R^2	0.86			0.88			0.88			0.88		
Due to Multicolin.	0.07			0.21			0.24			0.15		
Due to Regressors	0.79			0.67			0.64			0.73		
Adj. R^2	0.67			0.72			0.71			0.72		
Standard Error	6.11			11.57			18.60			37.98		
F statistic (D.F.)	4.54 (23,17)			5.53 (23,17)			5.24 (23,17)			5.49 (23,17)		

Table C-17

The Determinants of Sentence Severity for Robbery Convictees: Multnomah County, 1974

(Multivariate Regression Equation Results, Ordinary Least Squares Estimation)

							Sentence Severity Index						
	A			B			C			D		
Variable	Coef	T	η	Coef	T	η	Coef	T	η	Coef	T	η
Com. Ties Index	1.44	1.77	0.01	4.11	1.72	0.02	6.78	1.69	0.02	14.84	1.55	0.02
Age	-5.37	2.38	-0.38	-13.19	1.99	-0.57	-21.02	1.89	-0.65	-36.20	1.36	-0.59
Black	1.49	0.18	0.00	1.49	0.06	0.00	1.50	0.04	0.00	8.09	0.08	0.00
Other Minority	-3.96	0.50	-0.00	-10.60	0.46	-0.01	-17.24	0.45	-0.01	-28.24	0.31	-0.01
Min. P.R.	1.32	0.31	0.01	1.32	0.11	0.00	1.33	0.06	0.00	-1.20	0.02	-0.00
Maj. P.R.	14.31	3.15	0.0	42.72	3.21	0.11	71.14	3.19	0.14	143.05	2.68	0.14
Pris. P.R.	11.90	2.77	0.10	31.38	2.48	0.15	50.85	2.40	0.18	88.91	1.76	0.17
Jail Custody	10.27	2.15	0.25	23.09	1.65	0.34	35.91	1.53	0.38	63.68	1.14	0.36
Bail	8.14	1.29	0.03	13.53	0.73	0.03	18.92	0.61	0.03	53.91	0.72	0.04
O.R.	5.22	1.02	0.03	4.34	0.29	0.02	3.46	0.14	0.01	-6.88	0.11	-0.01
Ct. App. Coun.	-1.37	0.50	-0.02	-2.53	0.31	-0.02	-3.68	0.27	-0.02	-7.56	0.23	-0.03
Def. Ret. Coun.	-2.97	0.57	-0.01	-7.62	0.50	-0.02	-12.27	0.48	-0.02	4.60	0.08	0.00
Orig A(1°) Chgs.	7.16	1.99	0.29	19.58	1.86	0.48	32.00	1.81	0.56	57.88	1.37	0.53
Orig B(2°) Chgs.	17.39	1.64	0.03	54.07	1.73	0.06	90.76	1.74	0.07	212.68	1.70	0.09
Orig C(3°) Chgs.	1.46	0.15	0.00	4.05	0.14	0.00	6.65	0.14	0.00	-14.74	0.13	-0.00
Orig Misd. Chgs	0			0			0			0		
Chg. Red. Barg.	-10.74	2.04	-0.03	-31.33	2.03	-0.05	-51.93	2.00	-0.06	-93.94	1.51	-0.05
Count Red. Barg.	-22.15	1.71	-0.03	-61.43	1.61	-0.05	-100.71	1.58	-0.05	-127.33	0.83	-0.04
Sent. Barg.	-5.61	1.24	-0.02	-17.10	1.29	-0.04	-28.60	1.29	-0.05	-60.29	1.13	-0.05
Drop Oth. Case Barg.	3.37	1.02	0.03	6.63	0.68	0.04	9.89	0.61	0.04	32.77	0.84	0.07

Court Trial	-0.19	0.04	-0.00	-1.43	0.09	-0.00	-2.66	0.10	-0.00	-4.37	0.07	-0.00
Jury Trial	1.59	0.33	0.01	4.91	0.35	0.02	8.23	0.35	0.02	18.45	0.33	0.02
Mo. Fin. Dispo.	0.38	1.60	0.38	0.83	1.20	0.50	1.28	1.11	0.56	3.11	1.12	0.71
Constant	7.50	0.94		0.37	0.02		-6.76	0.17		-39.23	0.42	
R^2	0.59			0.55			0.54			0.46		
Due to Multicolin.	0.03			0.01			0.02			0.05		
Due to Regressors	0.61			0.54			0.52			0.41		
Adj. R^2	0.34			0.28			0.27			0.13		
Standard Error	8.40			24.67			41.34			98.90		
F statistic (D.F.)	2.37 (22,37)			2.06 (22,37)			1.98 (22,37)			1.42 (22,37)		

Table C-18

The Determinants of Sentence Severity for B&E Convictees: Dade County, 1974

(Multivariate Regression Equation Results, Ordinary Least Squares Estimation)

| | Sentence Severity Index | | | | | | | | | | | |
| | A | | | B | | | C | | | D | | |
Variable	Coef	T	η	Coef	T	η	Coef	T	η	Coef	T	η
Com. Ties Index	0.30	0.66	0.00	0.97	1.25	0.00	1.63	1.42	0.01	2.41	1.23	0.01
Age	0.78	0.48	0.10	1.44	0.53	0.17	2.10	0.52	0.22	1.40	0.20	0.10
Black	2.86	1.23	0.11	3.68	0.94	0.12	4.50	0.78	0.14	7.27	0.74	0.15
Other Minority	6.65	1.75	0.06	8.06	1.26	0.06	9.46	1.00	0.06	18.55	1.15	0.08
Min. P.R.	3.91	1.33	0.05	7.71	1.57	0.09	11.51	1.57	0.12	26.12	2.10	0.18
Maj. P.R.	8.52	3.03	0.13	13.73	2.91	0.19	18.94	2.71	0.24	29.56	2.48	0.26
Pris. P.R.	8.50	1.82	0.04	9.64	1.23	0.04	10.79	0.93	0.04	12.35	0.63	0.03
Jail Custody	3.36	0.89	0.07	12.35	1.96	0.22	21.34	2.28	0.34	36.31	2.28	0.40
Bail	-1.08	0.29	-0.04	1.71	0.28	0.05	4.50	0.49	0.13	8.81	0.57	0.18
O.R.	-1.09	0.27	-0.01	2.82	0.41	0.03	6.72	0.66	0.07	14.60	0.84	0.10
Ct. App. Coun.	6.79	1.05	0.01	3.48	0.32	0.01	0.17	0.01	0.00	0.16	0.01	0.00
Def. Ret. Coun.	3.34	1.12	0.04	2.79	0.56	0.03	2.24	0.30	0.02	2.22	0.18	0.02
Orig A(1°) Chgs.	9.80	2.38	0.03	32.42	4.70	0.09	55.05	5.38	0.14	133.76	7.68	0.24
Orig B(2°) Chgs.	0.96	0.49	0.07	4.71	1.45	0.30	8.46	1.75	0.49	20.96	2.55	0.85
Orig C(3°) Chgs.	1.26	0.81	0.07	0.47	0.18	0.02	-0.31	0.08	-0.01	-0.36	0.06	-0.01
Orig Misd. Chgs.	-1.84	0.78	-0.03	-3.35	0.85	-0.04	-4.86	0.83	-0.06	-5.00	0.50	-0.04
Off. in Dwell.	2.82	1.23	0.11	3.11	0.81	0.11	3.40	0.59	0.11	0.61	0.06	0.01
Chg. Red. Barg.	-6.47	1.89	-0.05	-7.62	1.32	-0.06	-8.76	1.03	-0.06	-14.31	0.98	-0.07
Count Red. Barg.	-0.48	0.16	-0.01	0.95	0.19	0.02	2.39	0.33	0.04	0.44	0.04	0.00
Court Trial	0.26	0.07	0.00	3.31	0.53	0.02	6.35	0.68	0.03	8.40	0.53	0.03

Jury Trial	10.47	1.70	0.02	14.57	1.41	0.03	18.67	1.22	0.03	25.63	0.98	0.03
Mo. Fin. Dispo.	−0.88	0.43	−0.15	−0.20	0.59	−0.31	−0.32	0.63	−0.43	−0.56	0.64	−0.53
Constant	4.88	0.68	−2.98	−0.25	0.60	−10.84				−24.26	0.79	
R^2	0.50			0.58			0.60			0.69		
Due to Multicolin.	0.12			0.15			0.15			0.14		
Due to Regressors	0.38			0.43			0.46			0.55		
Adj. R^2	0.28			0.40			0.43			0.55		
Standard Error	7.93			13.30			19.74			33.61		
F statistic (D.F.)	2.30 (22,50)			3.18 (22,50)			3.44 (22,50)			5.08 (22,50)		

Table C-19

The Determinants of Sentence Severity for B&E Convictees: Dade County, 1975

(Multivariate Regression Equation Results, Ordinary Least Squares Estimation)

| | | | | | | | Sentence Severity Index | | | | | |
| | A | | | B | | | C | | | D | | |
Variable	Coef	T	η	Coef	T	η	Coef	T	η	Coef	T	η
Com. Ties Index	-1.00	0.23	-0.00	-0.18	0.26	-0.00	-0.27	0.27	-0.00	0.99	0.47	0.00
Age	0.81	0.57	0.11	1.59	0.70	0.18	2.36	0.71	0.23	1.18	0.17	0.07
Black	1.78	0.90	0.07	2.39	0.76	0.08	2.99	0.65	0.09	-6.87	0.71	-0.13
Other Minority	-1.97	0.59	-0.02	-1.21	0.22	-0.01	-0.44	0.06	-0.00	-5.34	0.33	-0.02
Min. P.R.	3.52	1.53	0.06	4.50	1.22	0.63	5.46	1.02	0.07	13.96	1.24	0.10
Maj. P.R.	5.59	2.22	0.09	7.48	1.86	0.09	9.35	1.59	0.10	20.02	1.63	0.13
Pris. P.R.	9.06	2.56	0.07	18.15	3.21	0.11	27.22	3.31	0.14	45.80	2.66	0.15
Jail Custody	4.13	1.05	0.13	7.83	1.24	0.20	11.55	1.26	0.25	16.61	0.87	0.22
Bail	1.26	0.33	0.03	-0.20	0.03	-0.00	-1.65	0.19	-0.03	-1.83	1.00	-0.02
O.R.	0.85	0.21	0.01	-3.13	0.47	-0.04	-7.10	0.74	-0.07	-18.42	0.92	-0.11
Ct. App. Coun.	7.38	1.27	0.01	10.02	1.08	0.02	12.64	0.93	0.02	6.19	0.22	0.01
Def. Ret. Coun.	1.08	0.28	0.01	1.79	0.29	0.01	2.49	0.28	0.01	-4.26	0.23	-0.01
Orig A(1°) Chgs.	4.41	0.75	0.01	19.61	2.08	0.03	34.81	2.54	0.05	83.14	2.90	0.07
Orig B(2°) Chgs.	-0.43	0.24	-0.27	1.05	0.36	0.05	2.53	0.60	0.11	4.42	0.50	0.12
Orig C(3°) Chgs.	1.42	1.12	0.11	1.83	0.90	0.11	2.24	0.76	0.12	2.74	0.44	0.09
Orig Misd. Chgs.	-0.63	0.27	-0.01	-3.08	0.82	-0.04	-5.53	1.02	-0.63	-12.73	1.12	-0.09
Off. in Dwell.	6.42	3.39	0.26	11.31	3.73	0.38	16.18	3.67	0.46	25.29	2.75	0.44
Chg. Red. Barg.	-9.33	2.42	-0.04	-12.28	1.99	-0.05	-15.24	1.70	-0.05	-23.38	1.25	-0.05
Count Red. Barg.	-0.89	0.43	-0.02	0.11	0.03	0.00	1.09	0.23	0.02	-1.08	0.11	-0.01

	1	2	3	4	5	6	7	8	9	10	11	12
Court Trial	0.07	0.01	0.00	−0.98	0.13	0.00	−2.04	0.18	0.00	−5.61	0.24	−0.01
Jury Trial	0			0			0			0		
Mo. Fin. Dispo.	−0.29	1.82	−0.75	−0.64	2.50	−1.37	−0.98	2.65	−1.81	−1.68	2.17	−1.89
Constant	12.00	1.54		18.54	1.49		25.08	1.39		58.19	1.54	
R^2	0.49			0.58			0.60			0.51		
Due to Multicolin.	0.11			0.22			0.25			0.18		
Due to Regressors	0.37			0.36			0.35			0.33		
Adj. R^2	0.31			0.44			0.46			0.34		
Standard Error	7.37			11.79			17.15			35.85		
F statistic (D.F.)	2.71 (21,60)			4.00 (21,60)			4.32 (21,60)			2.99 (21,60)		

Table C-20

The Determinants of Sentence Severity for Robbery Convictees: Dade County, 1974

(Multivariate Regression Equation Results, Ordinary Least Squares Estimation)

Variable	Sentence Severity Index											
	A			B			C			D		
	Coef	T	η	Coef	T	η	Coef	T	η	Coef	T	η
Com. Ties Index	-0.54	0.42	-0.00	-1.05	0.39	-0.01	-1.55	0.36	-0.01	-2.08	0.21	-0.00
Age	1.78	0.52	0.15	-3.00	0.42	-0.15	-7.77	0.68	-0.28	-19.93	0.77	-0.38
Black	-4.92	0.99	-0.18	-10.07	0.97	-0.22	-15.22	0.92	-0.24	-36.56	0.98	-0.30
Other Minority	-22.25	1.19	-0.09	-48.64	2.29	-0.12	-75.03	2.21	-0.13	-150.44	1.96	-0.14
Min. P.R.	-3.82	0.88	-0.06	-20.13	2.22	-0.20	-36.44	2.52	-0.26	-88.90	2.71	-0.33
Maj. P.R.	6.36	0.97	0.05	-6.63	0.49	-0.03	-19.63	0.90	-0.06	-51.73	1.05	-0.09
Pris. P.R.	1.31	0.16	0.00	-1.75	0.10	-0.00	-4.80	0.18	-0.01	-16.75	0.27	-0.01
Jail Custody	18.61	1.53	0.86	24.14	0.95	0.67	29.67	0.73	0.59	47.63	0.52	0.39
Bail	2.30	0.16	0.01	-10.35	0.35	-0.02	-23.00	0.49	-0.02	-60.11	0.56	-0.03
O.R.	14.78	0.86	0.02	14.99	0.42	0.01	15.21	0.27	0.01	27.01	0.21	0.01
Ct. App. Coun.	4.62	0.32	0.00	12.81	0.43	0.01	21.01	0.44	0.01	46.95	0.43	0.01
Def. Ret. Coun.	-1.93	0.27	-0.01	-4.01	0.27	-0.02	-6.10	0.26	-0.02	-23.34	0.44	-0.34
Orig A(1°) Chgs.	1.33	0.52	0.09	6.15	1.15	0.25	10.97	1.28	0.32	26.49	1.36	0.40
Orig B(2°) Chgs.	1.58	0.42	0.03	-2.21	0.28	-0.02	-6.00	0.47	-0.05	-11.05	0.38	-0.04
Orig C(3°) Chgs.	0.09	0.01	0.00	3.19	0.18	0.01	6.29	0.22	0.01	18.62	0.29	0.02
Orig. Misd. Chgs.	8.97	0.63	0.01	-7.50	0.25	-0.01	-23.98	0.50	-0.02	-77.48	0.72	-0.03
Chg. Red. Barg.	-10.88	1.89	-0.09	-24.20	2.01	-0.13	-37.53	1.95	-0.15	-82.20	1.88	-0.17
Count Red. Barg.	-6.75	0.95	-0.06	-18.38	1.33	-0.10	-30.48	1.39	-0.12	-79.22	1.59	-0.16

Court Trial	-6.75	0.56	-0.01	-34.22	1.36	-0.03	-61.69	1.54	-0.04	-130.34	1.44	-0.05
Jury Trial	-3.91	0.35	-0.01	-14.75	0.63	-0.15	-25.59	0.69	-0.02	-60.12	0.71	0.22
Mo. Fin. Dispo.	0.37	1.01	0.45	0.85	1.10	0.62	1.32	1.08	0.69	2.83	1.02	0.77
Constant	-3.16		0.17	15.95		0.41	35.05		0.56	92.98		0.66
R^2	0.42			0.47			0.47			0.46		
Due to Multicolin.	0.17			0.16			0.13			0.09		
Due to Regressors	0.25			0.31			0.34			0.37		
Adj. R^2	0.13			0.20			0.21			0.18		
Standard Error	13.24			17.70			44.17			100.24		
F statistic (D.F.)	1.44 (21,41)			1.72 (21,41)			1.77 (21,41)			1.65 (21,41)		

Table C-21

The Determinants of Sentence Severity for Robbery Convictees: Dade County, 1975

(Multivariate Regression Equation Results, Ordinary Least Squares Estimation)

	Sentence Severity Index											
	A			B			C			D		
Variable	Coef	T	η	Coef	T	η	Coef	T	η	Coef	T	η
Com. Ties Index	-0.17	0.37	-0.00	0.58	0.67	0.00	1.33	0.94	0.00	5.65	1.52	0.00
Age	4.87	2.77	0.41	8.13	2.42	0.53	11.40	2.10	0.61	14.49	1.01	0.44
Black	5.64	2.16	0.18	9.67	1.93	0.24	13.69	1.69	0.27	30.91	1.45	0.35
Other Minority	10.23	1.46	0.01	21.61	1.61	0.02	32.98	1.52	0.03	70.37	1.23	0.04
Min. P.R.	-7.43	2.83	-0.11	-11.73	2.34	-0.14	-16.04	1.98	-0.15	-31.37	1.46	-0.17
Maj. P.R.	-3.14	0.93	-0.02	-10.98	1.70	-0.05	-18.83	1.81	-0.08	-22.78	0.83	-0.05
Pris. P.R.	-4.95	1.16	-0.02	-2.23	0.27	-0.01	0.49	0.04	0.00	70.15	2.00	0.09
Jail Custody	8.08	2.14	0.36	14.28	1.98	0.48	20.49	1.75	0.57	42.22	1.37	0.66
Bail	0.90	0.09	0.65	8.19	0.42	0.00	15.48	0.49	0.01	-9.59	0.12	-0.00
O.R.	3.51	0.39	0.00	2.44	0.14	0.01	1.37	0.05	0.00	10.93	0.15	0.00
Ct. App. Coun.	0.34	0.06	0.00	-2.02	0.19	-0.00	-4.37	0.25	-0.01	12.80	0.28	0.01
Def. Ret. Coun.	13.39	3.34	0.07	21.69	2.82	0.08	30.00	2.41	1.00	69.51	2.12	0.12
Orig A(1°) Chgs.	0.18	0.05	0.01	-13.68	2.10	-0.58	-27.54	2.62	-0.95	-70.43	2.53	-1.37
Orig B(2°) Chgs.	3.42	2.04	0.08	8.44	2.63	0.15	13.46	2.60	0.19	22.41	1.64	0.18
Orig C(3°) Chgs.	0.87	0.27	0.00	-4.66	0.75	-0.02	-10.19	1.02	-0.03	-39.98	1.51	-0.07
Orig Misd. Chgs	0			0			0			0		
Chg. Red. Barg.	-3.19	1.07	-0.03	2.90	0.51	0.02	8.99	0.98	0.05	19.51	0.80	0.06
Count Red. Barg.	-1.11	0.35	-0.01	-8.25	1.34	-0.06	-15.38	1.55	-1.00	-39.43	1.50	-0.14

	Model 1	Model 2	Model 3	Model 4
Court Trial	5.17 0.86 0.01	−2.63 0.23 −0.00	−10.42 −0.56 −0.01	−20.94 0.42 −0.01
Jury Trial	0	0	0	0
Mo. Fin. Dispo.	0.01 0.06 0.02	−0.24 0.74 −0.31	−0.49 0.93 −0.52	−1.09 0.78 −0.64
Constant	0.72 1.00	16.58 1.17	32.44 1.41	85.64 1.41
R^2	0.59	0.56	0.54	0.48
Due to Multicolin.	0.19	0.12	0.08	0.08
Due to Regressors	0.40	0.44	0.45	0.40
Adj. R^2	0.43	0.39	0.36	0.28
Standard Error	7.88	15.09	24.40	64.47
F statistic (D.F.)	3.65 (19,49)	3.32 (19,49)	2.99 (19,49)	2.37 (19,49)

Table C-22
The Determinants of Case Duration[a] for Robberies, Burglaries, All Felonies: Multnomah County, 1973
(Multivariate Regression Equation Results, Ordinary Least Squares Estimation)

Variable	Robberies COEF	T	η	Burglaries Coef	T	η	Variable	All Felonies Coef	T	η
Com. Ties Index	-0.32	0.10	-000	-0.66	0.16	-0.00	Pub. Defdr.	-24.33	2.07	-0.36
Age	18.77	1.54	0.54	-8.19	0.75	-0.26	No. Defs.	-15.51	1.09	-0.20
Black	7.51	0.48	0.02	23.07	1.09	0.05	Prop. Off.	-9.96	0.60	-0.08
Other Minority	5.11	0.17	0.00	8.02	0.11	0.00	Drug Off.	-35.33	0.70	-0.01
Min. P.R.	-23.44	1.27	-0.06	16.60	0.82	0.06	Other Off.	-13.34	0.35	-0.06
Maj. P.R.	-7.57	0.46	-0.03	3.67	0.16	0.01	Jail Cust.	0.19	0.01	0.00
Pris. P.R.	0.42	0.02	0.00	14.09	0.58	0.03	Bail (& O.R.)	-8.19	-0.54	-0.07
Jail Custody	58.95	1.77	0.57	-36.18	1.31	-0.27	Chg. Red. Bar.	-19.24	0.68	-0.04
Bail	41.11	1.13	0.09	-35.00	0.87	-0.04	Court Trial	-5.68	0.20	-0.01
O.R.	47.97	1.55	0.19	-20.72	0.66	-0.17	Jury Trial	-10.94	0.39	-0.14
Ct. App. Coun.	45.11	3.29	0.20	-0.87	0.04	-0.00	Dism. & Tri. Acq.	3.25	3.41	1.32
Def. Ret. Coun.	57.62	2.87	0.14	27.94	1.70	0.15	Mo. Fin. Disp.			
Orig A(1°) Chgs.	-6.19	0.67	-0.14	-13.92	0.50	-0.28				
Orig B(2°) Chgs.	0.14	0.01	0.00	22.44	0.94	0.03				
Orig C(3°) Chgs.	-39.64	1.93	-0.05	52.69	1.73	0.05				
Orig Misd. Chgs.	-4.03	0.11	-0.00	-33.16	1.14	-0.04				
Chg. Red. Barg.	16.82	0.79	0.07	-25.94	1.29	-0.19				
Count Red. Barg.	58.44	1.81	0.08	20.20	0.51	0.04				
Sent. Barg.	-11.77	-0.43	-0.02	-22.54	0.97	-0.06				
Drop Oth. Case Barg.	15.67	0.80	0.06	-20.13	1.04	-0.11				

Court Trial	−26.30	0.99	−0.03	−42.54	1.46	−0.05
Jury Trial	−9.95	0.38	−0.01	−42.52	1.31	−0.04
Dism. & Tri. Acq.	−6.72	0.34	−0.06	−54.33	2.51	−0.26
Mo. Fin. Dispo.	3.91	2.77	1.07	6.45	3.76	1.80
Constant	−100.87	1.98	29.42	0.54	26.81	0.63
R^2	0.48		0.40		0.24	
Due to Multicolin.	0.01		0.00		0.01	
Due to Regressors	0.47		0.40		0.22	
Adj. R^2	0.26		0.17		0.10	
Standard Error	46.71		58.27		47.64	
F statistic (D.F.)	2.22 (24,58)		1.77 (24,63)		1.72 (12,67)	

aElapsed time from arraignment to final disposition.

Table C-23
The Determinants of Case Duration[a] for Robberies, Burglaries, All Felonies: Multnomah County, 1974
(Multivariate Regression Equation Results, Ordinary Least Squares Estimation)

Variable	Robberies			Burglaries			Variable	All Felonies		
	Coef	T	η	Coef	T	η		Coef	T	η
Com. Ties Index	0.24	0.08	-0.00	-1.80	0.58	-0.00	Pub. Defdr.	-23.05	1.91	-0.17
Age	16.25	1.84	0.75	-3.31	0.31	-0.13	No. Defs.	4.07	0.27	0.03
Black	5.08	0.23	0.01	0.17	0.01	0.00	Prop. Off.	4.33	0.28	0.04
Other Minority	-12.73	0.38	-0.01	-9.26	0.17	-0.00	Drug Off.	24.85	0.65	0.01
Min. P.R.	-3.22	0.23	-0.01	-38.61	1.99	-0.08	Other Off.	-18.12	0.37	-0.12
Maj. P.R.	-8.66	0.50	-0.02	2.62	0.18	0.01	Jail Cust.	-16.30	0.34	-0.26
Pris. P.R.	-16.71	0.99	-0.08	-19.71	0.97	-0.06	Bail (& O.R.)	-30.76	1.98	-0.24
Jail Custody	20.40	1.28	0.30	18.16	0.88	0.15	Chg. Red. Barg.	28.67	0.95	0.06
Bail	19.82	0.84	0.04	6.71	0.26	0.02	Court Trial	173.98	1.82	0.05
O.R.	41.06	2.13	0.19	16.67	0.87	0.18	Jury Trial	-103.47	2.08	-0.96
Ct. App. Coun.	-7.14	0.66	-0.06	-2.08	0.17	-0.02	Dism. & Tri. Acq.	2.20	3.62	1.27
Def. Ret. Coun.	-15.02	0.74	-0.03	-13.71	0.75	-0.04	Mo. Fin. Disp.			
Orig A(1°) Chgs.	9.51	0.63	0.24	11.72	0.47	0.29				
Orig B(2°) Chgs.	8.31	0.19	0.01	24.57	1.01	0.01				
Orig C(3°) Chgs.	40.93	1.30	0.04	10.48	0.40	0.02				
Orig Misd. Chgs.	0			-39.26	1.31	-0.03				
Chg. Red. Barg.	29.62	1.27	0.04	-2.63	0.18	-0.01				
Count Red. Barg.	55.14	0.98	0.03	114.28	2.46	0.07				
Sent. Barg.	2.16	0.11	0.00	0.12	0.01	0.00				
Drop Oth. Case Barg.	-2.94	0.20	-0.01	-24.91	1.51	-0.13				

Court Trial	34.18	1.92	1.00	8.92	0.33	0.01
Jury Trial	32.86	1.92	0.12	48.50	2.46	0.10
Dism. & Tri. Acq.	−46.19	3.35	−0.26	−27.25	1.68	−0.13
Mo. Fin. Dispo.	1.00	1.63	0.60	2.07	3.33	1.28
Constant	−40.15	1.42	−20.35	0.51	95.75	1.42
R^2	0.53		0.42		0.29	
Due to Multicolin.	0.18		0.01		0.08	
Due to Regressors	0.35		0.40		0.37	
Adj. R^2	0.33		0.17		0.16	
Standard Error	39.07		43.75		46.49	
F statistic (D.F.)	2.67 (23,54)		1.69 (24,57)		2.24 (12,65)	

aElapsed time from arraignment to final disposition.

Table C-24

The Determinants of Case Duration[a] for Robberies, B&E Offenses, All Felonies: Dade County, 1974

(Multivariate Regression Equation Results, Ordinary Least Squares Estimation)

Variable	Robberies			B&E Offenses			Variable	All Felonies		
	Coef	T	η	Coef	T	η		Coef	T	η
Com. Ties Index	10.53	2.16	0.00	-3.97	0.96	-0.00	Pub. Defdr.	5.72	0.32	0.04
Age	-32.18	2.61	-0.49	11.99	0.91	0.26	No. Defs.	1.61	0.09	0.01
Black	2.58	0.13	0.02	46.73	2.33	0.29	Prop. Off.	-18.81	1.07	-1.00
Other Minority	37.57	1.06	0.03	61.18	2.14	0.10	Drug Off.	-20.55	0.92	-0.04
Min. P.R.	-13.82	0.81	-0.03	3.63	0.15	0.01	Other Off.	-130.08	1.80	-0.02
Maj. P.R.	14.58	0.56	0.02	32.20	1.29	0.07	Jail Cust.	19.22	0.63	-0.04
Pris. P.R.	18.91	0.60	0.01	4.00	0.11	0.00	Bail (& O.R.)	-1.37	0.05	-0.01
Jail Custody	39.63	1.15	0.30	-65.80	1.99	-0.20	Chg. Red. Bar.	-27.48	1.06	-0.03
Bail	111.77	2.77	0.09	-58.35	1.83	-0.38	Court Trial	30.46	0.93	0.02
O.R.	25.05	0.39	0.00	-18.85	0.52	-0.04	Jury Trial	22.95	0.66	0.02
Ct. App. Coun.	12.60	0.36	0.01	18.57	0.31	0.00	Dism. & Tri. Acq.	-20.32	0.68	-0.07
Def. Ret. Coun.	-2.63	0.09	-0.00	45.45	1.81	0.10	Mo. Fin. Disp.	6.19	6.07	1.47
Orig A(1°) Chgs.	13.29	1.10	0.14	-10.75	0.27	-0.00				
Orig B(2°) Chgs.	10.52	0.73	0.03	-2.56	0.15	-0.03				
Orig C(3°) Chgs.	20.17	0.72	0.02	1.90	0.14	0.02				
Orig Misd. Chgs.	-102.27	1.76	-0.02	0.58	0.03	0.00				
Chg. Red. Barg.	-12.71	0.49	-0.01	30.95	0.94	0.03				
Count Red. Barg.	-46.96	1.63	-0.05	-4.23	0.16	-0.01				
Court Trial	10.01	0.34	0.01	37.43	1.16	0.04				
Jury Trial	15.54	0.62	0.02	33.95	0.69	0.01				

	(1)	(2)	(3)
Dism. & Trial Acq.	−39.02 / 5.85	−0.11 / 1.14	1.34 / 5.00
Mo. Fin. Dispo.	1.89 / 5.75	31.07 / 5.93	0.09 / 1.56
Constant	−12.54 / 0.24	−73.11 / 1.41	−23.73 / 0.51
R^2	0.64	0.41	0.45
Due to Multicolin.	0.28	0.04	0.13
Due to Regressors	0.36	0.46	0.32
Adj. R^2	0.52	0.24	0.37
Standard Error	64.83	78.63	69.98
F statistic (D.F.)	5.59 (22,70)	2.32 (22,72)	5.40 (12,79)

aElapsed time from arraignment to final disposition.

Table C-25
The Determinants of Case Duration[a] for Robberies and B&E Offenses: Dade County, 1975[b]

(Multivariate Regression Equation Results, Ordinary Least Squares Estimation)

Variable	Robberies			B&E Offenses		
	Coef	T	η	*Coef*	T	η
Com. Ties Index	3.34	2.24	0.00	−0.22	0.09	0.00
Age	6.38	1.13	0.17	−2.78	0.34	−0.09
Black	−6.18	0.81	−0.06	9.60	0.87	0.09
Other Minority	0.78	0.05	0.00	12.19	0.65	0.02
Min. P.R.	−5.04	0.60	−0.02	18.70	1.55	0.08
Maj. P.R.	18.75	1.96	0.04	−6.08	0.44	−0.02
Pris. P.R.	−3.62	0.23	−0.00	25.88	1.28	0.04
Jail Custody	17.78	1.50	0.23	15.71	0.77	0.10
Bail	−1.68	0.06	−0.00	42.22	2.16	0.27
O.R.	44.52	1.38	0.01	60.78	2.82	0.20
Ct. App. Coun.	10.82	0.60	0.01	106.08	3.68	0.06
Def. Ret. Coun.	−22.51	2.10	−0.04	−10.59	0.52	−0.01
Orig A(1°) Chgs.	−28.42	3.00	−0.48	−19.80	0.57	−0.01
Orig B(2°) Chgs.	2.16	0.40	0.02	7.63	0.72	0.11
Orig C(3°) Chgs.	−18.50	1.68	−0.03	0.93	0.13	0.02
Orig Misd. Chgs.	−97.33	2.44	−0.02	−5.01	0.37	−0.02
Chg. Red. Barg.	−0.32	0.03	−0.00	−16.58	0.74	−0.02
Count Red. Barg.	−0.57	0.51	−0.00	15.62	1.29	0.07
Court Trial	20.70	1.41	0.02	6.45	0.22	0.00
Jury Trial	100.51	4.19	0.05	0		
Mo. Fin. Dispo.	1.88	4.96	0.89	2.64	3.70	1.54
Dism. & Tri. Acq.	−9.93	1.07	−0.04	34.15	1.99	0.07
Constant	17.85	0.89		−86.18	2.22	
R^2	0.58			0.46		
Due to Multicolin.	0.07			0.02		
Due to Regressors	0.50			0.45		
Adj. R^2	0.44			0.30		
Standard Error	29.13			44.11		
F statistic (D.F.)	4.37 (22,71)			2.90 (21,70)		

[a]Elapsed time from arraignment to final disposition.

[b]Because of the biases resulting from the time truncation in the sample of 1975 cases, we could estimate no regression equation for ALL FELONIES in that period.

Appendix D
Lists: Advisory Group Members and Practitioner Interviewees

Advisory Group Members

Louis Bergna
District Attorney, Santa Clara County
San Jose, California

Professor Alfred Blumstein
SUPA, Carnegie-Mellon University
Pittsburgh, Pennsylvania

The Honorable Winslow Christian
Justice of the California Court of Appeals
First Appellate District
San Francisco, California

Harry F. Connick
District Attorney
New Orleans, Louisiana

John Flynn
Attorney at Law
Phoenix, Arizona

Edward B. McConnell
Director, National Center for State Courts
Denver, Colorado

Sheldon Portman
Public Defender, Santa Clara County
San Jose, California

Harvey Solomon
Executive Director, Institute for Court Management
Denver, Colorado

Professor Harry Subin
New York University Law School
New York, New York

Preston Trimble
District Attorney, Cleveland County
Norman, Oklahoma

The Honorable Ernst John Watts
Dean, National Center for State Judiciary
Reno, Nevada

Jerry Wilson
Chief, Metropolitan Police Department (Retired)
Washington, D.C.

Criminal Justice Practitioner Interviewees

Judges

The Honorable Richard Hayden
Judge of the Los Angeles County
Superior Court

The Honorable Horace W. Gilmore
Judge of the Circuit Court (Wayne County)
Detroit, Michigan

The Honorable Leander J. Foley
Judge of the Circuit Court (Milwaukee County)
Milwaukee, Wisconsin

The Honorable Charles W. Halleck
Judge of the Superior Court
District of Columbia

The Honorable Warren P. Cunningham
Judge of the District Court
Houston, Texas

The Honorable Lee Duggan, Jr.
Judge of the District Court
Houston, Texas

The Honorable Andrew L. Jefferson
Judge of the District Court
Houston, Texas

The Honorable Robert Jones
Judge of the Multnomah County Court
Portland, Oregon

The Honorable Clifford Olson
Judge of the Multnomah County Court
Portland, Oregon

Court Administrators

Frank Zolin
  Executive Officer
  Los Angeles County Superior Court

Francis K. Cholko
  Director of Administrative Services
  Los Angeles County Superior Court

Wilbur S. McDuff
  Court Executive Officer
  Dade County Circuit Court
  Miami, Florida

Jack E. Thompson
  Court Administrator (Fulton County)
  Atlanta, Georgia

Arnold Malech
  Executive Officer
  Washington, D.C. Courts

Gordon W. Allison
  Superior Court Administrator
  Phoenix, Arizona

Lester Goodchild
  Chief Executive Officer
  Office of the New York City
    Administrative Judge
  New York, New York

Dr. John Jennings
  Director of Administrative Services
  Office of the New York City
    Administrative Judge
  New York, New York

James Murchison
  Court Administrator (Multnomah County)
  Portland, Oregon

Defense

John Van de Kamp
  Federal Public Defender (Now District Attorney, Los Angeles County)
  Los Angeles, California

John Flynn, Esq.[1]
  Attorney at Law
  Phoenix, Arizona

C. Anthony Friloux, Esq.
  Attorney at Law
  Houston, Texas

Myzell Sowell
  Chief Defender
  Legal Aid and Defender Association of Detroit
  Detroit, Michigan

Norman Lefstein
  Public Defender
  Washington, D.C.

James Hennings
  Public Defender (Multnomah County)
  Portland, Oregon

Prosecutors

Dominick R. Carnovale
  Chief, Criminal Division
  Office of Prosecuting Attorney (Wayne County)
  Detroit, Michigan

Ray Sinetar
  Chief, Preliminary Hearing Division
  Office of the Los Angeles County District Attorney
  Los Angeles, California

Barry Gross
  Special Assistant to State's Attorney
  Office of State's Attorney (Cook County)
  Chicago, Illinois

The Honorable Emmett Fitzpatrick
  District Attorney
  Philadelphia, Pennsylvania

The Honorable Harl Haas
  District Attorney (Multnomah County)
  Portland, Oregon

---

[1] Project Advisory Group Member.

Gary McClain
Chief Deputy District Attorney for
Criminal Matters (Multnomah County)
Portland, Oregon

The Honorable Roger Rook
District Attorney (Clackamas County)
Oregon City, Oregon

Academics

Harry Subin[2]
Professor of Law, New York University
(Former Assistant U.S. Attorney, Washington, D.C.)
New York, New York

Michael Lightfoot
Professor of Law, Loyola University
(Former Public Defender, Federal Public
Defender's Office, Los Angeles;
(Former Assistant U.S. Attorney, Los Angeles)

[2] Project Advisory Group Member.

Index

Index

315

CDS (Comprehensive Data System), 195

Charge bargaining. *See* Plea bargaining

Charges, multiple, 180

Charges, police vs. DA, 232-233

Charging accuracy, xxiii, 6, 44-47; and case audits, 171-172; Dade County, 184-185; interjurisdictional comparisons, 141, 154, 164; Multnomah County, 86-88, 127, 178-179

Charging threshold, xxii, 6, 39-44; interjurisdictional comparisons, 138, 139, 140-141, 164; Multnomah County, 80-86, 126, 127

Community ties of defendant, 62, 100, 148, 261

"Comparability" factors, 70, 136, 138-139, 140

Continuances, 94, 118, 119, 138, 166, 220; and contested/uncontested cases, 51, 116-117, 157, 160; data, 233-234; as delay measure, 51, 53, 91, 102n, 129

Conviction, determinants of, 263

Conviction, trial vs. straight plea, 63, 64, 109-111, 118, 119, 128, 129 153, 154

Conviction levels, 95-99, 111, 113, 145, 146-147, 165

Conviction probability, 46-47, 88, 129, 195

Conviction rates, 59, 60; and charging accuracy, 86-88, 141, 142; and evenhandedness, 103-110 *passim,* 149-156 *passim;* interjurisdictional comparisons, 137, 141, 142, 144, 149-156 *passim;* Multnomah County, 77, 79, 86-88, 96, 98-99, 103-112 *passim,* 128; and plea bargaining, 144, 173n; and pretrial custody status, 149, 150; and prior criminal record, 111, 112, 155, 156; and sentence variation, 96, 98-99

Convictions, multiple, 213, 222

Count bargaining. *See* Plea bargaining

Court activities, types of, 235n

Court calendar crowding, 118, 119, 130, 138, 148, 156, 161. *See also* Case backlog; Caseload

Court clerk logs, 122-123, 234-235

Court systems: Dade County, 219-227; Multnomah County, 210-219

Criminal justice system: Dade County, 219-227; and data analysis, 11-15; models, 17-18, 22-23, 46-47, 69; monitoring of, 173 (*See also* Case audits); Multnomah County, 210-219; quantitative descriptors, 15-20; standards and goals, xxi, 1-2, 18, 20-24, 32-36, 173

Criminal offense, nature of, 61, 63, 100, 101, 102, 128, 145, 148, 165, 178-179, 184-185

Criminal record categories, 62. *See also* Prior criminal record

Crowding: correctional facilities, 63, 64, 93n, 100, 101, 139, 148, 227, 263n; court calendar, 118, 119, 130, 138, 148, 156, 161

Dade County, Florida: case activity, 219-227 *passim;* case audit, 174, 183-187; Circuit Court, 220-223; criminal justice system, 219-227; data collection, 236-242; and Multnomah County compared, 131-167, 187-190; population and police manpower, 131, 132, 219; Pretrial Intervention Program, 225; Pretrial Release Program, 239; Public Defender and defense counsel compensation, 225-227; State Attorney, 223-225

Data collection, 8-9; availability and methodology, xxiv-xxv, xxvi-xxvii, 59, 193-194; Dade County, 236-242; information forms, 243-260; manual, 106n; Multnomah County, 122-126, 229-236; weighted caseload analysis, 122-126

Defendant: concessions to, 54-55, 60, 92, 94-95, 128, 180-182, 188n,

About the Authors

Sorrel Wildhorn has headed studies at Rand in the fields of criminal justice and energy policy research since 1968. Prior to 1968 he both directed and participated in studies in the national security field. He received degrees in aeronautical engineering from New York University and is a senior policy analyst at The Rand Corporation. He is the coauthor of *How to Save Gasoline: Public Policy Alternatives for the Automobile, Prosecution of Adult Felony Defendants: A Policy Perspective,* and *The Private Police: Security and Danger.*

Marvin M. Lavin is a member of the California Bar. He received the B.S. in mathematics, the M.S. in mathematical statistics, the M.B.A. from the University of Chicago, and the J.D. from Loyola University Law School (Los Angeles). He has both directed and participated in studies in the national security field for The Rand Corporation, the Department of Defense, and the University of Chicago. As a consultant to The Rand Corporation, his current special interest in criminal justice is the dangerous habitual offender.

Anthony Pascal is an economist who has specialized in policy analysis for many years at Rand as well as in the federal government, and during university appointments in California (UCLA, Stanford), Mexico, and Britain. He is currently Rand's Director of Human Resource Studies where his major responsibilities cover research on education and employment, race relations and urban problems. He has published articles and monographs in these fields of research, and his books include *Thinking About Cities* and *Racial Discrimination in Economic Life.* Pascal is American Editor of the journal *Urban Studies.*

Selected List of Rand Books

Averch, Harvey A., et al., *How Effective is Schooling? A Critical Review of Research.* Englewood Cliffs, N.J.: Educational Technology Publications, 1974.

Bagdikian, Ben H. *The Information Machines: Their Impact on Men and the Media.* New York: Harper and Row, 1971.

Bretz, Rudy. *A Taxonomy of Communication Media.* Englewood Cliffs, N.J.: Educational Technology Publications, 1971.

Carpenter-Huffman, P., R.C. Kletter, and R.K. Yin. *Cable Television: Developing Community Services.* New York: Crane, Russak and Company, 1975.

Cohen, Bernard and Jan M. Chaiken. *Police Background Characteristics and Performance.* Lexington, Mass.: Lexington Books, D.C. Heath and Company, 1972.

Dakley, Norman (ed.) *Studies in the Quality of Life: Delphi and Decision-making.* Lexington, Mass.: Lexington Books, D.C. Heath and Company, 1973.

DeSalvo, Joseph S. (ed.) *Perspectives on Regional Transportation Planning.* Lexington, Mass.: Lexington Books, D.C. Heath and Company, 1973.

Downs, Anthony. *Inside Bureaucracy.* Boston, Mass.: Little, Brown and Company, 1967.

Fisher, Gene H. *Cost Considerations in Systems Analysis.* New York: American Elsevier Publishing Company, 1971.

Greenwood, Peter W., Sorrel Wildhorn, Eugene C. Poggio, Michael J. Strumwasser, and Peter De Leon. *Prosecution Of Adult Felony Defendants: A Policy Perspective.* Lexington, Mass.: D.C. Heath and Company, 1976.

Jackson, Larry P., and William A. Johnson. *Protest by the Poor: The Welfare Rights Movement in New York City.* Lexington, Mass.: Lexington Books, D.C. Heath and Company, 1974.

Kakalik, James S., and Sorrel Wildhorn. *The Private Police: Security and Danger.* New York: Crane, and Company, Russak, Inc., 1977.

Levien, Roger E. (ed.) *The Emerging Technology: Instructional Uses of the Computer in Higher Education.* New York: McGraw-Hill Book Company, 1972.

McKean, Roland N. *Efficiency in Government through Systems Analysis: With Emphasis on Water Resource Development.* New York: John Wiley & Sons, Inc., 1958.

Meyer, John R., Martin Wohl, and John F. Kain. *The Urban Transportation Problem.* Cambridge, Mass.: Harvard University Press, 1965.

Pascal, Anthony H. (ed.) *Racial Discrimination in Economic Life.* Lexington Mass.: Lexington Books, D.C. Heath and Company, 1976.

Pascal, Anthony H. *Thinking about Cities: New Perspectives on Urban Problems.* Belmont, California: Dickenson Publishing Company, 1970.

Pincus, John (ed.) *School Finance in Transition: The Courts and Educational Reform.* Cambridge, Mass.: Ballinger Publishing Company, 1974.

Quade, Edward S. and Wayne I. Boucher. *Systems Analysis and Policy Planning: Applications in Defense.* New York: American Elsevier Publishing Company, 1968.

Quade, Edward S. *Analysis for Public Decisions.* New York: American Elsevier Publishing Company, 1975.

Sackman, Harold. *Delphi Critique: Expert Opinion, Forecasting, and Group Process.* Lexington, Mass.: Lexington Books, D.C. Heath and Company, 1975.

Sharpe, William F. *The Economics of Computers.* New York: Columbia University Press, 1969.

Wildhorn, Sorrel, Burke D. Burright, John H. Enns, Thomas F. Kirkwood. *How to Save Gasoline: Public Policy Alternatives.* Cambridge, Mass.: Ballinger Publications, Inc., 1976.

Williams, John D. *The Compleat Strategyst: Being a Primer on the Theory of Games of Strategy.* New York: McGraw-Hill Book Company, 1954.

Wirt, John G., Arnold J. Lieberman, and Roger E. Levien. *R&D Management.* Lexington, Mass.: Lexington Books, D.C. Heath and Company, 1975.

Yin, Robert K. and Douglas Yates, *Street-Level Governments: Assessing Decentralization and Urban Services.* Lexington, Mass.: D.C. Heath and Company, 1975.